The Psychology of Darśana Mālā

Other books from Narayana Gurukula !

Aitareya Upaniṣad: With the Original Text in Sanskrit and Roman Transliteration; by Muni Narayana Prasad.

The Bhagavad Gītā: A Sublime Hymn of Yoga. Translated from Sanskrit by Nataraja Guru, with explanatory Dialogue by Nitya Chaitanya Yati.

The Bṛhadāraṇyaka Upaniṣad: With Original Text in Roman Transliteration; by Nitya Chaitanya Yati (3 Vols.).

Experiencing One-World; by Nataraja Guru.

An Integrated Science of the Absolute: based on the Darśana Mālā (Garland of Visions) of Narayana Guru; translated by Nataraja Guru (2 Vols.).

Karma and Reincarnation: The Vedāntic Perspective; by Muni Narayana Prasad.

Kaṭha Upaniṣad: With the Original Text in Sanskrit and Roman Transliteration; by Muni Narayana Prasad.

The Kena Upaniṣad: With the Original Text in Sanskrit and Roman Translation; by Muni Narayana Prasad.

Love and Devotion; by Nitya Chaitanya Yati.

Muṇḍaka Upaniṣad: With the Original Text in Sanskrit and Roman Transliteration; by Muni Narayana Prasad.

Neither This Nor That But Aum; by Nitya Chaitanya Yati.

The Philosophy of Narayana Guru; by Muni Narayana Prasad.

Praśna Upaniṣad: With the Original Text in Sanskrit and Roman Transliteration; by Swami Muni Narayana Prasad.

The Taittirīya Upaniṣad: With the Original Text in Sanskrit and Roman Transliteration; by Muni Narayana Prasad.

That Alone, the Core of Wisdom: A Commentary on Ātmopadeśa Śatakam the One Hundred Verses of Self-Instruction of Narayana Guru; by Nitya Chaitanya Yati.

Vedānta Sūtras of Narayana Guru: with an English translation and Commentary; by Muni Narayana Prasad.

Wisdom — The Absolute is Adorable; by Nataraja Guru.

The Word of the Guru — The Life and Teaching of Guru Nārāyaṇa; by Nataraja Guru.

The Psychology of Darśanamālā

Nitya Chaitanya Yati

DK PRINTWORLD
Publishers of Indian Traditions

Cataloging in Publication Data — DK
[Courtesy: D.K. Agencies (P) Ltd. <docinfo@dkagencies.com>]

Nityacaitanya Yati, 1924-1999, **author.**
The psychology of Darśanamālā/ Nitya Chaitanya Yati.
pages cm
Includes text in Sanskrit (Devanagari and roman); translation in English.
Includes bibliographical references and index.
ISBN 9788124602546

1. Narayana Guru, 1856-1928. Darśanamālā.
2. Advaita. 3. Psychology and philosophy.
I. Narayana Guru, 1856-1928. Darśanamālā.
II. Narayana Guru, 1856-1928. Darśanamālā.
English. III. Title.

B132.A3N58 2017 DDC 181.482 23

ISBN: 978-81-246-0254-6
First published in 1987
Reprinted edition, 2004, 2017

Printed and published by:
D.K. Printworld (P) Ltd.
Regd. Office : *Vedaśrī*, F-395, Sudarshan Park
(Metro Station: Ramesh Nagar)
New Delhi - 110 015
Phones : (011) 2545 3975; 2546 6019
e-mail : indology@dkprintworld.com
Web : www.dkprintworld.com

Dedicated to My Friend
Sri N. Gangadharan in Appreciation of
His Love and Devotion

FOREWORD

The *Darśana Mālā*, or Garland of Visions, was one of the last major works of Narayana Guru, and was dictated by him about 1916. His disciple Swami Vidyananda transcribed the dictation, and made a short commentary of each verse.

Narayana Guru dictated the work in Sanskrit, but its original publication was in the Malayalam language. In 1948-49, Narayana Guru's disciple and successor, Nataraja Guru, translated the entire poem into English. This was printed in 1976 in *An Anthology of the Poems of Narayana Guru*, published by the Narayana Gurukula in Varkala.

This English version is used as the basis for the present commentary by Guru Nitya Chaitanya Yati, Nataraja Guru's successor as spiritual leader of the Narayana Gurukula. This volume thus embodies the combined work of the three gurus of the Narayana Gurukula.

Darśana Mālā consists of 100 verses, divided into ten chapters of ten verses each. Each chapter is a vision, complete in itself, and also forming part of the greater whole.

Darśana Mālā is an exceedingly compact and lucid expression of Narayana Guru's unitive vision. Each chapter is a seed of word-wisdom, containing within it the potential of a full unfolding. The nature of that unfolding will naturally depend on the soil in which the seed is sown.

Owing to its seminal nature, *Darśana Mālā* can be approached from many different points of view. Narayana Guru's immediate successor, Nataraja Guru, made *Darśana Mālā* the core and structure of his own monumental three-volume English work, *An Integrated Science of the Absolute*.

At Narayana Guru's behest, Nataraja Guru had been educated at the Sorbonne, where he studied under Henri Bergson and was immersed in the intellectual ferment of the new fields of quantum mathematics and relativity theory.

In his great commentary, Nataraja Guru reconciles and revalues the philosophical implications of the new Western physics by means of *Darśana Mālā*. He demonstrates the synthesis between the mystical vision of his Guru and the scientific findings of the new physicists and mathematicians of the West. Nataraja Guru takes *Darśana Mālā* from the philosophical and metaphysical point of view.

The present work, *Psychology of Darśana Mālā*, is in the same tradition. Guru Nitya Chaitanya Yati examines this unitive wisdom from the point of view of psychology. Nitya uses his own profound familiarity with Western psychological thought to create a synthesis that is available to Western readers. In this volume, Narayana Guru's uncompromisingly absolutist vision is expanded and amplified by reference to such diverse Western thinkers as Jung and St. John of the Cross, Kierkegaard and Lewis Carroll.

Nitya uses *Darśana Mālā* to explore and answer fundamental questions of human psychology: How do I come to experience this world? What is the nature of the transaction between I who experience and that which is experienced? How can I guide my actions?

As in all Nitya's works, *Psychology of Darśana Mālā* is infused with his characteristic compassion for the student. His commentary and examination are never merely for the sake of intellectual fancy. His eye is always on direct realization of the unitive life, approached through the mind, but not grasped by it.

Don Berry
Seattle, WA
U S A

GUIDE TO SANSKRIT PRONUNCIATION

Vowels

a pronounced like the u in "but"
ā like the a in "far"
i like the e in "me"
ī a longer sound, like the ee in 'beet"
u like the o in "to"
ū a longer sound, like the oo in "pool"
ṛ like the ri in "rig" (very short)
e like the a in "gate"
ai like the i in "high"
o like the o in "note"
au like the ou in "loud"

The Sanskrit alphabet has a beautiful structure. As the Sanskrit alphabet distinguishes more sounds than the English alphabet, it is useful to look at this structure to learn the correct pronunciation of the consonants. This will help to clarify the two main problems for the English speaker: aspiration and "the point of contact" (*sparśa*). For convenience we will use the vowel *a*, pronounced like the u in "but", to make the consonants articulate syllables. Read across from left to right.

Consonants

ka	*kha*	*ga*	*gha*	*ṅa*
ca	*cha*	*ja*	*jha*	*ña*
ṭa	*ṭha*	*ḍa*	*ḍha*	*ṇa*
ta	*tha*	*da*	*dha*	*na*
pa	*pha*	*ba*	*bha*	*ma*
ya	*ra*	*la*	*va*	
śa	*ṣa*	*sa*		
ha				

The first five groups of five consonants are arranged by points of contact in the vocal apparatus, proceeding from back to front. The points of contact are the velum, the soft palate, the hard palate, the teeth, and the lips, respectively. At the end of each series is a nasal sound made at that point of contact.

The second and fourth consonants in each of these first five series are aspirated. All the other consonants are unaspirated, with the exceptions of *śa, ṣa, sa,* and *ha.* To determine whether you aspirate a particular consonant, place your hand in front of your mouth. If you can feel your breath on your hand, that consonant is being aspirated. It is normal for English speakers to aspirate the "k", "c", "t", and "p" when these consonants come at the beginning of a word, but Sanskrit words could start either with an unaspirated syllable, like *ka*, or an aspirated syllable, like *kha*.

Pronounce the consonants as follows:

k as in "skip", *kh* like the k in "kiss", *g* as in "go" (always "hard"), *ṅ* like the ng in "sing", *c* like the ch in "eschew" (never a "k" or "s"), *ch* slightly harder, as in "much", *j* as in "jam", *ñ* as a gentle ny sound, like the *ñ* in the Spanish "Señor". The series starting with *ṭa* and the series starting with *ta* are distinguished by the respective position of the tongue in each series. The English "t" and "d" is often pronounced somewhere between the two positions. In the first (*ṭa*) series the tongue should be curled back further toward the roof of the mouth. In the second (*ta*) series the tip of the tongue should protrude slightly between the teeth. These sounds are characteristically "flatter" and less resonant than the preceding series. Go a little more gently than the usual English "t's" and "d's". Pronounce the *ṭ* and *t* as in "storm", (observing the different points of contact), the *ṭh* and *th* like the t in "tie", (not like the th in "think"), make the *ḍ, d, ṇ,* and *n* sounds as in English, but carefully observing the different points of contact. Pronounce *p* as in "spin", *ph* like the p in "pin", (not like the ph in "phase"), *b* as in "bear", *m* as in "my".

Note the nasals (*ṅ, ñ, ṇ, m*) go naturally with the corresponding consonants in the series they are in. Thus in the English words "hanker" and "anger" the "n" is pronounced like the Sanskrit *ṅ*, or as the ng in "sing". It is natural for "n" to precede "t" and "d" in words, as in "hunter" and "hinder". And it is natural for "m" to precede "p" and "b", as in "limp" and "lumber". The symbol here transliterated as *ṁ* is not technically a separate letter, and it is pronounced as the nasal appropriate to the consonant that immediately follows it. Thus, it is pronounced like the letter *ṅ* in the names *Śaṁkara* and *Sāṁkhya*, like the letter *ñ* in the name *Saṁjaya*, like the *n* in *saṁnyāsa*, and as *m* in *saṁbhavāmi* and *saṁyamya*. (It stands for the letter *m* not only when it precedes the consonants in the series beginning with *pa*, but also when it precedes any of the consonants which follow *ma* in the Sanskrit alphabet, and when it comes at the end of a word.)

Pronounce *y* as in "yes", *r* softly, something like the r in "drama", *l* as in "love", *v* with just the slightest contact between the upper teeth and the lower lip, (greater than that used for the w in "wile", and less than that used for the v in "vile"). Pronounce *ś* as a gentle sy sound, like the sh in "shove", *ṣ* with the tongue slightly further back, and slightly more aspirated, like the sh in "fish", *s* as in "so", *h* fully aspirated, as in "hope".

The symbol often found at the end of words and transliterated as *ḥ* is slightly aspirated, and echoes the vowel that just precedes it. It is always a very short sound, and so for the vowels *a* and *ai* the echo will be *i*, while for *o* and *au* it will be *u*. Examples: *devaḥ* pronounced as *devaha*, *devāḥ* pronounced as *devāha*, *devaiḥ* pronounced as *devaihi.* In all of these the very last syllable is extremely short.

There is really no English equivalent for the consonants *gh*, *jh*, *ḍh*, *dh*, and *bh*. Some rough approximations are: *gh* as in "loghouse" *jh* as in "hedgehog" (he*jh*og), *dh* as in "adhere", *ḍh* is the same aspirated *d* with the tongue further back on the palate, *bh* as in "abhor". They are not to be pronounced as two separate sounds, despite the form in which they are transliterated. These letters must be given the same strong aspiration that the letter "k", "c", "t", and "p" are given at the beginning of English words.

By carefully examining their position in the Sanskrit alphabet and saying the letters in order, you can get a feeling for their correct pronunciation. Any speaker of a modern Indian language could give assistance in learning to pronounce the letters of the Sanskrit alphabet, as words such as *dharma* (the first word in the Gita) are in their vocabularies.

ACKNOWLEDGEMENTS

In the year 1970 I gave a series of talks at the University of California, Los Angeles, on Altering States of Consciousness based on the *Bhāna Darśana* of Narayana Guru's *Darśana Mālā*. The talks were received with interest and sympathy. That helped me to see the psychological implications of Narayana Guru's teachings.

I was very intimately associated with Nataraja Guru during the years he was writing *The Integrated Science of the Absolute* based on the translation and commentary of the *Darśana Mālā*. A remark which Nataraja Guru wrote in the Preface of Volume I of the book was another incentive for me to take *Darśana Mālā* seriously. Guru wrote, "I have always kept Nitya Chaitanya Yati in my mind as a disciple who would benefit much from these writings." I read this line with gratitude and take it as Guru's blessings for me to dive deeply into the intricacies of Narayana Guru's *Darśana Mālā*. All through the work I felt the showering of the solemn blessings of both Narayana Guru and Nataraja Guru and I want to record here my heartfelt gratitude to these two pioneering masters.

When I commenced the work of writing down my commentary John Goodman from Sydney helped me by taking down dictation and typing the initial draft of the first two *Darśana*-s. Later I was helped by Dr. Peter Oppenheimer, Nancy Yielding, Sraddha Durand and Edda Walker. Another person who was very helpful in checking the Sanskrit verses and rendering the Sanskrit word meanings into English was John Stalling. Don Berry, one of the most well-known and much loved novelists of North America, was kind enough to read through the entire typescript and write a Foreword to the present work. I am very thankful to all these good friends.

The final typescript was edited and typed by my good friend and student Scott Teitsworth, of Portland, Oregon. He did the work so meticulously and with deep understanding that I felt much relieved of the hard work of scrutinizing every word and passage of this book. Without Scott's help this book would not have seen the light. So I have no words to express my gratitude to him.

Further, Scott offered to write an Introduction which would help the reader to handle the book meaningfully. This he has done with great care and sagacity. I am sure the reader will appreciate the guidelines given by Scott in his Introduction. For this act of love I thank him again.

When the typescript had to be shelved for many years for lack of funds, my good friend and fellow disciple, Sri N. Gangadharan came forward to offer me a sum of Rs. 50,000/- as donation. Without his help we would not have ventured to give the book to the printers. As Sri Gangadharan's gift came as a Providential gesture, my thanks to him is also an acknowledgement of the hand of God in presenting the book at a reasonable cost to the reader.

The laborious work of going through the galley proof was done by my associate and friend Vinod Vyas. We appreciate the good and careful work done by our experienced printers, The All India Press, Pondicherry.

All these friends, and many more whom I have not mentioned here are remembered with love and gratitude.

As Nataraja Guru has concluded his Preface to the *Integrated Science of the Absolute*, let me also "incline before the Absolute in everlasting adoration in the belief that in doing so I am in effect only adding glory to ourselves whose totality is no other than myself."

— Guru Nitya Chaitanya Yati
Narayana Gurukula,
Fernhill-643 004
Nilgiris, India.

April 1987.

Contents

INTRODUCTION

The Psychology of Darśanamālā is the *magnum opus* of Nitya Chaitanya Yati, an increasingly well-regarded Vedāntic philosopher and writer from South India. The work is presented as a commentary on the *Darśanamālā* of Narayana Guru, one of modern India's most brilliant mystic philosophers and poets. It was Narayana Guru who instructed Nataraja Guru, who in turn taught Nitya Chaitanya Yati, so there is a direct line of understanding represented in this book.

The Psychology of Darśanamālā is a thoroughgoing exposition of psychological states from the origin of individual consciousness to its extinction in nirvana. In the past, such large-scale undertakings have been to a greater or lesser extent heterogeneous and unsystematic. By using the elegant framework of *Darśanamālā* to properly organize the structure of the book, Guru Nitya has added an important dimension to this perennial study and at the same time made a significant contribution to the presentation of Indian psychology and philosophy. The reader will find that such a systematic presentation helps bring Indian psychology out of the realm of hypothetical speculation and into the arena of everyday life where it can be of immediate and practical use.

In the Spring of 1958, Nitya Chaitanya Yati was completing his Ph.D. thesis in social psychology at Bombay University. Just as he put the finishing touches on his work, entitled 'The problem of adjustment in the physically handicapped', his faculty guide moved to another university. The head of the Sociology Department had been a rival of Nitya's guide, in true scholastic fashion, and he proceeded to block his thesis presentation.

"You cannot present your thesis without a guide," he said.

"Then you present it for me, please," requested Nitya.

"I cannot. I was not your guide."

"Then will you appoint another guide for me?"

"No. The work is finished, so you cannot have a guide."

While Nitya was pondering and fuming over this catch-22, his spiritual teacher, Nataraja Guru, came to visit him. In his inimitable style, rather than give sympathy he upbraided his disciple.

"You have gotten all your information from American text-books," he said. "In ten years you will renounce all this borrowed knowledge."

It was almost exactly ten years later that Nitya, without his doctorate but now a Guru, perceiving many of the flaws of Western psychological technique, began formulating *The Psychology of Darśanamālā*.

The genius of the West has traditionally been expressed in an analytic methodology, developed in the ancient physical sciences. This has carried over into the modern field of psychology, where its application is more dubious than, for instance, in the categorization of animal species. A proper conception of the mind *in toto* is very much needed. Thousands of psychological studies are produced annually, painstakingly detailed and with great inner cohesion, but they fail to satisfy us because they do not belong to a meaningful picture of the psyche. They only depict isolated units of behaviour. 'What' is described from every possible angle, while the more fundamental question of 'why' is studiously avoided.

The process of breaking the subject down into smaller and smaller parts through analysis has led to such specialization by individuals that almost all of Western civilization is deeply dissociated from an integral understanding of the whole. The situation is aptly described in the classic story of the blind men and the elephant, where each imagines that he can accurately project the nature of the beast from the part he is in contact with, while disdaining the suggestions of a sighted person who can plainly see it is an elephant.

In India and some other parts of Asia the situation is the reverse. Intelligent thinkers have been contemplating the "big picture" for more than 5000 years, resulting in well-systematized schemes of synthetic, rather than analytic, reasoning. In contrast to the specialists in the West, every Indian is a philosopher, though often at the expense of everyday details. While the West is full of excellent plumbers who are unhappily divorced from their spirituality, India has an abundance of happily integrated people whose plumbing is permanently in a state of chaos.

While the twentieth century has seen some cross-pollination between the analytic and synthetic extremes, they generally remain entrenched as the rival polarized camps of materialism and spiritualism. Narayana Guru and his principal expositors, Nataraja Guru and Guru Nitya, maintain that the most beneficial attitude is one that combines the best of both in a dynamic conception. In the present work the common root where the material and spiritual worlds join is examined in some detail. In fact, the dialectical integration of the conceptual and the practical underlies the entire study of *Darśanamālā*.

In much of Narayana Guru's work, and especially *Darśanamālā*, there is a fusion of the best of modern scientific understanding with the traditional wisdom of India's ancient seers. This is in keeping with the purpose of a long line of Vedāntic revaluators. As humanity evolves there is a periodic need to restate the basic truths of life in a form that is relevant and comprehensible to the thought-patterns of a particular age. In Vedānta this is taken as a matter of course. There is a proud tradition of revaluation stretching back to the Upanishads. The Bhagavad Gita, written around 1000 BC, is an early and important example, and its continuing relevance is such that it is cited throughout the present work. Sankara revalued Vedānta in the context of the world of the first millennium AD, and Narayana Guru should be considered among the most important revaluators of the present era. The verticality of truth is such that Narayana Guru could modestly state, "what we have to say is what Sankara said." Or, as Nataraja Guru puts it with reference to the particular needs of the age of reason, "Narayana Guru has been able to state the gist of ancient Indian wisdom tradition in a manner lending itself to be integratively understood in a unified fashion." *The Psychology of Darśanamālā* is the distillation of this modern restatement of Vedāntic values into the specific field of psychology. Still, since mind as viewed here is the source of the entire universe insofar as it is knowable, psychology is a much broader subject in the Indian context than it is in the West, where mind is considered to be just one subject among thousands of independent categories.

No one will argue that the twentieth century has seen extremely rapid changes in virtually every facet of life. Even the freest thinkers of only 200 years past could not conceive of any part of the present way of life, let alone those of 1000 or 2000 years ago. Our sociological and technological development has vastly outpaced the adaptivity of philosophers. Such a time has a powerful need to have traditional wisdom interpreted in its own terms. Much of the current confusion and strife in the religious and political arenas can be traced to attempts to squeeze modern, global humanity into the confines of philosophies created for semi-barbaric tribal peoples of the distant past. It is high time for the kernels of eternal truth in those once-useful ideologies to be separated from the chaff of their historical trappings of tribal ethics and politico-economic power struggles, to be restated in the language of the present day.

In belief-systems where there is no provision for change one expects such conflicts, yet even in India, with its time-honored tradition of revaluation, there is tremendous resistance to the kind of opening up of entrenched attitudes recommended by Narayana Guru and his successors. Admittedly, and to their credit, they have hit hard at precisely the weakest points, where unquestioned habits have done the most to degrade human values. Like scar tissue over a wound it is here that society's skin tends to be the thickest. But the task of the revaluator is just this—to break us free of the horizontalized stasis of mind that sets in over the years, even against our best intentions, with fresh infusions of verticalized truth. For India this means philosophical surgery on the twin evils of the oppression of women and the maintenance of inflexible casteism, which is India's version of the more general problem of racism. While even the ancient and revered Bhagavad Gita mentions that Self-realization is not dependent on relative factors such as sex or caste, at least a *de facto* discrimination has been in operation well into the so-called modern era. It is often the case that theoretical truths only penetrate the hard shell of social conditioning through a prolonged process. Narayana Guru and Guru Nitya wish to make it clear that equality on the actual as well as the theoretical level is the birthright of every human being. How can one profess a universal and all-encompassing belief system and yet make slaves of women and children? How can we advocate freedom and liberation while building artificial barriers between arbitrary groups? Simple enough questions, but ones that are even now being rejected with vehemence and violence, not just in India but around the globe. What were reasonable patterns of understanding thousands of years ago have slowly lost their value-content to become a strait-jacket for the human soul. The subtle faults in those schemes, which through the years have been greatly magnified, are overdue for correction.

While the West fully shares the onus of racism and sexism, in fact all the isms, its deepest-rooted faith is placed in scientific skepticism rather than spiritual accepticism. In *The Psychology of Darśanamālā*, Guru Nitya demonstrates at great length the similarities between the attitudes of scientific materialism and religious theism. How both orientations emerge from a universal ground of consciousness is examined in the very first darsana of the book. He points out:

> As a result of the conditioning of the faithful by the established religions, and of the skeptics by the categoric statements of science, man has become bifurcated in his sense of his true beingness. Having thus separated him from his true ground — that substratum that gives rise to all beings — those responsible for this have largely repressed in him the sense of wonder and delight in which one who knows his true being lives all the time. Looking in vain for some religious statement or scientific formula which will neatly encompass the whole mystery of being, so that we can file it away in our box of consumer goods and calendar maxims, we have forgotten that the mystery we seek to penetrate is our own mystery.

From the absolutist perspective adopted in this book, religion and science are seen to be nearly indistinguishable in their philosophical limitations and their effects on the psyche. Nonetheless, at the horizontal level of everyday life these two systems are very much in opposition.

The renormalized structuralism revived by Narayana Guru, developed by Nataraja Guru, and used as a springboard by Guru Nitya in this work, provides a solution to this conflict-causing confusion of values. Truth is an eternal, vertical value, while its historical context is horizontal and undergoing constant evolution. Mistaken notions that horizontal values have the same eternal verity as absolute truth need to be sorted out by reference to an orderly scheme of correlation such as is presented here. Orthodox religious thinkers tend to give an eternal, vertical status to the transient horizontal factors making up a large bulk of their scriptures. Rationalist thinkers err in the opposite direction, so to speak, by attempting to include truth with the horizontal factors as limited by time and place. While both of these may be termed one-legged arguments that must sooner or later fall down due to their lack of balance in the integration of horizontal and vertical elements, at least the skeptic is less likely to burst from his ivory tower with sword flashing or guns blazing.

Narayana Guru was born August 20, 1854 just north of Trivandrum in Kerala State, South India, and died nearby in Varkala on September 20, 1928. During his lifetime he became a major force in the spiritual regeneration of his region, and is now becoming recognized throughout India as an important revaluator of Vedāntic wisdom. He lived a life of quiet yet intense contemplation in the forests and mountains of the South, where he scrupulously, even passionately, avoided the limelight. The few of his words that were recorded by his disciples are almost entirely in brief and cryptic verses given for the contemplation of those in his immediate circle. They are penetratingly absolutist and nondual. No explanatory concessions are made; the reader is expected to enter into the verses through his own meditation and substantial intellectual efforts. Such a writing style, coupled with his personal habit of walking away from people as soon as they gathered about him, is almost a guarantee of obscurity. We are exceedingly fortunate that Nitya Chaitanya Yati has both understood the contemplative insight compressed into Narayana Guru's poetry and is able to expand it into its proper scientific framework in a language that the reader can readily grasp.

Narayana Guru's disdain for fame actually serves to heighten his absolutist reputation for those who do become familiar with his life and works. Fame tends to water down and dilute the importance of great men and women, who must cater to the demands of their public. Certainly, those Indian pundits who have become well-known in the West have often purveyed a 'pop' message mixed with unabashed sensationalism that has attracted mainly the gullible and offended the scientific and philosophically-minded, who have the most to gain from an in-depth study of oriental contemplative science.

While a profound depth of non-dual philosophy is presented in various guises throughout Narayana Guru's recorded words, the highest degree of structural organization is to be found in *Darśanamālā*. Such a well-organized methodology is a real departure from the rather loose-knit tradition of South Indian composition to which his other major works like *Ātmopadeśa Śatakam* and *Svānubhavagīti* belong. Its thoroughness and scientific organization have made it the perfect vehicle for Guru Nitya's present exposition of Indian psychology as well as for Nataraja Guru's crowning achievement, *An Integrated Science of the Absolute*, which integrates science and mysticism over the skeletal structure of *Darśanamālā*.

Towards the end of his life, in 1916, Narayana Guru was asked by his disciples for a definitive work on Vedānta philosophy. This he agreed to do under certain guidelines. He would chant the work and Swami Vidyananda was to take it down. There were to be no repetitions. If he was asked for any he would stop. The disciples agreed to the conditions.

Early in the day the Guru would go for a walk, and Swami Vidyananda accompanied him carrying his water pot. With the Swami's hands thus engaged, Narayana Guru chanted ten verses, which Vidyananda would have to commit to memory. When the Guru finally took his water pot and wandered into the jungle, the Swami would immediately sit down and begin writing feverishly. Thus even the production of this timeless masterpiece was used as a tool to further the training of a disciple.

After this routine was repeated several times, Narayana Guru said simply, "That's all." He then asked Swami Vidyananda to read the verses back to him, and he gave his tacit approval. Finally he told his disciples that there were ten visions, gave their names, and titled the work *Darśanamālā.* Later, Vidyananda wrote a brief commentary on each verse that was based as closely as possible on the Guru's own words. It has been reproduced in *An Integrated Science of the Absolute*.

Darśanamālā is perhaps the work most suited to be used by the modern scientific thinker. The subject matter is consciousness, and the occasional reference to religious terms and deities is not intended to substantiate hierophantic notions, but rather to relate particular principles of the mind with their traditional symbols. Nothing is expected to be taken on faith, beyond the belief that much is to be gained by pondering over an idea that may not be immediately clear. In fact, Guru Nitya explicitly recommends that the reader maintain an attitude of healthy skepticism and critical scrutiny, both in his approach to this book and to his search in general.

The structure of the work is a marked advance over the heterogeneity of many other textbooks in either field of psychology or mystical contemplation, demonstrating a comprehensive overview of the entire subject where others have been busy building an edifice piece by piece. *Darśanamālā* means 'A Garland of Visions'. The garland likens consciousness to a series of ten flowers strung together on a golden thread, with a precious jewel pendant in the center. Each flower is a unitive vision, and is described with the utmost economy in ten succinct and evocative verses pregnant with implications.

Indeed, the image of the garland to epitomize consciousness by itself conveys a number of significant ideas. First, it is a decorative article of dress that is put on and taken off. The clear implication is that the essential Being wears consciousness as a kind of ornament for a time, and when it is removed the wearer remains unchanged. This allusion is in keeping with the Guru's absolutist perspective, and is typical of the vivid poetic imagery which infuses his writings. The perfection of the image is such that we can go on extracting meaning upon meaning: a garland is often given as a gift from one to another, just as we cannot claim to be the creators of consciousness, but rather receive it from the Unknown. It often marks a significant event or celebration, just as our life has an overriding importance to us, and deserves to be celebrated. Each stage of our conscious growth is so like a flower: complex, symmetrically beautiful, complete in itself; and its tinting reminds us of the coloration of our psyche with moods and biases. The golden thread that runs through the whole is an important image, implying an invisible continuity linking the stages of life into a meaningful progression. Even the shape of the garland as it hangs around the neck is significant. The first darsana begins high up on the shoulder with the very origins of consciousness, which may be taken either in general terms or in relation to the birth of the individual. This distinction is in any case minimized in Vedānta. There is a progressive development as the garland is traced in a graceful curve of increasing objectification and subjectification down to the pendant jewel at the center of the neck: the supreme teaching and keynote of the whole, *tadevasat*, "That alone exists."

Following this high point of awareness, as it were, the garland ascends toward the other shoulder. During this second half of the work, consciousness is progressively turning inwards again. Narayana Guru's highest ideal does not, therefore, come at the close of the work proper, but slightly before the end, in the fifth verse of *Nirvāṇa Darśana*:

> Having burned everything with the fire of wisdom,
> aiming the good of the world,
> doing action according to injunction,
> the knower of *brahma* remains firm in *brahma*.

In fulfillment of methodological requirements in keeping with the Indian tradition of a complete presentation, Narayana Guru then goes on to include the progressive extinction of consciousness in the absolute ground.

While it is possible that the garland, after it disappears behind the wearer's back, forms a complete loop to the first shoulder again, any such speculations are scrupulously avoided by both Narayana Guru and Guru Nitya. Their concern is a total presentation of consciousness, and no claims are made based on faith. Speculation on life after death, or any type of speculation, is placed by them in this work as belonging to a psychological reality based on the superimposition of personal values on universal values, and as such it is only a hindrance to the reduction and integration process that receives primacy here.

It is doubtful that we are extracting more symbolic meaning than is justified from Narayana Guru's metaphor of a garland. The reader will find throughout his work that the Guru's imagery — non-visual as well as visual — is a seed or kernel which, when watered and tended by the student's intellect and intuition, yields an impressive harvest of insight.

Briefly, the work is in two parts of five darsanas each. Part I may be said to deal with the origin and extroversion of consciousness, while Part II treats its introspection and remergence. The first darsana, *Adhyāropa*, presents the creation and essential structure of consciousness. Perception is examined in some detail, and is shown to be of the nature of projection or superimposition on the actual ground of being. The Vedāntic approach makes it clear that in this we all share a kind of generic defect in our awareness; the same is transformed by everyone into personal, specific variations which merit the attention of the psychiatrist only when they become exaggerated. As Guru Nitya says on page 79: "The world we think to be real has in fact very little objective reality. It is padded out in all directions with half-baked conceptual notions and hidebound prejudices." The aim of the second darsana, *Apavāda*, is to correct this universal condition through recognizing and refuting that which is false. In the course of this several dual aspects of existence are highlighted, including cause and effect, unity and multiplicity, and the self and the other. How the individual attains knowledge is also treated here.

The *Asatya Darśana* is based on the principle that the knowledge of what is false is the most potent way to eliminate it. Knowing how the unreal appears real to us, and how we substitute mental pictures for reality, can motivate us to undertake the discipline of correction for our own benefit instead of merely treating it as an interesting abstraction. Up to this point of the work there are parallels with conventional psychotherapy, as the subject matter is generally the correction of errors in cognition. Beyond this point *Darśanamālā* takes the reader further to discover his own true nature, something that has yet to come within the purview of the Western science of psychology.

The next four darsanas relate to a proper understanding of the world and the individual's place in it. When wrong notions are uprooted, there should be normalized notions offered to replace them. The *Māyā Darśana* presents a corrected perception of the empirical world and its transactional verity. How false suppositions proliferate into the manifold world and the negative factors which conceal truth from us are also within its scope. The *Bhāna Darśana* complements this with a normative notion of awareness in its several aspects, including the traditional scheme of a four-fold consciousness. This leads naturally to the great dictum *tad eva sat.* "That alone is" at the midpoint of the work, described by Nitya as "the precious pendant and secret key of the entire 'Garland of Visions'."

In the second half of *Darśanamālā*, Narayana Guru reverses the normal scientific methodology of seeking truth through its effects. He wants us to discover the original cause from which all effects follow. This can be viewed as the wholesale, as opposed to the piecemeal, approach. His disciple, Nataraja Guru, expressed seeking truth through the study of its effects as opening a door from the hinge side. Certainly it can be done, with a great effort, but isn't it easier to open it from the side of the latch? In *An Integrated Science of the Absolute*, (vol.I, p.239), Nataraja Guru describes this important difference between Parts I and II:

> The methodology and structuralism tacitly presupposed in the *Darśana Mālā* implies both a reduction and a construction by which multiplicity is first reduced to negative unity in the first five chapters. Both plurality and duality get abolished by a method of elimination of what is doubtful and unessential. Having touched the rock bottom of ontology by this negative reduction, the last five chapters aim at a more positive construction implying the normalizing of existence with its own rational subsistence. There is a construction implied in the method here by which ontology gets trans-

formed into a value-world where teleological first and final causes gain gradual primacy. Even at this stage of reconstruction there are always the Self and the non-Self involved as irreducible counterparts related by complementarity, reciprocity and cancellability.

The second part of *Darśanamālā* commences at the gross level of action with the *Karma Darśana.* Action is generally taken for granted, but it becomes elusively subtle when carefully examined. That we are actors initiating action is shown to be a faulty assumption that binds us in chains of misery-producing cause and effect. Our attachment to action transforms the I-consciousness from the source of awareness to an object of awareness. The remedy for this is to relinquish attachment by turning to the unmoved mover of the Self. Similarly, the *Jñāna Darśana* contrasts conditioned knowledge, based on I-consciousness, with the unconditioned knowledge that is free of I-consciousness. To arrive at a total awareness of the Self, the various forms of knowledge are given a philosophical structuring and value orientation. In the earlier darsanas, knowledge was viewed from the standpoint of how it affects the individual, while here it is given its absolute status in the overall scheme of existence. This completes the normalized vision of reality offered by Narayana Guru, setting the stage for the remergence in the blissful state of the Self described in the final three darsanas.

The *Bhakti Darśana* presents the science of values and their interrelationships. Certitude of awareness is gained through bhakti, defined as continuous contemplation of one's Self. This comes about by a resolution of duality that is an outcome of the unifying and focusing of the psyche through its natural interest and joyful devotion. Identification with the Self automatically dissipates the disturbances and restlessness caused by our conjunction with the non-Self. In the *Yoga Darśana* this joyful orientation to the Self is augmented with the intentional uprooting of binding tendencies like conceptualization based on name and form and the compulsive action arising from incipient memories. The aim is the total cessation of the part of consciousness that fluctuates and thereby automatically produces the duality of subject and object. A number of specific suggestions are made for putting this into practice. In these two darsanas the psyche is realigned with its Self, first through a bipolarity based on love and devotion and then through contemplative absorption.

The various grades of absorption in the totality of consciousness are discussed in the final vision, *Nirvāṇa Darśana.* Nirvana is here translated as extinction, meaning the extinction of limited awareness in the bliss of the Absolute. Still, the term 'extinction' can have some rather frightening connotations. It is important to realize that the final verses do not represent the goal of Narayana Guru's teaching, but are included to round out the thoroughgoing presentation of awareness that is required by the Guru's methodology as well as by Indian philosophical tradition. To misunderstand the significance of the last five verses could have a negative effect on the seeker. Nataraja Guru points out: "Here it is the inner enjoyment of the high value implied in the notion of the Absolute that serves as the diagnostic factor. The outer evidence of such enjoyment might be feeble in the eyes of an onlooker who is not conscious of the Bliss of contemplation of the Absolute." As stated earlier, Narayana Guru's highest ideal is closest to that given in the fifth verse, where the knower of the Absolute retains his realization while interacting with the world for its own benefit. This is poetically presented in verses 11 and 12 of his *Subrahmaṇya Kīrtanam*, in a free English translation by Guru Nitya:

> All discernible forms disappear where light is not paired with shadows, and all imaginations cease where beatitude reigns supreme. Such is the resplendance of your supreme state. It is as if your brilliance has swallowed the sun and the moon. Your lotus feet rest in the brilliant fire of the wisdom of the third eye. Oh Lord, reposed on the colourful wings of the phenomenal peacock, my supplication to you is not to disappear. The moon has gone beyond the horizon. With it also have gone the fantasizing dreams of the night. The sun has risen in the firmament. The moon and the shimmering stars are no more to be seen. It is a good time to immerse deeply into the depth of beatitude. Alas! That does not befit the occasion. It is not the time to be lost in spiritual absorption. Look, here is the world drowning in the dark ocean of misery. In body and mind millions are diseased. By drinking they have increased their torpor. These unfortunate wretches are to be roused from their drunken madness. Oh ye people, wake up now! It is time for you to enter into the cleansing river of eternal wisdom and perennial joy.

Narayana Guru was a living example of his own highest ideal.

The news that a person has attained Self-realization is common enough in India to cause barely a ripple of interest. What distiguishes the best from the generality is how that realization is lived and shared with humanity as a whole. The story of the Guru's life is an exciting and inspiring one, a drama of a quiet crusade to revitalize the highest of human values amongst a downtrodden people. But it is his role as a revaluator of wisdom that brings the Guru's influence out of a localized context and into the world arena. As put by Nataraja Guru in *The Word of the Guru* (p.61): "His method and approach to the subject of non-dual wisdom for the first time conforms not merely to 'objective' or 'critical' standards, but—and this is of epochal significance—even comes up to the requirements of a 'normative' or 'experimental' science, as far as that will probably ever be possible."

We are fortunate indeed that the fierce one-pointedness of contemplative withdrawal necessary for the Guru's realization was complemented by an unusually high intellectual ability and an extensive grounding in academic and spiritual classical literature. This and his later exposure to Western scientific thinking are combined in his momentous breakthrough in the form of a philosophical revaluation. In addition, the brilliance of his insight attracted some of India's most intelligent seekers to his ashram, and these have served to keep this revolutionary wisdom alive and growing. This includes his disciple Nataraja Guru, and his disciple Nitya Chaitanya Yati, who have dedicated their lives to the incorporation and extrapolation of the Guru's teachings. It is of more than passing interest to note that both of them chose *Darśanamālā* to form the core of their most definitive written works.

A well-known novelist once described his method of writing. First he writes a scene of one particular event, just a simple vignette of a few pages. Later he produces another scene, then more and more until he has a good-sized stack of them. All he needs to do is put them in a sequence with a few connecting sentences and he has his book.

Our everyday thinking is very much like the writing style of this novelist. We proceed in a linear fashion through a series of disjunct incidents seemingly held together by common characters and settings. The significance of each event depends solely on the particular context, and we derive the meaning of our life from the progression of several of them through time. This type of orientation to our surroundings becomes habitual as we progress through childhood, and is firmly fixed by the time we attain maturity.

In producing *Darśanamālā*, Narayana Guru had a very different perspective. Contemplating intensely for year upon year he evolved a unitive vision of the whole of the mind and its universe. Then, for the benefit of others, he divided his unitive awareness into major categories using a scientific methodology. This type of word production, where wisdom emerges from a holistic appreciation that transcends linear thinking, is called *darśana*. It is a philosophically presented mystical vision.

Our habitual mode of thinking becomes a major impediment when we seek to grasp the kind of word-wisdom found in *Darśanamālā*. Where our minds tend to follow a one-dimensional line, so to speak, we are confronted here with a multidimensional solid. Even with the able assistance of Guru Nitya providing a kind of interdimensional bridge, the reader must make an intensive effort in an unaccustomed direction in order to penetrate to the heart of it. Where reading a novel is natural and entertaining, assimilating *Darśanamālā* is a concentrated process, with the major rewards apparent only after a wholesale appreciation is attained.

If it were not for the compassionate guidance provided by Guru Nitya every step of the way, the work would undoubtedly remain the unappreciated masterpiece that it has been up to now. It most definitely requires an interpreter, for which role the Guru is eminently suited. Not only has he dived deeply into the mystery of the work's content, he has a sympathetic understanding of the point of view of the seeker gleaned from his worldwide exposure to bumbling students of every stripe. He never loses sight of the fact that the reader is a seeker of wisdom bent on self-improvement to achieve his own happiness, rather than an "armchair philosopher" with only a superficial interest.

The Psychology of Darśanamālā is not written to prove a point, but as a guidebook for seekers of Self-realization. Certain ideas which might be passionately defended in the average book of philosophy are taken here as a matter of course. The reader is expected to make the effort to grasp the meaning of what is offered, and the benefit will be in proportion to the effort expended. In this, the reader will be much better served by a leisurely and sympathetic approach. If he can take the time to absorb it verse by verse, perhaps spending even a day in reflection with each, adding as much of his own insight as possible, then he will discover the truly extraordinary nature of what is printed here. One hundred years of continuous contemplation by three of the modern world's most original and intelligent thinkers is encapsulated here, and one cannot hope to have it all in a week's casual perusal.

The intricacies and details of the structure of *Darśanamālā* are not especially examined in the present work, as Nataraja Guru has already done so with great thoroughness in *An Integrated Science of the Absolute.* For the student who is interested in discovering the full scope of *Darśanamālā*, *An Integrated Science of the Absolute* is eminently suited as a companion book to *The Psychology of Darśanamālā*. The former work covers the implications of *Darśanamālā* from the theoretical side, while the latter is more a practical guide for a personal search or self-examination based on Narayana Guru's visions.

Guru Nitya is an expert at explaining complicated ideas in ways that make them easily accessible. However, the reader should note that the disarming simplicity of his presentation belies the depth and radicality of the content of the present work. This is word-wisdom with the power to draw the mind out of hiding to discover for itself its true nature. The book is not for anyone clinging to the vested interests of their ego; it is for those who have already decided to give up their small comforts for a greater bliss and are prepared to make substantial efforts towards this end. *The Psychology of Darśanamālā* makes unusual demands on the reader, not through any exterior coercion or threats of damnation, but through "reason, steadily applied." Such a tool can be quite effective in unmasking the depth of one's being, which is well guarded by fear and psychological defense-mechanisms. On page 413 we read, "To those who are constantly under the spell of their ego-infatuation, forgetting or forgoing the ego is wrought with the fear of being destroyed. Such a prospect always brings to them a plaguing sense of insecurity. So they always prefer to have some sense object to be associated with, or other paranoiac people to make friends with. This emotional dependence and sense indulgence keeps the mind always at the periphery of consciousness, and it becomes incapacitated either to dive deep or to fly high." While it is quite proper to keep the bliss of the Absolute in mind in our goal-orientation, we should not forget that part of ourselves may be wholeheartedly opposed to the success of our quest.

Since this is by no means a beginning work in Vedānta, some familiarity with Sanskrit terminology on the part of the reader is assumed here. While almost everything is explained in detail within the text, a few peculiarities need to be pointed out beforehand.

It will be noted that the word 'self' is sometimes capitalized and sometimes not. These are two distinct terms. When capitalized, 'Self' refers to the universal or true 'I', defined as *sat-cit-ānanda*, existence-knowledge-bliss or value. It is the source of the 'self', the totality of parts that go to make up the individual. So 'self' is the individual, and 'Self' the absolute ground or being from which the individual emerges.

The focus of awareness within the self is called the I-consciousness. It is the monitor of the personality, and is colored by the social ego. This localized identification is the basis of polarization between the 'self' and the 'other', from which arise the manifold dualities of our perception. The text will examine this and the relationship of the self to the Self in great detail.

Generally speaking, consciousness is used here to include the entire range of existentiality, meaning both the conscious and the unconscious in the Western context. Awareness is the term which closely corresponds to the Western idea of consciousness. Unfortunately, due to the grounding of the author in Western as well as Eastern disciplines, such distinctions are not always adhered to. A perceptive reader should readily be able to note this from the context and make the appropriate adjustments.

The terms 'horizontal' and 'vertical' are used extensively in this work. They refer to the two axes of the cross or Cartesian coordinates, and while having their origination in the distant past, they have only recently been developed by Nataraja Guru into their proper philosophical stature as a frame of reference for wisdom. The interested student can turn to Nataraja Guru's writings for a more complete understanding of the subject. For the purposes of this introduction we need only say that vertical elements have an eternal quality, while horizontal ones belong to what is transient. Where the horizontal is conditioned, the vertical is unconditioned. Dual factors that may be integrated by this scheme include truth and supposition, spirit and matter, contemplation and action, oneness and multiplicity, and conception and perception. Christians intuitively use this relationship in the idea of the fatherhood of God and the brotherhood of Man. It forms the basis for the distinction between 'real' and 'actual' highlighted in this book.

The four states of consciousness according to Vedānta can also be superimposed on the coordinate axes. Waking consciousness, *jāgrat*, corresponds to the horizontal positive, while the dream state, *svapna*, is placed at the horizontal negative. *Suṣupti*, the deep sleep state, is placed at the vertical negative, and *turīya*, the transcendental, is represented by the vertical positive. Thus the horizontal covers the range of perceptual values from objectivity on the plus side to subjectivity on the negative, and the vertical comprises conceptual values which rise from the alpha to the omega in a graded series. Such is the frame of reference which comprises the core of the Science of the Absolute, of which *Darśanamālā* is a textbook.

As a biproduct of the emerging equality between the sexes, the word 'man' and its correlates 'he', 'him' and so on, have been recently called into question as perpetuating a sexual bias. Historically, 'man' has referred inclusively to both sexes, and has a rich and important etymological significance, being derived from the Sanskrit word Manu, the fourteen progenitors of mankind. In recognition of this neutrality, Old English had prefixes for each gender, of which the male was dropped and the female evolved into 'woman' over a period of time. The disappearance of the male prefix probably reflects the male dominance of this period, coupled with the Christian Church's effort to superimpose a male God on the face of the all-embracing Absolute. The process of rectifying this discrepancy has begun only lately, with the word 'person' replacing 'man' in compound words such as 'spokesperson', 'chairperson' and the like. However, it would be more fitting to extract the notion of 'male' from our concept of 'man' in the way that 'female' was during the European Dark Ages. Terms currently in use, such as 'he or she' and 'him/her', are unwieldy in sentences with four or five references, and must be considered intermediate steps in the development of proper terminology. It is hoped that a normalized language in respect to gender will be developed in the near future as a result of the current creative ferment. As stated earlier, the author fully supports the equal status of any and all subgroups within humanity. The Science of the Absolute is open to anyone, male or female, with an earnest desire to enter in to it. In the present work, therefore, the word 'man', and 'he', 'him' and 'his' referring to it, should be taken in the original all-inclusive sense, unless specifically excepted.

Quotations from Narayana Guru's writings found in the text are Guru Nitya's own translations. The maximum effort has been made by him to incorporate the subtle implications of the originals in a readable and poetic English, and the results speak for themselves. The frequent excerpts from the *Bhagavad Gita* are all Nataraja Guru's translations, in our opinion the finest rendered so far in the English language. They may be found in his commentary published by R & K Publishing House, New Delhi.

So now the stage is set and the actors have been introduced. The lights of phenomenality are dimmed down, and the crowd grows quiet. As the curtain raises, the audience is invited to participate in the fullest possible measure.

Scott Teitsworth
Portland, Oregon 1987

PART ONE

THE TEXT IN TRANSLATION

I. ADHYĀROPA DARŚANAM

1. It was in the beginning as if non-existence —
this world, like a dream; thereafter,
everything was projected
by the will alone of the Supreme Lord.

2. As incipient memory form alone, in the beginning,
this remained; thereafter, the Lord
projected with his *māyā*,
like a magician, the entire world.

3. Before origination this was
latent in him; thereafter, from him,
as sprout from seed, by his own
power it created itself alone.

4. The power, however, is of two kinds, known as
the bright and the dark; thus,
there is no coexistence between these,
as with light and darkness.

5. This, of mind-stuff alone, in the beginning
was accomplished, as if a painting,
with all the picturesqueness seen here,
by the Lord, like an artist.

6. Like potential yogic power,
in the beginning this was nature indeed;
thereafter, like a yogi, the Lord of the World
unfolded his magical powers.

7. When Self-knowledge shrinks,
then ignorance is fearful;
substantiation by name and form,
in the most terrible fashion, looms here, ghostlike.

8. This is terrible and empty of content,
like a phantom city;
even as such, the whole universe
is made as a wonder by the Primeval One.

9. From the sun, by stages, was not at all
how the world came to be; from the Self
this appeared all at once,
as one's vision comes in sleep.

10. He from whom this world manifested,
as a fig tree from a seed —
he is Brahmā, he is Śiva and Viṣṇu,
he is the Absolute, he alone is all.

II. APAVĀDA DARŚANAM

1. This world, which is of gross
and subtle form, comes from consciousness;
if it is affirmed, everything is existence through and through;
if it is denied, it is consciousness through and through.

2. Apart from cause there is no effect;
therefore, all this is unreal;
for the unreal, how can there be an origin?
Of the unoriginated, what dissolution?

3. That which has no origin or dissolution
is none other than the supreme Absolute;
through *māyā* the confusion arises that there is
origin and dissolution in the Self.

4. Because of its non-difference from cause,
how can an effect come to have existence?
By that, how can there be
the non-existence of cause also?

5. This which is unreal, being an effect,
has a cause; it is not the world,
but the Absolute alone that is real,
which a dull mind wrongly imagines to be unreal.

6. If one alone has reality,
how can one experience another's beingness?
To say that the real is in the real is tautology;
to say it is in the unreal is contradiction.

7. When all parts are separated
one by one, then one sees
everything as consciousness alone —
far from *māyā* — and not any other.

8. Consciousness alone, not another, shines;
therefore, there is nothing other than consciousness;
what does not shine — that is unreal;
and what is unreal — that does not shine.

9. *Ānanda* alone shines as real,
not anything else; therefore, everything
is *ānanda* through and through;
apart from *ānanda* nothing else is known.

10. All is indeed existence, consciousness, and pure happiness;
in this there is not even a trace of the many;
he who sees this as many
goes from death to death.

III. ASATYA DARŚANAM

1. All this is a permeation of mind,
   but mind is nowhere to be seen;
   in the same way, like blue and so on in the sky,
   the world is seen in the Self.

2. By ignorance, which is none other than the mind,
   all worlds are imagined;
   when by this knowledge dissolution comes,
   then everything becomes like a painting.

3. What expands here from darkness
   into a ghost to a coward —
   that world is seen by the wise
   as a dream-world of the wakeful state.

4. The visible is imagined by the will;
   the visible is seen only where there is will,
   and not where there is no will —
   like the snake in the rope.

5. There is no difference between will
   and mind; that mind, which is called
   ignorance and darkness, is a wonder,
   like Indra's magic.

6. To one who reasons correctly
   the world appears as a mirage in the Self;
   and to the indiscriminate, by confusion,
   a reflection looks as if it is real.

7. The Self does not, like milk, attain
   to another form; therefore, everything,
   as in the creation by Indra's magic,
   seems to be through superimposition.

8. *Māyā* alone is the primal cause of the world;
   by that which is none other than the
   wielder of *māyā* all this is created,
   like the unreal effects of psychic powers.

9. To the mature mind of the old the world appears
in the Self as a forest in the sky,
even as the unreal form of a puppet
seems otherwise to a child.

10. The One is real, not a second;
the unreal indeed appears to be real;
the *śivaliṅgam* is stone alone,
not a second made by the sculptor.

IV. MĀYĀ DARŚANAM

1. What is not known, that is *māyā*;
it alone shines as many forms:
vidyā, *avidyā*, *parā*, *aparā*,
tamas, *pradhāna*, and *prakṛti*.

2. Like the prior non-existence in the clay alone, before it is fashioned,
none other than the Absolute is known;
what is that Absolute is indeed
māyā, of indeterminate possibility.

3. The non-Self is unreal, the Self is real;
thus, the means by which such knowledge comes,
that is this *vidyā*, like the recognition
of the truth about rope and snake.

4. The Self is unreal, the non-Self is real;
thus, the means by which such knowledge comes,
that alone is *avidyā*, like the erroneous cognition
about rope and snake.

5. The senses, mind, intelligence,
five vital tendencies and such — that by which
they are specifically created as the subtle limbs
of the reasoning Self is *parā* alone.

6. Adopting these limbs, the reasoning Self
by its own *māyā* becomes deluded,
as if happy and unhappy;
in truth there is nothing at all.

7. That by which this world, which is indeed
the object of the senses, is specifically created
is *aparā* alone, which in the Self
permeates the eidetic imagery of the gross.

8. As ignorance of mother-of-pearl
is the basis of silver,
what is imagined in the Self —
that is known as *tamas*.

9. Just as a tree is wonderfully
latent in the seed,
all are in this; therefore, or by its
importance, it is called *pradhānam*.

10. As by its very nature it
diversifies the modalities marvellously,
this, of three-fold modality,
is well-known here as *prakṛti*.

V. BHĀNA DARŚANAM

1. Present within as without,
constantly fluttering like a bee,
awareness is divided into just two kinds:
generic and specific.

2. Gross, subtle, causal, and the fourth —
thus, the bases of awareness are of four kinds;
the same names
apply to awareness also.

3. See here: "I am the body;
this is a pot." Thus, based on the gross,
the awareness which is experienced,
that is considered to be the gross.

4. Here, such awareness as "body" and "pot,"
these are the specific;
similarly, "I," "this," and such
are to be remembered as the generic.

5. The senses, mind, intellect,
items of interest, and the five vital breaths —
the awareness which constitutes
the subtle nature of its basis is the subtle.

6. "I am ignorant" — such awareness
exemplifies the causal;
here, what is revealed as "I am" is the generic,
"ignorant" is the specific.

7. "I am the Absolute" — such awareness
is praised as the fourth;
here, the element "I am" is the generic,
and "the Absolute" is the specific.

8. Where there is awareness there is an object of awareness;
where there is no awareness there is no object of awareness;
thus, by agreement,
and also by difference, certitude comes.

9. As the eye does not see itself, even so
the Self by the Self; because the Self is not
an object of awareness, what the Self sees —
that indeed is the object of awareness.

10. What is the object of awareness, that is superimposed;
the non-superimposed is not an object of awareness;
what is superimposed, that is unreal;
what is not superimposed — That alone is real.

VI. KARMA DARŚANAM

1. The Self, through *māyā*, does
action by assuming many forms,
though detached and self-luminous,
like the *taijasa* in sleep.

2. I think, I speak, I grasp, I hear —
all such forms of action are done
by the Supreme Self
through the agency of consciousness and the *indriya*-s.

3. Prior to action the Self alone is;
nothing else is known;
therefore, actions are done
by itself with its own *māyā*.

4. The Self has some kind of power,
inseparable from it, difficult to define;
by that alone all actions are
projected in the actionless Self.

5. The Self is always detached alone;
by ignorance action is done as if attached;
"I am not acting" — thus,
the seer remains detached in action.

6. The one Self alone
burns as fire, blows as wind,
showers as rain, supports
as earth, and flows as river.

7. Going upward as *prāṇa*,
downward as *apāna*,
remaining actionless, the one alone
beats, murmurs, and pulsates in the nerves.

8. From the unmodulating Self,
and not another, the six aspects —
existence, birth, growth, change,
deterioration, and extinction — happen here.

9. In spite of action becoming self-accomplished
   by the psychic dynamism and the senses,
   the wise one knows, "I am the
   unattached *kūtastha*."

10. Because "I" is seen as an object of
    awareness, I-consciousness is also a superimposition,
    like the silver in the mother-of-pearl;
    above everything else, today and tomorrow, the one alone exists.

VII. JÑĀNA DARŚANAM

1. Knowledge is one indeed — unconditioned
and conditioned; that, devoid of
I-consciousness and so on,
is the knowledge which is unconditioned.

2. That knowledge modulated as I-consciousness inside,
likewise that which is modulated
as knowledge of thisness outside,
such knowledge is known as the conditioned.

3. That by which one experiences the witnessing of the non-Self,
such as I-consciousness and so on,
is Self-knowledge, by which alone
immortality is enjoyed.

4. That by which I-consciousness and innumerable
such effects, which belong to the non-Self,
are known, is said to be
knowledge of the non-Self.

5. When things are known as they are,
as in the knowledge of the truth of rope,
that is factual knowledge;
and fictitious when it is otherwise.

6. By the mere presence of which alone
everything is illuminated —
that is characterized as knowledge of
immediate perception, and also as inner perception.

7. That form of the modulation
of knowledge, by which the appraisal of
the possibility produced by concomitant inherence
is deduced, is inference.

8. On going near the object to be ascertained
and recognizing, "this is the form of the animal
whose marks have been heard of" — that by which
such knowledge comes is analogy.

9. The knowledge of "I am," "mine," and so on,
is individual knowledge;
the other, such as "that," "this," and so on,
is spoken of as sensory knowledge.

10. *Aum tat sat* — what is thus instructed,
arrived at as the union of the Absolute and the Self,
devoid of functions like willing —
that is said to be absolute knowledge.

VIII. BHAKTI DARŚANAM

1. Meditation on the Self is *bhakti.*
That by which the Self is blissful, with that,
the knower of the Self always meditates
upon the Self by the Self.

2. *Brahma* is meditated upon
because *Brahma* is blissful.
Constant meditation on *Brahma*
is known as *bhakti.*

3. *Ānanda* alone is meditated,
not misery by anyone any time.
That meditation which is blissful
is *bhakti*, it is instructed.

4. *Ātma* alone is *Brahma.*
The knower of the Self contemplates the *ātma*, not any other.
This thus meditating the Self
is named as *bhakti.*

5. *Ānanda, ātma* and *Brahma*—
such are the names of this alone, so it is said.
In whom there is such certitude of awareness,
he as a contemplative is well known.

6. I am *ānanda*, I am *Brahma*, I am *ātma*;
in such forms, for whom
there is always identification,
as a contemplative he is well known.

7. The wife does not merely worship the husband,
nor the husband, the wife.
By all, their *ānanda* alone is worshiped,
which resides in the sense interests.

8. Thus the wise man sees everywhere
nothing but the joy of the Self—
not even a little of anything else.
His *bhakti* indeed is the highest.

9. Towards the Father of the world,
to one's spiritual teacher, father, mother,
towards the founders of truth,
towards those who walk in the same path,

10. towards those who put down evil,
(and) to those who do good to all,
what sympathy there is, that is *bhakti*,
what here belonging to the supreme Self is the ultimate.

IX. YOGA DARŚANAM

1. That which always unites
and also gets united with *cidātma*,
which is in the form of restraining mind,
that is praised as *yoga*.

2. Where the seer, the sight and the seen
are not known, there the heart
should be joined while *vāsana* is present.
Such is *yoga* — thus the *yoga*-knower.

3. All this name and form is
Brahma indeed. Thus, in
the Absolute, mind always merges well.
This is ascertained as *yoga*.

4. By the modulation of consciousness
which is unbroken as in the streak of oil,
what incessant rejoicing is in the Self.
Such is *yoga* — this is the recognition of *yogi*-s.

5. To whichever mind goes, from all that
this should always be restrained,
and should be united in the Self —
this is *yoga*. In this should remain united.

6&7. *Saṅkalpa* — the cause of all disasters of mankind —
along with projections, should be uprooted
and incipient memories be restrained in the *ātma*.
What is seen has not the perceived
reality, because what is seen
is the seer itself. Who is thus united
in the seer, he is the best among *yoga*-knowers.

8. When mind, the bumble bee, sips
the honey-like sweetness of one's own bliss,
fluttering ceases and is drawn
into union by *yoga vāyu*.

9. When meditation is done with gaze between the eyebrows
and the tip of the tongue fixed above the uvula,
then happens *khecarī mudrā*,
which dispels torpor and fatigue.

10. In this world *yoga*, in short, is of
two forms — knowledge and *karma* — thus.
All forms of *yoga* are conclusively comprised
in these two descriptions of *yoga*.

X. NIRVĀṆA DARŚANAM

1. *Nirvāṇa* is of two kinds:
the pure and the impure.
That which is the pure is devoid of *vāsana*;
similarly, that is impure which is conjoined with *vāsana*.

2. Most pure, pure — thus
the pure is of two kinds, and similarly
the impure also is said to be
impure-pure and impure-impure.

3. The most pure is again of three kinds:
one in the superior, one in the more superior,
one in the most superior; and thus
the pure is established in the *brahma*-knower.

4. The impure-pure is devoid of *rajas* and *tamas*
and the other is with *rajas* and *tamas*.
The former is known to be in the seeker of liberation,
the latter in those who desire psychic attainment.

5. Having burned everything with the fire of wisdom,
aiming the good of the world,
doing action according to injunction,
the knower of *brahma* remains firm in *brahma*.

6. Having renounced all action,
always established in the Absolute,
who moves about the world merely to conduct bodily life —
he is the superior knower of *brahma*.

7. He knows only when informed by another,
does not know by himself —
such a person is the more superior.
He always enjoys absorption in the Absolute.

8. Not knowing anything by himself,
even when informed he remains so —
such a person is the most superior.
Always without modulation, he is *brahma* alone.

9. Of this, there is nothing avoidable and acceptable.
As for the Self, it shines by itself.
Thus having become certain, liberate.
Thereafter modulation does not repeat.

10. The one *brahma* alone is without a second;
nothing else is; there is no doubt.
Thus the knower should liberate from duality.
Thereafter he does not return.

I. ADHYĀROPA DARŚANAM

Cosmic Projection

Life is a continuous series of experiences. In the intervals between these experiences there arise, often unbidden, the links of memory. When the attention is not focused on some event in the external world, then one's attention is directed into the inner world of subjective reasoning and fancies. There one recalls the pleasures of the past, or experiences again its paranoiac nightmares. Living retrospectively, facing the events of the immediate present, or hopefully looking towards the future for some imagined fulfillment are all aspects of our attitude to life.

Each time the mind becomes aware of a concept there arises along with it a witnessing consciousness of the concept as the agent of its knower. This agent is recognized as "I." In the process of relating the concept to a percept, and after such objectivization, relation is established between the subject "I" and the objectivized concept-percept complex. It is in such an interrelationship of concept, percept, and the agent of awareness that knowledge is experienced.

Stimuli, on entering the senses below the threshold of consciousness, excite the interrogating faculty, causing concept after concept to arise in an effort to illumine and translate these stimuli into meaningful ensembles. This process can be described as that orientation of the mind which seeks to place each perceptive experience within the frame of reference of a relevant time-space continuum. To assist this orientation of the mind, every situation as it is perceived is penetrated with the questions, how, what, why, where, and when. Although consciousness flows without cessation, the mind introduces breaks in that flow in much the same way as commas and periods are used in the text on this page. Each element of judgement, so introduced, stands alone as a unit of understanding. When viewed in terms of logical relevancy or epistemological belongingness, several such units are interrelated and recognized by the mind as one whole. These complex units are very often confections which are admixtures of percepts arising from the external and the individual's subjective value sense.

When an inner idea envelops a seemingly perceptive situation, christening it with a definitive term and recognizing it as having the status of an objective percept, what arises in consciousness as the understanding of that object is called projection, or more conventionally, superimposition. In this respect we should note, however, that the substratum of the superimposed knowledge is totally concealed from us. We tend to describe such an experience in terms of objective sensory qualities or properties actually belonging to the perceived object. This we do in spite of the fact that all such qualities or properties are projected by our own automatic recall of concepts. Of course there is a mysterious element operating identically in all individuated minds that makes the compositions of concepts almost similar at the transactional level.

Just as a microscope cannot show the exact size of a virus in the smear on a slide except by supplementing the data with a mathematical deduction which the bacteriologist employs, we can only have access to what is presented in our consciousness. We cannot escape the fixed mechanism of the sensory system and the physiological and biochemical rules which regulate the psychophysics and psychobiochemistry of the mind. Considering these aspects, we have to agree that we wrongly identify our perceptions as exclusively belonging to the seemingly outside world.

As every aspect of our wakeful life is composed of an admixture of percepts and concepts, our conscious life becomes a curious alloy of appearances and our psychic reactions to them. The present chapter will be a critical examination of the basic experience on which the superstructure of individuation is erected. In a scientific treatise the method adopted is to go from what is known to what is unknown, and from the simple to the complex. Narayana Guru keeps such a method in mind as he presents his first philosophical vision, "The vision of the projection of the qualities of the non-Self onto the Self."

VERSE 1

āsīdagre 'sadevedam
bhuvanam svapnavat punaḥ
sasarja sarvam saṅkalpa-
mātreṇa parameśvaraḥ

It was in the beginning as if non-existence —
this world, like a dream; thereafter,
everything was projected
by the will alone of the Supreme Lord.

āsīt — it was
agre — in the beginning
asat eva — as if non-existence
idam — this
bhuvanam — world
svapnavat — like a dream
punaḥ — thereafter
sarvam — everything
sasarja — was projected
saṅkalpa mātreṇa — by the will alone
parameśvaraḥ — of the Supreme Lord

Here the subject matter is the world. The particular term that is used here for world is *bhuvanam*. The literal meaning of this word is "to be; to become; to be born or produced; to spring or proceed from; arise." (See Apte's *Sanskrit-English Dictionary*, p. 408). When a child emerges from his mother's womb, a world of variegated forms arises before him. Each time we fall asleep the world disappears as far as we are concerned, yet when we again awaken it reappears in all its previous detail. From where does this world come? How does it manifest? In the present verse these questions will be answered.

If we are to question the world, the world should in itself be sufficiently interesting to give us the incentive to do so. It is so, and that interest is the sense of wonder which comes when we contemplate our environment. Wonder arises from the uniqueness of an experience, but to repeat that experience again and again in the same way will blunt the edge of wonder. Familiarity brings, if not contempt, at least a diminution of interest. One exception to this is higher truth, which becomes all the more dear when one knows it intimately. Each time we are aware of what is happening around us, a new experience can bring with it a new sense of wonder or intrigue. Inherent in this wonder or sense of concern is the realization of the newness of the experience; newness and spontaneity are factors in the sense of wonder.

It is appropriate that our inquiry begins where this verse states, "before we knew the world it was as if it did not exist." When we consider past and future time, our point of reference is the present. The phrase "before we knew" can be considered only in its relativity to the present. The Sanskrit word for the present is *vartamānam*, and it can be separated into two parts, *vartan*, meaning "existing"; and *mānam*, meaning "in a measurable manner." What occurred in the past is no longer available for measurement, nor can any system of measurement be applied to what may occur in the future. In the sense in which the word is used here, "measurement" includes the making of observations, a mental scrutiny, and the formation of value judgements arising from our response to the nature of a given experience. The simplest form of judgement is to first predicate a subject with the appropriate attributes.

The English term "present tense" is, for our purposes, psychologically as relevant as the logical appropriateness of the word *vartamānam*. To become tense (as in the word "tension") indicates that the psychophysical organism is transforming itself into the psychological state of attention. An example often given is that of a cat contracting its body, thrashing its tail, and concentrating on a rat before pouncing on it. After the expected action is accomplished, the tension passes away, the body relaxes, and the attention is turned elsewhere. In short, the present tense changes into the past tense. The expectation of some event which may again produce a state of tension indicates the future tense.

In this verse we question the world of our experience: that which we see, hear, touch, taste and smell. If the world is to be available for empirical experience and judgement, we must assume it to exist in some manner before our experience of it. Hence the question, "Did this world exist before I became aware of it?" The answer is, "No, it did not exist as you now see it."

The Sanskrit term used to indicate that something exists is *sat*. When an experience is irrefutable, the dynamic of its persistence is called *sat*. Such an experience is an assertion of its beingness implied in the action of judgement. When we make the affirmation "it is," then "is" refers to the existential aspect of an experience. When the mind is unable to assert a positive existence, the Sanskrit term used is *asat*.

At this stage of our inquiry we should be certain that we understand the question before us. It is not that we question the existence, for example, of the solar system or the starry heavens, nor do we suggest that these didn't exist prior to the birth of any individual man. To fully penetrate the meaning of this world for me in terms of its existence I should ask myself, "What was this world in terms of its relativity to a self, namely myself, before I existed as a self to experience it?" In order to do this I must be able to postulate a self other than this purely psychological one which I seem to experience as my self. Is there a self which can be identified as my own, and which is not limited by the present, past and future, or the limitations of a physiological body? The answer to this will become clear as we proceed. For the moment, the question of my possible experience of the world before I existed can be answered by the Sanskrit phrase *āsīdagre'sadevedam bhuvanam.* Sanskrit grammar allows this to be read as either *asat eva* or *sat eva. Asat eva* means "as if non-existence," while *sat eva* means "as if existence." In the face of such an apparent contradiction, we are entitled to ask why the Guru uses an ambiguous term here. When we understand the full implication of these terms, the ambiguity melts away. The world did not exist for the person prior to his experiencing of it, therefore we can say "as if non-existence." Experience itself is an effect, and no effect can proceed except from a cause. Since there must have been a causal factor to produce the effect we can say, "as if existence."

Let us say a man designs in his mind the construction of a house. He has a mental picture of its dimensions, the number of rooms and their uses, its situation, decoration, and furnishings. He may picture the life of his family in that house, and even himself live with them a mental existence in a mental construction. But the house can be called an accomplished fact in the transactional sense only when it is transmuted from the mental world into the world of three-dimensional existence, built of substantial materials and with people inhabiting it. Yet the actual house could not have been brought into existence without the prior conception of it. Similarly, this world which I experience now exists as an integral part of my beingness. It may not have come as a consequent result of a person's prior concept, but in and through its continuous process of organization we see a steady, progressive actualization of logically reducible ideas of integrated forms and interrelationships of properties.

This room which I observe around me, the trees and flowers outside it, the blue sky seen through the window, and the far-off horizon are all parts of the same knowledge through which I am aware of this physical body and the psychological responses to pleasure and pain, joy and misery, hunger, fear and happiness, and so on. To make a dichotomy of internal and external worlds in knowledge is to create an artifical division of analytically ponderable ideas of values, which can serve only the purpose of explaining things psychologically. Following this train of thought, I should infer that any experience, or the ongoing totality of experience, is the sum of my several impressions and ideas woven into the fabric of my socially educated and conventionally structured understanding of the world.

However, one should be careful, for this kind of argument can come to resemble solipsism. If the world of my experience is entirely my own projection, how is it that most people will confirm my projections as having an empirical validity in their own experience? Where external objects are concerned there will be a very wide agreement as to their nature between myself and others. Is it possible for all to make an identical projection simultaneously?

A mathematician can calculate the exact distance from the earth to any planet within this solar system. Having done this, scientists and technicians can then construct an extremely complex physical artifact and dispatch it on so precise a course that it can be made to land on a predetermined spot on that planet. In the light of such an achievement, it is difficult to refute the existence of an actual space and a universally admissible time. Such an event cannot be explained as merely the result of an individual and private projection. To overcome this difficulty we have to postulate a universal mind which can lend its homogeneity to all individual minds.

At this point some people think of personifying nature, making cosmic laws look like the ingenious reasoning and scheming of a superman. Mystically inclined thinkers project the little-known cosmic functions as dictates of an anthropomorphic God. In this context we should guide our steps cautiously so as not to make either of these mistakes.

Such a universal mind as we have referred to is called *parameśvara. Param* means "Absolute." *Īśvara* is derived from the root *īṭ*, meaning "that which rules." In every unit of the experience of each individual this principle operates. Moreover, it does so in such a manner that all the parts of each experience are held together in a way which makes the whole experience unitively meaningful. This occurs in spite of the heterogeneous functioning of the parts. This principle can be seen to be of the same nature as creative intelligence, so it can manifest as the awareness of each individual mind. It is as if the Universal is observing itself through the action of a properly focused human mind. Another aspect of this universal mind is its ability to interpret visibles in terms of calculables.

Taking into account all these factors, it can be seen that the word *parameśvara* has a very appropriate usage in this context. What can blind us to the full appreciation of this is the unfortunate fact that our minds are conditioned by the myths and fables of ancient legends. Because of this, the word *parameśvara* may bring to our minds some irrelevant picture, such as that of a religious diety living in the Himalayas with matted hair and an iron trident in his hand. As a poetic fancy such an image may have some value, but it should not be confused with the scientifically structured usage of the term *parameśvara* as intended in this verse.

Seated before a Guru will be disciples who vary in the maturity of their understanding. It is appropriate therefore that instruction is given in words which make sense to both the novice and the mature scholar. While the young novice, who is familiar with legendary stories, is satisfied that the universe is created by God, known as *parameśvara*, the mature and erudite student meditates on the deep significance of the structure of each sound, which has been specially chosen by the Guru to impart his wisdom.

This is why, if we examine the source books of different *darśana*-s, we find them all given as collections of aphorisms. Aphorisms are cryptic statements sometimes presented in only a couple of phrases. For example, the second sūtra of the aphorisms of Bādarāyaṇa is *janmādyasya yataḥ*. The literal meaning is "birth etc. and such." In itself this phrase may not seem to make much sense. To help the student, Śankara wrote an elaborate commentary on every aphorism contained in Bādarāyana's *Brahma Sūtra*-s.

Now we have to carefully consider the statement, "This world was afterwards projected by *parameśvara* by his will alone, as if in a dream." All that we experience in dreams is structured in our mind from fragments of memories. The number of beads in a kaleidoscope is limited, but the patterns which may arise from the movements of the beads are endless. In the same manner, through the use of previously experienced impressions and their pleasurable or painful associations, the mind can weave dream after dream. The secret of the composition of dreams can baffle the creative genius of man. There seems to be no consistency in the structuring of dreams. In accordance with the value-dynamics involved, a concept can be projected into awareness by the presentation of symbols, the meanings of which are unfamiliar and apparently unrelated to anything we have seen or experienced before. An elephant may be reduced to the size of a mosquito, or human qualities given to a flower. Within the frame of reference of the dream world, the dreamer does not doubt the existence of any of the items in his dream. But when the dreamer wakes all is gone, and nothing exists other than himself. The world we see during the wakeful state also disappears from our awareness when we fall asleep. From this we can rightly infer that the world of appearance is a changing flux and that the only unchanging factor is the one witnessing consciousness. Of course, there is a constant element in the wakeful world of transaction that gives the contiguity to proceed from one wakeful experience to another period of wakeful experience. We have, however, to look for this mysterious element as a transpersonal factor.

In the present verse the Guru does not say that the world is dreamed by the individual. He attributes its existence to an overriding principle which, like the human mind, can project its ideas in such a cogent and coherent manner that it should be possible for anyone to gain some understanding from and about it.

If the world is like a dream, can it be called real? The answer is no, it is not real. But if the world is unreal, how could it have a creator? Are we not forced to say that if the effect is unreal, the cause also must be unreal?

This leads us to a position where the initial assertion of a creator as a reality is cancelled out by the unreality of the creation. This in turn brings us to the awareness of a numinous but indiscernible principle that is behind the phenomena of both creator and creation. So we are led to the conclusion that the status of such a reality has an existence which is established *in itself*, and which is independent of all other possible forms of existence.

As an alternative to the hypothesis of an independent creator creating the world with whatever means he has at his disposal, let us look at the very stuff called "world," which includes us also in it. Think of it unitively as one primeval substance. It should not be difficult to see how a substratum can remain the same in its essence, without any fundamental change, and yet transform itself into a variety of individuated forms. When physicists speak of the conservation of energy and the transformation of matter, they refer to the same truth. The unchanging substratum, which is willing its own transformation into the manifested world, in the present context is called *parameśvara*.

Spiritualists claim this primeval cause to be an absolute principle of Spirit. Materialists argue that the original cause is a primeval energy which is in no way different from matter. They say further that consciousness, which is apparently different from matter, is after all only a quality of organized matter. If we should ask both spiritualists and materialists to define and describe the exact nature of the primeval substance, they will postulate the same attributes to what they call the original cause. But neither will give up their claim that spiritualism or materialism is the definitive truth.

Materialism in India is at least as old as the Vedic culture, if not older. In the Upanishads, before the ideas of God or the Absolute or the Self are presented, the primeval world-substratum is defined as "irrefutable existence," or *sat*. This irrefutability of existence substantiates itself by its ability to impress on the human mind the qualities of its own existence. The fact of existence is impressed on consciousness as a certitude of the substantiality of existence. The awareness of that certitude, when it manifests in the human consciousness, is expressed on each occasion in the form of a meaning of the existence and its inherent value. When the same is observed in the frame of reference of an individual experience, it is called "affectivity."

From this we can see that the riṣis of India were not basically idealists, but were existentialists in an unlimited sense. They gave attention to existence, subsistence, and value. It is a matter for regret that even the best of Indian minds, such as that of Dr. Radhakrishnan, misunderstood this fact. He presented the teachings of the riṣis as "an idealist view of life."

For anything to assert its existence, it should be supported by the irrefutability of its own true beingness. If the existence of cloth is denied, then the existence of thread must be accepted; or if there is a denial of thread, then the reality of cotton will have to be accepted. It can never be established that a whole experience comes as though from nowhere, without some source of origin. Modern science proceeds towards the discovery of truth through the observation of sense-data. In addition, the senses are supplemented by mathematical tools. But even with this assistance, the senses inevitably come to the frontier of their limitations, beyond which they cannot be stretched. A scientist may claim that his observations are objective, but the fact remains that he arrives at his conclusions through calculations, some part of which will certainly be subjective.

In the days of people such as Karl Marx, the farthest point to which the physicist could go was the atom. The real war between spiritualists and materialists of that time was in trying to recognize what lay beyond the boundary of classical physics. The twentieth century ushered in another aspect of physics. Now we are unable to say that the field of the modern physicist is limited to the world of objective data alone. If we walk through the halls of modern science, such as physics, astrophysics, chemistry, biology, or psychology, we shall soon come up against a wall of uncertainty, and we shall be filled with a great sense of awe and wonder. Such an experience has changed at least some scientists into contemplatives. In the next verse Narayana Guru will refer to this world of awe and wonder.

VERSE 2

vāsanāmayam evādā-
vāsīd idam atha prabhuḥ
aśṛjan māyayā svasya
māyāvīvākhilam jagat

As incipient memory form alone, in the beginning,
this remained; thereafter, the Lord
projected with his *māyā*,
like a magician, the entire world.

vāsanāmayam eva — as incipient memory form alone
ādau — in the beginning
idam — this
āsīt — remained, existed, was
atha — thereafter
prabhuḥ — the Lord
aśṛjat — projected, created
svasya — with his own
māyayā — with *māyā*
māyāvī iva — like a magician
akhilam — the entire
jagat — world

When school children attend a chemistry class for the first time, the teacher may seek to inculcate in them a sense of wonder and interest in his science. For example, in a beaker of water he may have a piece of phosphorus. Taking it from the water he exposes it to air. After a few minutes it will fume and catch fire. Then he may take a piece of sodium which has been soaked in kerosene oil, and throw it in the water. As soon as it enters the water the sodium will burst into flame. Experiments such as these may stimulate the children to put searching questions to their teacher.

Magicians entertain and charlatans exploit ignorant people by the performance of tricks and illusions, the processes of which are not known to the onlookers, whose reactions are much the same as those of the children in our chemistry class — wonder and amazement. Everything that is presented to our senses has its own characteristic properties, and it is science which seeks to know the source of these properties. When common salt is analyzed, it proves to be a compound of sodium and chlorine, but in the pinch of salt which we taste we do not detect the natural properties of these two constituents. If we analyze still further, we come to the primeval state of particles or waves. There we shall find no distinction between those particles which are structured as sodium or chlorine.

In this discovery the natural question which comes to the mind is, "What is it that causes qualitative variation at the atomic level?" To answer this question we have to move into a more general branch of science called mathematics. In the realm of mathematics we no longer deal with things which are visible. Even with the use of the most powerful electron microscope we can penetrate the visible world only so far, and our findings are valid only within certain limits. When our inquiry is taken beyond the frontiers of the visible world, physics changes into metaphysics. Most scientists are unwilling to accept that their philosophical speculations are not strictly objective and are on a par with the shrewd guesses of philosophers.

Just as religion has its followers who swear by the pronouncements of one prophet or another, so also do people who are excited by scientific invention or technological progress satisfy themselves by shouting slogans in favor of science. The physicist tries to relate all forces to one physical entity. The biologist wants to show that all forms of life arise from a primitive principle of Life. Thus, unknown to themselves, scientists, like every one of us, are in need of a unitive principle to which all phenomena can be related. However, they do not wish to underline any one term as the first principle or first cause. They tend to leave this question as a mystery, while engendering the hope in their followers that some day in the future they will be able to realize this elusive first principle.

In the present verse Narayana Guru names this first principle or cause of the universe, *prabhu*. What stimulates the interest of the philosopher and scientist in questioning the phenomena of their experience is the element of mystery that transforms one form or one quality into another. This mysterious and veiling process is called *māyā* in Sanskrit. What is a mystery to a human mind can cause a variety of responses: wonder, delight, and fear or dread, among others. When the mysterious cause of leprosy was discovered and an antidote invented, there was universal rejoicing in those countries where leprosy had been a scourge. On the other hand, the mystery enshrouding the dreadful disease of cancer provokes a response of a more sinister and fearful kind. Thus *māyā* is a field where joy and sorrow, affection, and fear can all operate side by side. All scientific effort since the time of seers such as Atreya in India and Democritus in ancient Greece, upto and including the present-day study of outer space, has been directed towards unveiling the mystery of *māyā*.

It may seem to us as if *māyā* functions in a magical way. One who understands how to perform magic is no stranger to its secrets. The magician is the master of his mysterious world. As there is a secret to be mastered in the practice of magic, so also there is one to be penetrated if we are to understand the mystery and power of *māyā*. We can, for example, read in the ancient Indian epic *Mahābhārata* of people who travelled to the moon, there to undergo a period of intense ascetic discipline (*tapas*), and who later returned to the earth. Even during the first quarter of this century there might have been few who would have given credence to this claim. Nowadays, however, we cannot so readily dismiss the possibility of truth in that ancient teaching. Everywhere across the world people watched, through the medium of television, courageous Americans walking on the moon. Later they returned to also tell of their experiences. But such is the resistance of the human mind to change that some believe the whole operation to have been an elaborate hoax. The Flat Earth Society still has its protagonists. Those who understand to some extent how the moon landings were accomplished have to, that extent, understood a deep mystery. Thus, to know the secret helps us to consciously participate in a principle which continues to be a mystery to those who fail to understand it.

When we turn our attention from the mysteries of the physical and chemical worlds and focus it on a more intimate subject, that of our own personal life, we are confronted with a much deeper mystery. In the matter of behavior, for example, we seem often unpredictable even to ourselves. At one moment a person, in his love for someone, holds out a friendly hand as a gesture indicative of his inner emotions. At another time the same person can shriek and shout, becoming violent and destructive towards the one he claims to love. This can surprise those who are not familiar with the inconsistencies of that person's behavior. Human caprice can be likened to a piece of phosphorus, which when exposed to the air can suddenly and without warning burst into flame. In the case of phosphorus, the possibility of such a transformation is a latent chemical property; in a man it is latent as a potential psychological factor.

This potential or latent aspect, which enables one to have harmonious or discordant relations with others, and which often appears capricious to the onlooker, is described by the Sanskrit term *vāsana*. In one case the transformation is a chemical potential and in the other a psychological potential; there is no essential difference between the two. Narayana Guru attributes such potentiality to one generic, latent principle in the primeval substratum, recognized in the previous verse as *parameśvara*, and in the present one as *prabhu*. All possibilities in the universe, from the spinning of a nebula to the pollination of a flower, and including the composition of a symphony, are all latent in the *prabhu* as *vāsana*-s. *Prabhu* literally means, "that which becomes methodically and abundantly."

A candle will be seen to have a definite mass and form. We can see it, touch it, taste it, and smell it; we can weigh and measure it. A candle therefore is capable of giving us a very objective experience. At this point we do not perceive its latent luminous quality or its capacity to give out radiant heat, nor do we see the transmutability of form inherent in its composition. Now let us light our candle. At once we get both light and heat, and its mass and form begin to change. If we leave it alone it will appear to consume itself, and in time may almost or completely disappear as it burns away its own wax. Finally there may be no wax or only a small residue, no flame or heat, little if any mass, and a completely changed form. In much the same way camphor, if exposed to air, will also disappear. In these two examples we can see the transformation of a gross object into its subtle constituents. In the same manner an extremely subtle form may be changed into a gross form. Take, for example, the transmission of radiophotographs by a news agency. In a few minutes an event becomes a photographic record that is changed into electrical energy and further transformed into radio waves. These waves may be transmitted across the globe. The whole process is then reversed, and once again a visible photograph exists as an image on paper. The next verse is an elucidation of this principle.

VERSE 3

prāg utpatteridam svasmin
vilīnam atha vai svataḥ
bījādankuravat svasya
śaktirevāsṛjat svayam

Before origination this was
latent in him; thereafter, from him,
as sprout from seed, by his own
power it created itself alone.

prāk — before
utpatteḥ — origination
idam — this
vilīnam — was latent
svasmin — in him
atha vai — thereafter
svataḥ — from him
aṅkuravat — as sprout
bījāt — from seed
svasya śaktiḥ — by his own power
asṛjat — it created, it manifested
svayam eva — itself alone

In this verse the Guru uses an analogy different from those given in previous verses. If the world of empirical experience is described as being similar to a dream or to magic, one might tend to think of it as a shadowy nothing that may evaporate when one falls asleep, or when one turns away from the magician. The phenomenality of this world is not to be understood as a mere hallucination of the mind. To emphasize the factual and transactional validity of the world of wakeful experience, the Guru adopts here the simile of a tree germinated from a seed.

The meaning of the Sanskrit word *asṛjat* is not the same as the English word "creation." When a potter makes a pot he does not transform the original clay into a new material. From an amorphous lump he draws a shape consistent with general aesthetic and utilitarian values. This he calls a pot. This kind of transformation from the potential to the actual in Sanskrit is called *ādānam.* In the case of a seed, the transformation is effected by the creative power residing in the seed itself. The word *sṛj* means "pushing out, unfolding, or manifesting." It is a very apt term to describe the germination of a seed.

If a seed should be examined, and the potential tree looked for in it, not even the most powerful microscope will reveal any hint of the details of the tree lying latent within. The most primary forms of life, in its various manifestations, are so indistinct that merely to examine an unidentified form will not reveal whether it is going to be a fly, a barley plant, a black cat, or a philosopher. This idea is very humorously presented by Schrödinger in his book *What is Life?*

We have to postulate an indistinct cause as a point of departure on our journey toward some kind of certainty and understanding in this speculation. A static entity cannot be called a cause. If we visualize the dynamism involved in the cause-effect relationship, the cause would be placed at the negative pole or alpha point of an imaginary vertical axis. The effect would be placed at the positive pole or omega point of the same vertical axis. Millions of fertile sperms are contained in the semen of a male, and of that great number one may find its way into the appropriate ovum in a female womb. Now a cause is on its way to unfolding itself stage by stage. This simple event, which is physically concealed even from the couple engaged in the act of intercourse, becomes more and more complex. Even after objectifying itself in the external world as the birth of a living child, the cause may continue to assert itself for many more years, as the child is transformed through the stages of adulthood into old age. Such aspects of cosmic creation are not ephemeral, as are dreams or the workings of magic.

As a result of the conditioning of the faithful by the established religions, and of the skeptics by the categoric statements of science, man has become bifurcated in his sense of his true beingness. Having thus separated him from his true ground — that substratum which gives rise to all beings — those responsible for this have largely repressed in him the sense of wonder and delight in which one who knows his true being lives all the time. Looking in vain for some religious statement or scientific formula which will neatly encompass the whole mystery of being, so that we can file it away in our box of consumer goods and calendar maxims, we have forgotten that the mystery we seek to penetrate is our own mystery.

Everywhere the surging power of the mysterious primal cause can be seen in its perennial program of transformation. It will not be denied. A tree may take root in a small patch of earth among huge granite rocks. Slowly its roots will spread in the search for nourishment. In time those roots will split the great rocks as they push outwards, blindly impelled by the primeval force.

The wonders of the expressions of the substratum of being surround us on all sides. In the Sequoia National Park in America stands a living tree of gigantic size, which is reputed to be around 4000 years old. The *Rg veda*, claimed to be the earliest known literature of the civilized ancients, had not even been composed when this tree attained its maturity. When we see examples like this tree, how can we deny the concrete reality of this world the way we deny the reality of the snake seen in a piece of rope?

In the first two verses the Guru spoke of the primal cause as *parameśvara* and *prabhu.* In the present verse he uses the more impersonal term *svasmin*, which means "that causal factor from which all this has manifested." In the "Universal Prayer" of Narayana Guru he says:

> You are the act of creation, the creator,
> and the myriad variety of what is created;
> O God, are you not the very stuff
> of which everything is created?

From this it is clear that the Guru does not postulate God as a creator who stands outside the act of creation or the created world. As in the stages of the unfoldment of a tree — seed, germination, first sprout, the growth of branches, emergence of flowers, and the final fruition — all the developments arise from within the tree itself. Its own development was already inherent in it and is not the effect of any external cause. In this manner the Guru sees the whole development of creation proceeding from within itself, from a simple primal cause which yet contains the very programming which proliferates in complexity.

It is true that everything appearing in a dream comes from the imagination of the dreamer. But dreams have no contiguity. It is not possible to continue the dream of the previous night on the following one. The things which a magician seems to create cannot satisfy the transactional needs of our everyday life; only concrete experience can do that. The external world of man is what he himself can do, manipulate, transact, understand, or at any rate accept, because of his conditioning. There is much he can do, but for success he needs at least a minimum understanding of the uniformity of the laws which govern the world order. For example, he can pick apples from an apple tree year after year, and coconuts from a coconut tree month after month, but he cannot pick apples from a coconut tree. His external world needs some structuring of regularity, order, and predictability or he could not long survive in it.

A proper philosophical study should take into account the concrete facts of life and the problems arising from them. It is easy to say that the world is a projection, but it makes little sense if one does not follow this with an explanation of how the projection is experienced as a concrete fact. A philosophy which ignores this will not help us to emancipate our consciousness from the psychic colorations and social conditionings which perpetuate our misery.

When a seed is sown in moist earth it swells and bursts, and a tender shoot emerges which projects itself upward while the embryonic root system begins its downward projection. The newly sprouted plant seeks sunlight and the nourishment it can take in from the air. The root descends into the earth in its search for water, salts, and minerals. Part of the plant's organism is heliotropically oriented; the other part performs its functions geotropically. The metabolic function of the plant in the action of photosynthesis can occur only in the sunlit air, it cannot take place in the roots. On the other hand, only the root system can supply the plant with the necessary water and other nourishment found only in the earth. Thus, there is a complementarity between the two environments of light and darkness. In us also there is a similar dichotomy, of a conscious life with its voluntary functions and an unconscious life which is fully controlled by an autonomous system. The same can be seen also at the cosmic level, in the interplay between negative and positive forces. The Chinese philosophers speak of these as the principles of *yin* and *yang*. Narayana Guru will elaborate on this in the next verse.

VERSE 4

śaktistu dvividhā jñeyā
taijasī tāmasīti ca
sahavāso'nayor nāsti
tejastimirayoriva

The power, however, is of two kinds, known as
the bright and the dark; thus,
there is no coexistence between these,
as with light and darkness.

śaktiḥ — the power
tu — however
dvividhā — is of two kinds
jñeyā — known as
taijasī — the bright
ca — and
tāmasī — the dark
iti — thus
sahavāsaḥ nāsti — there is no coexistence
anayoḥ — between these
tejastimirayoḥ iva — as with light and darkness

The totality of forces unitively understood and presented in the first verse as *parameśvara*, in the second verse as *prabhu*, and in the third verse as *svasmin*, is here presented as the bright and the dark aspects of the Absolute, *taijasī* and *tāmasī*. To understand the implications of this verse we should look at it structurally. The structure adopted here is identical with that given in the *Māṇḍūkya Upaniṣad* as an explanation of the mystic syllable *AUM*. The word *AUM* contains three distinct intonations followed by silence. The three articulated sounds are *A* (pronounced "ah"), *U* (pronounced "oo"), and *M* (pronounced "mm").

The sound *A* symbolizes the empirical world of transactions, to which our mind relates itself as the subject. In this, the object of experience is considered as an entity separated from the subject. The world that is experienced is called *viśvam* in Sanskrit, the literal meaning of which is "the universe" or "the all-filling." When consciousness experiences awareness of the universe, and identifies itself as the knower of the universe, the self-identity arising out of that is called *viśva abhimāni.* Here we should remember the first verse of the *Advaita Dīpika,* in which the universe is defined as a composition of multitudinous names, concepts, and objects of interest.

We come to know an object of interest by remembering, hearing, or reading its name, and thus causing within ourselves its corresponding mental image. By relating a name to a form, the idea of it becomes a coordinated concept forever in our memory. Of itself the object of interest has no name. It is by our human deliberation that a name is attached to it, but the name thus given in no way modifies the nature or composition of the object. In the same way, the concepts surrounding our perception of an object arise only in the subject. Moreover, there is no guarantee that the concept has a one-to-one correspondence with all the properties of the object.

Concepts which were thought to be valid in past experiences may undergo a process of modification or correction as our knowledge becomes more intimate and precise. Thus, when a person passes from one experience to another of the same order, in a recurring series in which the same object or name is likely to repeat, the concept becomes modified. For example, the concepts surrounding the perception by a husband, as the subject, of his wife, as the object, are very likely to be modified as time passes. The wife also is likely to modify the conceptual framework through which she observes her husband. In both cases the objects remain what they were and are; only the concepts change. Thus it is that the nature and composition of an object can never be known to us in its own reality. When we view an object there arises in us a self-luminous concept, and we presume that is appropriate to consider the object as having that quality which the concept gives to it. As consciousness arises out of unconsciousness and recalls a little of its hidden aspect, so does the unknown allow some unveiling of itself to give us a glimpse of its nature.

Carl Jung makes certain divisions in the whole of subjective matter. He begins with two spheres, the physical and psychological. Then he divides the psychological world into two realms, the conscious and the unconscious. In the same way he divides the physical world into the known and the unknown. What is known in the physical world is minimal compared to the unlimited expanse of the universe, including whole galactic systems, that is unknown to us. And, although the unconscious is not to be taken as spatial, it has a depth which is also unfathomable. Even in the psycho-physical organism of an individual, the unconscious functions may be on the order of a million times more extensive than the voluntary ones.

Both Freud and Jung speak of the unconscious. Jung further speaks of the personal unconscious, the collective unconscious, and the archetypes. Jung maintains the view that there is no way of knowing anything of the unconscious until it manifests its contents in some manner, either in, or on the threshold, of the conscious.

As far as what is unknown in the physical world is concerned, there is no deliberate intention on the part of that unknown to keep knowledge of itself hidden from us. Man can expand his observations into what is now hidden from him, and fabricate for himself increasing numbers of methods to penetrate into the unknown. In any case, the known and the unknown cannot be thought of as being the same, by definition. And to speak of the unconscious is a contradiction in terms; we are not conscious of what is unconscious, therefore we cannot conceptualize about it, nor, strictly speaking, predicate its existence. Narayana Guru says that, like light and darkness, these two — the known and the unknown, or the conscious and the unconscious — cannot coexist at the same time in the same situation.

Thus far we have been discussing the implications of the first letter *A* of the mystic syllable *AUM*. The second letter, *U*, indicates a purely subjective state. The tree that we see before us in the wakeful state is illumined by a light external to itself, such as that radiating from the sun or reflected by the moon, or perhaps that of a fire. But the tree which we see in a dream is a self-luminous idea. The I-consciousness that witnesses a self-luminous idea and is affected by such an experience is called *taijasa abhimāni*. The world of this state of consciousness consists only of names and concepts. Here, the concepts relating to objects are experienced as perceptions in which the external aspects of the senses are not operating. However, we should not lose sight of the fact that whatever is experienced by us in both the wakeful and dream states is part of our conscious awareness.

A question arises here: what gives a dream the precision and clarity of objective perception, without the operation of sensory aids usual in such perception, and without the presence of an external object? We have already seen that within us are incipient memories associated with feelings such as pain and pleasure, and that these latent memories have the ability to present themselves to consciousness as impelling urges. It is a matter for speculation how these urges can create appropriate symbols, giving release to themselves through the dramatic presentation of assemblies composed of audio-visual memories. The aspect of consciousness we have termed *taijasa abhimāni* dominates this state of consciousness as the one who experiences again the projected situations of, for example, pain, pleasure, or indifference.

When we experience something in the wakeful state, where do the impressions created by that experience go upon its cessation? We know they do not leave us altogether; they become parts of the totality of our memories. And when we are in the dream state, as if from nowhere, many forms will appear to our consciousness. Where do these come from? There must be a hidden aspect of consciousness in which the impressions associated with experiences can be stored. From that same aspect of consciousness, called by us the unconscious, these impressions may be recalled. In the above-mentioned structural scheme, this aspect is indicated by the letter *M* in the syllable *AUM*.

The third state of consciousness is called *suṣupti*. We begin by asking, "What is the nature of the unconscious?" In Indian psychology, Vedānta and Yoga, the term "unconscious" is not used. Instead it is given as *avyākṛta*, which is derived from *vikāra*, meaning "undergoing transformation to assume a specific form." *Ākāra* means "form." Thus *avyākṛta* means "an indefinite state in non-manifestation." The opposite of this is *vyākṛta*. Strangely, this indistinct and static inertial state is called the causal consciousness. It is in constant resonance with the wakeful and dream states. In the wakeful and dream worlds the mind is permitted to attend to only one meaningful pattern at a time. These patterns are structured out of a select group of data taken either from the external world of objects or from the internal world of preregistered memories.

Before it can become a memory, an actual event or experience must undergo a psychic transformation. In Sanskrit this processing is called *samskaraṇ*. The literal meaning of this is "culturing." Often we are unable to account for some ingrained response or reactive conditioning displayed by ourselves or others, or some talent or aptitude which seems inherent in the genetic make-up of a person. Try as we may, we cannot find a cause for these sometimes very powerful traits in the present life of a person. Despite the most perfect childhood conditions, some aberration or negative reaction may persist in an individual throughout his life. Conversely, from the most unlikely circumstances a person may manifest a great and already highly developed talent or skill even in childhood. Apart from impressions cultured in this lifetime, one must bring with him at birth the essences of previously cultured experiences. These may result either from the chromosome structure inherited from the parents, or, as is the common belief in India, from a previous incarnation.

If the unconscious is seen as total darkness, how then does it operate as if with an awareness of the insecurity and possible destruction to which the organism and the individual self are exposed? Clearly, *something* seems interested in our welfare and takes adequate measures to enable us to avoid such threats. Here we have to accept the paradox or enigma of the unconscious operating as a superconsciousness.

In previous verses we have referred repeatedly to names and concepts. Let us imagine the setting of a flock of sheep grazing in a pasture which is adjacent to a forest. Out of the forest comes a large herd of elephants who, because of their size and numbers, appear as threatening as a black thundercloud. Such a scene may inspire an artist to interpret it on canvas, or a poet to picture it in beautiful verse. Neither the sheep nor the elephants depicted in the painting or the poem are real. And both the painter and the poet are limited in their expression by the medium in which they choose to work. Only the most subtle and advanced of painters would attempt to portray a flock of white sheep on a white canvas, using only white pigment. Nor would a painter normally attempt a picture of black elephants on a black canvas using only black pigment. Generally, the white color would be contrasted with the dark color.

For the presentation of the cosmic world it is also required that there be a complementarity of bright and dark forces. This example is given to correct an anomaly in the previous verse. There, too much emphasis was placed on the existential aspect of the world by using the analogy of a tree and its seed. In the present case the object is reduced to a picture of the object. The object is "out there," but is not independent of the mind which experiences it. This is further elaborated in the next verse.

VERSE 5

manomātram idam citra-
mivāgre sarvamīdṛśam
prāpayāmāsa vaicitryam
bhagavām citrakāravat

This, of mind-stuff alone, in the beginning
was accomplished, as if a painting,
with all the picturesqueness seen here,
by the Lord, like an artist.

idam — this
mano mātram — of mind-stuff alone
agre — in the beginning
prāpayāmāsa — was accomplished
citram iva — as if a painting
sarvam vaicitryam — with all the picturesqueness
īdṛśam — seen here
bhagavām — by the Lord
citrakāravat — like an artist

If an Indian should go to China, Africa, or Europe, he would find it difficult to distinguish one person from another in the country he was visiting. Yet in his own country he will recognize, without the need for concentrated effort, the distinguishing features of each individual. The inability of a visitor to distinguish one person from another in the country he visits may persist for a considerable length of time. Eventually, however, he will begin to notice the peculiarities which naturally exist between one man and the next. Every unit of individuation in the world has its own unique distinguishing marks. The variation that occurs in the uniqueness of individuals, who are parts of an uncountable plurality, is the main characteristic of nature. Śankara defines *māyā*, in his *Viveka cūḍāmaṇi*, as that which projects various and variegated impressions which are beginningless and of the form of ignorance.

The main aspect of distinction resides in form. All human beings have, of course, a generalized human form, while a monkey's form is somewhat different from that of man. Within the species *homo sapiens* we shall find considerable variations. For example, the basic Negroid type has black, crinkled hair, black skin, large lips, and a broad and somewhat flattened nose. For contrast we need only consider the Italian, whose features will in general tend to include a higher forehead than the Negroid, a more slender and aquiline nose, thinner lips, and a relatively pale skin. Even among those of the Latin type we shall find considerable differences between one man and another.

When we see the significance of these simple contrasts, we can take a further step and begin to view the entire world as a gallery of exhibits where all possible variations may be found. Before an artist can present a form, the idea corresponding to it has to exist in his mind as a necessary latent potential expression. Even the best artist may be reluctant to say that he can, through his medium, project exactly the form as originally conceived in his mind. The medium with which the artist works, such as paint, stone, clay, or metal, interacts with his mental image and the dexterity of his hand in order to fashion the work as intended. In addition, environmental and historical factors influence his mind. There is a continuing projection of the historical evolution of nature which is manifested up to any given point in time.

In this verse, the artist whom Narayana Guru has in mind is none other than the Supreme Lord. He is certainly unlike any other artist. This is because his art, or the manifestation of which he is the creator, is not to be considered as composed of distinct and separate entities. One should not see the manifestations of the Lord's art as though it were a series of photographic still pictures which have their own existence independent of the complete film of which they are, as it were, subjective parts before being objectified in the final print stage.

There is an ever-changing panorama, and every item in the grand picture undergoes six stages of becoming. These are existence, attainment of individual beingness, growth, change, disintegration, and disappearance. The final disappearance then allows for the appearance of new forms. This kind of cosmic art is unique in that it produces itself. In it the artist is not separated from his art.

The differences between an artistic production, a dream, and a magical performance should be clearly understood. In all three cases there should first be a latent idea which can become manifest. In the case of a dream or a magic show, the effect disappears when the dreamer wakes or the magician ends his performance. But a work of art may remain long after the artist has turned away from it to another expression of his work.

It is interesting to note the reason why Narayana Guru uses the word *bhagavān*. The word means "that power which can remain concealed or make itself overtly manifest." The following qualities are attributes of *bhagavān*: *aṇima*, "being atomic"; *laghima*, "becoming very subtle"; *mahima*, "becoming very gross"; *garima*, "to be concrete"; *prāpti*, "to achieve anything by mere volition"; *prākāmyam*, "experiencing the properties of an object without the actual presence of the object"; *īśitvam*, "the power to create, control, and protect"; *vaśitvam*, "to attract"; and finally *śrīmat*, "to be gracious."

When one appreciates a painting, he has no reason to question the artist's use of tones and colors. All the colors and tints, of whatever degrees of lightness or intensity, have their appropriate places in the picture.

In the world-picture there are three main aspects. First, a reflective function, which can mirror any feature of the cosmic picture and present it as a meaningful unit. Second, the colorful and formal manifestation of the picture, which portrays its moods and its various values. Third, a principle which veils or obstructs the clear vision of the underlying reality. These three aspects are known as the *triguṇa*, the three modalities; or *satva*, *rajas*, and *tamas*. If one understands the cosmic world-picture as being a creation of the Lord, using the triple modalities of nature as his medium, it will be easier to understand the contradiction between benevolence and malevolence, both of which aspects seem to be present in our day-to-day experience. We can glorify God for Jesus the Christ, who was sent by him to dwell among mankind and who is the embodiment of the Lord's love and compassion. Other great masters have also been looked upon as saviors or prophets. Be that as it may, we usually choose to forget that the same God created the devil also. In Indian iconography these contradictions are meaningfully conceived by presenting a delicate picture of the beautiful Sarasvati seated in a white lotus, playing melodies on a stringed instrument called a veeṇa. To complete the total picture, the serenity of Sarasvati has as its counterpart the terrible figure of Kāḷi, standing on a corpse and holding in one hand a scimitar and in the other a decapitated human head. If we can see all this as the aesthetic expression of an artist, then this may enable us to view the world in the same way, giving us a comprehensive viewpoint which will resolve many seeming paradoxes.

In the darkness of night, when a man passes by a graveyard, he may be fearful that some ghost or goblin will confront him. His mind will people the cemetery with spirits of the dead, and such is the negativity of the human mind that they will be seen as malevolent. He knows this to be a self-induced fear, and will do his best to reassure himself that there are, in fact, no ghosts. But deep within his mind lies a stratum of paranoia, and because of this he does not easily yield to rationality. If he sees the stump of a tree or hears a strange sound, his latent fear will cloak it with the vestments of a ghost. Then he will either flee or faint. In this case the man is hypnotized by his own latent fear. We can find examples of this form of self-hypnosis in every area of human experience, in the painful and the pleasurable, in the benign and the dreadful.

There are some who can produce a mass hallucination. Such people, using their hypnotic power, can create a common experience for all those who compose the audience. At such a time the experience of everyone present will reflect that of the hypnotist. There are some who can go even a step further; these are the yogis. In the Upanishads it is said, *yad dhyāyate tad bhavati*, which means "whatever is meditated upon, that one becomes." Yogis meditate upon the Lord or the Absolute. Identifying themselves completely with the Supreme, they can then participate in fashioning or altering aspects of the cosmic picture. In the next verse Narayana Guru will highlight this aspect of yogic power.

VERSE 6

āsīt prakṛtirevedam
yathā'dau yogavaibhavam
vyatanodatha yogīva
siddhijālam jagatpatiḥ

Like potential yogic power,
in the beginning this was nature indeed;
thereafter, like a yogi, the Lord of the World
unfolded his magical powers.

yathā — like
yogavaibhavam — potential yogic power
ādau — in the beginning
idam — this
āsīt — was
prakṛti eva — nature indeed
atha — thereafter
yogi iva — like a yogi
jagatpatiḥ — the Lord of the World
vyatanot — unfolded
siddhi jālam — his magical powers

In this verse Narayana Guru describes the substance of the universe as *prakṛti*. This Sanskrit term is usually translated as "nature," but its literal meaning is "that which proliferates." Here the nature of this universe is equated with the psychic power of a yogi. Only the yogi is real. What is manifested through the exercise of his powers has only a transient existence. The Lord of the Universe, who makes this world manifest, is here equated with the *yogi*. A special term, *jagatpatiḥ*, is used here to describe the nature of the Lord. *Jagat* is "that which is of the nature of flux or becoming." Thus *jagatpatiḥ* means "the principle of change." That which becomes a form and then changes into another form is *jagat*. But even the condition of flux cannot occur in a haphazard manner; therefore the law which governs change should itself be unchangeable. He who determines the law of change is called *jagatpatiḥ*.

According to Rāmānuja, the nature of the Supreme Principle is the transformation of itself into any modification it wills. He calls that capacity *bhāvarūpasvarūpa*, "of the intrinsic nature of assuming forms to suit the flux of becoming." But according to Śankara, the Supreme cannot be of the nature of that which changes itself into modalities. He is willing to admit, however, that it has the power to produce a magical effect of transference or transmutation without its own absolute beingness undergoing any change. Hence Śankara calls this world *bhāvarūpa*, but according to him this is not the intrinsic nature of the Lord.

In the first verse, the potential power of the Lord was equated with *saṅkalpa*, the imagination of the Lord. In the second verse the same power was described as *vāsana*, or incipient memories. The third verse identified that power with *śakti*, the two-fold power inherent in the Lord. Verse four was an elaboration of the same power of *śakti*. In the fifth verse the specific power of the Lord was described as *manas*, mind. Finally, in the present verse we have the power identified with *prakṛti*.

In the analogy of God as the universal artist and the world as his cosmic production, there is an important factor we must keep in mind. When an artist turns away from a work which he has just completed, the painting may still remain as a permanent feature of his studio. However, an hypothesis of the Vedāntin, that the world is a superimposition on the supreme Self, will fail if he agrees with the supposition that a superimposition can stand without its substratum.

A more correct example of superimposition is when one sees an illusory snake when in fact he is looking at an ordinary piece of rope. The proposition that the rope can be removed without disturbing one's experience of the snake is readily seen as false. If the rope is removed the snake goes with it. On the other hand we can say that God, through the exercise of his yogic power, creates the illusions of blue sky, mist-enshrouded mountains, singing birds, beautiful trees and flowers, the world of social transactions, and both heaven and hell. It is this power that remains as the substratum of all the illusory creations.

At the same time that God is involved in this world-production, he himself does not undergo any change. The apparent multiplicity of what is presented before us in the world can be attributed to a continuing erroneous judgement of the individual mind, which is itself affected by the cosmic illusion.

All beings in their normal condition of existence, from the insect world to mankind, are susceptible to fear. If one observes the activities of insects such as flies and ants, or birds and animals such as rabbits and deer, they will be seen to look fearfully around in every direction while engaged in their routines. Immediately after they sense danger or that their privacy might be invaded, they flee to another position. We don't know if fear is generated and experienced consciously, or if the sense of danger is merely instinctive, acting as a stimulus to reflex action.

All beings are fearful, but of all of them man is the most paranoiac. Great nations hastily stockpiling nuclear bombs and other weapons are confirming the fear that man has of his own nature when it is expressed as a corporate entity. In fact, the fears of nations are grounded on wrongful assumptions, hearsay, or at best a partial knowledge. In all of us lie incipient memories associated with painful experiences in our past. When these painful memories are reactivated, fear is very often the result.

Although we think through the action of our central nervous system, which is for the most part located in the brain, fear arises from one of the lowest synergic centers, near the coccyx, and is experienced at the navel. Even before the senses are aware of the actual image of danger, an unconscious power of vigilance flashes a message from the brain to the adrenal gland. Instantly this gland secretes adrenaline into the bloodstream, which carries it to the liver. There glycogen is released, supplying an immediate flow of increased energy throughout the body. The now chemically toxic blood stimulates the heart to greater than normal activity. The operation of the digestive system is suspended, and blood flows under increased pressure to the extremities, especially the feet, hands, brain, and jawbone. Now the organism is prepared to face and deal appropriately with what it senses as a threat. Depending on the normal psychological attitudes of the personality, the mood generated will be one of either "fight or flight." Both will be performed more effectively in this arousal of the organism.

With the possible exception of those skilled in the martial arts, a third state can exist for humans when they are confronted with extreme danger. For those in this state neither fight nor flight is possible. If the unconscious danger signal is immediately supplemented by sensory data indicating a fatally grave situation, the metabolic functioning of the body deteriorates. The man will not be able to move, or even raise his voice. He will stand paralyzed, and may even faint. If the fear is strong enough, or the man is inherently unstable, reason may be submerged and madness supervene.

It is in these kinds of experiences that the reasoning power of man becomes greatly minimized. If an ordinary situation of ignorance can cause such damage to our psychophysical organism, how much greater will be the fear generated in a living being when it becomes subject to the much more profound ignorance of nescience? In the next verse Narayana Guru will illustrate what happens to a person when his knowledge of the Self diminishes.

VERSE 7

yadā' tmavidyā sankoca-
stadā' vidyā bhayankaram;
nāmarūpātmana' tyartham
vibhātīha piśācavat

When Self-knowledge shrinks,
then ignorance is fearful;
substantiation by name and form,
in the most terrible fashion, looms here, ghost-like.

yadā — when
ātmavidyā — Self-knowledge
sankocaḥ — shrinks
tadā — then
avidyā — ignorance
bhayankaram — is fearful
ātmana — substantiation by
nāma — name
rūpa — form
atyartham — in the most terrible fashion
vibhāti — looms
iha — here
piśācavat — ghost-like

Once a man came to see Narayana Guru in his ashram. It was very late in the night when the man decided to return to his home. Seeing that the man was apprehensive, the Guru enquired whether he was afraid to walk home in the dark. The man admitted that he was. The Guru asked his devotee to describe exactly what it was that he was afraid of. To this the man could only say that he did not know. Then the Guru told him that he was afraid of the "other," and that if he could persuade himself to believe that nothing but himself existed, there would be nothing of which he could be afraid.

Often when people have to enter solitary places in darkness they are more afraid of the hypothetical dangers, such as ghosts or evil spirits, than they are of the possibly real threats such as snakes or wild animals. Ghosts and goblins have only a nominal existence in the world of semantics. Yet the myth-making faculty of the mind of man fabricates an image consistent with his conditioning to suit every word he hears spoken. To many people, concepts arising from no greater a reality than a name can become as real as empirical entities. Mr. Geoffrey Hodson, of the Theosophical Society, published an exciting and beautifully illustrated book describing his encounters with hundreds of devas and nature spirits. America has its legends of beings such as Big Foot, while in the Himalayan folklore the Abominable Snowman or yeti continues to flourish. Everywhere man's myth-making faculty is evident. Since we find such stories quite fascinating, the world population of ghosts increases every year.

The capacity to act in the physical world belongs only to properly organized physical beings which are guided or governed by consciousness. When a person dies, consciousness ceases to exist and the physical body disintegrates. Thereafter nothing remains as an entity which can transact with a physical body in this physical world. Fear of nonexistent entities arises because of nescience or ignorance. It is knowledge which creates; self and knowledge are identical. Apart from knowledge there is no separate entity anywhere which can be called a self.

When knowledge is circumscribed by the boundary of an "other," then the fear of that "other" can make the sphere of knowledge shrink. The idea of the "other" is saturated with fear. The only way to remove fear is to expand the horizon of knowledge until nothing remains beyond knowledge itself.

The idea of "other" arises because we are very much influenced by our individuation as an entity possessing a specific name and form. True knowledge can exist only when one has a transparency of vision which transcends the limitations of formal perceptions and nominal conceptions. The immediacy of cognition in a person is a referent recognized by him as "this." Every "this" can be connected with a conceptual predication. One says, "This is what I see; this is what I hear; this is what I like; this pains me; this is beautiful; this is ugly." There is no end to the formations of units in knowledge. Moreover, when such formations are taken as disjunct entities, the conscious "I" stands apart from all of them as a separated individual in an ocean of infinite "otherness."

This separative apperception is the result of a lack of contemplative discipline. Occasionally, even a noncontemplative person may have moments when he feels himself to be one with the universe, finding enjoyment in that happy state. When, for example, a man sees a pattern of blue lines on the petals of a pink flower, his world of interest can remain contemplatively concentrated in that flower. He may easily forget himself as the range of his consciousness shrinks to occupy only that space filled by the flower. In such a unitive experience his joy can transcend both space and time. It is as though there existed only a singular beingness without a second. In the same manner, depending on the nature of the object in which he has concentrated his being, his experience may be not one of joy but of terror. What in one case may be a song of joy, in another may be a shriek of unbearable dread. Still, in every case the value-interest of every item of knowledge arises from the continual, if usually unconscious, quest to be in tune with the blissful nature of the Self.

When we understand Self in this sense, the difference which exists between true knowledge and mere information will be plainly evident. Knowledge occurs only when there is a pure comprehension of the blissful awareness of existence. This possibility can be veiled by a mistaken identification of existence with nonexistence, knowledge with nescience, or the apprehension of responses such as disgust, fear, and nausea as value-factors.

When a mother sings a lullaby in a monotonous tone and rocks the cradle in a gentle rhythm, her child will fall asleep. In this case the sleep is induced by a form of hypnosis. Sleep is a state wherein one withdraws himself into an inertial condition. If the sleep is without the production of dreams, then consciousness is gathered and focused within, remaining in a blissful state. In this state there is no duality of the knower and the known. The joy in this case is very different from that experienced by one who enjoys a delicious meal, or embraces his beloved. Our reference here is not to anything in the nature of an event. According to Henri Bergson, an event is that which can be recalled from memory and relived in imagination. The joy of deep sleep cannot be recalled and relived. The so-called "memory" of it is the mental effort to give contiguity to one's I-consciousness.

In all other items of knowledge each event remains separated from the rest as a figural gestalt. The experience of unidentifiable bliss in deep sleep remains as a negative factor when consciousness returns to the alpha point of its source. There is the possibility in some for consciousness to free itself from specific transactional events and the fantasizing ideations of dreams, to remain poised in a state of unconditioned awareness without falling into the state of deep sleep. This is called the fourth state of consciousness — a state of pure transcendence. As this state is without finite limitations, it is called the pure state of Self. In fact the other three states occur within the state of pure consciousness, as modifications of consciousness, producing item after item of what is generally called knowledge or experience. We modify the state of pure consciousness, which is absolute truth, to produce the illusions which we mistakenly call reality. So habitually and continuously do we vary our focus of awareness, that few of us come to know that the pure state even exists. This is one of the tragic aspects of individuation. Narayana Guru gives a clearer picture of that tragedy in the next verse.

VERSE 8

bhayankaramidam sūnyam
vetāḷanagaram yathā
tathaiva viśvamakhilam
vyakarodadbhutam vibhuḥ

This is terrible and empty of content,
like a phantom city;
even as such, the whole universe
is made as a wonder by the Primeval One.

idam — this
bhayankaram — is terrible
sūnyam — empty of content
yathā — like
vetāḷanagaram — a phantom city
tatha eva — even as such
akhilam — the whole
viśvam — universe
vyakarot — is made
adbhutam — as a wonder
vibhuḥ — by the Primeval One

Vibhu means that which exists before the manifestation of something. The word *bhu* means "becoming" or "manifestation," though the reference here is not to the manifestation of this physical world. Before we can use the definitive "is" or "is not," a consciousness must exist which is capable of discerning transaction. To become or to manifest in this context is to be taken as becoming conscious of existence. Bishop Berkeley said, "*Esse est percipi*," (existence is perception). Here what is perceived should be understood in a wider sense than something merely being known. This view of Berkeley's is also shared by Vedāntins.

Philosophers of the Sānkhya system, however, take a different approach. To them existence is self-existent. That is to say, existence is grounded in and requires no other affirmation than the fact that it is. The basic unit of existence in Sānkhya philosophy is called *tanmātra*, the nearest translation of which is the Kantian "thing in itself." However, we should not press this comparison too far — *tanmātra* and "thing in itself" are not really the same. *Mātra* means metric or measurement, so *tanmātra* means "that which can be measured only by itself." It is that which is measured, the measurement, the method of measurement, and that which measures. If *tanmātra* is expressed in terms of bipolarity, then one pole is the subject who measures and the other pole is the object to be measured.

Primeval Spirit before the creation of the world is depicted as the infant Krishna, reclining on a fig leaf which floats on water, while sucking the big toe of his right foot. There is also a famous sculpture by Rodin of a child feeling with one finger a thorn stuck in the sole of his left foot. In all such ideograms we have the idea of an existence prior to its manifestatation.

If *vibhu* — that which is before manifestation — is to be understood as God, then He, or "That" should not be conceived as a being seated on a throne and bringing the world into manifestation by a single act of creation. Instead, we should conceive of knowledge as being imbued with infinite possibilities of expression. Every such possibility may be actualized by a certain inner necessity.

All aspects of life and their interrelations are brought before us here as a chain of events in which *vi* stands for causes and *bhu* stands for effects. From the dawn of human history, two questions which have been intrinsically of interest to man are, "Whence came this world?" and "Who am I?" All religions, including those of the primitive races, have tried to answer these questions as best they could. The modern science of physics has accepted Einstein's challenge to use an analytical approach in its attempt to answer the first question. Psychology, sociology, and allied disciplines are trying to answer the second.

A story about the origin of the world is given in the Tenth Mandala of the *Ṛg Veda Samhita* of the Aryans. In the Book of Genesis in the Old Testament we find a similar attempt to elucidate the same subject. The Australian aborigines, as well as the Semitic and pre-Christian European religions all have their own versions. A more scientific probe into this area of knowledge was first initiated by the Greek philosopher Thales, according to whom water existed before the universe was created. Thereafter, a number of such theories came from such thinkers as Anaximander, Anaximenes, Parmenides, Zeno, and Heraclitus.

Socrates considered such studies to be a waste of time, describing them as philosophies of dirt and mud. His belief was that the best area of study for man was his own self. Taking a lead from his master, Plato gave his attention to the study of self. But Aristotle,

Plato's own disciple, thought that man should give equal importance to the study of both physics and metaphysics.

At about the same time as the Greek philosophers, the scholars of the Sānkhya and Nyāya schools of India were perfecting their own studies of the visible world. In a general sense, all six systems of the orthodox Indian schools, as well as the materialistic school of the Cārvākas, considered it important to know the nature and meaning of the external world. During this period the Jains and Buddhists were more concerned with the immediate amelioration of human misery.

The Sānkhya philosophy introduced the teaching of the duality between spirit and creative nature. In general terms, spirit covers the field of the Self and creative nature that of the manifested world. These two concepts were accepted by most of the people of that time as a good platform on which to build a structure of philosophical inquiry. The concept of *prakṛti* was elaborated to cover the whole spectrum of manifestation, from the primary aspects of elements to the gross aspects of physical structuring in the world.

Meanwhile, in Europe the power of the Church was complete. Any movement toward free thinking was suppressed and became taboo. Scholasticism came into power, and many centuries passed before anyone dared to risk his life by propounding theories which sought to go further than the Book of Genesis. Then pioneers such as Copernicus and Galileo extended the vision of their fellowmen, enabling them to look deeper into the mystery of the manifested universe. The previously chaotic appearance of shimmering lights in the sky changed into a meaningful cosmos, as the true movements of planetary bodies became irrefutably clear to the eyes of mankind. Our present concepts of the evolution of the universe have progressed very far from those of Galileo's day. The increasing sophistication of scientific technology enables us to observe the birth of planets, beginning with the spin of a nebula, as well as the development of the human species.

The interest of mankind today is not confined to the gathering of information relating to the formation of the physical universe. What stimulates our immediate interest is the actual world that surrounds us. To pinpoint the nature of this aspect of the world we can refer to the Sanskrit word *vartamānam*, which means "present." The world presented to us as individuals is not the entire universe. It is a very limited environment of a relatively few square miles in area, and which belongs entirely to the present moment.

We can perhaps give it a time-span of a few hours. The problems arising from it are likely to be few and simple, but we complicate matters which should only arise from, and relate to, our individual environment, by hooking on to them the structuring of a vast and complex world. The world with which we complicate our responses to sensory input is the conditioning passed on to us from generation after generation. This conditioning arises from the store of information chronicled as the history of human endeavor and discovery — the story of man's encounters with nature and his fellow humans. Thus, the world we think to be real has in fact very little objective reality. It is padded out in all directions with half-baked conceptual notions and hidebound prejudices.

After due consideration, we can take this viewpoint a step further. Then we shall be in a position to readily agree with the stand Narayana Guru takes in this verse. The Guru says that what has been experienced by us in the past reasserts itself in the present in every situation, appearing as a frightening and ghostlike presence which haunts us in our transactions with the world. Two threatening aspects of life are our present ruminations on past experiences, which arouse regret and remorse, and the fear which arises when we contemplate the uncertainty of the future. Remorse related to the past and anxiety related to the future — so much of these overlap into the present that the world begins to look like the Inferno for a great many people.

Once Narayana Guru asked a disciple, who later became Nataraja Guru, to meditate upon the room in which he sat as though nothing existed outside of it. He wanted his disciple to practice living entirely in the present moment and circumstances. The here and now is always simple. It is a great wonder that we insist on complicating it, thereby introducing an element of dread, by linking it with a dead yesterday and an unknown tomorrow. This we do at the expense of our enjoyment of the present, which could otherwise be a loving and meaningful experience of the Self. To help save us from the tyranny of history and the assumptions arising from our view of human evolution, the Guru presents the next verse.

VERSE 9

arkādyathākramam viśvam
tathā naivedamātmanaḥ
supteriva prādurāsīd-
yugapatsvasya vīkṣayā

From the sun, by stages, was not at all
how the world came to be; from the Self
this appeared all at once,
as one's vision comes in sleep.

arkāt — from the sun
yathākramam — by stages
viśvam — the world
tathā — in this way, how
naiva — not at all, did not come to be
ātmanaḥ — from the Self
idam — this
prādurāsīt — appeared
yugapat — all at once
supteḥ iva svasya vīkṣayā — as one's vision comes in sleep

There is a mythological story in which the sun gave birth to space. Space then gave birth to air, air gave birth to fire, fire gave birth to water, and from water came the earth. Modern science theorizes about the formation of the universe in a somewhat similar manner when it speaks of an as yet unidentified energy passing through a series of modifications on its way to becoming manifest as this planet. This energy is expressed as a nebula, which becomes a star; the explosion of the star forms a planetary system; and finally the cooling of the planetary fires allows water and other liquids to condense, leading to the development of an environment and atmosphere conducive to the manifestation of life on some planet. However, the book from which our mythological story comes is not a textbook on cosmogony or astrophysics. Its subject is *vedānta śāstra*, the science of transcending the world of sensual knowledge to attain imperishable peace and happiness.

It may be that our concept of the term "world" is too abstract. The world with which we should concern ourselves is that which presents itself when we wake from sleep or emerge from an unconscious state. This world is composed not only of earth, water, fire, and air; we are also continually confronted by situations which demand from us meaningful reactions. Even in the dream our consciousness is moving from one situation to another. We comprehend these as gestalts. The world we see, in addition to its physical qualities, is also a complex structure of situations and responses, projected by ourselves to the extent that we are often unable to separate our sense of self from it. To connote the world that is presented to us as a ceaseless input of sense data, all relevant associations and concepts that lie buried in the unconscious must instantaneously enter our conscious awareness when required. If there is little or no aberration of consciousness, we can very quickly recognize not only the relevant informational details of the situation presented to us, but also how it will affect the preservation of our life, the continuing quality of our integrity, and the progress and unfoldment of the Self expressed as our own self. Our individual self and its interaction with the world is assessed always in this manner.

Even in a dream the gestalts presented to consciousness lack no details. Scenes such as the individual afloat on a stormy sea, climbing with much effort up a craggy mountain, or perhaps mingling with the crowd in a busy marketplace, will be complete in every detail of environment, mental assessment, and emotional response. There is only one world with which we interact, and in it we live consciously in both the wakeful and dream states. The state of dreamless sleep we have described before as the causal consciousness, which is structurally placed at the alpha point of the vertical axis of consciousness.

Dormant concepts, incipient memories, and psychological urges are all stockpiled in the causal consciousness, which is generally referred to by the all-inclusive term *suṣupti*. These potent factors in the causal consciousness cannot relate themselves to objects of wakeful consciousness without first modulating themselves to assume the qualities of the objects concerned. This modulation is of the self-luminous mind-stuff which is the innate luminous power of all individuated beings, presented earlier as *taijasī*.

We should recognize here that there is really no difference between dreams and subjective mental images. These mental images meet halfway, as it were, with the stimuli coming through the sensory screen-and-response mechanism as the input to consciousness of data relating to external objectivity. The interaction between a prestructured mental image and newly presented sense-data restructures the conscious picture into a finalized vision. This is described in this verse as the world presented to the self through the operation of its own vision.

If we do not find within ourselves the source and the engineering of the situations to which we present ourselves, then there is danger that we shall succumb to a fatalistic philosophy. Narayana Guru certainly does not subscribe to such an attitude of fatalism. For him, man is capable of creating, modifying, and resolving his own world. To be able to do this properly, man should know where and how his microcosmic being finds its placement in the macrocosmic world, which is conceived, sustained and eventually dissolved by the Supreme. In the Upanishads this Supreme is called *brahma.* Emerson calls it the Over-soul.

Some scriptures are of the greatest value to man in his quest for wisdom. The Bhagavad Gita, for example, is reputed to be a science of the Absolute, as well as a science of unitive living. In the *Darśanamālā*, Narayana Guru assists the student to simplify the complexity of the world by helping him to know the planet on which he stands, and by giving him a new angle of vision which he can use, together with a viewpoint he can adopt in every situation. Then he will have a correct perspective and understanding of the problems presented to him as they arise. This will change the world described as a "boundless ocean of misery" into one of clear knowledge and precise laws. Then his understanding of the world will be more correct and profound, and his ability to deal appropriately with problems which confront him will be much improved. From this individualistic point of vision the Guru passes to a universal one in the next verse.

VERSE 10

dhānādiva vaṭo yasmāt
prādurāsīdidam jagat
sa brahmā sa śivo viṣṇuḥ
sa paraḥ sarva eva saḥ

He from whom this world manifested,
as a fig tree from a seed —
he is Brahmā, he is Śiva and Viṣṇu,
he is the Absolute, he alone is all.

yasmāt — (he) from whom
idam jagat — this world
prādurāsīt — manifested
dhānāt iva vaṭaḥ — as a fig tree from a seed
saḥ brahmā — he is Brahmā
saḥ śivaḥ — he is Śiva
viṣṇuḥ — (and) Viṣṇu
saḥ — he is
paraḥ — the Absolute; literally "beyond"
sarva eva saḥ — he alone is all

It is imperative that scientists and philosophers adhere to a single unitive principle in their works. Without a central, normative idea to which everything can be related, scientific explanations are impossible. This is true also of philosophy, which should emphasize one fundamental truth, the understanding of which will illumine all other aspects of reality. Individual scientists may differ from each other in their private and personal beliefs, but in the present context of scientific investigations and discoveries all must agree, for example, that matter is a unitive principle which can be used to understand all physical phenomena.

A rose blooming in the morning, the dewdrops shining on its petals, the bee hovering around it, the sunbeams illuminating the flower, the poet enraptured by this beauty, the inspiration which arises in his mind, his joy expressed in words, and the linguistic characters by which his poetry is imprinted on paper — all these are aspects of the same matter. In the time of Newton, the entire universe was conceived of as being made up of atoms, structured as might be the grains of sand which make up a beach; that is, very numerous and lying close to one another. Yet after the advent of modern physics the whole concept of matter changed.

The scientific description of matter today can be likened to a handful of salt crystals lying in water. Some crystals are still visible, although in the process of dissolving, but most have already dissolved, thus changing their form and becoming part of an indistinct solvent. In the world of modern science matter is as mysterious to us as is spirit or God — it cannot be understood in its finest and ultimate form. Sometimes it appears as mass, but time and space are not different from it. It is also that which somehow manifests as consciousness, though when acting through the agency of the enigmatic *vāsana*-s it functions below the threshold of awareness. In short, matter has qualities similar to those described in the cosmic vision given to Arjuna by Kṛṣṇa, in chapter eleven of the Bhagavad Gita: it is indistinct, beautiful, horrid, plain, simple, awe-inspiring, and evasive.

Today the physicist has come to a decision concerning the fundamental nature of matter; it is either a particle or a wave-form. As it is necessary that the science of physics should be structured on the basis of a single normative idea, there is common consent among physicists that the particle and the wave-form are the same. This is like saying a fixed location and the constant movement of that location are one and the same thing. In any case the scientist is unable to substantiate his monistic view that there is only one truth.

When we come to the philosopher, he has first to decide whether his method is valid for the pursuit of truth, and he should establish the criteria he will use to decide the verity of the truth he wishes to come to in his search. Mere personal conviction is not sufficient to validate truth. Inherent in the nature of truth is a universal acceptance of it. In order to substantiate the universal recognition of his beliefs, the philosopher should inform his public what the normative idea was which he used to arrive at the truth he propounds. That normative idea should be valid enough to enable it to be adopted as a universal measuring rod.

For there to be a general agreement among all peoples there should be a simultaneity in the intellectual functioning of individual minds in spite of all personal differences. Moreover, there should be a common parameter which can be used to prove to every mind the validity of a truth, when that parameter is used by every individual. When one speaks to another person, he takes it for granted that the capacity of the other mind is the same as his own. In fact this is very often not the case. How is it that sometimes the best argument of one man can seem totally irrelevant and unacceptable to another? It is because each has a different standpoint and angle of vision, which lead to diverse assessments of the same situation. Is there some way by which everyone can be brought to the same point of view? The answer is yes, there is such a way. The method is direct perception, unmodified by conditioning or mental aberration. When able to use this method, all people of goodwill can set aside individual or racial conditioning and dispassionately accept explanations of the physical world as it is presented to the senses. The Indian analogy for this is a gooseberry in the palm of one's hand. This means: I hold the fruit in my hand and directly perceive it; how, therefore, can I doubt its existence?

René Descartes, the French mathematician, and David Hume, the English philosopher, give this same idea in other ways. According to Descartes, all items of explanation come under the headings of either fact or opinion. People may disagree with regard to their opinions, but when it comes to matters of fact there must be universal agreement. According to Hume, the compulsion to agree can arise from either a psychological or a logical necessity. The former may arise from a religious conviction, a fixed notion, a blind spot in the mind, uncritical acceptance, association of events, superstition, or prejudice. Here there can be differences of opinion. But an imperative may arise that is born of logical necessity. This imperative will compel everyone to accept the same truth. Even the theory of cause and effect approved by scientists is, according to Hume, based solely on a psychological necessity.

The ultimate conviction of truth is a certitude which can be termed as being self-evident. Thus the final criterion as to whether something is true rests with the self itself. In mathematics this would be called an axiom. As an example of what is axiomatic let us consider the geometric triangle. It is axiomatic in that only if there are three fixed points connected by three lines can we draw a triangle. Our mind will reject the possibility of any alternative ways of producing a triangle. An axiom is an example of logical necessity. Both scientist and philosopher accept a mathematical homogeneity in the structure of the macrocosmic world, which seems to be external to the self. The human faculty of intellect is capable of discovering the cosmic structure in both its macrocosmic and microscopic aspects, and of reducing it to mathematical pictures such as logarithms or propositional calculus. How the *Logos* can relate itself to the *arithmos* is a major discovery, giving the human mind the capacity to understand a greater mystery to which the mind itself belongs, both as a structural part and in its operational dynamics.

Apart from a wholesale intellectual approach there is an alternative way to appreciate the totality of this world-experience. It is to approach the adorable Absolute with a warm and devotional feeling engendered in one's heart. This approach from the heart, though a very private and personal matter, is shared by all, including the scientist and philosopher. The limitations of experimental science and theoretical speculation bring an enquiring mind to a certain frontier of imagination. Beyond that lies the vast expanse of human ignorance.

At this point it is likely that the quest for truth will emerge from the heart in the form of an appeal to a higher source of understanding. This will have the quality of a prayer. Here one enters into "the cloud of unknowing," or what St. John of the Cross calls "the dark night of the soul." It is here that a skeptic may be transformed into a believer. An aircraft may be coming in to land on an airfield shrouded in dense fog, with only radar to guide the pilot. He must trust his instruments and the remote voice from the control tower, and make what mental calculations he can. He must approach what he thinks is the runway, cut back the speed of his aircraft, and commit it irrevocably to contact with the ground. And he must do all this in the firm belief that everything will turn out for the best. What he does blindly, but with an intuitive certainty of the validity of his calculations, will have a good and safe ending. Perhaps only once in a million such operations will a disaster occur. The lives we conduct from day to day are not so very different from this analogy of the jet pilot. If, allowing our intuition to inform us, we too make every possible effort to penetrate the mystery of truth, then it is very likely that we shall eventually do so. We share this grace of intuition with all creatures of nature and with the vegetative life. It is from this deep source that the bumblebee, for example, finds his own guidance back and forth between his hive and the distant flowers from which he is to gather honey.

When a religious person makes the statement that God creates, sustains, and recalls, the apparent irrationality of this exceeds even the most preposterous claims which scientists think to be rational. Narayana Guru wrote the *Darśanamālā* with the beliefs of the Indian people as its background. The one Supreme Truth which generates, sustains, and dissolves is described in this present verse as Brahmā, Viṣṇu, and Śiva, respectively. That Truth, which is looked for and spoken of by scientists, philosophers, and psychologists, is the same as that which is approached with reverence and spoken of with humility by theologians. As this truth is beyond our comprehension, the Guru describes it as *parā*. And as there is nothing else that can be spoken of, he also describes it as the All.

Cosmic Projection

Applied Psychology

What is taken for granted as a life experience, when carefully examined, will reveal itself to be a superimposition. A superimposition implies a ground upon which something alien to its nature is transposed or imposed. The ground of our experience is what we call "I", although the I we talk about or ponder over is not the ground, but only a semantic symbol which is colored by what is superimposed on it. Thus the transactional I is as much alien to the beingness of the ground as what is fictitiously projected upon it. All of the various kinds of reasoning are inefficient for cutting through the matrix of projections because conceptual word-images are used, which, by affinity of semantic associations, get entangled with the verbal content of the reasoning mind and float along with the stream of verbal concepts rather than penetrating to the bottom, which is beyond the reach of concepts and untainted by memories of the past. One must go again and again to the bottom of one's experience, carefully avoiding all habitual chains of reasoning.

The crust of our consciousness is formally structured with a relation-relata complex. Our empirical ego, which is also the semantically structured I-consciousness, is the invisible thread which holds together all ideas, sensations, and feelings to form the gestalt of the moment. An integral part of this gestalt is a certain pattern of reasoning and its given coloration of mood, which time and again is recognized as one's mind. Thus, on the whole both the mind and its monitoring I-consciousness are camouflages that conceal from us the true ground, which can be equated with the prior nothingness of what is being experienced. The Self, or the true I, is therefore to be understood as the anterior absence of what is present. It implies within its structured content the paradoxical contradiction of the coexistence of both beingness and nothingness. When Ramana Maharshi advised his followers to repeatedly ask the question "Who am I?", his intention was to make them go beyond all semantic exercises and not hang on the crutches of reasoning, so that they could experience directly the nothingness of nothing being cancelled by the being of beingness. So, in order to be precise, we should add here in parenthesis (forgive the use of words and forget that it has been said).

If we hear a statement such as, "It is raining. It is so beautiful I feel like crying," our immediate reaction is to ask why one should cry for having experienced beauty. The "why" we put here as an interrogation is typical of our mode of reasoning. We ask why because we think that everything in the world is interrelated as cause and effect. In the West the entire edifice of science is built on the fundamental notion of cause and effect. When Hume questioned the validity of that notion, many did not understand why he refused cause its legitimate place in the logic of relationship. Later, however, Immanuel Kant recognized Hume's wisdom, saying that his skepticism had roused him from his own philosophical slumber. As we mentioned earlier, Hume maintained that there are certain logical imperatives, such as the impossibility of conceiving of a triangle with anything less than three sides. This is a mathematical necessity, a logical imperative. There is no logical imperative, however, in the fact that heat flows from a warm substance to a cold one, because we can conceive the opposite. Our habitual recognition that heat is the cause of warmth is necessitated by a psychological compulsion. Most of what we call cause and effect are pairs of sequential occurrences in which the antecedent is believed to be the cause and the consequent the effect. In many cases such a surmise is not warranted by a logical necessity.

Should everything necessarily be related this way? Should this be the only way of understanding relationship? What is the difference between what and why? Kierkegaard, the father of modern existentialism, questions the disproportionate importance assigned to reason in all matters of experience. What are the other constituents of experience?

Let us think of the element of reason as our inner light. In this light we see several elements of our experiences; reason is our tool to specify these elements as it highlights each unit as a value factor. Let us take joy as one such unit. The recognition of joy occurs as a conscious appreciation of its existence in our awareness. Awareness and the state of joy are now related as a matter of psychological affinity. We recognize not only the element of joy, but also the fact that we are joyous, and the recognition of being joyous is immediately promoted as a main aspect of our experience. The recognition "I am joyous" is a secondary representation of the primal happening of pure joy. We have thus rationalized our experience, and it is brought forth as a representative image of our understanding of the spontaneous occurrence of the state of pure joy.

It has become almost impossible for an adult to have at-one-ment with his or her original and spontaneous experience except on rare occasions, as when we experience a musical rhapsody, mystical frenzy, poetic vision, a sexual orgasm, or spiritual absorption. The eagerness to know what is going on impels the mind to give a running commentary, as it were, of all inner experiences, by remolding the experience into a conceptual framework of words. Words are manufactured to suit as parts of speech. Parts of speech are designed by the grammarian and the logician, and both of them are cold-blooded pragmatists. To clothe an experience in all its richness, mystics, musicians, poets, and for that matter all those who are endowed with a high degree of sensibility, have to choose mediums other than precisely connoted words, as, for instance, icons, ideograms, symbols, or even emotionally surcharged theatrical gestalts and pregnant forms of silence. So when those of us who are not as brilliant as such creative geniuses have to formulate a linguistic expression for what is being felt, we struggle for words and then look for the most approximate one; this makes the experience more and more meager as we practically mutilate it in our own conscious appraisal of it. By doing this we make our conscious recognition sophisticated. This sophistication is what is referred to here as superimposition.

The intention of the first *darśana* is to give us the discipline of recognizing our general experience as a superimposition, and then to work our way into the primal state previously mentioned as the ground of all experiences.

Kierkegaard refers to the crossroads of our lives which present themselves to us repeatedly. Each such occurrence is experienced as a confrontation, which forces us to make a decision. A decision may not be reached even after considerable effort; this is the time when one becomes most acutely conscious of his existence. According to Kierkegaard, this is existence in its most dynamic sense. His next question is, how much of our existence do we know? When we experience the existence of I, it is not an altogether rational recognition, because most of what is felt as our own existence is not clear to us. There is a central reference which we recognize as I; there is a great clarity about that, but it is only one aspect of existence. How big is the field of personal existence? We don't know. When we say I, how deep is its ground? At what sublime dimension does it become evanescent? What structural complexity does it assume from moment to moment? We do not know. This is our honest answer.

As individuals we make deliberations, and we consider a good number of our decisions to be freely made choices. In order to choose we should have a norm. Only in rare cases, such as when a judge weighs evidence and considers the requirements of a statute, or when a theoretical scientist or philosopher considers the feasibility of an inference, does the norm or criterion loom large as a substantial factor. In most situations of paradoxical or enigmatic expositions of contradicting values, where the demands of decision-making are pressing and often chaotic, even the most deliberately conceived move actually evolves by itself due to the forces of circumstance. These are what Kierkegaard calls indetermined decisions. Most of our decisions come under this category.

We think of I as a rational element in us because we are conscious of it. Let us see how this I is related to its ground. What is there before anything is experienced? We may say nothing. Out of nothingness, thingness comes to us. So what is nothing? It is the prior absence of things. Before a pot is made out of clay, there is a prior absence of it in the clay. The prior absence of the pot is the nothingness of it, and from that absence arises the thingness of it. Thus, if something has to come, there has to be a possibility of it, but that prior possibility remains unknown. All our experiences have their prior absences in that unknown which is the ground of all.

By silencing our mind we can go back to our own prior absence. This is not, however, meant to be an intellectual process. It is accomplished by a process of reduction, though not a reduction in the sense in which it is suggested by Husserl or Jaspers. The type of reduction suggested here is the kind performed by a yogi. We have hands for working and legs for walking or moving. When a yogi sits quietly he does not use his legs or his hands. The hand is an instrument. If it is not functioning, the mere structure of it alone does not make it a hand. The plastic hand of a doll is also called a hand, but is it one? Is a plastic flower a flower? No. It is a chemical substance molded into a form that bears some similarity to a hand or flower. It may look like a hand or flower, but even structurally it is not true to the original. When we go beyond it, when we reduce the function of the hand, we go from what it can do to nothingness. The same with the legs. This means we sit quietly. If we also make this happen to our mind by not feeding it with memories and by not hooking one association to another, then functionally the body and the mind come to a certain nothingness. It is in this nothingness that we find the ground. We do not see the ground, we are the ground.

This ground or nothingness is not a total nothingness; it has certain potentials. When these potentials become actual, we think of them as the cause and the actuality as the effect. Now let us again forget the tyranny of language. At what stage is there a cause and at what stage does it become an effect? We can imagine our physical growth. Could we draw a line somewhere and say that up to this point in our growth was the cause and thereafter the effect began manifesting? After the prior absence of the foetus there comes into being a single cell, the zygote, which then starts to multiply. Can we stop there and say that that was the cause and the rest is the effect? No. The replication of the cell is done as if by memory, like a habit. It is as if this organism has done it so many times before that it has become instituted in it as a habitual function. This is what is called incipient memory. The incipient memory need not necessarily be the memory of what we recall in our mind. It is a potential in the ground itself. Our meditation is to reach the ground as well as the potentials in it.

Why should we bother to seek the ground? It is because at the conscious level in which we live our life we have no control, since that level is already manifested. If we want to do something with the primeval dynamics, we should go to the area which is still in the process of being manifested. The further we go into the unmanifested potentials, the greater is our control. How do we go about this? Let us go into our own personal experience, our own life. What problems are we confronting now? What kind of personal relationships do we have with others? What makes us cry? What makes us laugh? What inspires us to write poetry, or paint, or do any creative work? What inhibits us? What gives us courage? These are the areas that have become fully manifested. We should try to predicate the "what" in these questions.

Let us look at the paintings of three artists, Bosch, Goya, and Van Gogh, who belonged to different lifestyles and times, and who had different attitudes, moods, and expressions. Like Goya, Bosch uses the Biblical background of God, Hell, and the Day of Judgement for the representation of his art, but in him we see a skeptical person who was very satirical. Van Gogh is deeply religious in his expression. He would never make fun of anything that was of a religious nature; whatever was said in the Bible was a great reality to him, even though his religion was not that of the Church. Goya is not a mere chronicler, as has often been suggested; he was aware of the grotesque as well as the beautiful and he made a balance of these two aspects.

Why does one person make a somewhat grotesque representation and another use a more sublime way of presenting the same subject? Why did Van Gogh give so much attention to the peasants — the potato eaters for instance? We see a depth of compassion in his paintings. They are not like paintings, but more like messages, reminders. He seems to call our attention to some deep and sublime human value. In each person we see the special function of incipient memory, the potential that is lying buried within.

We began with nothingness. Then we found that nothingness is the prior absence of things that are manifesting, and that if there is a prior absence of what is manifesting then the potentiality of that which has to manifest is there. To understand ourselves we should know our ground, the nothingness, the scratch from which we began. Understanding is a complex process of comprehension where our emotions understand our emotions, our reason understands our reason, and our unconscious inner mechanism understands the unconscious totality to which it belongs. The principle of homogeneity is to be applied at each level so as to include and interrelate the entire content of our experience. One way of doing this is to conceive of our life as a series of pulsations, and to watch the centripetal and centrifugal contractions and expansions.

In order to visualize life as a pulsation and to meditate on it, we should imagine three concentric circles about a central point, as shown:

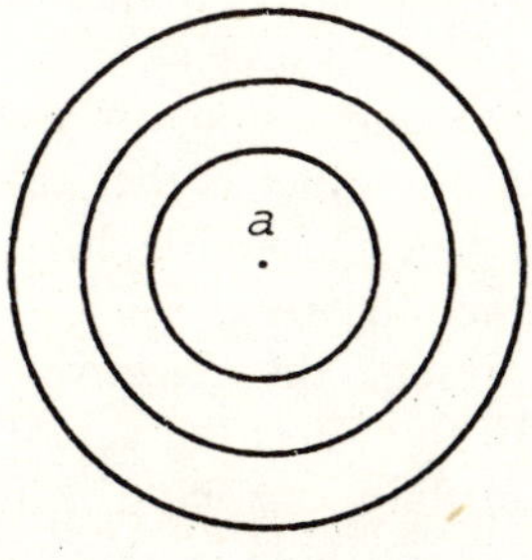

The central locus is marked *a* and stands for the alpha point or ground, which in one sense is nothingness and in another sense is the absolute value, the *summum bonum.* The Buddhists prefer to conceive of it as a pure state of nothingness, which they call *nirvāna* or *nibbāna.* The Vedāntins prefer to recognize this as pure beingness of absolute value, which they call *ānanda.* In either case this is the source of all, and is also the final culmination to which everything moves. This movement is what we have already described as a pulsation.

The small circle surrounding the center is to be understood as the repository of all incipient memories. In this first *darśana*, Narayana Guru compares the operation of the incipient memory to a dreamer who creates out of his unconscious self a wide variety of forms and events, and who becomes affected, pleasantly or unpleasantly, by interacting or reacting to the value significance of whatever is symbolized by the dream. The second analogy he gives is that of a magician showing many tricks. The only difference here is that the magician forgets his identity and becomes awed and bewildered by the magic he is showing to himself. The third analogy is the unfoldment of a tree from a seed. The fourth analogy is of an artist who gives a visual expression to whatever is presented to his mind in the form of mental imagery. The fifth analogy is that of a yogi who produces psychic phenomena by unfolding his psychic potentials. The sixth analogy is that of an ignorant man who becomes afraid of being surrounded by ghosts and goblins because of his timidity and fear. Narayana Guru uses several analogies so that they can all be put together to complement each other. In one sense or other all these qualities can be observed in the incipient memories that lie buried in the core of our unconscious self.

The second circle suggests the field of the threshold of our consciousness, from which consciousness expands to the frontiers of objectivity. Two ambivalent forces operate here like positive and negative energies. One fills the subjective consciousness with hope, courage, love, empathy, compassion, a sense of beauty, and many similar positive values; the other is the stifling, depressive energy that comes again and again like a dark cloud to fill one's mind with anguish, nausea, and helplessness.

The outer circle represents the objective and empirical world of all our transactions. In fact, it is the actual world we see around ourselves. From the farthest star we can imagine to the smallest pebble under our feet, everything in this world comes within this circle.

The first movement of pulsation arises from the alpha point, provoking incipient memories to wake up and gather the momentum to push through the subjective world of desires, fantasies, and deliberation, in order to become an actuality in the objective world. As all through this movement the primal momentum comes from *ānanda* or the ground of values, its actualization in the empirical world is experienced in terms of affectivity. This is the reliving of a memory. The experience changes into a subjective impression, contracting from the outer circle to the middle circle, then transforms into a seeded potential to reoccupy the unconscious core as a continuing incipient memory. The momentum which carried it all through is again reabsorbed into the alpha point. Thus, the omega and the alpha are both at the identical center.

This is exactly what we experience in our daily lives. In this let us include all the people involved and all the problems, our emotions and reasonings, our arguments and inspirations, the areas of interest to which our mind is easily drawn, and the fears and revulsions we have. All this and then again go back into that nothingness.

Life implies a binary function between our being and nothingness. What happens in between the being and the nothingness is what Sartre calls the becoming. The becoming should be the tool of our meditation, not to achieve anything but to have a comprehension of the *modus operandi* of our life process.

The next factor in our system is the vital urge. The vital urge has its origin in incipient memory. An incipient memory is a pre-established habit, which remains in the system as a potential waiting for an opportune moment to actualize once again as a manifested reality. Conscious deliberation is not an imperative to initiate the actualization of the incipient memory. Before a person becomes conscious of an urge or need the incipient memory unlocks many hidden reservoirs of inner forces, which, for example, stimulate the glandular system and turn on the secretion of hormones. Thus only half of the story of the reaching forward from nothingness to beingness is shared with our conscious mind. If by some chance the actualizing incipient memory is stifled or represesed by a counter-memory, all that we come to experience is perhaps a muffled uneasiness, or a dark and choking depression, or even an irrational outburst of hysteria. We will never consciously know what triggered the irrational anguish of the psyche.

There can be a prospective follow-up of an experience or a retrospective examination. Suppose a man feels the urgency of making a drastic decision, such as the shifting of his residence from his family home to an apartment, in order to effect a break followed by a legal separation from his wife. He wants to do this in two weeks. The time he suggests to his mind corresponds with a likely period of absence of his wife from the rest of the family. The decision came up with all its urgency as he was driving back from the airport after seeing his wife off to visit a relative in another city. From this point, if he retrospects and tries to understand the origin of the problem, he is faced with the uphill task of clearing his thoughts from the dark and torrential current of shame, guilt, self-pity, anger and frustration. Should he somehow manage to steer his way out of this mess to the source of his memory, he would come across different strands of memory interlaced into a bittersweet pattern. The will to justify his stand and the rationalizing of his guilt are likely to interfere with his search, and will recreate the memory inexactly by drawing curtains on what he does not want to see, yet the fear of a leak-out of incidents which are utterly shameful to him will highlight the memories of the same. In these memories one can definitely spot the archetypal intentionality of phenomenal creation as suggested by Narayana Guru in his first six analogies of the *adhyāropa darśana*: the dreamlike, myth-making fantasies; the actualization of latent potentials favored by ignorance and passion, and commonly shared by all; the fecund thrust of the will to live as seen in the bursting of a germinating seed and its consequent irresistible growth into a tree; the overwhelming aesthetic sense which so lowers the frontiers between fact and fiction that poetic fancies and wishful fantasies can stand on a par with the stern facts of life; and the crippling fear of hypothetical ghostly projections born of ignorance, that can create a kind of third world, as it were, fit for a neurotic or a schizoid.

After going upstream for a while through gorges and ravines, surrounded by beautiful panoramas, frightful and dismal overgrowth, and arid desert lands swept by the irrational gusts of sandstorms, he will start to complain of poor vision. Now he has come to the checkpoint—thus far and no further. What he faces at this point is not nothingness, but the black box of incipient memories. He is close to the core, but the core is forbidden to consciousness.

If our subject is to make a prospective follow-up of his problem he must face his own mind, which transforms itself into a crowd voicing the questions of his wife and children, near relatives and friends, his enemies and marriage counselors; it presents the phony legal claims raised by his and his wife's attorneys, the moral issues put forth by the priest, the suspicious voice of the devil, and the stern look of God from the uncompromising and all-seeing seat of judgement. (The person under discussion here is a God-fearing Christian).

Even at its best, no expression represents the total potential of an urge. And whether it is an outburst of an inner conflict or the manifestation of a creative urge, all our expressions stem from our incipient memories propelled by a vital urge.

Next we come to the polarization of bright and dark forces. What appears to be bright to the generality is not necessarily bright, and what seems to be dark to most people may not, in fact, be dark at all. It takes time for a person to sort out his or her dark and bright energies. The negative and the positive, the dark, *tāmasī*, and the bright, *taijasī*, *yin* and *yang*, interplay and interlace in different degrees in all forms of manifestation. Here, however, we are concerned only with that aspect which affects our psyche.

Although cosmic sociology is a new term in Western science, in India it has been a commonly accepted belief from the days of the Vedas that a man's personal life reflects the longitudinal and latitudinal conjugation of the cosmo-sociologic intentionality of karma, and the interacting forces of that phenomenon swirl around each pulsating unit of life with a unique pattern.

The following account, given by a student in a class assignment, illustrates what we want to say about the dark and bright forces making a pronounced impact on us:

> Christianity played a big role in my life, as I was always seeking and at the same time pleasing my family. I could never understand why, when I was very young, I would cry when the congregation would rise to sing hymns. Standing between my parents, I would sing, but every time I would feel such an overwhelming sense of depression, anxiety and fear that I could not contain my emotions. I know now what I was feeling. Somewhere in my past I either witnessed or experienced great suffering as a result of a belief. But when the suffering occurred, all feelings of holiness and grace disappeared and I was left with nothing but false impressions and an overcoming self-weakness. I had become so blinded by concepts (structured religion), I neglected to take the time to strengthen myself. Achieving perfection is not falling on the shoulders of other people's values, but to recognize your own and live by them.

> Truth does not lie on one narrow path — it lies on many paths and what you make of it depends on how many lessons you have learned and how aware you are of intangible concepts from past experiences.

This woman's experience is typical. The explanation she gives is also typical of the times, in the sense that psychoanalysts explain away all emotional conflicts as the direct outcome of childhood shocks. We should consider this. Meanwhile we should note that what came upon her as a dark force ultimately changed her mind to a positive attitude towards life.

In *Strindberg und Van Gogh*, Karl Jaspers says:

> It is not only increased productivity — precipitated by the excited condition — which, among other things, lead to the discovery of new (artistic) tools and thus to an enrichment of the artist's language; but new forces also emerge which in their turn objectify themselves, forces which are spiritual, i.e. neither sick nor healthy, but which thrive in the soil of disease.

He further observes:

> A striking fact is that today some outstanding personalities who became schizophrenics, exert an influence through works dating from their schizophrenic period.[1]

Although this might sound provocative to professional psychiatrists, Jaspers' question on schizophrenia is pertinent. He is asking if there is not something unique in these works of schizophrenic personalities, something that has a specific character with a defined place in the cosmos of spirituality, but which materializes in reality only if and when the conditions are created by the process of the disease.

What seems at first to assail a person as his darkness can be a virile source of spiritual dynamics, which can ultimately transform him from a conventional conformist into a genuine being fully committed and dedicated to a truthful life — the existential validity of which arises from the very essence of his beingness. When one is ultimately in resonance with his own vertical nature, he may emerge in the society as a dark threat to its prestructured stability and a challenge to its social norms. The truthful man makes his breakthrough and causes serious dents in the shell or crust of society.

Sooner or later, others who love and aspire to the same truth turn to the voice of the rebel; they read prophecy and promise in his words. In this case what appears in the beginning as a dark force confronting the individual finally proves to be a fresh lease of life coming from the perennial fountain-source of the Eternal, the ground of all.

This darkness has another side. It spells tragedy when it smothers all traces of sanity. In the *Chāndogya Upaniṣad*, fear is described as a conditional consequence of darkness and ignorance. According to the *Bṛhadāraṇyaka Upaniṣad*, even the Cosmic Person experienced fear upon finding himself alone immediately after his manifestation. Loneliness causes fear. The Cosmic Person overcame his fear by asking himself, "If there is nothing else but me, what am I afraid of?" It is from the other that fear comes. The risis believed in the redressal of fear by cultivating the right attitude.

Modern psychologists identify fear with anxiety and phobia. Anxiety suggests strangulation. In his earliest formulations, Freud considered anxiety to be the outcome of repressed somatic sexual tensions. He believed that libidinal images which were perceived as dangerous were repressed, and that the libidinal energy was cut off from normal expression and transformed with anxiety. He later replaced this notion with the much broader conception of anxiety as a signal for danger, distinguishing between objective anxiety (fear) and neurotic anxiety — depending on whether the danger came from the outside world or from internal impulses.

According to Wolpe, an operational definition given to anxiety is that it is the autonomic response pattern characteristic of a particular individual organism after the administration of a noxious stimulus. The autonomic events that make up an anxiety response are predominantly functions of the sympathetic division of the autonomic nervous system. Common manifestations of the sympathetic response are an increased heart rate, raised blood pressure, increased respiratory rate, sweating of the palms, dilation of pupils, and dryness of the mouth. Common parasympathetic responses are diarrhoea, nausea, vomiting, and frequency of urination.

In the *Bhagavad Gita*, Vyasa gives a symptomatic description of a similar state of Arjuna as follows:

> My limbs fail and my mouth dries up, my body trembles and my hair stands on end. The bow slips from my hand and my skin feels as if burning all over, and I am unable to stand and my mind is whirling round, as it were. (Ch. 1. v. 29,30)[2]

In all the Upanishads wisdom and realization of the Self are characterized as the attaining of the state of fearlessness. Freeing oneself from fear is given minute attention in the third section of the *Bṛhadāraṇyaka Upaniṣad.* The principles that illuminate, *indha*, and animate, *virāj*, come together in each individuated person. This coming together is described as similar to the synchronization of the light that comes from the right eye, *indha*, and the light from the left eye, *virāj*. The gross body, in which these powers manifest, is maintained by the essence of nourishment processed and evenly administered by *prāṇa*. The union of *indha* and *virāj* is in the heart, from where a network of minute conductors of energy, called *hita*, runs in all directions. This is similar to a nerve which is as fine as a hair split into a thousand parts. The organism conducts itself by reacting to the solar energy, electromagnetic field, entropy, the word-dynamics of interpersonal communication, and by maintaining its core in the spirit of the Self. The Self extends in all directions and is meditated upon as *neti neti*, "not this, not this." The individuated self moves ambivalently between the inner light, *antar jyoti*, and applied reason, *vijñāna* in conjunction with *buddhi*. It operates overtly in the mind, which is considered to be a reflection of the Self in the physical counterpart of the embodied self.

When this subtle network of the conductors of energy is affected by the white, blue, brown, green, and red serums of the nerves, it becomes afflicted with the past conditionings of the individual, and the mind is drawn to the non-Self, which is characterized by desire and the urge to engage in activities that gratify desire or are of a compulsive nature. As a result of this the individual is again and again exposed to self-delusions, which result in fear and anxiety.

The individuated consciousness alternates between the empirical limit and the sublimity of infinity. At the empirical level, the physical reality draws it to identify with the properties of several sensory data and with the compulsion to act so as to ease the system from the pressure of necessities. Both the wakeful experience and the dream experience rest on the modifications of the mind brought about by its past iniquities, as is evidenced by their painful nature. Thus fear is a deep-seated ignorance or conditioning, and it can be rectified only by reclaiming the self from the vicissitudes of ignorance.

The Upanishadic theory of the *hita* that operates as a liaison between the self and the serum of the nerves has some resemblance to the Haemic theory of knowledge, of which Warren S. McCulloch gives a short account in *A historical introduction to the postulational foundation of Experimental Epistemology*. Early Greeks postulated entities called "mixtures." One of these is what Aristotle called *conate pneuma*, an airy blood postulated by the Hippocratic school. Atomists and Greek Empiricists also had their versions of mixtures; of these the latter's theory of the "perfect mixture" is considered as the natural cause of conception, formation, and the growth of progeny. According to McCulloch, this is the precursor to the shuffling of genes, first postulated by Mendel to explain the frequency of occurrence of traits in phenotypes.

In the mixture postulated to explain knowledge, Aristotle treats the knower and the known in equal counterparts, as when a hand grasps an object and it conforms to the object, "the fulls of the one filling the hollows of the other," just as the signet impresses the seal onto the wax. McCulloch says:

> In the form and proportions determined by the impression, the elements (earth, air, fire and water) of the known mix with those of the knower. This mixture forms in the blood of the knower. The veins, anastomizing, mix the blood from various parts of the knower, and the final mixture takes place in the heart. Such was the cardiocentric theory of knowledge. The nerves were only reins to govern the muscles, and the brain a phlegm to cool the blood.[3]

The *hita* theory of the Upanishads finds other affinities in the nervous theory of knowledge postulated by Alcmeon around 450 B.C., who based everything human on pairs of opposites; and, much later, in the theory of Renè Descartes, who postulated that:

1) nerves were composed of parallel tubes too fine to be seen individually by him even under a magnifying glass;
2) each tube was filled with liquid in which pulses of hydraulic pressure went from the brain and spinal marrow to muscles, causing them to contract; and
3) each tube had a fine thread in it, which, as the muscle contracted, signaled back to the central nervous system to close down the valve.[4]

The complete picture of the *hita* theory is approximated a bit better by adding to the above postulates the current theory of the electrical excitation and inhibition of nerves, which enables one "to understand the interaction of impulses afferent along separate fibers on their way to a terminal cell or cells."[5]

To raise consciousness to the Absolute, arrived at through *neti neti* from the ambivalent world of the *hita* that is intertwined with the physical world of the serums — which are almost identical with the present day theory of chromosomes and the nucleotides of memory bits of at least three million years of biologic history — one should learn the art of transcendental reduction. Fritjof Capra writes in *The Tao of Physics* of such possible transcendence even in physics by going to a higher dimension: the fourth dimensional space-time. He says:

> Space and time themselves are two concepts which had seemed entirely different, but have been unified in relativistic physics. This fundamental unity is the basis of the unification of the opposite concepts mentioned above. Like the unity of opposites experienced by the mystics, it takes place on a "higher plane," i.e. in a higher dimension, and like that experienced by the mystic it is a dynamic unity, because the relativistic space-time reality is an intrinsically dynamic reality where objects are also processes and all forms are dynamic patterns.[6]

The James-Lange theory of emotion is unceremoniously dismissed by Walter Cannon; he gave no attention to the unconscious origin of the arousal of the visceral response. Albert Ax, in *Psychosomatic Medicine*, speaks of norepinephrene and the increases in blood rate and blood pressure associated with anger and fear, accompanied by a visceral reaction of an increased breathing rate, known to be produced by epinephrine. It is now recognized that norepinephrene and epinephrine are the distinguishing chemical components of anger and fear respectively. Compared to the James-Lange theory, the Cannon-Bard theory and Lashey's view of the function of the thalamus — which according to him controls the various patterns of emotional expression — are not at all conclusive.

While modern scientists play with their gadgets and wrangle over the issue, we can work on transcending our basic fear by meditation on our inner light, *antar jyoti*. In the Bhagavad Gita we are given a formula to work with:

> — slowly, slowly, activities should be brought to a standstill by reason steadily applied, establishing the mind reflexively in the Self, without thinking of anything whatever.
>
> Whatever causes the changeful, unsteady mind to go out (again and again), from each such, restraining (it again and again), it should ever be led to the side of the Self.

> Such a yogi, verily, of calmed mind, of pacified passion, who has become the Absolute, and free from all dross, comes to supreme happiness. (Ch. VI v. 25–27)[7]

The immediacy of our life shades off into contemporary convictions and conventions. The sanctions of society are part of an historical evolution. History itself is a confection of the thoughts, beliefs, and actions of a number of people over the centuries, which are expressed in literature, art, music, and monuments. Beneath the overt growth of history lies buried humanity's perennial dream, which we sometimes recognize as myth. Jaspers calls this the original cipher, the primal language of transcendence. According to Jung, myth is a fact of life, though the world picture it produces is not consistent with our rational and objective view of things. He says:

> The instinctive, archaic basis of the mind is a matter of plain objective fact and is no more dependent upon individual experience or personal choice than is the inherited structure and functioning of the brain or any other organ. Just as the body has its evolutionary history and shows clear traces of the various evolutionary stages, so too does the psyche.[8]

Narayana Guru refers to this archaic basis when he compares the cosmos to the unfoldment of a seed into a huge and ever-spreading banyan tree. He equates that seed with Brahma the creator, Viṣṇu the nourisher, and Śiva the destroyer. Besides all these mythical figures he also refers to the Absolute, the All. The myth of creation is as old as man. The Rig Veda, the oldest known literature of the world, describes it as follows:

> What was the wood, what was the tree,
> from which heaven and earth were hewn?
> Let the sages inquire within their minds. (X:81:4)

The *viśva karman*, the All-Creator, who made the world from the unknown tree, did so as follows:

> Sacrificing as a wise sacrificer,
> Our father entered into all these beings;
> Striving for blessings through prayer,
> Hiding his origin, he went into the lower world.
> Yet what and who has served him
> As a resting-place and a support?

The Rig Veda proceeds to answer these questions: *Puruṣa* (Man, Anthropos) was the primal being who

> encompassed the earth on all sides.
> and ruled over the region of the heart.[9] (X:90)

Jung reads into this myth his archetypal concept of the Mother principle. He says:

> As the all-encompassing world-soul, Puruṣa has a maternal character, for he represents the original "dawn state" of the psyche: he is the encompasser and the encompassed, mother and unborn child, an undifferentiated, unconscious state of primal being. As such a condition must be terminated, and as it is at the same time an object of regressive longing, it must be sacrificed in order that discriminated entities — i.e. conscious contents — may come into being.[10]

Jaspers sees the formation of three tiers of language originating from what he calls the original cipher:

1) the primal language of transcendence has in it the embodiment of these ciphers in myths and philosophies,
2) metaphysical reality realized in thought and symbols forms a second original language, and
3) the connection of the previous two languages takes place in the union of transcendence and immanence, as well as *Existenz* and reason, which enlightens and makes intelligible the message transmitted.

What Jaspers attempted to do was what Jung referred to as turning toward the primal myth with a regressive longing to return to it. According to Jaspers, the task of philosophy is to carry the original cipher, to lead us back to the immediate language of Being.

The attitude that Narayana Guru recommends is neither regression to the primal cause nor progression towards the finitude of the individual existence that ultimately lapses into the void of death, but to cancel the *parā*, the absolute One, with *sarva eva saḥ*, all that are — or as Kant conceived it, "the numerous intelligible egos." In this *darśana* both birth and death are placed within the mythical reality of a cosmic dream, a grand magic, a superb psychic feat, and the ontologic verity of a cycle that emerges from a seed to remerge once again into a seed.

The mere knowledge that there is a myth under our feet or that we are confronted with ciphers that cannot be deciphered does not help anyone. Jaspers recognizes attempts to interpret myths or ciphers when he considers art as a "meditation of the reading of ciphers in nature, in history and in man, provided that the meditation occurs at the intuitive, not the speculative, level."[11]

In the matter of turning to the myth for light, resigning ourselves to intuition can lead us to fanciful imaginings and beliefs. This is dangerous. For this reason, in Plato's dialogue "Euthyphro," Socrates categorically denies his belief in the myth when it is taken literally. The appeal that Socrates makes to reason is fully upheld by the ṛiṣis of the Upanishads. The whole of the *Darśanamālā* is an attempt to clearly steer our way through the fog of all three languages that Jaspers spoke of, so that we can obtain a transparency of vision which will put us in touch with the primal language of transcendence, the metaphysical reality realized in thought and symbols, and the language of reason that reveals, in apodictic terms, the meaning of existence.

I. ADHYĀROPA DARŚANAM

1 *The Philosophy of Karl Jaspers*, Open Court, 1976, p. 447

2 Nataraja Guru, Bhagavad Gita, R & K Publishing House, Delhi Ch. I, v, 29, 30, p. 92.

3 Warren S. McCulloch, *Embodiments of Mind*, M.I.T. Press, 1970, p. 360

4 Ibid., p. 363

5 Ibid., p. 365

6 Fritjof Capra, *The Tao of Physics*, Shambala, 1975, p. 150

7 Nataraja Guru, Bhagavad Gita, R & K Publishing House, Delhi Ch. VI, V, 25–27, p. 300-301.

8 Carl Jung, *Symbols of Transformation*, Bollingen Series XX, Princeton University Press, 1956 p. 29.

9 Ibid., p. 416

10 Ibid., p. 417

11 Karl Jaspers, *Philosophy*, p. 840

II. APAVĀDA DARŚANAM

Truth by Consistent Refutation of the False

Every man has his own fundamental convictions. When he incorporates a new item of knowledge or an extension of understanding into his already existing knowledge-structure he examines the validity of the new input in the light of his fundamental conviction. According to some the Self alone is real. For them the Self is a spiritual entity, and nothing can be countenanced which seems to lie outside it. For this reason they cannot tolerate materialism. On the other hand, materialists think it an irrational superstition to accept the so-called Self, which no one has ever seen. They believe the human race cannot make adequate progress when blindfolded by religious superstition, so they consider it their duty to eradicate the superstitions of spirituality from the minds of men.

These two arguments are opposed. In the same manner, and sometimes using the same arguments to justify their propositions, some believe in the existence of a supreme Person or God, while others deny the existence of such a Being. So spiritualists accept the existence of God, but materialists deny it. Both groups try to prove their stand with the aid of reason. If we examine the intention of these contending forces, we shall see that their apparent differences contain a large measure of agreement. Both sides want truth to prevail; both want the mind to be systematically directed towards truth, so that whatever an individual does will be consistent with a truthful conviction; both hold that only truth will set man free from incorrect beliefs and wrongful conditioning; and both want their votaries to be happy. In addition, both spiritualists and materialists believe they should share happiness with others and work towards the perpetuation of peace, justice, love, and happiness for all through the achievement of the goals of their philosophies.

What both groups are trying most sincerely to do is remove false notions or wrongly indoctrinated convictions. It is wonderful to see that except for doctrinal points there is almost complete agreement between them. The systematic method of correcting a false notion is in Sanskrit called *apavāda*. When the qualities or properties of one thing are wrongly projected or superimposed on another it is called *adhyāropa. Apavāda* is the antidote for *adhyāropa.* Thus *apavāda* is a philosophical method used to reclaim and reestablish truth. After clearly presenting various aspects of the mental projections we are prone to make because of our ignorance and the limitations imposed by our generic psychophysical nature, Narayana Guru wants now to provide us with a method with which we can eradicate from our minds all false identifications.

We have already said that a spiritual believer wants to prove that the Self is the only reality, and that the most direct way to experience its blissful nature is to remove the ignorance of mind which obscures that reality. If a man comes to know this reality he will see everything as a manifestation of the Self, and such a realization will automatically make him a lover of the manifested world. So far as his interpersonal relationships are concerned he will neither hate nor wish to possess or dominate anyone, for he will see all men as manifestations of the one Self. If all men saw the Self everywhere we would live in a world of absolute peace, with a spontaneous sharing of joy and happiness. It is the spiritualists who are on the right track. Of this there can be no doubt, if we compare the worlds which result from the practices of spirituality or materialism.

When we come to the materialists, we see that for them there is only matter. This same matter in its most elaborate and complex form is the totality of nature. All sentient beings are part of nature. And nature being anxious, as it were, to propogate itself, is careful always to nourish the bodies and minds of beings. Mind is only a quality of the highly organized nervous systems of beings who have evolved from less sophisticated living bodies. As growth and development in the process of evolution is uneven because of geographical and physical conditions, in the process of time a basic difference between men becomes apparent — the difference between the strong and the weak. The history of human evolution is a painful record of the exploitation of the weak by the strong. In lower forms of life the weak are eaten by the strong for sustenence, not from caprice or cruelty for its own sake. But man uses the endowment of his superior intelligence as a powerful instrument to enslave and exploit his weaker brethren.

The will to live is a dynamic force. It can assert itself as a physical force, as the dynamics of emotion, or as the intelligent exercise of power. All these expressions of force are used by men to destroy and exploit by shameful manipulation the weaker sections of his species.

As a result of this, mankind has formed itself into separatist groups — races, classes, and various kinds of primitive communities.

Materialists believe that the whole of mankind could be molded into one classless society. They believe that if people can be persuaded of their essential sameness, in that they are all parts of the same whole which is nature, and if their behavioural patterns are corrected by radical methods, then it will be possible to establish the ideal classless society. In such a world, humanity as a class would be considered as one and the same entity. Thus the happiness of that entity would ensure the happiness of the society, and of all its members. This sounds quite similar to the spiritualists' goal.

When we compare the doctrines, aims, and methods proposed to achieve these goals by both the spiritualists and the materialists, then the materialists may be amazed and not a little discomforted to see there are no essential differences between the two groups. The continuing warfare between them arises from the obscuration caused by a confusion of tongues. As Bertrand Russell rightly said: "Man can never attain lasting peace without finding adequate measures to solve his semantic problems."

Unfortunately, prejudices cannot be easily eradicated. But *apavāda* is an effective method we can use for this purpose. It addresses itself both to prejudices arising from misguided spiritual enthusiasms, and to those stemming from the slogan-chanting exaggerations of materialism. The "emperio criticism" of Lenin is a good example of the application of *apavāda* in the effective integration of earlier schools of materialism.

Narayana Guru opens this *Apavāda Darśanam* with the following verse:

VERSE 1

caitanyād āgatam sthūla-
sūkṣmātmakam idam jagat
asti ced sadghanam sarvam
nāsti ced asti cidghanam

This world, which is of gross
and subtle form, comes from consciousness;
if it is affirmed, everything is existence through and through;
if it is denied, it is consciousness through and through.

idam — this
jagad — world
sthūla sūkṣmātmakam — which is of gross and subtle form
āgatam — comes
caitanyāt — from consciousness
asti cet — if it is affirmed
sarvam — everything
sadghanam — existence through and through
nāsti cet — if it is denied
asti cidghanam — is consciousness through and through

The Self exists; matter exists. What is common to both cases is the predication "exists." When a person says, "This exists," he is describing the existential aspect of an experience, and, as far as he is concerned, is describing the experience itself. What he experiences is the action of a subjective consciousness interacting with an entity. The entity can be the immediate presence of an object seen as external to himself, it can be a barely distinguishable feeling arising from where, he knows not or a strong emotion which floods his being, or even the presence of an idea in his mind.

Close scrutiny of the statement "the Self exists" will show the simple meaning of it. It means only that one has in mind the vivid experience of a certain quality of awareness to which he gives the name "Self." Another will say, "Matter exists." He too refers to a subjective entity experienced as a quality of awareness to which he gives the name "matter." Regardless of the terms given in each case to the subjective entity, the quality of the two experiences may be very similar: in both cases they refer only to the experience of a specific configuration of awareness in the respective minds. Awareness in Sanskrit is called *caitanya*.

"Here is a book. It is an interesting book." No one would suppose these two statements could be capable of causing any controversy. "The weight of this book is two pounds. It contains five hundred leaves of paper, and every page has something printed on it in black ink." These are facts about the book which can be verified or repudiated by anyone who examines it. Observation and verification are methods by which one obtains specific information. With this in hand, what was previously an awareness related to a subjective entity, in this case "book," becomes now that quality of awareness called "certitude" in relation to it.

The second statement about our book, that it is interesting, cannot be as universally accepted as the statement concerning the weight of it. The enjoyment of the special style of the book and the ideas it presents is the result of an interaction between the reader's own conscious ideation and belief-structures, together with the incipient memories which condition him in a certain way, and the conceptual imagery which the author has presented. When a reader finds the book interesting, he then goes beyond it. His mind becomes holistically oriented toward the transformation it experienced through the modifications effected in its structuring by its interaction with the objectified ideas of the author.

Now we have two sets of ideas about the same book. One pertains to its gross aspect, the other to its subtle aspect. The Sanskrit term for gross is *sthūla*, and for subtle is *sūkṣma*. *Sthūla* is that kind of knowledge which is structured with impressions derived from our sensory system, for example, form, color, physical dimension, weight, and so on. The awareness which is *sūkṣma* is a form of comprehension arrived at by relating concepts which exist as ideas in the mind, without much reference to the presence of objective data. Even when a physical object is present in its gross aspect, one can transcend the physical impression cast by the object on the senses and lift one's mind to subtle planes of varied significance and meaning.

In a general sense we can say that the existence of what is gross is an external factor in our conscious life, while the existence of the subtle can be considered as internal. Gross objects belong to the public world, subtle objects to one's own personal and private experience. That which is experienced as being external is called "objective." If we are driving an automobile and see a tree fallen across the highway and blocking our path, we must stop if we are to avoid disaster. While it is true at that moment that our conscious awareness is centered on the tree, nevertheless there exists also on the periphery of awareness a quality of concreteness. The concreteness which is inherent in the construction of the automobile is also inherent in the tree. If the two were to come together at speed, disaster must inevitably follow. The impact of a physical object on a human body can cause a painful bruise or dislocation.

If a man experiences a breach of trust or rejection by a beloved, or finds himself in a situation where he is being abused or insulted, all such experiences are subjective and occur only in his own mind. But despite the psychological origin of such experiences, they cannot easily be brushed aside. Such an incident can affect one's digestion and appetite, and may even prevent one from sleeping.

It is evident that man can be affected by both gross and subtle entities. Events in the gross world of objectivity and psychological factors in the subtle world of subjectivity can in both cases upset equanimity and even coherence. These distinctions between gross and subtle should not be held too rigidly. Clearly, although these distinctions can be drawn, they are in fact and in operation experienced by the same consciousness. And both are generated by modifications of the awareness of the consciousness. Hence Narayana Guru says, *caitanyād āgatam sthūlasūkṣmātmakam idam jagat*.

When a person says "it is," the reference can be to either a gross or a subtle entity. The perceiver experiences the irrefutability of the awareness of existence; this is why he uses the definitive term "is." In either case, whether the entity of his experience is gross or subtle, the experience is existentially valid. But suppose the same person uses the phrase "it is not." Here the pertinent question is: what is it that is not? Before the existence of a thing can be denied, one must first conceptualize the existence of it in order to be able to deny it. In the subjective and objective worlds of consciousness what does not exist cannot be said to be in a condition of nonexistence. Only after the act of conceptualization can one say that nothing is present which warrants the cognition corresponding to that particular concept. Such a statement cannot arise from a mental vacuum, The whole statement therefore belongs to the subjective world of pure concepts.

When people say, "God exists," they have in mind a normative idea and belief-structure of what God is. They experience in their emotional life a sense of wonder and adoration toward the concept of God, and in the external manifestation of inner values they see a perfect correspondence with the subjective concept. For them the one-to-one correspondence between the normative idea-structure and the objective existential experience is accepted as the existence and very often the proof of existence of God.

When others say, "There is no God," they too conceptualize an idea structure to use as a criterion to verify the possible existence of God. In this they will include such items as perfect order, uncompromising justice, a clear revelation of absolute truthfulness, the compassionate protection of all beings, and so on. After forming this structure and including in it other values of a purely conceptual nature, they look for a one-to-one correspondence in the world of objectivity. Unfortunately, what they have structured in their minds as God has little or nothing corresponding to it in the external world, so they vehemently deny the existence of God. Their experience is a purely subjective awareness of ideas.

So it is that when Narayana Guru says *asti cet sadghanam*, it has the same meaning as an affirmative "yes," and as such is a reference to an existent verity. And when the Guru says *nāsti ced asti cidghanam*, it has the meaning of a negative "no," and is a reference to a subjective experience of ideation. The Guru calls "existence" *sadghanam*, and "ideation" he calls *cidghanam*. In both of the above cases concerning the existence of God, the people resorted to the criterion of a normative idea-structure to say yes or no. The God who is asserted to be real and the God who is denied reality are both only byproducts of the reasoning faculty. If the proponents of this argument had known they were quarreling only about the incompatibility of their ideational structures — a merely semantic issue — they might have agreed to suspend hostilities.

When the people who were indigenous to the area called Arabia propounded the great truth in their own language, *la ilah il Allah*, its complementary truth was uttered by the seers of India, *sarvam khalvidam brahma*. Unfortunately, these nearly identical doctrines pronouncing the truth of one Divine Principle have given rise not to a unity of peoples, but to hostility and bloodshed. Even today India is a country divided against itself as the result of fanatical partisanship to one presentation or the other of the same truth. Throughout recorded world history terrible things have been done by man to man in the name of religion, and words have usually been the medium used to inflame unworthy passions.

Words such as "democracy" and "socialism" are the expressions of hypostatic concepts which have only a subsistential verity but which are treated as existential realities. This type of misunderstanding gave rise to the recent tragedy of war in Vietnam. American and Vietnamese youths by the hundreds of thousands fought, and many died, for the preservation of hypostatic concepts. The whole ridiculous and tragic confrontation was to decide the meanings of the words democracy and socialism. It is not surprising that the issue remains undecided.

Once upon a time a wise king named Vikramaditya ruled ancient India. On a certain day the king was presiding over an important banquet when a woman came into his court. She was a well-known harlot in addition to being very wealthy and beautiful. Entering the banquet hall, she approached the throne on which the king sat enjoying the revels. Upon reaching the king, she prostrated before him and burst into tears. The king asked her why she wept. She told him and the assembled court that a certain man from the town came to her in a dream the previous night, enjoyed her favors, and left without paying the usual fee. Now she begged the king to compel the man to pay her a thousand gold coins.

The whole incident of the harlot and her lover took place in a dream, but despite this the king sent for the man. He was to attend on the king at once, and bring with him one thousand gold coins. This man was known to all as one of great virtue. As ordered by the king, he came and laid the purse of money before his ruler. The king then asked an aide to bring him a piece of stout cord and a mirror. The purse full of money was then held suspended by the cord over the mirror, which was placed face upwards on the floor. All present could see the purse reflected in the mirror.

Now the king spoke to the harlot. First he acknowledged the validity of her claim, in that her client did come to her and did leave without making payment. But then he pointed out that the whole incident had taken place in a dream. In the dream the man had enjoyed her; in the dream he had left without making payment. "Was this in fact so?" asked the king. The woman agreed and again asked for her fee. "Indeed," said the king, "You shall be paid. But you received this man in the subtle world of the dream state, not in the gross world of the wakeful. What you earned in the dream shall now be paid in the coin of that realm. Take your due and go; it is the purse you see reflected in the mirror."

This story draws a definite line of demarcation between the world of transactions, which may be called objective reality, and the world of dream, which may be called subjective illusion. Illusion can be the cause of much misery when our level of understanding is low.

Let us imagine a scene where two men, Peter and Thomas, are sitting in a room with its door and windows closed. Peter speaks to his friend, "What would you do if you were suddenly changed into a snake, and I changed into a mongoose and pounced on you?" (A mongoose will always kill a snake in a fight). If Thomas is susceptible to the subjective effects of imagination, he may well become disturbed and even horrified. The imagined metamorphosis of himself into a snake and his dear friend into his killer may be too much for him to accept calmly, but if he has a firm understanding of the difference between the transactional and illusory worlds he will dismiss such a suggestion as being ridiculous.

When the question of conscious awareness at the gross and subtle levels is considered, it is necessary that one should have a proper understanding of what is truly existent and what is merely fanciful imagery of the mind. The differences between what is existent and what is fancy should never become blurred in our experience of events or situations, or in our assessment of individuals and our relationships with them, if we are to retain psychological health. This is even more important if we are to have any hope of penetrating the mysteries of the esoteric. What is hidden from us now will remain so if we cannot distinguish between what exists and what does not.

Human misery is wrongly thought to arise merely from human action. In fact, it is the effect of a basic illusion which is cosmic in its dimensions, and an all-pervading ignorance which has no beginning in the sense that we can say mankind began. This illusion and ignorance is fundamental to the emergence, structuring, and ongoing development of the cosmos. It cannot therefore be attacked in a piecemeal fashion. If it is to be reversed, it must be done in a radical and wholesale manner, and this is not possible without resorting to an efficient methodology. Narayana Guru presents us with such an effective method in the next verse.

VERSE 2

anyanna kāraṇāt kāryam
asadetadato'khilam
asataḥ kathamutpatti-
ranutpannasya ko layaḥ?

Apart from cause there is no effect;
therefore, all this is unreal;
for the unreal, how can there be an origin?
Of the unoriginated, what dissolution?

anyat —apart from
kāraṇāt — cause
na kāryam — there is no effect
ataḥ — therefore
etat akhilam — all this
asat — is unreal
asataḥ — for the unreal
katham — how
utpattiḥ — origin
anutpannasya — of the unoriginated
kaḥ — what
layaḥ — dissolution

In 1976 a multi-billionaire died in America. Doctors recorded the grim fact that his death was due to undernourishment. Because of his great wealth, no material comfort was denied him—certainly he did not lack the means to buy food. But the poor man suffered from an intense fear of bacteria and viruses. For him everything was polluted, including the very air he breathed. Food was a great source of worry to him: his phobia made every mouthful seem unclean. He even refused to handle a newspaper, so the news was read aloud to him. Yet by no criteria could he be called an unintelligent man. He had built a vast business empire, and had many inventions to his credit; he was perhaps even qualified to be called a genius. Naturally he was able to buy the best specialized medical attention the world had to offer. But skilled though his physicians undoubtedly were, they could offer him no relief for his condition. This was because they could not eradicate the cause of his fears. They could not detect the germs and bacteria which terrified him, because they did not exist in reality. Being unable to detect them, they could not destroy them.

How could it be possible to eradicate something which has no origin? The fantasies of dirt and pollution arose in the mind of the sick man as mental images based entirely on irrational ideation. They were his own subjective creation, yet to him they were real enough. Here we see the effects of a subjective experience causing apprehension or elation in the mind of an individual. This particular type of experience is one which cannot be shared with other individuals. In Sanskrit it is called *pratibhāsam.*

Objective empirical experience and subjective illusory experience are both creations of the same mind. The primary material which is fashioned into images that are both empirically valid as well as illusory is consciousness. In either case it is the same consciousness. We make a mistake if we suppose that consciousness in itself is of different kinds. This can be readily understood if we consider the nature of memory. What is experienced as an actuality in the objective world afterwards becomes transformed into a memory. There is no qualitative difference between memories, whether they are of an illusory experience at the subjective level of consciousness or of an actual event in the physical world.

In the transactional world, the memory of a previous experience, the experience of an immediately perceived event in the present, and the actualization when it occurs of what was an anticipated possibility in the future, all show a subjective resemblance. If we therefore take an experience related to a single event or situation in the physical world, which passed through the stages of anticipation, actualization, and transfer to the memory structure, we see that what may have appeared to be a series of isolated experiential entities is in fact one contiguous whole, not much affected by the passage of time.

All experience in the empirical world is "of" something — the object and the experience of it are not usually felt to be one. But in fact all experience is subjective, though we do not usually realize it. For most people, what appears to be a flow of experiences relating to the passage of time gives them the feeling that the empirical world is independent of their subjective consciousness.

Let us suppose that we are in a theater, watching a film of people engaged in various events in a beautiful countryside. What happens on the screen before us will be seen and experienced as one continuous whole. But if we penetrate to the source of what we see, all that will be found is a static light focused in a beam and a plastic translucent strip of cinematographic film imprinted with many separate still pictures. When the still pictures pass through the light beam at a speed which is greater than the time required for a visual image in the eye to disintegrate (sixteen images per second), the consecutive still pictures projected onto the screen are seen by the eye as one continuous action. And although the music and speech we hear emanates from a sound system — the loudspeakers of which are some distance from the screen — the sound and visual image become synchronized in our mind as one experience. Enchanting though this may be to the cinema addict, what is happening should really be seen as a defect in our nervous system. But we don't question the validity of the experience.

It is for this reason the Buddhists designate our world as being of empirical and interdependent origination, *pratītya samutpannam* — that is to say, an aggregate of sensory impressions. An example given in a Buddhist text illustrates this point. A lamp is burning. When we look at the flame we do not see the mechanism of its production. The flame arises from the combustion of cotton fibers which are saturated with oil. There is a continuous supply of oil which is consumed, and a continuous disintegration of the fiber into a fine ash or soot. From one moment to the next the constituents of the flame are new. New oil rises to the top of the wick and is burnt, and new fibres turn to ash. Thus, the flame itself can at any given point in time be said to be a new one, though to our vision it seems to be one continuous flame. We make no distinction in the experience from one moment to the next. In fact, however, it is a series of impressions, one leading into and producing the next; in other words they are interdependent. It is a contiguous series of flames, not one flame.

We can look at life from the point of view of biophysics. For example, we can take a case of simple mental arithmetic. A person, through the process of addition, arrives at the sum of two plus two, which is four. Simple though this may appear to us, in fact a complex series of functions operating below the threshold of consciousness has occurred. The molecular structure and functioning of the brain has to be modified at a speed much faster than can usually be observed. A specific restructuring of molecules produces, then raises into consciousness, the answer requested in the addition of the numbers. In the next moment we may consciously subtract one number from another, as in two minus two, thus arriving at the difference of zero. Again the entire molecular pattern is restructured, though we are not aware of the process. Thus, even in the physical aspect of our organism we are not the same, in terms of structuring, from one moment to the next. As Heraclitus said, "It is not possible to step into the same river twice." From moment to moment man, like the river, is different.

What we experience as the world at any given moment is the sum total of the effects produced by the whole organism. The world is the sum total of the experiences of our own organism projected in such a way as to seem external to that organism. In the present verse the Guru calls this "the non-difference of the effect from the cause." In his work, *Creative Evolution*, Henri Bergson describes this as the historical evolute of each moment.

Cause and effect are not two entities, they are the two poles of complementary events or situations. It is not possible, for example, to think of "child" as an entity existing without the complementary "parent." No child is parentless, and the parents in turn, when children, had parents themselves. So irrefutable is this system that even in religious mythology it cannot be discounted. Even the greatest of spiritual heroes were not the products of a discontinuous structuring. Although the Christian Church can deny the incarnation of Jesus as being the result of normal human sexual union, it cannot produce him from nowhere as the result of nothing. He had to have a mother, and she had somehow to be impregnated. Thus the union of the Holy Ghost and Mary becomes the cause and Jesus the effect. Even the Church cannot totally evade the laws which govern manifestation, though it does its best to do so. Without a cause there cannot be an effect. Equally the effect is necessary if there is to be a cause. Without an effect there cannot have been a cause.

Some say the world is unreal. If this is so, and because the world is an effect, or rather, the result of a series of effects, then the cause or series of causes must also be unreal. To say the unreal has existence or did exist, or had origin either in reality or unreality, is to construct a fairy tale for children, as in the *Yoga Vāsiṣṭha*. There, a foster mother narrated stories to children who had no ability to discern truth from falsehood. In regard to the unreality or otherwise of the world, if something has not originated, then the question of its dissolution cannot arise.

In these questions, as in every other, what may seem to be an impenetrable mystery becomes crystal clear after the acquisition of sufficient knowledge. As far as the world is concerned knowledge is an imaginary entity. But this is not to say that it is unreal. Knowledge is indispensable at every level of our existence. Even for illusion or misunderstanding, some knowledge is necessary. We can question everything, but we cannot question knowledge; without knowledge we can question nothing. Still, most people are satisfied to have and propound a type of knowledge that from an enlightened viewpoint can be seen to be more properly described as ignorance.

We might now ask, "What is the use of knowledge?" The answer is that it dispels fear and anxiety, misery, unhappiness, ignorance and illusion, and gives us an entirely different understanding of life and the world and of ourselves. We understand at last what the universe is, how it came into being, who created it and how the "creator" came into being, how it is sustained, and the laws which govern its manifestation. And so far as the empirical world is concerned, we are able to see beyond its appearance of reality to the subsistent ground from which it arises in ourselves. This brings a peace and certitude unknown to most people.

The Tamil people of India have a folk song which is relevant to the question here. It goes like this:

> On the tip of a thorn, three ponds were dug.
> Two were dug in the rock which had no springs,
> one had no water.
> Three men were paid to dig the pond which had no water;
> one had no hands, and the other two no legs.
> To the man with no hands three cows were given,
> two were barren, one gave birth to no calf,
> so he had no milk.
> The cow who had no calf was given three
> pastures to graze on. Two were covered with rocks,
> the other had no grass.

This song, though manifestly absurd, produces merriment in those who listen to it sung. Though it refers to a series of tragedies its very aspect of the ridiculous makes us laugh. A man of realization feels a similar kind of humour when he watches the emptiness and ridiculousness of the world-game. He no more takes the world seriously than we do the song. We see the events in the song as absurd illusory fabrications of the imagination, and so we laugh. The man of realization looks at the world and laughs for the same reason. This illustrates a transcendental knowledge not available to the great majority of persons, just as our knowledge transcends the ineptitudes portrayed in the song.

In the first chapter of the Bhagavad Gita, Arjuna is moved to beat his breast in the agony of his confusion. He turns to Kṛṣṇa, the Guru, and says he can see for his family and friends nothing but slaughter and doom. He weeps like a child. But Kṛṣṇa, when he observes this, merely smiles. Kṛṣṇa, the Guru, and Arjuna, the disciple, were about the same age as far as years go. Their dialogue took place as they stood between opposing armies, with arrows and other missiles flying from both sides close over their heads. In this situation, so fraught with tension, uncertainty, and danger, why did one man weep and the other smile with a serene confidence? The answer is the secret which is implied in the present verse.

When we are small children our parents are delighted to see us correctly recognizing objects and other people. Parents carefully teach children the names of people and things, and how to recognize the values in situations and events. For the most part what they teach arises from their own conditioning, the distillation of their life experiences, and the belief-systems structured from their hopes and fears. Above all they teach us name and form. Again and again they repeat the teaching to make sure we have memorized it. When we in turn become adults we are fully convinced of the reality of a world of actuality, constituted of countless things, each having a different name and form. But our view of the world is really only a conditioned subjective reaction to sensory input.

When we think of the human organism, we first usually identify ourselves as a physical body. We experience mind as operating within that body, and within the mind we experience a focal point of attention which is recognized as the I-consciousness. Keeping the I-consciousness as a nucleus and the external shape of the body as the outer limit, a personality is structured. This personality is experienced as being limited in size and influence, and as being separated from the rest of what constitutes our world. We experience self as a small individual in a world of immense dimensions. When one who is self-structured like this wishes to learn about what is called the Self, he naturally thinks of it as being confined to one branch of knowledge, as are history, geography, chemistry and biology. This attitude is the most dangerous and harmful stumbling block, which can impede the progress of even the most earnest seeker of truth.

The enquiry in which we, as genuine seekers of truth, are engaged in is not much concerned with the subject — or object-matter of our world experience. It concerns itself more with the turning of the student inwards towards himself in an effort to penetrate the cosmic mystery expressed as his own mystery. There are a number of what may be called instruments or tools which will assist one in discerning what is true. But the present study is not an exercise in the use of tools or methods. What we are studying is that very knowledge which is itself the basic instrument and expression of all knowledge.

A foetus in the womb or a person in the condition of deep sleep are both unaware of any duality of subject and object. Such a dichotomy occurs only in the wakeful and dream states of a fully developed human organism. Narayana Guru, in an equation using an allegoric ideogram, comments on this. In his "Universal Prayer" he says:

> As ocean, wave, wind and depth,
> let us within see the scheme
> of us, nescience,
> your glory and you.

Only at the horizontal level of the empirical world do we experience the phenomena of plurality. When our awareness is verticalized toward the omega point of the Absolute there is only the experience of a unitive state. In that state the experiential quality is one of awe and wonder. And in that state the distinction of the knower and what is known does not exist. In the empirical world of transactions and the subjective and illusory world of fantasy we can experience the individualized variations arising from the ceaseless modifications of continuing impressions. When we stand at sea level we can see the differences in wave forms: small ripples, a choppy sea, cresting waves, and giant rollers are all plainly visible. The plurality of wave forms is caused by the unending modifications of a body of water. In much the same way, all the things we experience as the external world or as the world of dreams are the unceasing manifestations of our own primary consciousness. This is further examined in the next verse.

VERSE 3

yasyotpattir layo nāsti
tat param brahma ne'tarat
utpattiśca layo'stīti
bhramatyātmani māyayā

That which has no origin or dissolution
is none other than the supreme Absolute;
through *māyā* the confusion arises that there is
origin and dissolution in the Self.

tat — that
yasya — which
na asti — has no
utpattiḥ — origin
layaḥ — dissolution
na itarat — is none other than
param brahma — the supreme Absolute
māyayā — through *māyā*
bhramati — confusion arises
asti iti — that there is
ca utpattiḥ —- origin and
layaḥ — dissolution
ātmani — in the Self

Because of the confusion caused by and inherent in the negative phenomenal power (*māyā*), one experiences the illusion of origin and dissolution in the individuated self. Those who have received a modern academic training will be unlikely to understand what is meant here by "confusion." But there are some enlightened thinkers among contemporary scientists. Sir Arthur Eddington, for example, refers to the universe as nothing but "folds and fringes in the space-time continuum." He speaks in the same language as would a Vedāntin. To understand and experience the reality of space and time one has to apply the mind in an unconventional way. As the mind penetrates new dimensions of consciousness, and our sense of individual self is diminished, conscious awareness itself becomes the mystery and therefore also the answer to what now seems mysterious.

To a person in Australia, India is in the west and America in the east. But to an African, India is to the east and America to the west.

A statement such as, "My house is on the left-hand side of the road," is meaningless unless it is first explained from which direction the viewpoint is taken. All expressions of reference to distance or direction, such as up, down, near, or far, relate always to a subjective point of reference first established in the mind. And when we say "time" we are really referring to a sequence in our mind.

The concepts of space and time are useful to us for our orientation in the perceived world, but the orientation is happeing only in our mind. The question of the reality of space becomes even more interesting if we take into account the distinctions between psychologically projected space, mathematically computed space, and hypothetical physical space, about all of which we can only make presumptions.

If one stands on a hilltop at night when the sky is clear, many constellations of stars can be seen in our own galaxy, the Milky Way. The horizon will be very wide, and space will seem infinite. No one would think of the immense vastness of space as a projection of the mind.

It is true that the light coming from the starry heavens is not created by us. But the retina of the human eye is such that it can cover a very wide area when all the light waves passing through the lens of the eye are made to converge to a point. When light passes beyond this focal point, it again diverges and creates an image which is just big enough to be contained within the retina. The retina is made up of rods and cones which are receptors ready to be stimulated in tune with the frequency of the light waves. This kicks up electrical impulses in the optic nerve, and from that point what passes on to the visual area of the brain is not light but nerve impulses. These impulses are screened, controlled, measured, and directed by the cortex of the brain, so that the visual memory of the associated area can be recalled to provide for conceptual complementarity, thus structuring a pattern of awareness that makes sense to that particular consciousness.

All this is not nearly as simple as it would seem. The biophysicist also has something to contribute to the study of this area. The complicated molecular functioning of the brain takes place as if it had behind it a mysterious operator who is assembling the molecules in terms of a selective structuralism that has relevancy to the individual's memories of the past and expectations or apprehensions of the future.

We do not know the exact psychochemistry that produces the

sense of colour, tone, shape, and so on, in our awareness. In fact, when we think we are seeing the Milky Way we are actually only seeing a miniature version of it appearing within the field of our own gray matter. Although it does not seem so to man, it is here that we have one of the greatest miracles. When awareness presents a picture to the individuated consciousness, the miniature version which has been structured in the brain is enlarged according to a certain scale of perspectives and is also presented in such a wonderful manner that it looks as if it were infinitely far away. This experience of space is what we call psychological space.

An astrophysicist can sit in his office, and through the use of mathematical equations arrive at a sense of space which he will express as a number of light-years. A light-year is the distance light travels in one calendar year. The physicist uses this method to express not only distance but time. A star, he will say, is a given number of light-years away from Earth. Such immense time spans and distances have a quality of fantasy. It is said that light travels at a speed of 186,000 miles per second. Based on a year of 365 days, a light-year is 5,865, 696,000,000 miles. Let us now take this serious figure and add an arbitrary number of miles, say 333, and 2 yards. Does this make any change in one's time sense? Light-years are a scientific myth in terms of objectivity, and should be relegated to the realm of fantasy. This is what is known as mathematically computed space.

Apart from the psychologically projected and the mathematically computed experiences of space, there is a mysterious factor which compels the mind of man to conceive of space. Man has not discovered any way of jumping out of his psychological outfit and rational speculation to find any means to solve this mystery. What he experiences is at once real and unreal, hence it is called *sat-asat*. The Absolute is *sat*, "that which exists." But *māyā* is indefinable in that it is impossible for the mind to conceptualize "it is" and "it is not" at one and the same time.

In this chapter the Guru is not asking us to add to the already very many perceptual and conceptual patterns we have created. Instead, he is asking us to get rid of them so that we can go back to our primal consciousness. In his "Universal Prayer" Narayana Guru says:

> Are you not *māya*, the wielder of *māyā*,
> and also the rejoicer in *māyā*?

Are you not the True One who,
having removed *māyā*, grants the Supreme Union?

Here the disperser of *māyā* is not postulated as an outside factor. The mind which can structure a gestalt can also unstructure it.

The phenomenal world and the life experienced in it can be expressed in one word: *līla*. It means "playful sport." Children at play become absorbed in what they are doing as if the make-believe situations are reality to them. From old materials they may erect a shelter and furnish it with a few odd boxes. Then they play the game called "mothers and fathers." They create fantasy children, and feed and care for them. Suddenly interest will fade and they will stop the game and leave, with no regrets, for fresh fields to conquer. The game is a seeming reality for them, but when it is finished the attachment to it is finished also, and the experience of the game as reality ceases. They know it is a game. In the world, adults also play similar games, but with one important difference: they take the game seriously, and for them it is reality indeed. Their attachment to the games of the world is total, whether the games are negative or positive. For the very great majority of people, illusion is taken as a lifelong reality.

The *Apavāda Darśana* looks at life as a sport or a passing show. But every game has its rules, and these must be recognized as valid within the frame of reference of the game. When the game is in progress we should play by the rules, indeed we must do so if it is to come to a logical conclusion in the external world. At the same time the more serious part of the mind can safely be kept aloof from the world-games, remaining unaffected by success or failure in those games. Such games, which collectively we call "life," are played on the periphery of consciousness and—relative to what might be called the deeper center of consciousness — are illusory indeed.

The Upanishads repeatedly say that mind is the cause of both bondage and liberation. Superimposition establishes the state of bondage, while the systematic denial of superimposed falsehood brings one to the state of liberation. Human life can be a very enjoyable confection of moods. In classical Indian literature and the visual arts, nine basic human moods are recognized. According to this classification one may feel pleased, displeased, angered, pacified, afraid, awed, emboldened, compassionate, and erotic. Combinations of these moods give rise to the innumerable variations of expression. Each basic mood has its own value vision. The urge to bring into objective realization a particular value transformation comes when the whole psyche is colored by the nature of that particular value.

When a young lover looks at the world, everything is seen as a symbolic expression of love. A man who is filled with fear sees nothing but danger around him. We impregnate the external world with our own values. On closer scrutiny, it is not difficult to see that all values are derived from one central value, which is none other than *ānanda* — happiness, pure and simple.

Our moods reflect the possible reality of values or an immanent threat to our interest. What we call experience is an effect, a consequent factor. At the causal pole there resides the blissful nature of the Self.

Between a dominant value and its existential actualization, awareness has an active role to play. If awareness is coloured by a negative apprehension, it obscures the presence of a value. Then the natural bliss of the Self and its existential experience are separated by ignorance.

Everyone experiences irrational fears and frustrations throughout a lifetime. This shows that the ignorance we speak of is not merely a defect of the individual mind. There is a generic aspect of nescience which affects all individual beings in one way or another. Generic ignorance conceals the true nature of things or of the Self from all people alike. This veiling aspect is called *āvaraṇa*.

In addition, this same nescience can condition all minds to simultaneously project the same falsehood. This is called *vikṣepa*. All of us see the sky as a blue dome above. We know that there is no such dome and no such blue color. Still, even the best physicist cannot escape from the impression of a blue dome-like sky above his head. This is but one example of the mass projection of falsehood.

Everything we think we see is the illusory result of the action of those elements of consciousness called *āvaraṇa* and *vikṣepa*. From this it is evident that we should at all times keep the mind actively engaged in a continuous process of the reduction of projected anomalies. Such an understanding through reduction can and will, if properly done, lead to an unbroken experience of the sweet and blissful serenity of the Self.

VERSE 4

kāraṇā vyatiriktatvāt
kāryasya kathamastitā
bhavatyataḥ kāraṇasya
kathamasti ca nāstitā?

Because of its non-difference from cause,
how can an effect come to have existence?
By that, how can there be
the non-existence of cause also?

vyatiriktatvāt — because of its non-difference from
kāraṇā — cause
katham — how can
kāryasya — an effect
bhavati — come to have
astitā — existence
ataḥ — by that
katham asti — how can there be
nāstitā — the non-existence
kāraṇasya — of cause
ca — also

For human beings nothing is more important than the experiencing of this world. We could categorize thousands of items which come under the heading "experiencing this world." For example: problems of relationship with parents and family members, friends, workmates, and neighbours; the transference of giving and receiving; arguments which may lead to fighting or litigation; diseases of the body and mind; social and religious obligations and rituals; moments of inspiration or jubilation; and unexpected experiences which leave behind a sense of wonder or repulsion.

There is an actuality about experiences in the world, and for the most part they cannot be avoided. If we are told that the world and our experiences in it are unreal, and if we take the statement seriously, we shall be faced with a sense of deprivation and the stability of our individuated structure may be threatened. If we are told it is all unreal, then where do we turn? We know no other reality than of this world.

It seems to almost all of us that we are creatures of this world and inextricable parts of its structuring. We are members of society with obligations to ourselves, our families, and the state. If the world is not real, where does this leave us? Can it be wrong to care for one's parents? It would certainly seem to be a wasted effort if they were unreal. Should a man not be responsible to nurture and educate his children? Should all the schools and universities be closed, the courts of justice be dismantled, and the production of goods and services cease? Can it be shameful or a waste of time to enjoy the beauty of a sunrise, to write poetry or music, to paint, or to sing?

If we treat all these and many more of the stimulating and creative activities of our life as being merely the aspects of an abysmal ignorance, then our life will become truncated and meaningless. Even if an experience is transient, like the beauty of a rainbow, the stimulating affection of a friendship, or the enjoyment of some sporting activity, it contains an element of truth which is itself not transient.

In the case of the awareness of an experience, of its beauty, and of our enjoyment of that beauty, all items of awareness have their existence in knowledge. When we speak of bliss we ought to speak of our awareness of that bliss, or to be more precise, of the quality of that awareness. It is the quality of our awareness at any given moment which gives our experience of that moment its particular flavour. The aspect of consciousness known to us as awareness has the inherent power, if it is conditioned correctly, to change the potential morbidity of an experience into an actualized delight. Very much power to shape our own experiential destiny lies in our own hands if we care to exercise it. We experience our own projection of what is called "the world." Either individually, or joining with others in a mass projection, it is we who create the world. And what we have made, we can alter and unmake.

If we ourselves become the expression of true knowledge, we can change what is now a world of unreality into a different world of reality. Whether we actually see what is real, or see what we wrongly believe to be real, depends on the extent to which we have experienced ourselves as reality, that is, as the living Self.

With an enlightened consciousness we can eradicate the spurious duality of cause and effect, together with all the ills and problems which arise from such an apprehension of duality. But we cannot altogether efface the existence of that primal principle which inscrutably programs into consciousness the many dualities, such as subject and object, cause and effect, knower and known, observer and observed, enjoyer and enjoyed, and so on. This nondesignated primal principle of existence cannot be named, but for the sake of convenience in communication we call it the Absolute. Here we must depend on what is called "surface evidence." The existence that is evidenced has no outer criteria by which such an existence can be proved.

An event cannot be conceived, nor can the experience of it last for more than a moment, without one knowing irrefutably the existence of awareness. The examination of a number of instances in which one was selfconsciously aware of one's existence, that is to say of existence as an experiential actuality, will make it easier to understand that every item of awareness is experienced as an affectation of awareness. If the affectation is one of psychological pain or misery, then its placement in space and time is easily forgotten. We tend to repress into the unconscious the memories of what in the past gave us pain. And if the affectation is one of joy, then many dichotomies, such as the knower and the known and the enjoyer and the enjoyed, are transcended without effort.

Since the Self is in its most true nature transcendent, we can deduce from the above that the nature of Self-existing awareness is blissful. Despite the multitudinous expressions of itself, the Self is one; and the awareness of its existence is experienced as bliss when the individuated self becomes consciously what it always was—the universal Self. Even in the transactional world we can see that joy leads to expansiveness, cohesion, and unification. In short, joy is a unitive experience, while misery leads to the desolation of separateness and disunity. When the self deviates from a blissful awareness of itself, then automatically is initiated the need for the lost joy of the Absolute which is intuitively felt by the individual. This is experienced within consciousness as the phenomenal transforming into the numinous.

A poor man goes to the market with a basket of fresh oranges and sits by the roadside hoping to sell them. After a while all his oranges are sold. Now, content with the outcome of his enterprise, he goes home with a pocketful of money. But what he really did was exchange food, which his family could have eaten, for pieces of paper and imprinted metal. His family cannot eat money. But both he and his customers are happy. Out of the transaction each was able to realize the value most important to him at that time, the customer with the "use value" and the vendor with the "exchange value."

When a need is imperative, in this case to obtain a refreshing orange, a person is motivated by the use value. When several needs are to be satisfied, then the exchange value becomes very useful.

Values change from moment to moment. The vendor, previously concerned with exchange value, now wishes to purchase food for his family, and so he becomes motivated by the use value. Constant change can be said to be the only unchanging aspect of manifestation. If we examine the events and experiences in our life, we shall see that there is a rhythmic flow in an ascending spiral pattern in which certain types of events seem to recur again and again and intermeshing with this is a figure eight pattern of movement in which the real flows into the unreal, and the unreal into the real.

If we look at transactional events or experiences in isolation, the whole business of life may well appear meaningless and without purpose. But if we can relate all events in the flux of life to the golden thread of joy, which is the manifested Self, then we see only the Real ever shining in the gloom of what seem to be the constantly altering phases of real and unreal aspects of the phenomenal world.

We are normally unable to discriminate between what is real and what is unreal. And even that lack of discrimination varies from a state of translucency to one of opacity. Sometimes for a brief moment we may think we have glimpsed reality, but then again the veil drops. The "purpose" of the Absolute is to everywhere experience its own existence in that form of universal consciousness called the Self. When that is achieved, then translucency and opacity give way to transparency.

In this vision the Guru is helping us to develop a transparent insight which will always reveal the one abiding truth now obscured by the passing shadows of the phenomenal world. Without this transparency, even the most apparently satisfactory life is dull and insipid and full of irrational tribulation. The Guru will elaborate on this in the next verse.

VERSE 5

kāryatvādasato'syāsti
kāraṇam nahyato jagat
brahmaiva tarhi sadasa-
diti muhyati mandadhīḥ

This which is unreal, being an effect,
has a cause; it is not the world,
but the Absolute alone that is real,
which a dull mind wrongly imagines to be unreal.

asya — this
asataḥ — which is unreal
kāryatvāt — being an effect
asti — has
kāraṇam — a cause
ataḥ — it is
nahi — not
jagat — the world, the phenomena
tarhi — but
brahma eva — the Absolute alone
sat — what is real
manda dhīḥ — a dull mind
muhyati — wrongly imagines
asat iti — to be unreal

In the world of transactions our experience is holistic. It is only psychologists who for convenience analyze and speak of it in terms such as cognition (*asti*), connation (*bhāti*), and affection (*priya*). When consciousness is expressed as awareness, even as the first faint comprehension of an object, event, person, or idea, it comprises in it the idea of existence, an intimation of its general nature, and the dynamism to affect the perceiver in a positive or negative way.

In commenting on the previous verse we took the example of a man who exchanged oranges for money. When we look at such a transaction, we can clearly see how a human being interacts with nature and how he discovers values — in this case use and exchange values — and by his own action creates a whole chain of action and reaction leading from one set of values into another. Karl

Marx, in his book *Das Kapital*, uses twenty pages to explain this phenomenon. First, he outlines the difference between other beings and men in his discussion of man's interaction with nature. He says:

> We have to consider labour in a form peculiar to the human species. A spider carries on operations resembling those of a weaver; and many a human architect is put to shame by the skill with which a bee constructs her cell. But what from the very first distinguishes the most incompetent human architect from the best of bees, is that the architect has built a cell in his head before he constructs it in wax.

It is strange that such a hard-core materialist should unconsciously give priority to ideation before action. Marx goes on to make a very fine observation of the whole process of our creative reaction. He continues:

> In the labour process, therefore, man's activity, with the help of the instruments of labour, brings about changes in the subject matter of labour, changes intentionally effected. The process disappears in the product. The product is a use-value, materially supplied by nature, and adapted to human wants by a change of form. The labour has become incorporated with the subject matter of labour. Labour has been materialized, and the subject matter of labour has been elaborated. That which in the labourer appeared as movement, now appears in the product in a resting phase, as 'being' instead of 'becoming.' The worker has spun, and the product is his web.
>
> If we regard the whole labour process from the outlook of its result, the product, then both the instrument of labour and the subject matter of labour assume the aspect of means of production, and labour itself assumes the aspect of productive labour.
>
> Though a use-value issues from the labour process in the form of a product, other use-values, the products of earlier labour processes, enter into the present labour process as means of production. The use-value which is the product of one labour process, becomes means of production in another.[1]

The complex phenomena of socioeconomics, biochemistry, physical chemistry, and astrophysics are pregnant with endless ramifications and details. But if we trace the whole process of their emergence, from the most immediate in the series of phenomenal effects backwards in time to their one primeval causal factor, we shall eventually come to a terminus. This terminus is none other than what was described in the previous chapter as the binary function of primeval creative energy, which contains within itself a positive aspect of brightness and a negative aspect of darkness, or *taijasī* and *tāmasī*.

Narayana Guru, in his *Cit Jadangal*, "Thought and Inertia," summarizes the subject matter in one verse:

> Mind first, then smell, and wakefully all five
> up to the joyous numinous is the spirit's domain of mind-stuff made;
> from earth we touch to darkness' boundary — alas! —
> inertia gross extends. These twain do all comprise. (v.4)

At this point it will be useful to recall Jung's concept of the unconscious and the unknown as the sources of the conscious and the known, which we have already described elsewhere. The status of a phenomenon is that it exists for a little while in a condition of developing beginningness, then that state disappears as the next phase is entered. We have seen that this explanation of the flux of life is easily acceptable both to Vedāntins such as Narayana Guru and materialists like Karl Marx.

Another aspect of the discussion which is equally universal is that which says that the human mind is affected, and its structuring modified, by existential knowledge. Such an affection of mentation is an inducement for the mind to react, and its reaction is always oriented towards the avoidance of pain and the attainment of happiness.

The search for happiness is unfortunately very much restricted by economists, who appear to see the highest values in life as questions of supply and demand in the world of physical wants. It is true that man is very much occupied with the satisfaction of his physical needs, such as the preservation of life, shelter, sustenance, security from natural hazards, the compulsive need for action, and so on. But if he is to develop his full human potential, man must also satisfy other needs. These include companionship, the recognition of his worth and value as a person, the mysterious prompting which makes him seek to understand the nature of his own being and his relationship with universal being, and many more. The needs in this second class are more complex than the generalized theories of biologists, for example, seem to indicate. Man's psychological and specific problems are more complex and interrelated than what is known in the world of socio-economics.

In all his oscillations of needs and satisfactions, man again and again comes to the experience of happiness that gives him a sense of peace and restfulness. This resting place is what is termed here the Absolute or Self. And this experience, or the possibility of it, is common not only to mankind but to all sentient beings. The Guru describes it as the only unchanging reality, which serves as a substratum in the whole process of becoming.

If an observer says that there are eight people in a room besides himself, this would be a descriptive statement of an immediate perception. It would, however, be an incomplete statement. In the actuality of the perception, what is meant by "eight"? That is to say, what is the meaning of "eight" other than the superficial one of number. Let us assume the observer amplifies his statement by saying that three people sit to his left; their names are Tom, Dick, and Harry. Does the mere act of perception help him to relate these names to the visual images he has in mind of these people? Do the names have a relation to the physical act of seeing? Suppose the name of each man is changed to that of one of the other men—Dick, for example, becomes Harry. The men remain as before and the observer's visual images of them remain as before. Can we expect the changes in names to be the cause of some aberration in the observer's physical action of seeing? From where does the concept come to support the idea indicated by the word "eight"? What makes the name Tom relevant to that particular person? Our usage of words is habitual. If the name "mouse" had been bestowed on the elephant centuries ago, and the name "elephant" on the mouse, then those are the designations which would be in common use today. As has been said before, "The map is not the territory." Is elephant the name bestowed on the beast? If our observer said that Dick was the second, and a woman named Edith was the eighth person in the group, what special qualities should those two have to be second and eighth respectively? Normally one would not raise any of these questions. As with most things, we take names and descriptions, and the actions of perception and conceptualization for granted, without any consideration of the how or why of them.

In the situation of the eight people and the observer there is a coming together of perceptions supported by external data and concepts arising from the causal consciousness. In synchronizing these two groups of mental entities — one arising in conscious awareness, the other emerging from below the threshold of consciousness — to form a meaningful whole, the mind adopts certain structural devices. These devices belong to pigeonholes within the scheme of understanding, such as "generalization," "abstraction," "elimination of the irrelevant," "categorization," "organization," *et cetera.*

In this chapter the Guru does not want to leave anything unquestioned. This is reminiscent of Descartes' *Meditations.* Bacon and Descartes were the first among modern Western philosophers to open the era of critical skepticism. Descartes succeeded in evolving a systematic methodology to differentiate facts from opinions. In that system he eliminated those items of knowledge which failed to impress their categorical certitude.

In the example given above, we called Dick the second person and Edith the eighth for our own convenience. This type of knowledge falls into the category of supposition. In this chapter the Guru directs us to try our best to attain to a clear and precise vision of the Self, without getting caught in the cobwebs of fancies and superimpositions.

Descartes arrived at an axiomatic basis for his methodical system of thought, and expressed it as *cogito ergo sum,* "I think, therefore I am." In this axiom the certitude of the self arises from the self itself. Jean-Paul Sartre wrote a book called *Being and Nothingness* to refute the stand of Descartes. He denied the "categorical certitude," saying that when it is said that A is A, it looks like begging the question.

Two possible paradoxes confronting philosophical speculation of this sort are tautology and contradiction. We have already shown how necessary it is for both scientist and philosopher to have in mind one fundamental truth to act as a ground from which all other truths may arise.

If we give the world of superimpositions the status of absolute truth, then consciously or unconsciously we are accepting a double standard. That can result in contradiction. Here the Guru wants us to discipline ourselves to be as uncompromising as possible when it comes to giving our conclusive verdict in furtherance of the only truth. In the next verse he examines the two paradoxes, tautology and contradiction, mentioned above.

VERSE 6

ekasyaivāsti sattā ce-
danyasyāsau kva vidyate?
satyastyātmāśreyo yadya-
pyasati syādasambhavaḥ

If one alone has reality,
how can one experience another's beingness?
To say that the real is in the real is tautology;
to say it is in the unreal is contradiction.

ced — if
ekasya eva — one alone
sattā asti — has reality
kva vidyate — how can one experience
anyasya asau — another's beingness
sati asti — (to say) the real is in the real
ātmāśreyaḥ — is tautology; dependent on itself
yadi api — to say it
asati — (is in) the unreal
asambhavaḥ syāt — is contradiction; inconsistent or impossible

From the previous verse we have come to know that the world of empirical experience is structured in our own minds. The constituent factors of that structuring include sense-data drawn from memories, psychological urges arising from incipient memories, and names and nomenclature, all of which are arbitrarily assigned in the formation of concepts. In addition there is a structural device of ideation based on whatever meaningful correlation is adopted by the individual mind. This structuring of correlation is shared more or less universally with other individuated minds, while still being in part the recorded data of the personal history of the individual concerned. It is through the action of this conditioned structure that a normal individual mind can communicate ideas which can to some extent be reproduced in another mind. However, the complete communication of one's total experiential awareness to another individual remains impossible

When consciously experiencing an ensemble of mental entities, the mind is able to separate one item from another. In doing this, the I-consciousness that serves as a nucleus for all units of experience retains its own identity. This sense of the I-identity is experienced as separate from the characteristic uniqueness of each item of knowledge. And though the experience of individual identity is not present during the condition of deep sleep, it is the first thing to be reconstituted upon waking. Thus a person retains the I-consciousness from the first emergence of his distinctive consciousness as an infant until the moment of its disappearance at death.

A young child does not have a complex structured ego as the nucleus of its personal awareness. However, it slowly develops an individuated consciousness and personal ego, which in the process of time becomes conditioned by and part of the social dimension of consciousness. Even in the absence of all sensory data, the mind can turn to the self-luminous I-center and examine the meaning of nature and the worthwhileness of all thoughts and feelings.

In short, this is the only area of consciousness which can assure certitude. At one and the same time it is the ultimate criterion of judgement and the consciousness which applies that criterion. To introduce other criteria or another methodology to prove what is self-evident will result only in the logical fallacy of tautology. And if one fully understands that the only real existence is the Self, then to attribute reality to transient projections of the mind will result in contradiction. Accepting this as the final truth, the world of perceptions should be treated as non-Self and its so-called reality should be refuted.

Our senses have limitations beyond a certain range. For example, for each of us there is a distance beyond which nothing will be seen distinctly by our physical vision. The mechanism of our ears can make audible to us only those sound waves which oscillate within a certain range of frequencies. Our sense of smell is considerably less acute than that of many animals. Without the direct contact of our tongue being involved, we can taste nothing. And our senses have other defects. Things which are very small are invisible to us, and things which are very large cannot be seen in their entirety if we stand close to them. And there are defects in the senses even between individuals: one man may have a red-green deficiency in regards to the general consensus of color harmonics, another may see no color at all, a third may have monocular vision and a fourth may be blind.

Under the circumstances of this limitation of the senses even among those with the very finest of sensory structures, man, who is generally speaking eager to increase his knowledge, augments the range of his senses by the use of mechanical appliances. With these accessories our world of perception is considerably extended. Because of the tremendous advances in science and technology over the last few decades, we have gone very far beyond our previous sensory boundaries in the macrocosmic and microscopic worlds. No one can directly perceive the terrain of the planet Mars, but the extension of our sight in the form of a camera attached to the American spacecraft which landed on that actual location enables us to see details of the ground with ease. And now microphonic transmitters smaller than a shirt button can be concealed in rooms to record conversations inaudible to us if we were twenty yards away, yet reproduced with full fidelity for a listener a thousand miles away. Thus do we extend our senses of sight and hearing.

But wonderful though the technological advances of man may be, there remains an unknown that is infinite and far beyond the reach of the radio telescope or the electron microscope. Even in this region the adventurous spirit of man will not accept defeat. He decides to accept a compromise. The watchword of the British Academy of Science is: "We believe what we see." But now scientists have gone beyond that and agree that what lies beyond the range of our senses, even beyond the reach of the appliances which so greatly extend that range, can be known through the methodology of statistical approximation. Although the physicist does not yet know the exact nature of a particle, he can produce a deductive model of what is an approximation from a highly quantified unit.

This type of compromise has left the scientist with no justification for his previous claim of objective certitude. Heisenberg was honest and humble enough to announce to the world his belief that what awaits the scientific world is the principle of uncertainty.

Man, unfortunately, has a boundless vanity; to him there is nothing more important or of greater value than his individual self. If he is outside on a starry night he may admire the celestial panorama, but in general he seems to feel that it is all a drama staged for his personal benefit. Awe and wonder are not often among his feelings. Yet the glorious panorama he sees is only a small fraction of the total grandeur of the universe.

Although scientists hold the view that the universe, though not infinite, is very big, that bigness is beyond normal human comprehension. The forces emitted from the bodies which can be seen to form the universe, and those forces from unknown sources such as the neutrino, can never be controlled and manipulated in experimental laboratories. So it is that beyond a certain stage the scientist links arms with the philosopher, and both enter the realm of theoretical speculation. Their investigations lead from the gross to the subtle, and from the subtle to the mysterious. The scientist cannot remain for long in this unconfined area for fear of being ostracized by his professional community, so he usually denies the implications of it and falls back.

Of all men who as scientists have shown unparalleled courage, C.G. Jung must be reckoned among the bravest. He risked his professional reputation, and sometimes his sanity, and reached out almost to the fringe of what is possible. He stood in awe and wonder at what he discovered. Time and time again he had to tread the razor's edge between the known and the unknown. Time and time again his scientific conditioning and belief systems were imperiled, until finally he withdrew from the inescapable conclusions of what he had discovered, on the plea that he was a scientist. No one should criticize him for this. Of all men in this present era, his penetration of the unknown and his contribution to man's understanding of himself have been of incalculable value.

According to the Upanishads there are only two methods by which man can come to know truth. One is annexing the certitude of the truth of experiencing one unit to another such experience, and thus knowing the whole universe to be a manifestation of one and the same truth. The second is denying the falsehood of the countless facets of the kaleidoscopic presentation of the phenomena of perceptual experiences. This denial culminates in a total abolition of all individual things, and in the experiencing of a wonder in the Unspeakable, which reveals itself to be the basic reality of the enquiring mind.

The analytical approach to the discernment of reality, which generally is accepted by scientists, is examined in the next verse.

VERSE 7

vibhajyāvayavam sarva-
mekaikam tatra dṛśyate
cinmātramakhilam nānya-
diti māyā vidūragam

When all parts are separated
one by one, then one sees
everything as consciousness alone —
far from *māyā* — and not any other.

sarvam — all
avayavam — parts
vibhajya — separated
eka ekam — one by one
tatra — then
dṛśyate — one sees
akhilam — everything
cinmātram — as consciousness alone
māyā vidūragam — this is far from *māyā*
na anyat iti — and not any other

From a piece of cloth the threads can be pulled out, one after another, until no cloth remains. Now the thread itself can be untwisted and unwound until only a heap of cotton fiber is left. Every fiber can then be destructured until the heap of fiber is no more. In the laboratory the constituents of the fiber can be separated and revealed. When this is done the name "cotton" is no longer applicable. And when the limits of our instruments have been reached, still we can continue to analyze the subject in the subjective realm of ideation and speculation. In this case we have gone from the gross manifestation of cotton cloth to the subtle manifestations of mental entities. This process can be repeated in actuality or by analogy with anything manifested in the world of physical objectivity: it can all be reduced to its subtle beginnings in mentation.

A serious penetration of the meaning and workings of the external world must inevitably take us step by step into the sources of our own subjective causes. What may at first appear to be infinite and immeasurable shrinks into a point of acute awareness, and it is located as the centre of consciousness. Without knowing the pulsation of this consciousness, which can converge or contract to a point of awareness that is infinitesimally smaller than a conceivable mathematical point, and which can also expand with variegated forms, shapes, colors, and names into an infinite universe, one will be unable to wipe off the misery of life in a wholesale manner. Piecemeal techniques or shortcuts are of little help, though they may give a momentary respite.

Narayana Guru did not begin his spiritual life as an evangelist of wisdom. First he withdrew himself from everyone and everything. For more than a decade he examined the life-style of his fellow men. Then he withdrew from the world. After that he withdrew from the physical body. Finally he withdrew from the tumult and feverishness of the mind. Eventually came the experience of the realization that his own being was none other than Being itself, which is the One manifested as the All. Only after the actualization of this experience had saturated and transformed his emotions, thought, volitions, and specific identity did the Guru begin to reveal his gospel of love and unitive understanding.

When we wake in the morning, the aureole of the rising sun in the oriental sky with its crimson decoration welcomes us to the experiences of a new day of life. Every morning life is given to us again. Later in the night sleep comes with its inaudible lullaby and, without conscious volition, we lose our identity in its oblivion. Between waking and sleeping we act out our roles on the stage of life. Our day is filled with roles, moods, attitudes, and experiences which give us pleasure or pain, or to which we are indifferent. Even the greatest seer must attend to the natural functions of his body, and for the sake of retaining that body he must take nourishment. No matter who or what a person is, his physical organism is subject to the demands of unavoidable physical laws. When this is so obvious to everyone, how can we take seriously the statement made by some that the objective world is unreal?

There is a school of thought totally opposed to Vedānta. This is the Indian school of materialism. But there is one testimony of truth which is accepted by both Vedāntins and materialists: the validity of immediate perception. According to the Indian school of materialism, known as the Cārvākas, the only valid testimony is perception. When a man sees a cow and says, "This is a cow," he is relying on his immediate perception. A materialist would confirm the validity of what he experiences. But let us say the same man builds and lights a fire. Seated by the fire he experiences the association of smoke with fire. Afterwards, if he sees smoke, the previous associations are reactivated and he makes the inference of fire. The Cārvākas would not consider inference a valid assumption. According to them it is a case of a partial perception from the past. They would say that the difference between immediate perception and inference is that in a case of inference only half of the experience is immediate and the other half is of the nature of recall.

If one were to say that an okapi looks like a giraffe with the stripes of a zebra, such a testimony would be called analogical. According to the Cārvākas analogy is also inadmissible, since it is no more than the combination of two partial perceptions into one.

For most people the testimony of authority, such as is propounded by scriptures or recorded in an encyclopedia, would be taken as the recorded perception of a reliable person, and therefore is valid. This view is also unacceptable to the Cārvakas. They will accept as valid no testimony other than that of one's own immediate perception.

Vedāntins interpret perception in a very different way from the materialists. In the book *Vedānta Paribhāṣa* by Dharmarāja Adhvarindra, testimony is defined as "that which gives certitude." According to this author, valid knowledge is that knowledge which is new and is not contradicted by a previously established primary truth. Since one of the criteria is that for knowledge to be valid it must be new, then what was previously experienced may have been true when it was experienced, but because of the passage of time it must now be relegated to the status of memory. Memory has no immediacy, therefore nothing is gained by its recall.

Here a question arises. When a person looks at a pot, the pot comes into view at the first moment of perception. It cannot therefore be the object of new knowledge from the second moment onwards. Should we consider our continuing experience of the pot as valid knowledge or not? In reply, Adhvarindra says it is an arbitrary judgement to break up an experience into discontinuous segments or moments of time. Consciousness, he says, is one continuous flow and is to be treated as one, so long as it continues as a living experiential gestalt.

Adhvarindra also examines the question of the validity of perception. Vedāntins hold the view that everything other than the Absolute is unreal. Since what we experience through the action of our senses is not the Absolute, is it therefore unreal? Adhvarindra answers this objection by saying that everything in the world of transactions is real and continues to be real until the person's consciousness is overwhelmed by its identity with Brahma, the Absolute. Relative factors become unreal only when they are contrasted with the Absolute.

Perception is classified into four categories by the Vedāntins: *pratyakṣam*, *apratyakṣam*, *aparokṣam*, and *parokṣam*. What we see or know as a result of the direct application of our senses, that is to say immediate perception, is *pratyakṣam*. When the senses are out of commission and no knowledge is derived from them, that is to say that a state of non-perception exists, it is called *apratyakṣam*. When a person gains total certitude without reference to the action of his senses or to the results of conscious mentation, that is called intuition or *aparokṣam*. And when knowledge is gained through the assistance of another person it is called indirect perception or *parokṣam*. Of these four categories, knowledge of the Self and the Absolute comes under that of intuition. A useful reference book for further study of this subject is Śankara's *Aparokṣa Anubhūti*, "The Ecstatic Intuition of Certitude."

Before giving further examples of the differences which exist between direct and indirect perception, we should know more about the general Vedāntic concept of perception. A pot is not a self-luminous entity. It cannot itself project, through the action of self-lumonisity, its own image onto the retina of our eye. What is not illumined the eye cannot see; for the pot to be seen light must fall on it. When the pot is illuminated it is not the pot that the eye sees, it is the light waves reflected from it. The eye does not see objects, it sees only light.

In nature, only those things having a similar nature or a complementarity of nature can come together. This is called the principle of homogeneity. The seeing eye and the seen world are complementary aspects of a universal homogeneous principle. This principle is looked on by the Vedāntins as "unbroken, continuously flowing, primal consciousness," *avichinna tailadhārāvat*.

When an aspect of this flow of consciousness is circumlimited by a specific focus of consciousness which experiences itself as an I-identity, then the individuated ego is formed. This ego sense accumulates impression after impression of similar circumlimitations in consciousness. These become incipient memories with value-affectivity, or simply units of information which can be recalled to conscious awareness.

When the ego is structured, it develops the faculty of discernment. The individual becomes an entity which is complete in itself when the mind marks out its own boundary of individuality. Then there exists what the mind feels to be its individuated self, and, standing in opposition to that self, what it looks upon as "other." Just as the individuation of "I" arose from a circumlimitation of consciousness, so the objects of perception are similar circumlimitations in the universal homogeneous principle of consciousness.

Perception, according to Vedānta, is a temporary transference of the circumlimitation of the ego consciousness to become identical with the modulations of any unit which becomes an object of perception. So close is this identification of the knower with the known that it is not possible to say whether we manifest ourselves as a "pot-identity," or whether the pot is formulating itself where we experience the I-identity. Thus, perception in Vedānta is an indiscernible confection of the observer and the observed happening within the realm of the Absolute. It is an experience of an apparent duality within the ambit of the non-dual Absolute. This is why the Guru says a close scrutiny of the apparent reality of things restores all individuated objects to their primeval status as the Absolute. When viewed from this standpoint, *māyā* becomes irrelevant.

In the next verse the Guru examines the nature of universal consciousness, presented here as a homogeneous principle.

VERSE 8

cideva nānyadābhāti
citaḥ paramato nahi
yacca nābhāti tadasa-
dyadasattanna bhāti ca

Consciousness alone, not another, shines;
therefore, there is nothing other than consciousness;
what does not shine — that is unreal;
and what is unreal — that does not shine.

cit — consciousness
eva — alone
na anyat — not another
ābhāti — shines
ataḥ — therefore
param nahi — (there is) nothing other than
citaḥ — consciousness
yat ca na ābhāti — what does not shine
tat — that is
asat — unreal
ca — and
yat — what is
asat — unreal
na bhāti — that does not shine

It is knowledge alone that shines. If something does exist, but is beyond the range of our knowledge, it does not exist for us. Our consciousness remains unaffected by what is beyond the scope of our knowledge. That which does not shine or reveal itself in terms of existence is nonexistent. Nonexistence cannot assert its beingness in any way.

If it is the quality of knowledge to reveal itself, everything we perceive or conceive is a revelation of knowledge mirrored as a mental image. In that case should we look upon everything we see as the same as the Self? It is to remove this doubt that we have already given the concept of perception as expounded in Vedāntic texts such as the *Vedānta Paribhāṣa* in our commentary on the previous verse. Since everything we perceive has this quality of self-illuminated existence, all that enters the field of empirical knowledge and subjective imagination should be seen as the Self, tainted by the negativity of nescience. The substratum of nescience is the Self. In this sense, realization is not anything to be newly gained. As all individuated beings are manifestations of the Self, they do not have to go anywhere to discover it. Unfortunately for us there is a veil of ignorance which creates the illusion of a dichotomy between the Self that is seeing and the Self that is seen. All we are asked to do by the Guru is to rectify this veiling ignorance of the individuated self.

In the ninth and tenth verses following, the Guru describes the Self as *ānanda*, which can be translated as pure bliss, happiness, or the *summum bonum* of all values. The goal of the present study is to release ourselves from the perennial chain of human misery, and to establish ourselves in a state of happiness which is not transient. Turning away, repudiating, or fleeing are methods adopted to escape pain. Drawing closer, and using techniques of sharing or communication are indications that pleasure is being experienced. Pain germinates fear; pleasure brings hope. Of these two major propensities, fear and hope, it is fear that dominates both the conscious and subconscious mind. Hope arises from that stratum of existence which is truth itself — that is, the blissful Self. Hope asserts itself again and again as the will to live, the will to seek, and the will to actualize. Actualization of the highest possible values, or the realization of the Self, dispels fear. As an example, the experience of perfect love does indeed "cast out fear."

When a child is afraid it turns to the protection and reassurance of its parents to allay its fears and restore security. Most people need to feel secure, to have a secure emotional and even physical base. Without that security, man in general finds it difficult or impossible to cope with the problems of living. Home and family are examples of secure bases. Man seeks God for a similar security.

As human beings we seek a secure place wherein we can enjoy peace and happiness in freedom from the fear that someone or some event can destroy it. In the *Taittirīya Upaniṣad*, Hume's translation, we read:

> In the beginning, verily, this (world) was non-existent.
> Therefrom, verily, Being (*sat*) was produced.
> That made itself a Soul (*ātma*).
> Therefore it is called the well-done.
> . . .For truly when one finds fearlessness as a
> foundation in that which is invisible, bodiless,

undefined, non-based, then he has reached fearlessness.
(Section II: 7)[2]

Thus the highest form of happiness is not any kind of excitement, as in the case of pleasure, but total fearlessness. Man is not afraid in the state of deep sleep, because at that time there is no ego nor any ideation giving rise to names and forms which may be experienced as threatening entities by him. But fear may return when he enters the dream state or awakens. To become established in fearlessness in all the four modified states of consciousness is another way of stating the main goal.

Here we are not just engaged in theorizing. All self-realized people are fearless, and fearlessly accept what life brings to them. When Jesus was about to go to the houses of the high priests of Jerusalem, his disciple Peter was very much afraid for his safety. Peter envisioned the great tragedy that was awaiting Jesus if he should go. With good intentions he tried to dissuade him, but Jesus was not any less aware of the sinister intentions of the high priests and King Herod. Despite this knowledge, Jesus said to Peter, "Satan, get thee behind."[3]

Socrates knew the consequences of accepting his sentence and drinking the hemlock. Even when offered the opportunity of escape by his close disciples, that noble soul smilingly accepted death.

When Alexander the Great overpowered King Purorus of Punjab, he became fascinated with the yogis of India. He forceably took a score of them with him on his return to Macedonia. There he wanted to exhibit the superiority of the spiritual worth of these men to his own people, so he asked the yogis to give a demonstration of their ability. They asked him to have prepared and lighted a huge bonfire in the center of the stadium. Watched by a large crowd, the yogis walked around the fire several times, chanting hymns in praise of the Supreme which is both visible and invisible. Then, one after another, they entered the fire and were consumed. This was too much for Alexander's understanding, with the result that he then and there relinquished his ambition to conquer India.

Such a story should not surprise us. In recent years more than one Buddhist monk has gone placidly to his death in a public self-immolation by fire as a means of political criticism. There are many examples in India of enlightened men such as Sri Ramakrishna, Narayana Guru, Mahatma Gandhi, Ramana Maharshi, and Nataraja Guru who accepted the horrors often accompanying phenomenal death with a smiling equanimity, as if it were a matter of course.

If the Upanishads are the revealed scriptures of realization which includes just such a freedom from the fears which beset ordinary men, it is no wonder that Schopenhauer described them as an inspiration during his life, and expected them to be his consolation at the time of death.

In *Ātmōpadēśa Śatakam* (One Hundred Verses of Self-Instruction) by Narayana Guru, we read:

> Knowledge, to know its own nature here,
> has become earth and the other elements;
> spiralling up, back, and turning round,
> like a glowing twig it is ever turning. (v. 33)

And further:

> Existing in knowledge, as the being of non-being,
> countless sparks arise, causing the appearance of the world;
> so, apart from knowledge there is not another thing;
> thus one should know; this knowledge bestows the state of oneness. (v. 89)[4]

If these verses are examined, we shall see the idea put forward of the Self transforming itself into all that is seen and experienced. At the same time we are reminded of the experiencing self. It is an inner sense of identity, that is, the Self experiencing itself, which removes from the mind all forms of anxiety and fear.

After a systematic application of the method of reduction, the Guru comes to the idea of the true nature of the Self, which is *ānanda*. This he states in the two remaining verses of the chapter.

VERSES 9 & 10

ānanda evāsti bhāti
nānyaḥ kaścidato'khilam
ānandaghanamanyanna
vinā'nandena vidyate

sarvam hi saccidānandam
neha nān'sti kiñcana
yaḥ paśyatīha nāneva
mṛtyor mṛtyum sa gacchati

Ānanda alone shines as real,
not anything else; therefore, everything
is *ānanda* through and through;
apart from *ānanda* nothing else is known.

All is indeed existence, consciousness, and pure happiness;
in this there is not even a trace of the many;
he who sees this as many
goes from death to death.

(9) *ānanda* — made up of *a* — total, encompassing; and *nand* — a root of *nandati*, to rejoice, or *nandayati*, to gladden or bless
eva — alone
asti bhāti — shines as real
na anyaḥ kaścit — not anything else
ataḥ — therefore
akhilam — everything
ānandaghanam — *ānanda* through and through
ānandena vinā — apart from *ānanda*
na anyat na — nothing else
vidyate — is known

(10) *sarvam hi* — all is indeed
sat cit ānanda — existence, consciousness, pure happiness
iha — in this
na asti kiñcana — there is not even a trace of
nāna — the many
saḥ — he
yaḥ — who

paśyati — sees
iha nāna — this as many
gacchatiḥ — goes
mṛtyoḥ — from death
mṛtyum — to death

To help us understand the meaning of these two verses, let us ponder the meaning of darkness. What is the substance of darkness? The usual explanation is that darkness is the absence of light. When a candle is lit in a dark room, darkness instantly disappears. Sri Ramakrishna takes this example as being a perfect analogy to depict the advent of knowledge. A person may be living a life of ignorance, but when knowledge dawns upon him his realization is total.

In the Bhagavad Gita, Nataraja Guru's translation, Kṛṣṇa says:

> Even if one of very evil actions should worship Me with a devotion exclusive of all else, he should be accounted to be good all the same merely by the fact that he has a properly settled determination. (IX, V. 30)

And further:

> In such (a path) there is no forfeiture of any merit nor is there involved any demerit by transgression. Even a little of such a way of life saves one from great apprehension. (II, V.40)[5]

From a contemplative penetration of the meanings of these verses we can see the negative nature of ignorance and the positive nature of wisdom. In the first verse quoted here, it is said that if a man who is of the most evil nature decides to tread the path of virtue, then from the moment he determines this all his previous sins disappear. This shows the negative aspect of a nonrighteousness born of ignorance, which is identical with spiritual darkness.

The second verse shows a positive content of spiritual awareness. Such an attitude, if adopted, makes life easier for us to live as our faculties become illumined and wisdom prevails. Kṛṣṇa says that even the slightest entry into such a way of life conforming to wisdom can transform one's life completely. This is the same as the saying of Jesus that "a little leaven leaveneth the whole lump."[6]

Here in these two concluding verses of *Apavāda Darśana*, Narayana Guru wants us to recognize that truth is nothing other than happiness. Happiness is that which sustains the value of everything in life. When life is permeated with happiness it is the same as saying it is beautiful. The beauty of the Self is its unalloyed bliss. This bliss permeates the knowledge of the Self.

This proposition, however, does not correspond to our everyday experience. Again and again we are caught in the grip of painful problems which we find hard to resolve.

There are three kinds of pains to which we are exposed. Firstly, we are helpless creatures exposed to various kinds of insecurity in our life on earth, which is ruled by universal laws. Most of the time we are at a loss to comprehend the functional secret of these laws. At this stage man turns to the Unknown with prayers of supplication. He thinks of a supernatural Being or God, and seeks its (His) succor. This first field which eludes man's comprehension is called *ādhidaivikam*.

Secondly, we are challenged by the extremities of nature. For our sustenence we have to depend on the food we grow or gather from the earth and sea. In all such endeavors we have to tame nature in one way or another. Nature does not change her laws, so man has to adapt himself to live in harmony with nature. In this process man changes, and discovers many devices to make nature less difficult to cope with. This is the field of empirical transactions, called *ādhibhautikam*.

The third source of misery is man himself. No one is a greater enemy to man than his own self. By hardening one's ego and blindfolding oneself with prejudices of all sorts, man cuts off communication with others and makes it impossible to have any sensible transaction with others of his kind. Many ills of the body and mind are created by one's own ignorance. The field in which man is confined to problems perpetuated by himself and other members of his society is called *ādhimānuṣikam*.

Thus, all miseries of man arise from these three sources of ignorance. The all-encompassing term for this ignorance is *avidya*.

We have already noted that the negative aspect of the Absolute is nothing but darkness. Earlier we said that darkness is not only the mere absence of light; it has a dynamism which paradoxically makes us believe the real to be unreal and the unreal to be real. Even the best marathon runner will fumble and find it difficult to run with the same pace if he is asked to run in utter darkness. This will be so even if the runner is assured he can do so fearlessly.

All our organs of action are centrally coordinated with our visual faculty. Even though a blind man cannot see, he still turns his head in the direction from which a sound comes. Those who have studied the psychosomatic behavior of the blind know how all behavioral movements bring a sort of psychophysical tension to the visual area. What the sun is to the world, the eye is to the body; and what the eye is to the body, knowledge is to the individual being.

Darkness helps the ignorant mind to project threatening situations. If a bruise is sustained by the body it will always heal by itself if left alone, but the paranoia of the mind interferes with it and makes it a source of misery. Lack of faith or trust in a friend is blown out of all proportion to become another source of misery. Thus, the capacity of ignorance to reveal a pattern of threat is tremendous.

The Guru recommends not only a withdrawal from the world of ignorance; it is also expected that we will make a progressive ascent from one state of happiness to another. When we light one candle in a room, the light is of one candlepower. When a thousand candles are added to it, the whole room will be flooded with light. This means that light and darkness can remain close together in a physical sense, although in principle light is opposed to darkness. In the same way, a mind can have bright thoughts and can also be surrounded by monstrous and demonic moods, attitudes, and intentions.

To help give such a progression to the mind, we are invited to a treatise on *ānanda*, or bliss, as given in the *Taittirīya Upaniṣad.* The second section, called *brahmānanda valli*, "Bliss of the Absolute," says:

> Let there be a youth, a good (*sādhu*) youth, well read, very quick, very firm, very strong.
> Let this whole earth be full of wealth for him. That is one human bliss.
>
> A hundred human blisses are one bliss of the human *gandharva*-s (genii) — also of a man who is versed in the scriptures and who is not smitten with desire. (*anuvāka 8*)[7]

A *mānuṣyagandharva* is a man who has high sensibility to take from the physical world the beautiful essence of enjoyable entities, and who has the ability to avoid the hardships of life. It is possible to go from one grade of happiness to another higher grade up to the tenth, at which stage the happiness attained is known as *brahmānandam*, or the Absolute bliss. This is within the grasp of those well versed in the scriptures and who are not busy attending to desires.

Every day should be an exercise in raising our own self from one degree of happiness to another. Spiritual progress means making today better than yesterday, and assuring oneself that tomorrow will be even better. The *Darśanamālā* was not written by Narayana Guru to cater to the curiosity of an armchair philosopher. It is not meant for mere discussion. The Guru calls it a *darśana* — a philosophical and mystical vision.

Philosophy in the West has assumed the nature of a discipline of logical speculation. This is to be contrasted with the speculative vision of a mind like that of Jesus Christ. He had a penetration of vision which was not built up on a series of syllogisms. When we listen to his word, our hearts reverberate in unison with the truth of what he proclaimed. The truth of it can be put to the acid test of action, it can be assailed by logical reasoning, but it cannot be altered or modified by a speculative mind. This kind of seeing is called *darśana*.

Narayana Guru gives the *Apavāda Darśana* with the same authority. He assures us of redemption from the clutches of ignorance while also promising us the positive path of ascending the mount of eternal bliss.

If truth is hidden and untruth is veiling it, one can never reach the truth without first removing the veil of this ignorance. As the Guru is convinced of this, he invites us to the third *darśana*, which is the envisioning of falsehood. The very knowledge of falsehood is the most efficient method to eliminate it. In modern psychological therapy, the psychoanalyst tries to spot the cause of a hidden malady. That in itself is the treatment. Here is where the method adopted by Narayana Guru goes beyond that of conventional psychotherapy. The psychologist leaves the patient at this point. He does not help him to go further and see what he truly is. In the remaining *darśana*-s, the Guru does just this.

II. APAVĀDA DARŚANAM

[1] Karl Marx, *Das Kapital*, Dent & Sons, New York, p. 173

[2] R.E. Hume, *Thirteen Principal Upanishads*, *Brahmānanda Valli*, *anuvāka 7*. Oxford University Press. p. 287

[3] *The Bible*, St. Luke 22:31–33

[4] Nitya Chaitanya Yati, *Neither This nor That But Aum*, Vikas, 1982, p. 67 & 191

[5] Nataraja Guru, *The Bhagavad Gita*, R & K Publishing House, 1973, p. 409 & 147

[6] *The Bible*, Corinthians 5:6

[7] R.E. Hume, *Thirteen Principal Upanishads*, Oxford University Press. *Taittirīya Upanishad*, II, *Brahmānanda Valli*, *anuvāka 8*, p. 279.

III. ASATYA DARŚANAM

A Vision of Nonexistence

In the previous chapter, ignorance was equated with the state of darkness. Darkness is not a static, unchanging state; it is an effect simultaneously occuring with the cessation of light. To understand the relevance of this simile in which we equate ignorance with darkness, we should make a careful study of both the structure and function of the mind.

What is the general nature of mind? It is not merely a stimulus-response device, since there are states of mind which precede the stimulation of the senses. Also there are states which continue even after the response is made. In fact, these states decide the volume, depth, intensity, and value implications of the responses that appear at the surface of the mind as awareness. These apperceptive states of mind are holistic expressions of the total personality of each person. Responses are colored by the combined effect of the person's past memories and futuristic expectations prevailing at any given time.

A continuous stream of memories is always passing through a person's awareness. Many of them go unnoticed, while some are recognized, a few are relived, and some are critically reviewed to assess their affective connotation. This is happening all the time, except when we are in deep sleep, although deep sleep is also a functional state of mind. We have an extensive dependence on our past memory for both the purposes of reasoning and of responding to sensory stimulation. Memory gives the right bearing to every passing thought or sensation so that it finds its appropriate place in the structuring of a meaningful situation. Again, it is the value implied in the associated memories of the past which goes a long way in making a person decide one way or the other in determining a course of action. In short, memory is associated with reasoning, feeling, and willing.

Where does this memory reside? Is there in the brain anything like a magnetic tape on which experiences are impressed so that it can give feedback whenever we want to have recourse to a past event? For this to be the case, there should be a stable biochemical arrangement in the gray matter which should remain intact in spite of the constant decay and replenishing of the organic cells of the brain. The fact remains that at least a few people in their eighties and nineties can clearly recall childhood memories, when on all physiological counts the biophysical and biochemical ingredients of their organisms have undergone considerable change.

In recent years physiologists, psychologists, biochemists, and biophysicists have put forward a number of hypothetical postulations to account for the persistence of memory. So far, no such postulate has become sufficiently impressive to prove the validity of their theories.

In religion, most of the inexplicable factors are relegated to the domain of God. Scientists use the blanket term "nature" to cover up most of their ignorance. The most convenient word that has come to the psychologist to explain all such phenomena is "the unconscious." Memories are said to be residing in the unconscious when they are not required. On recalling them, they show up from the depths of the unconscious.

However, there is a disadvantage in accepting this theory of the unconscious. The only instrument which can make any kind of probe in any realm is the conscious mind. The unconscious, by the very definition of that term, should be beyond the reach of consciousness. This being the case, it looks ridiculous for someone to claim that he has an insight into the structural details of the unconscious.

Indian psychologists do not think in terms of the conscious and the unconscious. According to them, mind is equated with nature. It has no consciousness of its own. Consciousness is the essential quality of the Self or Spirit, while the mind is merely an instrument of the Self. This instrument has three kinds of modalities, called ***guṇa***-s, which can be altered so very ingeneously that they cause a wide variation in the range of consciousness.

The first of these modalities is called *satva* — the pure and clear quality of nature which mirrors the existential and value significance of any specifically constituted thing or situation. *Rajas* is the second modality, which can animate a situation to have kinetic effects. It also can rouse emotional colorations, and thus gives exaggerated dimensions to both the existential purport and the value significance of experiences. By and large the most significant role is played by the third modality, *tamas*. It is an inertial binding force which can couple itself with either *satva* or *rajas*. Its inertial quality can stabilize a situation so that the temporal sequences can be reduced to the minimum. This comes in handy for making a span of interest somewhat static, so that one will not find life to be a fleeting experience. The opacity of *tamas* can shield away from consciousness whatever is not relevant or is opposed to the prevailing interest of the moment.

As the human mind shares these three modalities with the rest of nature, they are to be treated as universal phenomena.

Memories are shielded and preserved by *tamas*. This close association of *tamas* with memory shows a near identity of incipient memories with ignorance. Incipient memories are called *vāsana*-s, and ignorance is called *avidyā*. In both the systems of Vedānta and Yoga, *vāsana* and *avidyā* are sometimes treated as interchangeable terms.

In the state of deep sleep, *tamas* is said to be operating as a total veiling principle that envelops both *satva* and *rajas*. Consequently, there is no mirroring of any particular thing or idea other than the *satva* being focused on the pure and luminous nature of the Self. In this case the ego does not function, but there is the experiencing of the great calm of the pure spirit.

Tamas can also aid in the selective structuring of meaningful ensembles or gestalts. When a certain value factor of an incipient memory is being promoted to gratify itself in a favorable environment, *tamas* can provide it with a protective cover so that there will not be any interference from other interests during that span of experience. When the attention of the mind is about to be detached from its object and directed to another, *tamas* puts a blindfold on the focus of attention which allows a new train of thought to seep into the realm of consciousness without giving a chance for the conscious ego to realize that a distraction is already effected.

Just as a picture cannot be successfully projected onto a white screen in brilliant sunlight, even so man cannot experience the phenomenality of the external world and his several worlds of subjective fantasy without there being nurtured in him the darkness of ignorance. In fact, the *tamas* of cosmic nature is inside and outside. It is no wonder that it plays such a mighty role in the operation of the individuated psyche.

For this reason Narayana Guru, in the third *darśana* of the present work, places before us a number of examples to make us familiar with all the implications of what he calls darkness and ignorance, that is, *tamas* and *avidyā*. The examples given in this *darśana* are to be seriously meditated upon. In order to be able to decipher the subtleties of the differences given in each analogy, we must continuously remember that this is not a safe ground for us to engage in fanciful speculation. Holding fast to the Guru's hand, we must go step by step into the interior castle of our realization.

"Reality" is a term which is not used in quite the same sense by everybody. A religious person is likely to say that his particular scripture expresses all that can be known of what is real. But a physicist may be slightly amused by the same scripture, while a professed atheist might be outraged. For many people, reality is what they see.

Let us consider the reality of the human state. As far as can be judged, someone lying in a deep coma or in a state of profound and dreamless sleep appears to have no problems arising from any physical sensation or mental ideation. In the present chapter our reference is not to such a state. To use the language of Jean-Paul Sartre, what the Guru wants to consider here is "human reality." For Sartre, human reality is a nauseating experience because of its characteristic enigmatic presentation: its continuous series of contradictions such as pain and pleasure, fact and fiction, and transiency and persistence, to mention only a few.

Buddhists look at the so-called human reality as only a pseudo-reality of a phenomenon which is the expression of a universal condition of sorrow (*duḥkha*). The Bhagavad Gita also describes the world as an abode of sorrow and transiency, *duḥkhālayam aśāśvatam* (VIII: 15). Christianity, in its turn, paints a gloomy picture of the condition of man on earth with its insistence upon varieties of sins, including an original sin which is shared by the entire human race. If one takes seriously what his preceptors say and loses heart, then his condition can be described as most lamentable.

In *Darśanamālā*, Narayana Guru is not much interested in the analysis of man's woeful condition of ignorance. He is interested in imparting a positive discipline called *ātmavidya* — a Sanskrit term meaning "knowledge of the *ātma* or Self." It is only through the acquisition of true knowledge that man can be freed from what he sees as nauseating or sorrowful conditions which are bound to arise during the span of his conscious life on earth. *Ātmavidya* is a discipline of understanding evolved by seers over a period of thousands of years, and they have found it to be effective in releasing individuals from the negative conditions arising from ignorance.

Conditions such as pain and pleasure are experiences that arise only within the field of consciousness. Both the field and the experiences arising out of it as a result of its modifications are designated as the mind. What we here describe as consciousness is to be understood as having the dual qualities of the apprehension of objects seen as external to the self, and the simultaneous comprehension of mental entities such as ideas, concepts, images, and belief systems.

Apprehension of objects comes under the general category of perception, while comprehension may be seen as coming under the general category of conceptualization. All these terms contain within themselves a certain dynamism which can, so to speak, cast a spell over awareness in much the same manner as hypnosis. Awareness becomes circumlimited and identifies itself with a particular image structure as soon as a term evokes in us its formal image as a specific unit of awareness in consciousness. We should adopt an attitude of wary skepticism coupled with relentlessly critical scrutiny when seeking the path of our intended search for the nature and meaning of mind. It is paradoxical that the mind which brings all kinds of bondage and suffering can also lend itself to be the most efficient weapon to prove, analyze, scrutinize, and lay bare the truth of itself.

The term "human misery" is a generalization including my own misery, your sorrow, and the problems of other persons. This means we are concerned with the consciousness that is manifested as individuated awareness as well as consciousness expressed as the collective or the universal.

According to Sartre, there must be some form of existence which is antecedent to the essence of any experience. He prefers not to call this existence "God," but he is willing to qualify it as "Godlike Beingness." We need not get into a controversy with Sartre, but his "Beingness" is no more helpful than "mind." So it is advisable that we deal with the word "mind" even though it is now appearing to us as vague, ambiguous, and somewhat strange.

If "mind" as a general term does not allow for an easy penetration of its meaning, we shall have to turn to a direct examination of the facts concerning mental experiences. These facts of which we speak can have the quality of being real or fictitious. In the mental realm, fact and fiction may be inextricably intertwined or can manifest in such an amorphous manner that we may not be able to discern one from another.

In our search for a starting point, or some fundamental principle on which we can have a firm footing, we shall have to take the risk of making a plunge into the unknown. From the darkness of the unknown and from the mystery of the unconscious will arise our first glimpse of the intimation of an awareness. However intangible the origin of this awareness is, we should step onto it as the alpha point of our search. This kind of awareness can be called "eidetic."

A child may visualize an indiscernible feeling and may use his crayon on a paper in a random fashion. After having done so, he may contemplate the result with rapt pleasure, and then may see in what he has drawn an elephant or a flower or a country scene. Here the child is having an eidetic experience of his own projections. A further example of the eidetic is when someone continues to experience the presence of a limb even after that part of his body has been amputated.

The eidetic can present itself on two levels of the horizontalized world-field. As the positive aspect it has the status of being factual; as the negative it presents itself as a psychic presentiment. Schematically, it can be presented somewhat as given below:

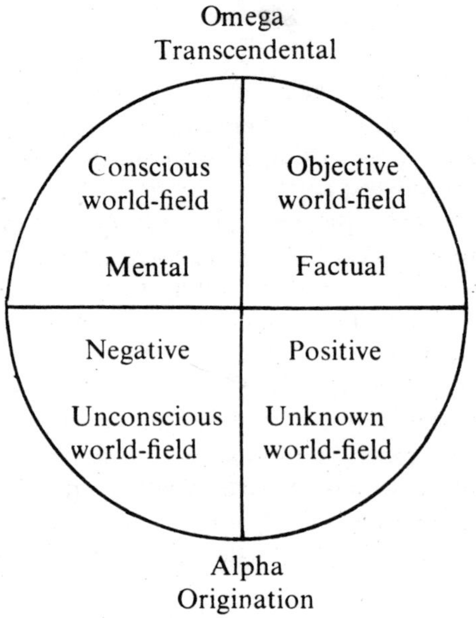

Here the eidetic consciousness can be seen as having four aspects or dimensions, and a vertical and horizontal orientation. The psychic becomes the minus pole and the factual the plus pole of the horizontal, empirical world of experience, corresponding to the subjective and objective levels of projection respectively. At the negative alpha pole, the first modification of consciousness — signalling the origination of an individuated awareness — begins a movement up the vertical pole to culminate in the omega point of the transcendental or universalized consciousness. From the universal or transcendental consciousness there arises a counterpart to the individuation of awareness moving downward. The awareness from the alpha point and the awareness from the omega point meet at the center. The whole pulsation of awareness operates in the individual from this central point of conjunction. This enables the individual to contract consciousness to a pinpoint of awareness, and also to expand it simultaneously to locate that specific experience as an integral part of a universal field of experience. This is like a constant dialogue going on between the dual principles of immanence and transcendence.

If you can follow the instruction of the Guru thus far, you can also comprehend how the individuated self can become universal.

Now let us go deeper in our scrutiny of these four aspects of consciousness. On the side of the factual, consciousness is individuated in a person, who in turn is aware of relating himself to the individuated consciousness of other persons. Thus, individuals relate to each other. Individuals also experience the sense of relating to objects seen as external to the subject. Through perceptions of and relations with people and objects, a person shares in and contributes to a general consensus of opinion regarding the nature and attributes of the beings and objects which constitute the world. There is a general agreement concerning existential factors. This universality of consent is the main factor which gives to this category of consciousness its recognition as being factual. Should some members of society raise questions or doubts concerning what are generally held to be facts, then the society will put into operation long established methods of investigation to reestablish certitude in the minds of its members.

When a person turns away from the facts of the empirical world to his psychic presentiments, he is entering into his own private domain of experience. This area covers a wide range of experiences such as sensations, feelings, moods, thoughts, visions, and fantasies.

These can interact with the factual, established by collective consent, or can remain confined to the individual mind as an exclusively personal form of consciousness. In either case, the reaction may cause personal problems of mental agitation. These agitations can be pleasant or unpleasant. This polarized field existing between the factual and the psychic can be seen as a hinterland of consciousness lying between the edietic origination and the transcendental.

What has eluded the comprehension of philosophers, psychologists, and theologians is an understanding of the real and fundamental cause, which gives rise to the presentation of an eidetic origination of consciousness, together with that which can release consciousness from the inhibitory clutches of the seemingly factual and psychic into the realm of transcendence.

Having established a general background in terms of reference for our study of the mind, let us now examine the *Asatya Darśana*. This is the third in the series of the ten philosophical visions of Narayana Guru.

VERSE 1

manomayamidam sarvam
na manaḥ kvāpi vidyate
ato vyomnīva nīlādi
dṛśyate jagadātamani

All this is a permeation of mind,
but mind is nowhere to be seen;
in the same way, like the blue and so on in the sky,
the world is seen in the Self.

sarvam idam — all this
manomayam — is a permeation of mind
manaḥ — mind
kvāpi na — is nowhere
vidyate — to be seen
ataḥ — in the same way
nīlādi iva — like the blue and so on
vyomni — in the sky
jagat — the world
dṛśyate — is seen
ātmani — in the Self

In the introduction to this *darśana* we have given a general idea of the structure of consciousness. We see it as a phenomenal structuring arising out of the mysterious depths of a primeval darkness. This structuring becomes horizontalized as a binary function consisting either of a subject-object duality or as a subjective state witnessed by a focus of consciousness experienced as "I". In either case the notion of the knower as "I" is detachable from the known.

In the two earlier *darśana*-s the Guru has established that everything perceived and conceived is basically the manifestation of one's own consciousness. But we are still uncertain about what it is that causes perceptual images to arise as experiences of definite forms, colors, and other sensory data. We are somewhat trapped, because the only mechanism available to us for the examination of how our mind works is that very mind itself.

Immanuel Kant points out that we cannot jump out of our mind and senses to know exactly what an object is before its image is adulterated with the biophysical and psychochemical peculiarities of our brain-stuff. According to Heisenberg, a physical entity cannot be scrutinized without the act of scrutiny disturbing its structure. In the same way, we can say that we can never perceive anything without causing agitation and disturbance in our own motor-sensory system.

When moving from one life situation to another, what we actually experience is the result of a kaleidoscopic shake-up of the psychophysical structure. The effect thus produced is known to us as a conscious experience. Even if such an experience is not sharply defined, we have at the very least an awareness, however vague it may be, of the object of perception or the subjective ideation. In every experience, whether subjective or objective, there is some awareness of an "I' which is distinct from both what is known and the act of knowing.

In our usage of "I" there is often confusion. Take, for example, the statements, "I am aware of this table," and, "I am aware of my love." The confusion here is centered around the preposition "of." Love is a specific quality of awareness — that is to say, awareness is colored and modified by the feeling-response to which we give the name "love." In this case awareness is not an activity separately taking place in the mind and then becoming interconnected with another activity called "love." Love is a component of awareness, as for that matter are anger, hatred, sorrow, joy, and contentment. Thus the preposition "of" has no factual status. The usage is necessitated only by the syntactics of structuring grammatically correct sentences.

Similarly, the awareness of the table also should be reduced to the formation of an image in the mind which is projected into a psychologically structured space. We presume that there is a real, solid table existing where we are experiencing the perception of it, but there is no way to verify this. Again, our experience is constituted of several modulated qualities of consciousness. In other words, there is no pure awareness experienced at any time which is nonmodulated.

In this verse, the Guru first highlights the common experience shared by all, that is to say the existential experiencing of generally known things and ideas. This he does by turning our minds towards the consideration of these phenomena. After stating that all experiences, whether seen by us as subjective or objective, are of the mind, he asks us to make a critical search for the mind itself. When the mind looks for itself it vanishes like a phantom, leaving behind only sensations, ideations, conceptual images, and sensory impressions.

When Schrödinger spoke of the world as a construct happening in the brain with percepts, concepts, and memories, he missed one thing.[1] This was pointed out later by John C. Lilly in his book *Programming and Metaprogramming in the Human Bio-Computer*.[2] There he asks this pertinent question: "If all that we experience is programmed and computerized by the human bio-computer, who is the programmer of that computer?" This vital question, the most fundamental question we can ask, was overlooked or disregarded by scientists for a long time. Let us ask it again: "Who is programming the mind?"

Narayana Guru was careful to present a programmer before turning our attention to what is programmed in the individuated mind. The program is the storage bank of incipient memories. And, as far as the collective consciousness is concerned, it is the universal Will which is the substratum of all existence, order, development, and purpose. The several shades of meaning attributable to the universal Will are given in the two previous *darśana*-s. In the present verse the Guru speaks of it again as the dormant will of the Self.

The example given here is the erroneous projection of blue color in the sky. In what is called "the sky" there is nothing specific, other than the interspace between bodies that are mutually exclusive. In that sense sky is everywhere. But what is sky really, and where is it located?

We see jet planes flying into the sky and disappearing in the blue, but when we ourselves fly in a similar plane we do not see it anytime entering any blue area in the sky. According to the astronauts who have gone into outer space, what they have experienced is an utter darkness and not anything blue. In fact, the blue color of the sky is to be seen more in the biochemical function of the brain than in any space external to the body. It is a complex phenomenon generated in our own visual area. The action of light waves on the retina of the eye, their transformation into electrical impulses, the passage of these charges through the neurons of the brain, the complicated molecular activity that causes various biochemical changes, and the resultant psychological response to the incoming sensory data, produces the experience of seeing the blue sky "out there."

If we critically examine them, even the red carpet, the green lawn, and the beautiful roses will also share the fate of the ephemeral blue sky in being relegated to the domain of fiction.

"Sky" as a factor experienced as external to the human organism is the result of a collective hallucinatory projection described in the preceding chapter as *vikṣepa*. Even the scientist who knows the complex function of the brain is not very much impressed by his knowledge when he goes to the ice cream parlor and insists on strawberry flavored ice cream.

When we are subjected to a collective hallucination we are completely carried away by the similarity of responses in a number of individual minds. When a sensitive person reads the poem of Hermann Hesse in which he writies:

> Is my sorrow a sorrow to you
> My death, a death
> Do you feel from my love, my grief
> Just a breath, just an echo. . .?

the rest of the world reciprocates because mankind is truly one kind. The individual mind is part of the collective mind.

We can prove that the world-experience of man is illusory, but that does not help us very much to escape from its tragic spell until it becomes completely transparent to us in what manner the Self is veiled, and how projection manifests in all the individual cases of the experience of entities with names and forms which seem to exist within the framework of time and space, with inner relationships such as cause and effect, and with whatever is treated dualistically as other than one's own Self.

In the next verse the Guru focuses his attention on the aspect of mind as ignorance.

VERSE 2

manaso'nanyayā sarvam
kalpyate'vidyayā jagat
vidyayā'sau layam yāti
tadā'lekhyam ivākhilam

By ignorance, which is none other than the mind,
all worlds are imagined;
when by this knowledge dissolution comes,
then everything becomes like a painting.

avidyayā — by ignorance
ananyayā — which is none other than
manasaḥ — mind
sarvam jagat — all worlds
kalpyate — are imagined
asau vidyayā — when by this knowledge
layam yāti — dissolution comes
tada — then
akhilam — everything
alekhyam iva — like a painting

When we are children we find great meaning and pleasure in toys. Wooden and plastic toys give us much joy, and we fiercely defend these possessions from other children. But children are also a part of the inexorable will to growth and development that animates the universe. As some maturity begins to come, children find less satisfaction in toys and discard them as if they were never significant. The collective will turns their attention away from balls to other children.

Passing through puberty into adolescence, the attention of the young becomes more intensely focused on one person, and their relationships with others become casual. Now love fills the horizon, and the term "falling in love" becomes of the utmost significance. At this stage the mind creates endless fantasies about the beloved until consciousness becomes saturated with the attributes of the beloved. From the mind also arise doubts, fears, and negative fantasies. Life becomes meaningless if love is not returned, and blissful if love is reciprocated. When the relationship is broken, the very presence of a previously loved person becomes annoying.

At this stage one retrospects, and thinks of the broken love affair as a rotten mistake of the past.

Affectivity is a two-sided coin. Love, worship, fidelity, kindness, and beauty are inscribed on one face. On the other we find hatred, anger, repudiation, lack of faith, meanness, and ugliness. It is from the same mind that both these responses arise. As the coin flips, one may repeat again the same kind of mistake thinking that the soul-mate has finally been discovered.

When old age comes, this kind of fantasy leaves the mind, and a new awareness dawns that all the achievements of youth and middle age were of little worth. The desire for peace and the need for spiritual security turn the mind away from all worldly values.

When we review life like this, we can see that the world that we live in is generated by our own fantasizing mind. We live mostly in a fantasized world of values generated by the mind — a mind which is not very clear about what is true or untrue, and what is of real worth or not. Throughout, an element of pleasure, a spark of joy, a dream of attaining greater happiness, operates as the dynamic for creating one fantasy after another. Finally, if it so happens that a person discovers within himself that there is an abiding bliss which is none other than the beingness of his own Self, only then will he see that the world he looked upon as real was merely a creation of his mind.

People who keep journals of their own daily moods, reactions, ambitions, pursuits, and dealings with other people have the feeling that they are recording every day a correct version of the world they are living in. After a few years, when they retrospect and read the same pages, they realize how mistaken their actions were and how they looked upon things of little value as being the most important in life.

This tendency of the mind to breed false values into its own fantasy is described in this verse as *avidyā*, ignorance. Corresponding to this individual experience of fantasy there are collective fantasies. The whole world was excited with wonder and thrilled with joy when a certain man, Yuri Gagarin, was sent into outer space and brought back to earth alive. Several millions of dollars (in his case, rubles) were spent to make this possible. Afterwards, when greater achievements such as the moon landing were made, a mere orbiting of the earth turned out to be of comparatively little importance. When moon walking and rendezvous in space became common, people started becoming bored of even watching them on television. These are examples of collective fantasies.

There are also tragic examples of such collective fantasies, such as when a whole group of people are made to believe that they are superior to other people or races, and they tune their destiny to rule over the world. World War II was precipitated by Nietzche's theory of the Superman, which made Adolph Hitler power crazy. Religious fanaticism is another example of collective fantasizing. Thus, both at the individual and collective levels, sheer ignorance is weaving and fabricating worlds of lies one after the other.

Omar Khayyam presents in his *Rubaiyat* a sarcastic caricature of human follies. Great prophets and saviors like Gautama Buddha, Jesus Christ, and Muhammad also tried to turn the individuated consciousness away from being caught in the cobwebs of ignorance. But their enthusiastic followers began building castles of nescience around the personalities of these people, as well as their spoken or recorded word. Thus the perpetuation of ignorance triumphs over the hidden splendors of the Self.

In this verse Narayana Guru gives us hope to ward off frustration. A person who is endowed with the power of discrimination will be able to learn from his own mistakes that he is a victim of projections arising out of his own imagination. There is the danger, even after realizing the folly of one's situation, that when the mind is filled with desire and craving it has the power to draw a dark blanket over the recognition of previous failure, which could otherwise guard the individual against making a fresh attempt in the same wrong direction.

In the Bhagavad Gita, Kṛṣṇa says that the mind will recoil from its fantasizing of imaginary pleasures only after realizing the absolute nature of the supreme Self:

> Objective interests revert without the relish for them on starving the embodied (of them). Even the (residual) relish reverts on the One Beyond being sighted. (II: 59)[3]

In the following verse the Guru will point out to us a negative principle which has the power to keep the truth veiled from the mind.

VERSE 3

vijṛmbhate yattamaso
bhīroriha piśācavat
tadidam jāgrati svapna-
lokavad dṛśyate buddhaiḥ

What expands here from darkness
into a ghost to a coward —
that world is seen by the wise
as a dream-world of the wakeful state.

yad — what
vijṛmbhate — expands
iha — here
tamasaḥ — from darkness
piśācavat — into a ghost
bhīroḥ — to a coward
tad idam — that world (lit. that this)
dṛśyate — is seen
buddhaiḥ — by the wise
svapna lokavat — a dream world
jāgrati — of the wakeful state

Life is an enigma which we live between a positive urge for life and a destructive principle which is at once aiding and hindering the possibility of growth. The first cell that is formed in the womb cannot grow unless it breaks. Proliferation in nature is at the cost of destroying what already exists. A child cannot remain as a child if it wants to grow into a youth, and before the appearance of fruit the petals must wither off the tree. Life is a movement which is steadily going on from birth to death. The urge to live and the possibilities of growing and changing fill the mind with hope. The occasional awareness that life is continually moving toward death brings fear to us. In short, our life oscillates between hope and fear.

In a previous chapter we discussed the elements of fear, and so do not want to elaborate on that here. However, it is very important to know that fear is intrinsically related with want the Guru terms in this chapter as *tamas*, or inertial darkness. The Self is treated here as opposed to this negative principle of inertial darkness.

As an intriguing anecdote we turn to the Gospel according to St. John. It speaks of the death and resurrection of Lazarus, who was the brother of Mary and Martha of Bethany. When a person came to Jesus and reported to him of a fatal illness that might rob Lazarus of his life, Jesus remained very cool. Lazarus was his best friend, but he didn't pay any attention to his possible death. After Lazarus was dead and buried, Jesus then said he would go and wake him up from his sleep. Thomas, Jesus' skeptical disciple, thought it ridiculous to go to a man who is buried with the intention of reviving him. When Jesus came to the Bethany city gate, Martha rushed to him with her unconsoled grief and complained to him that her brother would not have died if only he had been with him. When Jesus comforted her by saying that Lazarus would be resurrected, she took it very lightly, knowing that on Doomsday all dead souls would resurrect. Jesus corrected her, and assured her that he was not speaking of that kind of resurrection. Instead he said, "I am the resurrection, and the life; he that believeth in me, though he were dead, yet shall he live. And whosoever liveth and believeth in me shall never die. Believest thou this?" (11 : 25, 26).[4] He waited there until Mary came to him with a supplication to revive Lazarus. Mary came, and addressed him as a teacher and publicly proclaimed her faith in the grace of God. Then Jesus went to the grave and got the stones removed and asked Lazarus to wake up and come out of the tomb. Lazarus responded instantly.

To modern ears, such a story will sound like a fabricated myth. On the other hand, a Vedāntin would accept St. John's version as a beautiful allegory to understand eternal life in contrast to the emergence, submergence, and remergence of life in the unceasing flux of becoming.

In the Bhagavad Gita, Kṛṣṇa gives several versions of the meaning of life and death to Arjuna. On one occasion he says:

> What is unreal cannot have being, and non-being cannot be real; the conclusion in regard to both these has been known to philosophers. (II : 16)[5]

In other words, what *is* will never cease to be, and what is *not* can never exist. If we accept the verity of that dictum, then either we are or we are not. If we are, then we exist for all time. If we are not, then there is no need to fear of becoming nonexistent at any time.

Arjuna was not quite convinced by this argument, so Kṛṣṇa put forward another. He told him that anything that manifests is sure to dissolve. As it is a process of transformation, that which disappears will surely remanifest as a further elaboration of the principle of becoming. A child never weeps for having grown into an adolescent, and it only pleases a youth when he is no longer an adolescent. You cannot stop life from passing on to old age, decay, and death.

Arjuna still was afraid to look at the empirical truth of becoming as an unavoidable fact. To allay his fears, Kṛṣṇa moved on to another argument. In each moment there is the birth of a life situation. It perishes at the end of the same moment. The terminating situation gives way only for the next emerging moment to have a fresh presentation of life with all its multifarious values.

These are inevitable aspects when you look at life from the side of the gross world in its physical manifestation. There is another way of looking at life. That is from the angle of its beingness. In one of the Psalms of the Old Testament it says:

> For a thousand years in thy sight are but as yesterday when it is past, and as a watch in the night. (Psalm 90: 4)[6]

Plato spoke of this as the "eternal present." The same idea is repeated in verse 15 of *Ātmōpadēśa Śatakam*:

> To the blessed ones who have sucked the milk of *para*,
> ten thousand years is but a moment;
> but if knowledge succumbs to *apara prakṛti*,
> half a second seems like a thousand years.[7]

What is so very positive to the empirical scientist is a world of nescience for the Vedāntins. The mysterious Unknown, which is still considered to be a prohibited field for the positive sciences, is looked upon as the only reality that is worthwhile to be known by the Vedāntin. A verse from the Gita relates to this point:

> What is night for all creatures, the one of self-control keeps awake therein; wherein all creatures are wakeful, that is night for the sage-recluse who sees. (II: 69)[8]

In the next verse, the Guru is going to elaborate on the operational dynamics of negativity which we experience as our volition, and which further elaborates itself into the imagery of fantasy.

VERSE 4

sankalpa kalpitam dṛśyam
sankalpo yatra vidyate
dṛśyam tatra ca nānyatra
kutracidrajju sarpavat

The visible is imagined by the will;
the visible is seen only where there is will,
and not where there is no will —
like the snake in the rope.

dṛśyam — the visible
kalpitam — is imagined
sankalpaḥ — (by the) will
dṛśyam — the visible
vidyate — is seen
yatra tatra — only where there is
sankalpaḥ — will
ca — and
na anyatra kutra cit — not where there is no will
(*cit* is used for "will" here)
rajju sarpavat — like the snake in the rope

In the three previous verses we have seen that mind is an aggregate of impressions, thoughts, feelings, moods, and apprehensions of all kinds. Each experience is visualized as a meaningful unit which has the potential to produce a total effect of making the individual pleased or displeased. The effect can be one of pleasure, of pain, of interest or disinterest. The total phenomenon is called mind, just as a group of trees is called a forest or a number of people is called an assembly. General terms have no content other than what is derived from the particular constituents.

Earlier, we mentioned the need for a programmer behind the very many programs in consciousness, which we call wakeful experiences and dream experiences. We have also pointed out in the previous verse that an individual person is always torn between the dualities of hope and fear. The essential nature of an individual self is to treasure its identify as the most valuable reality on earth. All sentient beings share with man the great eagerness to preserve the continuity of life. There is nothing wrong with imagining that self-preservation is the greatest of all natural instincts.

Self-preservation presents itself in the form of maneuvering tactics. When there is a threat, this instinct forces the individual to withdraw, flee, stand in abeyance, or make a frontal attack. Cringing, crying, and adopting various measures of an underdog are also aspects of the instinct of self-preservation.

On the positive side, this instinct induces a person to seek nourishment, and to establish his existential or exaggerated image in the mind of others. The striving to gain name, fame, and power are prompted by it. The most dynamic of the functions of self-preservation operates as an almost separate major instinct called sex. Reproducing another of the same species can assure one's own continuation even after the cessation of the individual's bodily existence.

After all, the individual self is only a superimposition on the universal Self. Hence, it is no wonder that the individual self always seeks the imperishable reality of the universal Self. When the self is circumlimited by physical adjuncts which are essentially of the nature of flux, it is very much impressed with the fact of growth, change, decay, and death. At the physical level transformation is unavoidable. This is what causes so much apprehension in the individual mind. It is as if an eternal struggle is initiated from the very moment of the dawn of consciousness between a positive factor that is favoring the continued awareness of existence and a negative factor which is threatening its abolishment.

The interaction between these two factors is termed ignorance. The example used in this verse is the mode of operation of ignorance whereby a piece of rope is mistaken for a snake in the twilight, a common experience in India. For such a misapprehension there should be four factors:

1) the person's fear of snakes
2) the previously formulated image of "snake"
3) lack of proper light
4) a piece of rope which is somewhat similar in size and shape to a snake

In these four factors only the piece of rope has existential verity. The prevalence of darkness creates an ideal situation for the projection of a presentiment. The presentiment is a previously acquired image associated with fear. The whole coloration of the situation is derived from fear. If the element of darkness is removed, the snake also vanishes. This will automatically banish from the mind the presence of the snake and the fear relating to it. When this happens, one realizes the utter folly of seeing a snake where it was not.

The darkness mentioned here is only a metaphoric darkness. It can come in the form of lust, greed, suspicion, hatred, or attachment. Each of these brands of darkness have their own particular group of promptings and compositions of mental images.

A question arises: why do we not do away with the whole world if it is only an illusory projection? The Guru says that it would be possible if the world were only one's own singular projection. But unfortunately it is not. It is a universal projection.

Let us examine the difference between an individual projection and a universal projection. Say a number of individuals gather together in their own capacity, and decide to draw up a constitution to form a nation. At this point everybody has his say in the matter. Each person has his own sovereign will. In the act of enfranchisement, the sovereignity of each individual will be surrendered in principle to the collective whole. One person out of the entire group is chosen to be the chief executive, and thereafter he represents the sovereign will of the people. This person can now exercise his will either to honor an individual or to reject him. Although the individual's consent brought the sovereign to power, he is utterly helpless as a single individual to abolish this power, which is based on a universal projection. He now has to abide by the will of the supreme sovereign of the state.

It is individual minds operating as intrinsic links of a corporate whole which produces the world phenomenon, hence the transactional world enjoys a status which is different from that of a private fancy. Looking upon the world and its transactional reality this way, it poses a problem that appears impossible to resolve: if we are all subjected to a universal ignorance, how can we ever free ourselves from its clutches? A way is suggested in the Bhagavad Gita, where Kṛṣṇa says:

> Become one with Me; be devoted to Me; sacrifice to Me; bow down to Me; unifying thus yourself, you shall surely come to Me; your supreme Goal none other than Me. (IX: 34)[9]

Although this verse is often interpreted theistically as becoming devoted to God, when it is interpreted philosophically the theistic coloration looks only incidental. When an individual transcends his body limitations, social conditionings, and psychic colorations, his consciousness widens its horizons and gains the qualities of being universal. This is how the idea of becoming of one mind is to be understood. Additionally, the individual's devotion in the social context is in the procurement of his personal happiness. When this is given up in favor of an altruistic dedication to effect universal harmony and the sharing of joy with all, it can be interpreted as devotion to the Absolute.

Ignorant man sacrifices his health, time, and talents for the realization of his private ends. When the same is done more openly for universal benefit, it becomes a sacrifice to the Absolute. Bowing down to the Lord can be understood as consistently emphasizing a universal value in preference to the transient pleasures of the world. As a result, the individual becomes unified with the Absolute. When one promotes himself to this level of understanding, it is possible to convert, in one's mind at least, both the appearance and meaning of this world into something that can be easily accepted as one of precious values. The world is no longer frightening to one with such a vision.

When there is such a possibility before us, how is it that man fails to know this, leaving himself so much exposed to a demonic world wrought with fear? The Guru is going to examine this in the next verse.

VERSE 5

saṅkalpa manasoḥ kaści-
nnahi bhedo'sti yanmanaḥ
tadavidyā tamaḥ prakhya-
mindrajālamivādbhutam

There is no difference between will
and mind; that mind, which is called
ignorance and darkness, is a wonder,
like Indra's magic.

kaścit nahi asti — there is no
bhedaḥ — difference
saṅkalpa manasoḥ — will and mind
yat manaḥ tat — that mind which is
prakhyam — called
avidyā — ignorance
tamaḥ — darkness
adbhutam — is a wonder
indra jālam iva — like Indra's magic

We began this *darśana* with the question, "Where is mind?" When we look for mind, what comes to our attention is one of the many impressions, or in other words, an experience of awareness. In Sanskrit the act of giving a specific form to consciousness is called *saṅkalpa*. Usually it is translated as "will." As willing is an act of volition, such as when one is determined to say or do something or to become steadfast in a certain judgement, it lacks the wider connotation of the Sanskrit term *saṅkalpa*.

Saṅkalpa is somewhat equivalent to the drawing of a blueprint in consciousness which will lead to the actualization of an event, the attainment of a state, the acquisition of a desired object, or to the establishment of a new relationship with oneself or with another person at some time in the future. These do have an element of will implied in them. That is why *saṅkalpa* is usually translated as will.

Saṅkalpa carries with it a probability factor, and it is most likely that the desire to actualize it may bring it about. But it is also possible for desires to arise in consciousness which by their intrinsic nature are highly improbable. The ignorance of the individual, coupled with a rational myopia caused by infatuation, may easily convince him that what is willed is not at all improbable. In spite of this improbability, a person may try hard to actualize a desire and will fail to achieve it. In this aspect, the desiring imagination of the person is called *vikalpa*. Both probability and improbability are promoted with the desire to actualize, whereas the person sees nothing but probability due to his infatuated imagination. The infatuation is directly related to one of the many incipient memories, which we have referred to earlier as *vāsana*. Thus, both *saṅkalpa* and *vikalpa* are born of *vāsana*.

In this connection, we should think of the generic incipient memory of the universal mind and the specific memories of the individual mind. The whole gamut of universal incipient memories is called *tamas*, while the totality of each individual's incipient memories is called *avidyā*. They are respectively translated here as darkness and ignorance.

In the stream of consciousness we go from one situational awareness to another. In the *Vyāsa Bhāṣya* of the Patañjali *Yoga Sūtras*, a unit of consciousness which comes in the form of serialized awareness is called *prakhya*. In the present context *prakhya* can be a collective awareness, such as of the blue in the sky. It is experienced by all. A *prakhya* which is of the individual mind can be a frustrating nightmare. To expand our awareness of the term, we should also understand *sthiti* and *pravṛtti*. *Sthiti* means "becoming stable," so as to remain as a fact of experience for awhile. When the whole awareness is permeated by the qualities of what is presented to it, the individual as a whole undergoes a kinetic transformation. This is experienced as a mental agitation, a state of excitement, or an overt action, and is called *pravṛtti*.

In short, the emergence of an awareness, its meaningful persistence, and the interaction of subject and object with it, can be equated to what modern psychologists call a "gestalt." A gestalt can remain as an open gestalt until the nucleus of it fades out. The nucleus is always a projected value. Although the true source of the value is the Self, when it is transferred to a thought or a passing event the transiency of the medium into which it is superimposed can make it vanish.

The total effect is one of magic. The Guru calls it *indrajāla*. The word *indra* is derived from *indriya*. The *indriya*-s are the senses. What is perceived by the senses cannot be precisely located as an event occurring inside the brain or outside the body. Philosophy and psychology differ very much in deciding the status of what is perceived by the senses. According to the Vedāntin, when a pot is perceived, the pot is where it is seen and also it is purely an experience within. Hence they call it *anirvacanīya*, "something which can never be determined." For this reason, sense perception is like a magical phenomenon. As mind is considered to be a principle of orientation that is putting together varied sense impressions into a meaningful whole, it is called *indra*, "the Lord of the senses."

Mind is thus capable of producing magical effects in which there are individual projections generated with the help of private symbols. When the experience is exclusively personal and difficult to be communicated, there is a greater chance of it being an improbability born of personal darkness. This contrasts with the awareness of an enlightened mind, which can also be an experience that is not easily shared with others. Here we are not dealing with what is happening at a transactional level. We have two more chapters yet to go before discussing such matters.

Although the world is generally treated as unreal in Vedāntic literature, again and again there come exhortations from the great masters to do good to the world and to maintain the harmony of world order. This is called *loka saṅgraha*. Both in *Bhakti Darśana* and *Nirvāṇa Darśana*, the Guru tells us of the necessity to relate to the world in a meaningful way. Great masters like Kṛṣṇa, Christ, Buddha, and the Prophet have all desired peace on earth and fellowship between human beings. These good works are also *saṅkalpa*-s but they are qualified as *satya saṅkalpa*, desirable imagination that can be true in all probability.

Unfortunately, most of us are motivated by personal gains, and are so veiled by our personal ignorance that we draw thick ego boundaries and separate ourselves from the rest of the world phenomena. As a result of this darkness, the "other" can assume a fancied image which makes the individual hanker after it and thus become subject to infatuation. This brings about false hope after false hope, like that of a thirsty man going from one mirage to another. Such an unfortunate person runs after shadows, which results in mounting frustration. The "other" can also assume a demonic form, engendering in the person an element of fear. The fear grows from moment to moment until it becomes a paranoia that can assume gigantic proportions. These are classic examples of *vikalpa*.

On the whole, mind can be equated to a joint product of individual growth and collectively produced *saṅkalpa*-s and *vikalpa*-s, which have the general effect of a magic that can alternate between the experiencing of wonder and the experiencing of fear. The Guru examines the nature of this magical effect in the next verse.

VERSE 6

marīcikāvat prājñasya
jagadātmani bhāsate
bālasya satyamiti ca
pratibimbamiva bhramāt

To one who reasons correctly
the world appears as a mirage in the Self;
and to the indiscriminate, by confusion,
a reflection looks as if it is real.

prājñasya — one who reasons correctly
jagat — the world
bhāsate — appears
marīcikāvat — as a mirage
ātmani — in the Self
ca — and
bālasya — the indiscriminate
bhramāt — by confusion
pratibimbam — a reflection
satyam iti ca iva — looks as if it is real

There is a story that an artist approached the Neo-Platonic philosopher, Plotinus, with the intention of painting his picture. When he asked the philosopher's permission, he received the reply, "Why do you want to make an image of an image?" In Sanskrit a sculptured image is called *bimbam. Pratibimbam* means an image of an image.

According to Plato, what we see here has only a shadowy status. He made a distinction between the world of visibles and the world of intelligibles. To illustrate this theory of the shadowy world he included an allegory in the *Republic.* [10] Briefly, the allegory describes all thinking beings as living in a dark cave. Behind us there is a fire which casts our shadow on a wall that we are facing. There is a one-to-one correspondence between us and our shadows, and by association we recognize our own shadow. As we do not see ourselves in the light, the shadow is identified as our real self. People take their shadow existence for granted.

At some moment, one may feel the urge to turn away from the shadow and look toward the light. Only at that time does the person realize that he is bound and that his senses are turned toward the shadow. When he struggles to turn away from the shadows, his bondage is experienced with greater intensity. Others who have not the least idea of the light that is casting the shadow look upon this man as foolish. All the same, that person becomes more and more convinced that he can attain no peace without realizing the truth.

Finally he breaks the bondage, and recognizes that he lives in a cave with all his fellow beings. He falls at every step, and when he tries to walk out of the cave it is with the greatest difficulty. As he ascends the path leading him out of the cave, he comes to the crest of the hill from which he can see the blazing sun. As he is only used to the dim light of the cave, he stands blinded for a little while. Then he sees in the sun's light the real archetypes of things. Now he is convinced that worldly experience has only a shadowy status. He takes compassion on the people lost in the dark cave, and he reenters it to turn others on also to what he found for himself: the more truthful world of the intelligibles.

Narayana Guru does not go all the way with Plato. He does not make the division between the visibles and the intelligibles. To him, the only world we experience is the confusion of the conceptual and the perceptual. This is given in verse 20 of *Ātmōpadēśa Śatakam*:

> Other than this the world has no reality;
> "there is" — all such that people say is without reflection;
> even if to a numbskull it appears to be a snake,
> will a fresh flower garland ever become a serpent?[11]

On reading this verse, one may mistakenly think that the Guru is in agreement with the materialists when they say that this visible world is the only reality. But this is not so. This verse should be read together with the previous verse, in which the Guru categorically refutes the reality of the world of inertial matter. There he emphasizes the fact that "prime substance is all there is."

The subject of appearance and reality is brought up again in verses 80 and 85 of the same composition:

> Like rest and motion, how can contraries such as creation,
> existence and dissolution coexist in one place?
> There is no validity for these three anywhere; when this is
> considered, earth and such are mere words.

> No shadow exists independent of an actual form;
> as there is no original form anywhere for the existing world,

it is neither shadow nor substance;
everything that is seen is like a snake painted by a master.[12]

What is important to notice in these verses is that the ground of all appearances is given as the Self. When the child is seeing his own image in a mirror and in his confusion takes it for a second person, both the seer of that vision and the confusion about it are coming from his own reality. Without the child there cannot be any reflection, and the duality creeps in between him and his image by a a lack of recognition.

The word "recognition" is given here in a very meaningful sense. The Self cognizes itself only when it is in its primeval state. In this state it is a pure awareness of blissful existence. What the child cognizes is only a transient body which has the quality of inertial matter. This cognition is defective. It is only an assumed self, like an assumed lake in a desert. The true Self will reveal itself only by an act of re-cognizing, used here in the truest sense of the word.

In this verse, the particular word chosen by the Guru for a wise man is *prājña*. According to the Āgama of Gaudapada's *Māṇḍūkya Kārika*, *prajña* is a mass of consciousness. It is one alone that is known in all the three states of consciousness: the wakeful, dream, and deep sleep. Modification of this consciousness can come in the form of percepts, concepts, and memories. In all these states the only reality is the mass of consciousness which is personified here as *prajña*.

Ego is pronounced as a conscious agent cognizing forms of the wakeful world, and in that state the agent stands in contradistinction with what it is seeing as a world of objects. The same ego changes into a passive factor when it occurs in the dream state, without the maneuvering power to employ any direction to the act of cognition. When it goes beyond these two states, the personal identification of ego diffuses and comes to its own truer nature as a mass of consciousness. If this egoless state becomes a stable state of consciousness, even when there are the apparent alterations coming to the state of consciousness as surface phenomena, the person continues to be benefited by a recognition of his *prajña* state. This remains even when he plays roles of the agent of the dream and agent of the world-vision as an empirical fact.

VERSE 7

ātmā na kṣīravadyāti
rūpāntaram ato'khilam
vivartamindrajālena
vidyate nirmitam yathā

The Self does not, like milk, attain
to another form; therefore, everything,
as in the creation by Indra's magic,
seems to be through superimposition.

ātmā — the Self
na — does not
kṣīravat — like milk
yāti — attain to
rūpāntaram — another form
ataḥ — therefore
akhilam — everything
yathā nirmitam — as in the creation
indrajālena — by Indra's magic
vidyate — seems to be
vivartam — through superimposition

In the Bhagavad Gita the Lord says:

> Abandoning all *dharma*-s, come to Me, the One, for refuge;
> I shall absolve you from all sins; do not despair. (XVIII: 66)[13]

When the word *dharma* is translated as "religion," it may sound like all religions are being derided. But if we stick to the strict philosophical meaning of *dharma* as the principle of becoming, and contrast it with *brahma*, the principle of unchanging beingness, we get a deeper and wider meaning.

In the *Ātmōpadēśa Śatakam*, Narayana Guru speaks of the difference between intuitive knowledge and discursive knowledge. In verse 36 the Guru says:

> The power of knowledge is endless;
> the end of all this can be marked as "sameness" and "the other"; thus, in this way, there are two divisions; in this, merging the other with sameness,
> one should remain awake to that clear state of being.[14]

The above two verses are essentially of the same meaning. What is seen as the many are the modifications of the One. Here a question arises: "Does the One transform itself into the many, or is it only seen as the many?"

When we perceive the external world with our eyes, it assumes the qualities of having form and color. These are the visual images of what is seen. We do not know whether the external world has the forms exactly as we see them or has the colors it seems to have. After all, our visual world results from the impact of light, and that light appears to us as objects. The fact that we see objects does not alter the substantial reality of light. This is why the Guru qualifies the world as existing as eidetic (*vivartam*), and not a real transformation of any substance as such.

Seeing light of a certain frequency of vibration as red belongs to two forms of *dharma*. The psychobiochemistry of the brain is such that the quality of "red" arises when the impact of light on it is of a certain quantum. This is the *dharma* of the operational nature of the brain. Light has the *dharma* of having varying frequencies. These two become contributory factors in producing the joint effect of a red color in a visualized object or patch of color. In either case we are not seeing the thing in which these *dharma*-s are believed to inhere. Instead we are calling to our mind the thing in itself by combining two sets of *dharma*. This act of combination or composition of *dharma* is derived from two poles: the faculty of perception and the object of perception. This accounts for the act of seeing, which is a unit in the process of becoming. What is said of visual imagery here is also true of the other four sensory experiences we have.

It is obvious that we are making two superimpositions: a superimposition of the property of sense organs (*indriyadharma*), and the property of the object of perception (*viṣayadharma*). In fact, neither this sense faculty nor the light undergoes any substantial change. If they do change, such as milk turning into curd, then we could have treated the examples as a case of *pariṇāma*, evolution. In *pariṇāma* one thing changes into another, both formally and qualitatively.

Qualitative monists, such as the followers of Rāmānuja, and categorists of the process of actualization, such as the followers of Madhva, both give priority to *dharma* as an absolute necessity before relating oneself to *brahma*, the Absolute. This is evident in their respective interpretations of the first aphorism of Bādarāyana's *Brahma Sūtra*. The *sūtra* says: *athāto brahma jijñāsa*, "Then, therefore, the enquiry into Absolute."[15] The word "then" is interpreted by Rāmānuja as "after having understood *dharma*": *dharmajijñā sānantaram brahma jijñāsa.*[16] Śankara wrote an elaborate commentary on this aphorism, as if he anticipated that somebody at some time would make such an interpretation. He categorically announced that it is unnecessary to be disciplined in the *karma kānda* of the Vedas — that is, the ritual portion — in order to become endowed with the realization of the Absolute as recorded in the history of Indian philosophy.

There exists a polemic between those who emphasize *dharma* as a prerequisite to know *brahma* and those who abandon that aspect, treating it as only incidental. The first group is called *pariṇāmavādin*, evolutionists, and the second are those who support the view that the phenomenal world is only a superimposition. Here in the *Asatya Darśana* Narayana Guru supports the theory of superimposition, describing it as *indrajālena vidyate.*

We have already seen that the mind, which makes ensembles out of sensory data, can excel the performance of any magician. If we see three points placed in an irregular pattern the mind will interpret this as being a triangle. In actuality there is no triangle there, but the mind cannot escape the temptation of making an ensemble out of it. Taken in this sense the whole world is a continual effect of the ceaseless composition of the creative mind, like the performance of a magician.

All this comes under the sway of *dharma*. Our performances vary when we adhere to *dharma*, because it has the blinding effect of veiling from us the innate oneness of the Self, or, in its totality, of what we call *brahma*. In his *Advaita Dīpika*, Narayana Guru comments on the fact that the reality of the thread loses itself in the cloth, as does the water in the waves. Even so the reality of *brahma* is lost in the imaginary mirage of the phenomenal universe.[17]

The Guru is now preparing us for the next *darśana*, which is on *māyā*. From the present verse he is leading us towards this important concept.

VERSE 8

māyaiva jagatāmādi-
kāraṇam nirmitam tayā
sarvam hi māyino nānya-
dasatyam siddhijālavat

Māyā alone is the primal cause of the world;
by that which is none other than the
wielder of *māyā* all this is created,
like the unreal effects of psychic powers.

māyā eva — *māyā* alone
ādikāraṇam — is the primal cause
jagatām — of the world
tayā hi — by that
na anyat — which is none other than
māyinaḥ — the wielder of *māyā*
sarvam — all this
nirmitam — is created
asatyam siddhijālavat — like the unreal effects of psychic powers

We are all familiar with optical illusions. At the time of experiencing the illusion it looks real. Being an illusion it cannot remain the same way all the time, so that one soon discovers the fallacy of it. On discovering the fallacy, the impression of reality vanishes.

There are certain fallacies which can persist at the optical level, and these can only be detected through a process of deduction. For instance, if we put a straight rod or pencil into a glass half filled with water, the part of the rod or pencil in the water will be seen as slightly bent. When we pull it out of the water, it looks straight again. By comparing the two states we come to know of the fallacy of vision in this case. When the cause of this is looked into, we see the same phenomenon happening every time we put something straight into a glass of water. This is caused by the refraction of light, which varies from medium to medium, such as air, water, gasoline, and so forth.

Here there are two factors to be noticed: the first is the effect produced by refraction and the other is the refraction itself. Refraction is a universal principle which can affect the optical vision of all people. The principle of refraction is one of the many laws of nature. What we call "nature" here is nothing but the sum total of several such causal factors which produce similar effects on the minds of people, and even on the people themselves. These various effects can produce the joint effect of an apparently stable state of things, and we are impressed by this "factual" consistency. As a result it gains a transactional verity. But, as in the case of the optical illusion, apparent factuality can prove to be fictitious when a careful scrutiny is made.

It was by one such scrutiny that scientists arrived at the notion of refraction. Physicists have now compiled an index of refraction, so that they can understand and deduce from that index what medium is causing a certain refraction. In the same manner, *māyā* is to be treated as a refractive index of the degree of deviation in the erroneous transactions of life. In this way the man of realization can deduce from the collective effect of the world consciousness the only reality, which is that of the Self. Then the transactional world loses its power of compulsion, and one can attain freedom from what appears to be the empirical world. In such a state he knows that there is no world other than the Self.

VERSE 9

vibhāti viśvam vṛddhasya
viyadvanamivātmani
asatyam putrikārūpam
bālasyeva viparyayam

To the mature mind of the old the world appears
in the Self as a forest in the sky,
even as the unreal form a puppet
seems otherwise to a child.

vṛddhasya — to the mature mind of the old
viśvam — the world, everything
vibhāti — appears
ātmani — in the Self
viyadvanam — as a forest in the sky
eva — even as
asatyam — the unreal
putrikā rūpam — form of a puppet
viparyayam — (seems) otherwise
bālasya — to a child

Human life ranges between childhood and old age. The most prominent instinct in a child's overt life is the curiosity to know the external world. When the child is at the stage of becoming familiar with forms, sounds, movements, and the situational grouping of things, in order to gain an orientation of meaningful ensembles that can evoke the sense of wonder, he makes little distinction between a living object and an inert one. Out of indistinct and chaotic conglomerations of forms and sounds the child has to create ensembles that can give expression to his innate incipient memories belonging to major moods in life, like joy, fear, wonder, and frustration.

The myth-making tendency, the fantasizing of forms and situations, and the spinning of stories, along with many disjunct dreams, form in the child's stream of consciousness. The child does not draw a line between fact and fiction. Many parents complain that their children are incorrigible in telling lies. This is only because the parent does not understand the child's mind. They have already forgotten how they themselves experienced fictitious and fantasized imagery when they were children. Elders, including parents, sometimes take advantage of the capacity of a child to believe fictitious things.

According to Śankara, an illusion disproves itself by becoming ineffective in showing the intrinsic qualities or potential reactions of factual things or events. For instance, the mud pie made by a child satisfies only an imaginary hunger; when real hunger comes, the child throws away the mud pie and goes to the mother. Likewise, the silver that is seen in mother-of-pearl cannot be used to make a piece of jewelry.

As the child grows he will discover that there is a deceptive element in his experiences which is capable of thwarting his hopes and bringing them to dissatisfaction or frustration. When other similar occasions arise in life, the growing child becomes wary of so readily accepting things. Skepticism grows; truth and falsehood are thereafter sorted out with increasing precision. When the child grows into a mature youth, the critical acumen is applied to everything. Transactions become rigid. Definitive criteria are employed to safeguard the verity of facts.

Even a young person has to face a complex world of emotional fantasies, generated by the instincts of sex or self-preservation. Sexual fantasies make the mind romantic, and it attributes to the loved one many imaginary qualities. In this case also, the principle of efficiency acts as a reliable criterion to test the factuality of things believed to be true. When lovers begin getting into each other's need to respond to their several demands, transactions reveal the inefficaciousness of their assumptions. As a result, disillusionment comes.

The instinct of self-preservation exaggerates the sense of insecurity and prompts the need to find measures by which one can have economic, social, moral, and spiritual security. These exaggerated needs of the mind push the person into various avenues of activity, which should more aptly be called *karma* — actions prompted by desire — and desires born of ignorance.

The negative aspect of the instinct of preservation produces many forms of irrational fear. When such fear is intensified, a person may even go insane. Even in normal persons there are several hidden pathological tendencies, and even in "noble" sentiments, such as love or devotion, the operating dynamic can be a pathological sense of insecurity. This is a predominant factor in women when they grow old and lose their bargaining powers of physical appearance and sexual charm. People who make a living with their creative powers are also very apprehensive of old age. In old age the external world becomes anemic or barren and devoid of values.

Inner maturity that is not vitiated by pathological tendencies turns naturally from the external world to a more abiding reality which is seen in the Self. In this stage of life the mind of a person is at the extreme opposite pole of the child's visualization. All transactions of life are once again treated as make-believe, though of a reverse order. The principle drive of life, known as *rati* (the capacity to interact with objects of pleasure and projected value-visions) disappears, and in its place *arati* comes. *Arati* is total indifference to all kinds of aids, physical or mental. At this stage a person can easily become indifferent and withdrawn; *arati* leads to death. But if the mature person is wise, there arises a natural consciousness out of the subjective promptings to seek happiness and situations that bring fulfillment out of dissatisfaction. Duality fades out, the blissful nature of the Self slowly or suddenly becomes unveiled, and wisdom prevails. The revealed reality of the Self is the only factor that remains thereafter unassailed by the ravages of changing forms. Out of the ever changing flux the beingness of pure duration emerges. This aspect will be further discussed in the next chapter.

VERSE 10

ekam satyam na dvitīyam
hysatyam bhāti satyavat
śilaiva śivaliṅgam na
dvitīyam śilpinā kṛtam

The One is real, not a second;
the unreal indeed appears to be real;
the *śivaliṅgam* is stone alone,
not a second made by the sculptor.

ekam — the One
satyam — is real
dvitīyam na — not a second
asatyam hi — the unreal indeed
bhāti — appears
satyavat — to be real
śivaliṅgam — the *śivaliṅgam*
śila eva — is stone alone
dvitīyam na — not a second
śilpinā kṛtam — made by the sculptor

Nature is fecund. In her act of generation she proliferates several species, and they endlessly multiply into as many various kinds as possible. Nature's possibilities are endless.

In the act of generation there is an implied polarization of the sperm and the ovum. The sperm is like the positive nucleus of an egg and the ovum is like the nourishing albumen. The albumen gets absorbed into the nucleus and then transforms into a chicken. The chick that comes out of an egg can be a cock or a hen. Thus it bears upon itself the stamp of masculine or feminine.

A language has to provide for these primary classifications of all generated beings into male or female, and when the division is obscure or indistinct language stands confused in its neutrality. Thus we have the masculine, feminine, and neutral genders.

The Sanskrit term for gender is *liṅga*. In one aspect it points to the general distinction which is usually ascertained by looking at the genitals of a newborn baby. Hence the word *liṅga* has become synonymous with the genital organ. In common parlance, "man" also includes woman. Thus, *liṅga* can also imply what is termed in Sanskrit *yoni*: the female genital organ. This meaning is only dervied from an indicative incidence of semantics.

The main operational meaning of *liṅga* is the application of a conceptualized idea expressed through the medium of a proto-linguistic ideogram, such as a sign or symbol, or through the metalinguistic expression of a name. When we understand the full implication of *liṅga* in this way, the word *śivaliṅgam* as a phallic emblem of Śiva turns out to be a narrow meaning. Śiva stands for the indescribable reality without beginning or end, which by its own nature is awareness through and through, and which is peaceful due to its having no modifications whatsoever. Even the term "un-nameable" is a name; the qualification "indescribable" is already a description. When the indescribable is indicated with a sign or symbol, it becomes *śivaliṅgam.*

In India the *śivaliṅgam* is an icon carved out of stone by a sculptor, which is used as a protolinguistic expression of the omnipresent auspiciousness of everlasting, existential beauty. Just as children may see a motor car, a dog, or a man in a piece of wood, adults also use the crutches of icons as pegs to hang their ideas on.

In the previous nine verses of the *Asatya Darśanam*, it was clearly shown to us that our notion of the world is eidetic. In the *śivaliṅgam* there is neither a phallic emblem nor the auspicious Absolute—it is only a piece of stone, but the sculptor can visualize the indescribable Absolute in it.

Before the sculptor begins to work on a stone he conceives the idea of the symbol that is to represent for him and others the idea of the Absolute. He knows pretty well that the attributes of the Divine, such as timelessness, omniscience, and omnipresence can never be adequately presented through his craftsmanship. These eternal values in his mind belong to the vertical order. The medium and the craft used to convert the medium into a message belong to the horizontal order. In the *śivaliṅgam*, which he carves out of a stone, he combines his vertical value parameter and the horizontal craft and medium into a single holistic expression.

This kind of protolinguistic ideogram is not confined to the followers of Śiva. In the Christian form of worship such symbolic expressions are used extensively. In C. G. Jung's *Man and His Symbols* we can see the extensive use of symbolic representations by people belonging to all cultures and times. Metaphors, similes, and other allegoric expressions used in language differ from the stone-wrought image of the *śivaliṅgam* only in the medium selected by the exponent.

Still, there is always the possibility of people of lesser intuitive perception missing the message and looking upon the material artifact as a reality in itself. The great crusade made by the prophet Muhammad and his followers against idolatry is in its truest purport a call to recognize the essence. Yet even in such a noble endeavor, fanatical enthusiasts missed the message and have come to the same level as the idolators in looking at the artifact as an object of hatred.

This chapter is mainly to focus our attention on sifting the unreal from the real.

It is with the best of intentions that one begins to set out in the search for truth. As the search is directed by a finite mind using the finite doors of perception and the limited concepts of word images, sooner or later the seeker is likely to confine his final summation of truth as a fixed entity visualized by the individual's mind. This is in no way different from the sculptor deciding to express his visualization of the Absolute in the form of a *śivaliṅgam*. It certainly helps him and another person of identical vision to sense the Absolute by extrapolating the meaning of the symbol beyond the scope of the man-made artifact, as well as by interpolating into the medium the purest of notions that can never be confined to any form or name.

Even after making such a rational assessment of the several pitfalls that we may come across in the world of names and forms, there is no guarantee that such knowledge will spare us from conditionings. We began this chapter by saying that all that *is*, is the mind. Unless one transcends the conditioned operation of the mind he will again and again come back, through the back door as it were, to the same world of ignorance that he is trying to escape by adopting one device after another. Empirical perception can be erroneous or valid, but in either case it comes under the category of relativity. That is why modern scientists like Einstein, Planck, and Heisenberg are discrediting the possibility of attaining any final version of truth. The riṣis of India are not pessimistic about the realization of truth. They do not identify the Self with the mind. By knowing the Self, one becomes truth. This point is going to be elaborated in the next chapter.

III. AŚATYA DARŚANAM

1 Erwin Schrödinger, *What is Life? Mind and Matter*, Cambridge University Press, p. 99

2 John C. Lilly, *Programming and Metaprogramming in the Human Biocomputer*, The Julian Press, New York, read pages 1-17.

3 Nataraja Guru, *The Bhagavad Gita*, R & K Publishing House, Delhi, p. 166

4 The Bible, *The Gospel According to John*, 11. 25-26

5 Nataraja Guru, *The Bhagavad Gita*, R & K Publishing House, Delhi, p. 124

6 The Bible, *Psalms*, 90. 4

7 Nitya Chaitanya Yati, *Neither This Nor That but Aum*, Vikas, Delhi, p. 31

8 Nataraja Guru, *The Bhagavad Gita*, R & K Publishing House, Delhi, p. 172

9 ibid, p. 415

10 Plato, *Collected Dialogues*, Bollingen Series, Princeton, Rep. 7. 514, p. 747

11 Nitya Chaitanya Yati, *Neither This Nor That but Aum*, Vikas, Delhi, p. 41

12 ibid, p. 169, 180

13 Nataraja Guru, *Bhagavad Gita*, R & K Publishing House, Delhi, p. 705

14 Nitya Chaitanya Yati, *Neither This Nor That but Aum*, Vikas, Delhi, p. 73

15 *Badarayana — The Vedanta Sutras of*, Part 1, Trans. George Thibaut, Dover Publications Inc., New York, p. 9

16 *Sri Ramanuja — Sri Bhasya*, Trans. M. Rangacharya, Vol. 1, p. 2 — 24

17 *An Anthology of the Poems of Narayana Guru*, Trans. Nataraja Guru, p. 26-27

IV. MĀYĀ DARŚANAM

A Vision of Non-being Beingness

In Western psychology the whole sphere of human experience is divided into two parts: that which belongs to consciousness and that which can be attributed to the unconscious. The conscious covers a large field of experiences, including sensations, feelings, fantasies, dreams, passive observation, critical observation, active reasoning, conscious volition, and various kinds of conflicts only partially experienced at the level of awareness. The unconscious is said to operate in a very much wider field, and to have a depth that is not fathomable to normal human awareness. What occurs in the conscious sphere of mind and experience is indicative of causal factors presumed to be lying hidden in the depths of the unconscious.

Indian poets conceive of the nature of the primal cause of manifestation and the imperatives arising from the unconscious through the use of richly meaningful ideograms and symbols of mythology. The main theme of the genesis of cosmic consciousness elaborated through such poetry is personified as *sadāśiva*. In Sanskrit, *sadā* means "always," while *śiva* is synonymous with a state of equipoise or perfect harmony. Thus, this state exists when no distinction is drawn between awareness and nonawareness, or between the conscious and the unconscious. In other words, the primeval state is indistinct and passive. Yet all manifestations in consciousness are attributable to the intelligence and purposiveness that remain hidden and dormant in this indistinct, original Being.

When we examine the miraculous operations of our own psychophysical systems, we might well be wonderstruck by the evidence of such ingenuity shown by the unknown functional intelligence that manages the affairs of our everyday life, such as body building, respiration, blood circulation, digestion of food, and elimination of wastes. Automatic functions which are totally unknown to most of us maintain the smooth working of our organism and keep it in a condition which allows us to cope with all the demands of life. No man-made machine is nearly as complex or beautifully designed and engineered as the aggregate of systems known as the human organism. The hidden knowledge concerning the factors which maintain our organism, lying at the very substratum of the world order, is called *śudhajñānam*, or pure knowledge.

This pure knowledge, or *logos*, which is identical with what St. John calls the Word of God, while retaining the homogeneity of all things, also expresses itself through heterogeneous functions. This aspect of the existential prime mover of all cosmic functions is called *parameśvara*. Further, the world order of collective experience and our own individual experiences can be looked at from the aspect of an aggregate or admixture of effects. Here we are confronted by the obvious phenomenality of things. This last aspect is called *māyāśakti*, which can be translated as "the force which gives rise to and sustains the nescience or ignorance that perpetuates the affectivity of the mind by attaching to it the seeming reality of names and forms."

The present *darśana* will be a critical study of both the noumenon and the phenomenon. In the previous *darśana*, Narayana Guru gave us an efficient method for the discernment of the real from the unreal. In this *darśana* he gives directions, the use of which will enable us to discern the truthful basis of superimpositions of falsehood. He helps us to recognize and extract the real from the unreal, in both the absolute and relative senses, and he helps us to have a correct perception of the empirical world and its transactional verity. In addition, he reveals the negative factors which obscure and conceal truth from us.

VERSE 1

na vidyate yā sā māyā
vidyā'vidyā parā'parā
tamaḥ pradhānam prakṛtir-
bahudhā saiva bhāsate

What is not known, that is *māyā*;
it alone shines as many forms:
vidyā, avidyā, parā, aparā,
tamas, pradhāna, and *prakṛti.*

ya — what is
na vidyate — not known
sā māyā — that is *māyā*
sa eva — it alone
bhāsate — shines
(*iti*) *bahudhā* — as many forms
vidyā — knowledge in the true and absolute sense
avidyā — ignorance, in the sense of relativistic notions, opinions, and conditioned reflexes
parā — consciousness pertaining to the reasoning self, mind, and senses; with which one discerns happiness and sorrow
aparā — the unconscious and instinctive self that is instrumental in carrying out all physical and biological functions
tamaḥ — the state of confusion in which the discriminative power of the reasoning self is at its lowest
pradhānam — the prime potency, such as of a seed to develop into a tree or a big-bang that can cause an expanding universe
prakṛti — that which has the tendency to proliferate, replicate, and cause endless varieties of mutations

In any experience in which there is an element of mystery there are two functions. One is the emergence of something out of an unknown factor. The other is the disappearance of what seemed to be factual into another unknown factor. In either or both the emergence and remergence, we experience the positivity of pleasure or the negativity of pain. To an uniformed mind there may well be an element of mystery in the majestic appearance of the golden disc of the sun at dawn. The banishing of darkness would undoubtedly induce in the observer a positive pleasure. Sunrise is usually an enjoyable experience for everyone. But the mysterious and unheralded formation of a cancerous growth in a human body is likely to be experienced as a negative despair and pain. Both these cases are examples of emergence.

A beloved person with whom we relate every day, and on whom we depend in many ways, may suddenly disappear from the environment to become a "missing person," or may suddenly, with no warning illness, pass away in death, leaving us heartbroken. Remergence in this case has a negative aspect. But a threatening menace, such as a bad disease, an unhappy life situation, or some natural hazard, may disappear for no apparent reason. In this case remergence will bring peace and consolation, and thus it becomes a positive factor.

When we survey the events, situations, and existential experiences of life, we can see that it is a continuously changing pattern of mysterious emergences and equally mysterious remergences. Life on Earth can be compared to a vast ocean, over whose surface roll the emerging waves of birth and the re-emerging ripples of death. Birth and death, heat and cold, pain and pleasure, victory and defeat, fame and disgrace — all such dual aspects of life come as ceaseless agitations of our objective and subjective consciousness. There is a sense in which the wave or agitation in consciousness exists for a moment with an identity of its own, but in the next moment it is gone as if it had never been. For this reason we can say that an experience *is*, yet it *is not*. And since "the world" is merely an aggregate of experiences or, more correctly, of the projections of subjective experiences, we can say it also is and is not. That which makes only an appearance and has no substantial existence is termed *māyā* in this *darśana*.

In this very first verse the Guru introduces us to eight aspects of our personal and empirical consciousness. These are: the principles of negation (*māyā*), knowledge (*vidyā*), ignorance (*avidyā*), transcendence (*parā*), immanence (*aparā*), darkness (*tamas*), primal potency (*pradhāna*), and nature (*prakṛti*). In subsequent verses the Guru defines each of these terms and illustrates the concepts with appropriate similies.

Western logicians may think it odd to treat negation as a category. Yet from the Indian point of view, negation is as much a category as substance, quality, time, action, or relationship, for instance. The Sanskrit term for category is *padārtha*. *Pada* means an articulated word. When written, a word assumes another quality: it becomes a word-symbol. But whether articulated or written, a word should have meaning relevant to the subject under discussion. Hence, *padārtha* means "that which gives a definite connotation on hearing or reading it." Words such as "solid" rock or "running" water bring to our mind the idea of something concrete. Descriptive words such as "hot" or "cold" introduce the idea of quality. In the same way, words which in themselves contain the quality of negation do make sense. We can say, for example, "Socrates is not here" — a statement of fact in which "Socrates" and "here" are both negated. Therefore negation is included in Indian logic as a category.

Vedāntins further speak of four kinds of negation:

1) *prāgābhāva* — Before a potter fashions a pot from clay, there is in the clay a prior absence of the pot. The negation in this case is the prior existence of the pot in the clay. It is the anterior cognition of negation.
2) *pradhvamsvābhāva* — If a pot is made, but before firing it is reduced again to an amorphous lump of clay, this is the negation of the pot by its destruction. Here negation stands for the annihilation of identity. It is posterior negation based on the principle of the destruction of identity.
3) *anyonyābhāva* — When milk turns into curds, that which was milk is now absent; only the curds exist. Before the milk is curdled there is the absence of curds. In this case there is a reciprocal complementarity of negativity.
4) *atyantābhāva* — In a lump of granite there is no trace of milk. Here we have a negation arising from the total absence of one thing in another.

It is useful to know which kind of negation is relevant in any situation where one employs the method of agreement, the method of disagreement, the method of agreement and difference, or the method of residue. We shall have occasion to discuss this later. In the next verse the Guru leads us further into the study of negation or non-being.

VERSE 2

prāgutpatteryathā'bhāvo
mṛdeva brahmaṇaḥ pṛthak
na vidyate brahma hi ya
sā māyā'meya vaibhavā

Like the prior nonexistence in the clay alone, before it is fashioned,
none other than the Absolute is known;
what is that Absolute is indeed
māyā, of indeterminate possibility.

yathā — like
abhāvaḥ — the prior nonexistence
mṛt eva — in the clay alone
prāk utpatteḥ — before it is fashioned
na pṛthak — none other than
brahmaṇaḥ — the Absolute
vidyate — is known
yā brahma — what is that Absolute
sā hi māyā — is indeed *māyā*
ameya — of indeterminate
vaibhavā — possibility

The material used in the manufacture of a pot is clay, but it is evident that there is no pot in the clay as such. How does the clay change into a pot? Apart from the material cause, three other major factors operate: the intentionality of the potter; his efficiency in making a pot; and the required instruments, such as the potter's wheel. To be more precise about the material cause we should include the water used to moisten the clay, any ingredients added to make it stable, and the glazes used in firing. Associated with the potter's instruments there may be other contributory features, including delivery of the clay, the kiln, the fuel for heating it, and so on.

In Aristotelian logic, the four main causes of any effect are the material cause, efficient cause, instrumental cause, and final cause. In Vedānta, the basic principles of the efficient, instrumental, and final causes are all contained in one cause. This cause is looked upon as the occasional cause of creation. Again, in Vedānta the material cause is not the equivalent of that of Western logic. It is called *upādāna*. The concept of *upādāna* contains within itself not only the material, but also the inherent possibilities of everything that might be fashioned from it. A pot would be seen as only one of those things.

Clay, as a material from which a pot may be formed, has an existential status. However, the possibility of a pot being produced is only a phenomenological intention in the mind of the potter. The absence of a pot in the clay does not rule out the possibility of a pot being made from it. This possibility of a pot — the prior non-existence of it — implies the promise of a future pot. Although it may seem strange that the factor of nonexistence can change into an existential factor, this is exactly what happens in all creative processes.

The poet who writes a poem, the artist who paints a picture, a sculptor who carves a sculpture, a playwright who produces a drama, as well as the entrepreneur who becomes wealthy and powerful — all begin their role at the negative alpha pole of consciousness. The examples here, and many more which could be cited, are examples of the imaginations of people becoming sufficiently dynamic to produce individualized items or structures of an empirical utility or a transactional validity. The same is also true of the universal mind, beginning at the alpha pole of the nonexistence of the world in the Absolute.

The universal volition can promote one, or many, or all of the possibilities of manifestation, from their indiscernible potentiality to their factual existence. The result is the world we universally share as a common reality. Possibility alone does not vouchsafe actualization. Out of a hundred possibilities there can arise many ratios of the probable and the improbable. Even out of the probable only a certain proportion finally become actualized. In one sense we can say it is *māyā* that it is the enigmatic factor which plays the vital role in the making of possibilities, impossibilities, probabilities and improbabilities. Unfortunately, poetic descriptions of *māyā* have created in the minds of many people several concepts of mythical personification. For many, *māyā* has become a mythical, personalized face, such as the devil in Christian theology, or a kind of uncouth and ludicrous Shakespearian Puck.

When viewed from a mathematical standpoint, *māyā* cannot be seen as an entity. When we retrospectively examine the events in our life, it is possible to see how unexpected occurrences have given it definite directions. We may have been going along placidly in our accustomed manner and direction, when a new factor was introduced — perhaps a person, some item of information, or a sudden insight — and everything began to change. Life took on a new meaning and direction, and many of its components fell away to be replaced by different ones. Sometimes a complete and radical change occurs in our lifestyle. Looking back we can see how many of what we thought were highly qualified probabilities turned out to be only possibilities that came to nothing, while what we thought to be only the faintest of possibilities became actualized, revealing a high probability factor we had overlooked. Because of this inability to predict the course of events, mankind in general often sees the negative aspect of the Absolute as a benign Providence when things go well, or as a malignant Fate when things go badly. On the whole we have to admit that it is indiscernible.

In the next two verses the Guru will distinguish between right knowledge and fallacious perception.

VERSE 3

anātmā na sadātmā sa-
diti vidyotate yayā
sā vidyeyam yathā rajju-
sarpatattvāvadhāraṇam

The non-Self is unreal, the Self is real
thus, the means by which such knowledge comes,
that is this *vidyā*, like the recognition
of the truth about rope and snake.

anātmā — the non-Self
na sat — is unreal
ātmā — the Self
sat — is real
iti — thus
yayā — the means by which
vidyotate — such knowledge comes
sā — that is
iyam vidyā — this *vidyā*
yathā — like
tattvāvadhāraṇam — the recognition of the truth
rajju sarpaḥ — about rope and snake

In the world of personal and subjective experiences we encounter certain facts that are valid as personal knowledge; the remainder belong to the categories of fantasy and illusion. The valid items are: first, the personal identity of one's I-consciousness together with its supportive structures, so long as those structures are not merely fantasies. Then come the logically and mathematically structured thoughts or reasoning, which can be expressed to other people without contradicting universally accepted norms of logic or principles of mathematics. There is a further category of subjective experience that can be considered to be fundamentally valid. Intuitive experience of the Self is an example. Usually the contents of this category cannot be easily or adequately conveyed to others.

In the transactional world one apprehends the duality of subject and object. Here one can have right or wrong knowledge concerning the appearances which make up the world. When someone sees an object or situation as having the same form or aspects that others see, then the perception attains to the world of actuality and is considered to be right knowledge.

Illusions spring from a variety of causes. It may be that the sensory equipment of an individual is in some way defective. There may be some derangement of the mind, or the central nervous system may be polluted with intoxicants or narcotics. In such cases, although the subject's experience belongs not to the subjective world of dreams but to the wakeful state, the experiences must be considered as wrong knowledge.

On the whole, our experiences can be classified under the general headings of "factual" and "fictitious." We can say something is factual when its existence can be substantiated with objective evidence or logically valid reasoning. In the world of actuality, exactitude is the criterion by which we can decide whether our perception is right or wrong. When we call a spade a spade, there is a one-to-one correspondence between the actuality of the objective spade and our subjective idea of it. This kind of knowledge is called *yathārtha*, which means "making sense or meaning of a thing as it actually exists."

Yathārtha has various extensions of meaning. For example, *yathārthajñāna*, meaning "the knowledge of the actual," should be distinguished from *paramārthajñāna*, which means "the knowledge of ultimate meaning." *Parā* is "ultimate," *artha* is "meaning." *Yathārtha*, the knowledge that relates to the world of actuality, is in no way comparable to *paramārthajñāna*. The world of actuality has only a relative reality. When that reality is methodically examined in an attempt to arrive at its absolute nature, the world of actuality is bound to appear shadowy.

When a chemist calls common salt "sodium chloride," he is describing it in terms of actuality. And for all normal operations of his science in the empirical world this description would be sufficient. But he may wish to penetrate further into the matter; his curiosity may impel him to seek the fundamental nature of sodium chloride. Soon he will exhaust what is to be known at the actual level of science concerning the meanings of sodium and chloride. He will pass through the findings of atomic physics, and at last arrive at the inescapable idea of a primal source or sources of energy. It is here that he will enter the realm of mystery where the methods of science come to a hopeless dead end. In respect of common salt, calling it sodium chloride is to describe the actuality of the substance at the transactional level. To designate salt as waves or frequencies of primal energy is to describe the real beingness of it.

The entire world of transaction, along with whatever is of empirical knowledge, comes under the category of the actual. To apprehend the real, one has to transcend the transactional. At the transactional level the only reality is the Self alone. In comparison to the Self, the transactional world is unreal. Therefore "right knowledge," mentioned in this verse as *vidyā*, can only be knowledge of the Self.

This verse has reference to three aphorisms of an enigmatic nature given in the *Īśāvāsya Upaniṣad:*

> Into blind darkness enter they
> That worship ignorance;
> Into darkness greater than that, as it were, they
> That delight in knowledge.
>
> Other, indeed, they say, than knowledge!
> Other, they say, than non-knowledge!
> — Thus we have heard it from the wise (*ahīra*)
> Who to us have explained It.
>
> Knowledge and non-knowledge —
> He who this pair conjointly (*saha*) knows,
> With non-knowledge passing over death,
> With knowledge wins the immortal. (v.9-11)[1]

Those who rejoice in the world of ignorance live in darkness. Those who take delight in the world of knowledge live, as it were, in a greater darkness. The resultant effect of ignorance is one thing, but the resultant effect of knowledge is quite another. Those who know the secret of ignorance transcend death, and those who know the secret of knowledge attain to immortality. Such is the explicit teaching of the above verses.

In these *mantra*-s of the Upanishad it is easy for us to understand that a man who delights in ignorance should live in darkness. But when it is said that one who delights in knowledge lives in a greater darkness, we are faced with a paradox. What is termed here as ignorance is the world of transactions, where we are concerned only with the factual and objective entities of that world. Pragmatic people who take pride in their down-to-earth attitude miss most, if not all, of the sublime values of life. Wordsworth complains of such people:

> The world is too much with us; late and soon,
> Getting and spending, we lay waste our powers:
> Little we see in nature that is ours;
> We have given our hearts away, a sordid boon!
>
> (Sonnet VIII)[2]

Without having in them an element of transcendence, worldly transactions can become very prosaic and spiritually unrewarding. For many people, music, poetry, and the fine arts become meaningful only at the level of commercial propositions.

Conversely, it is possible for some who turn to the pursuit of wisdom to completely lose touch with the empirical world. A man may be dedicated to high ethical or aesthetic principles, yet may lack the ability to actualize the values inherent in such principles. The famous novel *Don Quixote*, by Miguel de Cervantes, depicts the life of such a man. The hero of the book suffers ridicule from almost everyone, and his blindly obstinate adherence to his principles makes him a menace to himself and to others. One's personality can become lopsided when the search for knowledge ends up in theoretical speculation. So it is that despite a life of dedication to the highest principles, such an individual is here described as living in a greater darkness than ignorance.

As embodied creatures inhabiting the terrestrial plane, we all have to share in transactional life. The world of transactions is also the world of action, and action is almost certain to create reaction. In the third chapter of the Bhagavad Gita it is said that action is unavoidable for even the most enlightened of men. Merely to live in the world is to have to engage in action.[3] Our lives are therefore filled with the chains of actions and reactions. Attachment, bondage, rivalry, competition—all these are aspects of life in the transactional world.

An intelligent person should ask: "What is it that compels me to act?" As he seeks to understand his own state, enquiry will disclose to him first that action is preceded by volition. Then he will see that volition is preceded by desire, and that desire is born from the preference for pleasure and the avoidance of pain. Pleasure is a quality of awareness that reflects the element of happiness, which in truth belongs to the Self. If the seeker understands this, he will realize that he should turn his attention inward into his own being to find true and lasting happiness, instead of seeking it through the gratification of his senses in the world external to himself. When one gains this knowledge, he naturally curtails all activities in which he previously engaged which are born of the confusion arising from the ignorance of his projected values. Then he is saved from the world of transient values that the *Īśāvāsya Upaniṣad* describes as darkness.

It is for this reason that the *Īśāvāsya Upaniṣad* says that a man who knows the secret of ignorance will transcend death. A wise man who is initiated into the secrets of the ultimate meaning of life and the reality of the Self should also know how he can bring the light of his wisdom to bear on everything that happens. The best examples of the application of wisdom in transactional life can be seen in the personal lifestyles of men like Gautama Buddha and Lao Tzu. In the Bhagavad Gita it is said that a wise man should not disturb the world, nor should he be disturbed by it. [4] When the wisdom of a man is sound, he lives in a state of transcendence without neglecting his role in the world of transactions. The *Īśāvāsya Upaniṣad* speaks of such a man as one who becomes immortal in wisdom.

VERSE 4

ātmā na sadānātmā sa-
diti vidyotate yayā
saivāvidyā yathā rajju-
sarpayorayathārthadṛk

The Self is unreal, the non-Self is real;
thus, the means by which such knowledge comes,
that alone is *avidyā*, like the erroneous cognition
about rope and snake.

ātmā — the Self
na sat — is unreal
anātmā — the non-Self
sat — is real
iti — thus
yayā — the means by which
vidyotate — such knowledge comes
sa eva avidyā — that alone is *avidyā*
yathā — like
ayathārtha dṛk — the erroneous cognition
rajju sarpayoḥ — about rope and snake

The Self described in the previous verse cannot be comprehended in the same way in which objects are perceived by the senses or concepts are comprehended by the mind. In all such experiences, the agency of the I-consciousness retains its identity. This causes a very illusory separation between the I-consciousness and the object of knowledge, whether it be external or internal. From childhood onwards, the personal identity of the embodied self can be recognized by its capacity to will and control all the activities that can possibly arise from the operation of the five organs of sense and the five organs of action.

When one speaks of himself as "I," the image he has is an amalgam of the physical body, the senses, the mind, and the I-consciousness. He takes all these to form a single identity. Every person treats another individual as having a separate identity and as being similar in all important respects to himself. Just as a man experiences himself as being real, so does he also give the quality of reality to others. The same principle is extended to inanimate objects, such as a stone or body of water, and to animate beings, such as animals or birds. Such a person does not make a distinction in his mind between the real (*paramārtha*) and the actual (*yathārtha*), for the simple reason that he is unable to do so. The effect of this is that the reality of the Self is erroneously attributed to the non-Self. This action will not seem unnatural to most.

There are several schools of thought which do not question the reality of things as such. These include the materialists and the existentialists. At the empirical level the world is perceived according to the actions of the senses. From incoming sensory data the world is structured, restructured, and projected as though external to the individual. It is the certitude arising from the operation of his senses and the input of data which vouchsafes for the ordinary man the reality of the objects of perception.

The composition of the world is not so simple as we think it to be. One cannot relate to an object, another person, an event, or even a sound without being to some extent affected. The dynamics of affection surge up from the depths of an unconscious state which is the seedbed of countless incipient memories. Thus the essence of existence becomes a matter for concern, because we are not, as we usually believe, the conscious masters of our own responses to experiences. Our reactions to situations produce varying gestalts. From this it should be evident that the false identity of the I-consciousness, together with the conditioned activity of the psycho-physical organism, do not leave the incoming sensory data unmodified. Each situation gains a psychic or social coloration, and thus, on the whole, life becomes a continually changing matrix made favorably or adversely meaningful by the actions of our latent tendencies.

Hope, fear, love, elation, depression, a sense of guilt or insecurity, and many other states of mind come into being as though they are alternatives between the possibilities of extreme pain, on the one hand, and supreme joy on the other. This state of alternation is described in the *Bṛhadāraṇyaka Upaniṣad* as being like a fish swimming in a stream who swims from one side of the stream to the other, touching the two banks alternately. A person who is immersed in this kind of affective involvement, with both the encounters in his external world and the compositions of meaningful situations created by the fancies of his own mind, is described in this verse as a man of ignorance, or *avidyā*.

In the next verse the Guru takes us a step further toward Self-knowledge.

VERSE 5

indriyāṇi mano buddhi-
pañcaprāṇādayo yayā
visṛjyante saiva parā
sukṣmāngāni cidātmanaḥ

The senses, mind, intelligence,
five vital tendencies and such — that by which
they are specifically created as the subtle limbs
of the reasoning Self is *parā* alone.

indriyāṇi — the senses
manaḥ — mind
buddhi — intelligence
pañca prāṇa — the five vital tendencies
ādayaḥ — and such
sa yayā — that by which
visṛjyante — they are specifically created
sukṣmāngāni — as the subtle limbs of
cidātmanaḥ — the reasoning Self
eva parā — is *parā* alone

As individuals we place ourselves as integral units within a cosmic frame of reference. Compared to the complexity and immensity of the cosmos, the individual is a negligible, tiny speck. Even so, we seek to understand the nature and mechanics of the cosmos. The seemingly infinite universe is understood in terms of such qualities as our small, though penetrative, consciousness can conceive. There is only one absolute consciousness, and that is the universal; yet there prevails a homogeneity in consciousness that is common to both our personal consciousness and to cosmic consciousness. The individuated consciousness is called *jīva*, "the living one." The cosmic consciousness is called *brahma*, "the all-inclusive, all-comprehensive totality of consciousness." Although the pure aspect of absolute consciousness is necessarily transcendent, it operates, so to speak, as if by an inherent, negative principle whereby it can project the individuation of consciousness.

The individual organism manifests with and through the action of a motor-sensory system activated by five vital tendencies. When individuation becomes a manifested reality, its operations are motivated with the help of a mind that can interrogate, receive impressions from the senses, and produce meaningful ensembles which can be retained in memory. Recall is then possible of any such recorded impression for the purpose of orientation. The same mind is also engaged in the making of decisions in an affective manner based on its conclusive judgement of the values involved in each item of experience.

Because of the homogeneity of the individual consciousness with the transcendent Absolute, it is possible for the individuated self to intuitively know its original and true nature, and to raise itself to the same transcendent level. The word *parā* used in this verse should not be confused with the pure transcendent, which is identical with the Absolute. The Guru is referring here to that aspect of *māyā* which operates as a negative potential force even at the level of transcendence.

A question may arise here: "Why are the senses and organs of action described as the subtle limbs of the individuated consciousness?" When we think of the five senses, what comes to mind are the physical eyes, ears, nose, tongue, and skin, which is sensitive to touch. These physical organs as such do not indicate the qualities of a state of perception during deep sleep or in a coma. Consciousness at these times is not animating the physical body. Hence, the physical aspects of the senses are to be treated only as efficient adjuncts to enable awareness to carry out the operations appertaining to elusive and subtle decisions, which at the conscious or unconscious levels are made by the individuated self.

Consciousness is called immanent (*aparā*) in an attempt to explain the mystery of the physical organism behaving as though it were permeated with consciousness; and, moreover, to explain how subtle, non-material ideas can be articulated through that organism. So far as transcendence (*parā*) is concerned, it becomes meaningful only when it refers to a reality which transcends all the requirements of the flux of becoming in the space-time continuum. Fundamental truths, conceived, experienced, and enjoyed by great spiritual masters, including the seers of the Upanishads, Gautama Buddha, and Jesus the Christ, continue to assert the dynamics of their word power even though these physical persons have reintegrated and moved away from the flux of becoming.

It is clear, then, that this aspect of *māyā* has the power to take us to the sublimity of transcendental heights, and also to bog down the individuated consciousness with all the wretchedness that is characteristic of the physical anomalies of the embodied state. This is further examined by the Guru in the next verse.

VERSE 6

angānyetānyavaṣṭabhya
sukhī duḥkhīva muhyati
cidātmā māyayā svasya
tattvato'sti na kiñcana

Adopting these limbs, the reasoning Self
by its own *māyā* becomes deluded,
as if happy or unhappy;
in truth there is nothing at all.

avaṣṭabhya — adopting
etāni angāni — these limbs
cidātmā — the reasoning Self
svasya — by its own
māyayā — *māyā*
muhyati — becomes deluded
sukhī duḥkhī iva — as if happy or unhappy
tattvataḥ — in truth
kiñcana na asti — there is nothing at all

All theistic religions — for example, Judaism, Christianity, Islam, and the Śaivite and Vaiṣnavite religions of India — think of an unblemished and divine Supreme God as being the first cause of everything. According to religious theists, the world is created by the most perfect God; yet, as anyone can plainly see, it is strangely full of imperfections. Our life on Earth is sometimes pleasurable, sometimes painful, sometimes ludicrous or boring. For most it is certainly conditioned, restrictive, and without freedom. If the first cause is good, pure, beautiful and peaceful, then how can such a God produce something which must be in disharmony with his own nature?

Everyone who subscribes to the idea of a benign God also hopes or believes that one day, usually after death, the worshiper and his God will be together in some imagined heaven where all is peace and goodness. Even non-theistic religions, such as Buddhism and Marxism, further the aspiration that man can one day achieve a state which is devoid of physical and social bitterness.

The little spark of consciousness that arises in us must have come from the purest of all sources of consciousness. This source is called "God" by the theologians, "the Absolute" by philosophers, and "a mysterious intelligence" by naturalists. If our own consciousness is part of the universal inheritance of the purest source of consciousness, what is it that pollutes it? This question, which is anxiously asked by the religious, generates the imperative necessity to account for all the negative experiences of life.

The Semitic religions, in an effort to answer this question, have created and adopted a hateful satanic principle as a counterpoint to balance the benevolence of God. In Vedānta, the negative principle inherent in the First Cause is assigned to phenomenality. Although *māyā* — the nescience which is the phenomenal — is sometimes personified as a feminine principle, when it comes to discussing it at a metaphysical level it is treated as being a negative counterpoint of the transcendent Absolute. At the level of transcendence there is no experience of pain or pleasure, but there is a pulsation of manifestation in that state of consciousness.

The state of consciousness that is expressed as manifestation is described by some schools as the Absolute expiring and inspiring. When the Absolute "expires" the universe comes into existence; when it "inspires" the universe disappears in the blissful oneness of the Absolute. In the Bhagavad Gita this aspect is treated as that which comes and goes. Kṛṣṇa advises Arjuna not to bemoan anything which is of a transient nature, and everything except the transcendent Absolute itself is of a transient nature. We should maintain a state of equanimity in all situations, knowing that everything is transient and in a state of continual change, including ourselves.[5]

In this and the previous verse, what puzzles our minds is locating the cause of the phenomenal in the transcendent, which is called *parā*. This verse also is to be understood in the light of the explanations we have given in the previous one. In the next verse the Guru takes us a step further in the understanding of immanence (*aparā*) and transcendence (*parā*).

VERSE 7

indriyāṇām hi viṣayaḥ
prapañco'yam visṛjyate
yayā saivā'parā'dhyātmā-
sthūlasaṅkalpanāmayī

That by which this world, which is indeed
the object of the senses, is specifically created
is *aparā* alone, which in the Self
permeates the eidetic imagery of the gross.

yayā — that by which
ayam prapañcaḥ — this world
indriyānām hi viṣayaḥ — which is indeed the object of the senses
visṛjyate — is specifically created
sa aparā — is *aparā*
eva — alone
adhyātma — which in the Self
mayī — permeates
saṅkalpa — the eidetic imagery
sthūla — of the gross

From an examination of the causal aspect of the cosmos, we now come to the familiar world of our day-to-day existence. When we experience something as being external to ourselves, it is from the incoming sensory data, processed by the mind, that the experience arises. We turn our senses toward the objects of perception, and each object is identified as being separated from every other object. Objects are identified as entities having a concrete existence as well as uniquely special qualities. Among the several qualities which constitute an object, the most primary and fundamental quality is considered to be that which gives uniqueness to the object. This fundamental quality or attribute is called the "differentia." Several objects having the same differentia are classified under one heading, known as the "species." A number of coordinated species are grouped under the more general classification of "genus." A species is defined by stating its differentia and the genus to which it belongs. The genus of "animal" is one in which the species of man, monkey, cow and tiger are all coordinated. Man is defined as *homo sapiens*, belonging to the genus animal. Although the terms given here are concepts, when we hear words such as man, *homo sapiens*, tiger or cow, we think of the entities associated with the names as being objective factors external to ourselves.

In the two previous verses we have referred to a negative principle of phenomenality which occurs as the counterpart of the Absolute. In the present verse this negative principle is given the content of actuality. It is called *aparā*. The difference between the Sanskrit words *param* and *parā* is a very subtle one. *Parā* means "the other." *Param* means "the ultimate." But the word *parā*, when conjoined with the word *brahma* (the Absolute) as *parabrahma*, can give the meaning of "the transcendent Absolute." To give the meaning "ultimate Self" or "absolute Self," the word usage is *param* with *ātma;* (the Self), as *paramātma*. Thus, the word *parā* can refer to the all-inclusive Absolute as a transcendental principle, as well as to the causal factor of phenomenality which is enigmatically related to the Absolute.

The same ambiguity can also be seen in the words *aparam* and *aparā*. In the compound-word *aparabrahma* the reference is to the phenomenal world, but it can also indirectly imply that the immanent world is not really other than the transcendental. This is the crux of the paradox which philosophers, theologians, and the common man find most difficult to resolve with exactitude.

Our physical body is closer to us than anything else in the world. There is no doubt in our minds that it is objective, gross, and concrete. The demands made by the body are the most intimate experiences in human life. But, as with many other objects seen by us in the phenomenal world, much of what we believe concerning the physical body is merely assumptive. Without the use of mirrors we cannot see the back side of the body, and since what is then seen is not the actual body we cannot be sure of the verity of the image. As for what is inside the skull and the remainder of the body, that is all presumption. The brain tissues with their electrical frequencies, the nervous system, arterial and capillary systems, and the operation of the organs — all this we take for granted because we have been told it is so. If another body is opened, deliberately or by accident, then we can peer inside it; but that is another body, not our own. We cannot look inside ourselves; at any rate most of us cannot.

It is not difficult to prove that the objectivity and concreteness of our physical body is at most skin deep. The hand we see holding this book is only a sensory impression to which the collective agrees to give the name "hand." Is it not strange that we should conjecture the reality of our own objective existence merely on the basis of a number of assumptions?

Narayana Guru here uses the word *sthūlasaṅkalpanāmayī*, which means "the universalized concept of concreteness." In short, we have an idea of the gross and an idea of the subtle. Of these two, the idea of the gross enjoys a collective acceptance that is itself proof of the homogeneity of the universal concreteness. This is why the term *aparā* is chosen here. It can mean "the other" and also "the not-other." To an unimaginative person, all objective entities exist separately and each has its own differentiating qualities. In that world of objectivity there can be birth and death, pain and pleasure, growth and decay. But an imaginative person, though still experiencing the world of objectivity, can comprehend the idea of an ultimate unity that is transcendentally real.

Each time ordinary men experience pleasure they become more firmly rooted in allegiance to the illusory world of sensory impressions and mental projections of fantasies. Such people, and that includes almost everyone, are unlikely to forsake transient pleasures and turn away from the phenomenal to seek the consolation of the non-transient transcendental. But pleasure can become repetitive and stale, and in any case must soon give way to pain. If sufficient growth toward maturity eventuates, we begin to see life from a different viewpoint. Then transient pleasures cease to allure us, and we are impelled to turn away from the immanent and transactional world when we taste the bitterness of the undependable flux of phenomenal becoming. That men should choose the lower, when they could as easily choose the higher, is very strange. It is the negativity of the universal ignorance and the implacable demands of nature that make us do this. That aspect of *māyā* which again and again brings a false reassurance to our minds to accept the verdict of the senses, and to stand by all the obligations and changing patterns of our day-to-day life, is here classified as the *aparā* aspect of *māyā*.

In the following verse the Guru tries again to lead us into a true vision of the world of objectified ignorance.

VERSE 8

śuktikāyām yathā'jñānam
rajatasya yadātmani
kalpitasya nidānam ta-
ttama ityavagamyate

As ignorance of mother-of-pearl
is the basis of silver,
what is imagined in the Self —
that is known as *tamas.*

yathā — as
ajñānam — ignorance
śuktikāyām — of mother-of-pearl
nidānam — is the basis
rajatasya — of silver
yad — what is
kalpitasya — imagined
ātmani — in the Self
tat iti — that is
avagamyate — known as
tamaḥ — *tamas*

Consciousness alternates between the dual states of brightness and darkness in varying intensities and combinations. If a man should be walking in the sunshine at midday, even if his road should be a lonely mountain track and he should be alone, it is not likely that he will fear the onslaught of prowling ghosts or goblins. The same man might tremble with fear when walking the same road alone at night. This shows a change which the mind undergoes when confronted with darkness. Physical darkness is symbolic of a more profound darkness that can affect the mind as a psychological dread. Light is symbolic of the banishment of fear and the establishment of security, just as the "light" of the presence of our parents reassures us as children. To a person afraid of economic uncertainty, a bank balance with an amount of four or five figures can bring the sunshine of security. And to one craving for love, the assurance of trust and faith from a beloved can be as delightful as basking in a similar sunshine. In the phenomenal experience of the world, light and darkness thus assume varying forms. It is not exactly the form which decides its power to illuminate or darken our minds.

As we grow and change, we continue to make evaluations and revaluations of whatever we and the world around us consider to be valuable. As a result, constant and sometimes radical changes occur in our personal vision of values.

One cannot evaluate or revalue without adopting a normative notion of fundamental values. When given the option to save from death the condemned fellow, Barabbas, or the spiritual master who was the light of the world, Jesus, the Jews exercised their option in favor of the crucifixion of Jesus. The Jewish mob, and Jesus — who preferred to die rather than to concede to the relativistic Jewish norms — both held to their normative notions of what was right. The Jews were obsessed by the socio-political oppression imposed on them by their Roman masters, so they looked upon Jesus as the Messiah whom the prophets had said would come to bring about a political redemption. They became frustrated and angry when Jesus bracketed them and the Gentiles together as all the children of God in need of spiritual redemption.

Most of our social norms are based on the vested interests of groups which themselves have a historical relevancy. The light we try to derive from the relativistic notions inherent in our social norms is at best only the light of half truths. On the other hand, the light to which the riṣis wanted to turn, to which the Buddha turned for his illumination, for which Jesus pledged his life, and in the name of which the Prophet recorded the immortal words of the Quran, is the pure light of the Absolute. Until our mind is flooded with this uncompromising light of truth and justice, compassion and love, we will not see how faulty our stand is.

The example given in this verse is the silver seen in the mother-of-pearl. The sight of the silver certainly pleases the mind of the observer, but when light is brought to shine on the mother-of-pearl the silver in it vanishes. This can be very frustrating. We are exposed to such experiences on many occasions during our lifetime. Disillusionment in matters such as the accumulation of riches, mistaking infatuation for love, and treating scholarship as wisdom are only a few cases which remind us of how we are deceived day after day by the veiling power of our own psychic darkness.

In this context one should realize the efficacy of truth as the most dynamic principle to dispel darkness. When we turn to God or to a master, we are seeking light to dispel the innate darkness of *māyā*, described in this verse as *tamas*.

VERSE 9

dhīyate'smin prakarṣeṇa
bīje vṛkṣa ivākhilam
ataḥ prādhānyato vā'sya
pradhānam iti kathyate

Just as a tree wonderfully is
latent in the seed, all are in this;
therefore, or by its importance,
it is called *pradhānam.*

iva — just as
vṛkṣaḥ — a tree
prakarṣeṇa — wonderfully
dhīyate — is latent
bīje — in the seed
asmin akhilam — all are in this
ataḥ — therefore
vā asya — or by its
prādhānyataḥ — importance
iti kathyataḥ — it is called
pradhānam — *pradhānam*

The Gospel according to St. John begins this way:

> In the beginning was the Word, and the Word was with God, and the Word was God.
>
> The same was in the beginning with God.
>
> All things were made by Him; and without Him was not anything made that was made.
>
> In Him was life; and the life was the light of men. And the light shineth in darkness, and the darkness comprehended it not. (I: 1-5)[6]

St. John makes a departure from the conventional way of writing chronicles. Although he was cryptic and his words need elucidation, the few words quoted above contain the key to the understanding of the relationship between the transcendental and the immanent.

In the Book of Genesis the opening sentences are:

> In the beginning God created the heaven and the earth.
>
> And the earth was without form, and void;
> and darkness was upon the face of the deep. And
> the Spirit of God moved upon the face of the waters.
> (I: 1-2)[7]

St. John also could have begun his Gospel with a reference to God, but he preferred to mention the Word first and then to identify it with God. The Word aspect is also implied in the third verse of Genesis given below:

> And God said, "Let there be light"; and there was light.
>
> And God saw the light, that it was good; and God divided the light from the darkness. (I: 3-4)[8]

The element of wisdom underlying both the Book of Genesis and St. John's Gospel is the same. In both there is reference to the Word, or *logos*, that can bring into manifestation the world of gross and concrete actuality and in both there is reference to the dual principle of light and darkness in which darkness has the opacity to reject the positive power of light. The Biblical language is of a mystical order and does not pretend to a scientific clarity. Even so, the suggestions given in the above quotations can be of immense help to anyone blessed with the faculty of intuition. They will help him to understand the major riddle of spirit versus matter which confronts us in the fields of religion and science.

From the English version of St. John's Gospel it is a little difficult to understand the exact concept of the Word as it occurred in the mind of St. John. He was a contemporary of Philo Judea, who at that time was engaged in a commentary on the Jewish scriptures in the light of Platonic philosophy. After Jesus' death, St. John, who was then about twenty years of age, joined Philo as a disciple. Until the coming of Philo, the Greek notion of the *logos* was an impersonal principle. It was Philo who gave the *logos* a personified status. If we agree with the descriptions of the *logos* given by Heraclitus and Plato,[9] we shall think of it as a totality of intelligence operating in and through the entire gamut of the universal and world manifestation and the process of creation.

The Word is an idea. How then does it translate itself into the manifested world of the actual? In reference to this question, it is said that on the front gate of Plato's Academy was affixed a prominent statement. This laid down the condition for admission of students to his school: it was restricted to those who were initiated into the secrets of geometry.

The relation between logic and mathematics is intrinsic and infinite. The *Principia Mathematica* of Bertrand Russell and Alfred North Whitehead, and the *Tractatus* of Wittgenstein are books which throw light on this subject. The perennial nature of the problem can thus be seen confronting both religious philosophers and scientific speculators. In the same manner, the questions of how spirit becomes transformed into matter and how matter becomes able to efficiently articulate the voice of spirit are major problems that no one in the religious, philosophic, or scientific fields can bypass. Very special attention is given to these problems by all the major schools of the Indian philosophical systems. Of these, particular mention should be made of the *darśana*-s of Sānkhya and Nyāya, and both the schools of Mīmāmsa, the Pūrva and Uttara (Vedānta).

The word *pradhānam*, which is given in the present verse as the primeval cause of manifestation, stands on a par with the Word of St. John and the Grecian concepts of the *logos* and *arithmos*, which come together to create the three dimensions known to the world of geometry. We can give an example from an experience that is very common in the world. A young girl in puberty generally has a strong instinct to nurse her own child. Such an instinct, which parents are quick to foster and encourage, can be seen even in very young girls in the meticulous, maternal care they give to dolls. In older girls, this previously unconscious urge now enters the conscious awareness in the form of fantasies, as they become physically capable of childbearing.

As far as the probable mate who can make her dream come true is concerned, he exists *in absentia* in every male. Whenever the girl burns with a conscious or unconscious urge for her mate, she experiences only his absence. Sometimes she may fancy that she sees a glimpse of the hypothetical mate in this man or that one. Everywhere life seems pregnant with possibilities. Her own brain waves seem to resonate, as it were, with cosmic vibrations in a conspiracy to further the possibility of bringing her into union with the potential father of the baby. Eventually the dream turns into an actual child, the unique product of her specific womb, to whom she has given the breath of life, and who turns to her for the sustenence — both physical and psychological — that only she can give.

Unlike the theologian, the philosopher, and the scientist, the new mother does not care to know how her fantasy materialized into the actuality of a child.

We have three options here. The first is to put our faith in St. John, and take it for granted that God was after all intelligent: he created everything, the child included, with the dynamics of his Word-power. The dual factors mentioned by St. John at the beginning of his Gospel — life and light, and light and darkness — are enough for us to understand both the transcendental and the immanent. Every cell in our body pulsates with light, yet we are in the dark as to the nature and purpose of that pulsation. At the same time, there is a great light in us that can soar high on the wings of the Muses and pay veneration to the highest values of the Self. It can also dive very deep into the depths of the mystery of our soul. Both these aspects must be put together to enable us to understand the nature of the Word, which St. John presents as not only of the world, but also of God. Unfortunately for the enlightenment of their followers, Christian theologians have made a complete mess of this sublime teaching.

Our second option is to turn to geometry. The study of geometry will lead us from the first dimension to the second, and from that to the third. In recent years the contemporary heirs of the ancient mathematicians have added a fourth dimension, and most recently extended that on to the "nth" dimension. Let us begin our discussion with the idea of the mathematical point. It can be conceived, but can it also be perceived? The point can be said to have location, but not the attributes of length, width, or height. It is only an idea or mathematical concept. However, this idea is in no way inferior to that which arose in the mind of God when he said, "Let there be light."

The nature and meaning of the mathematical point is difficult to communicate. If a child were to ask a teacher to do so, that is to say, to impart his private conception of a point, all the teacher could do would be to verbalize analogies, or to falsely represent it by putting a dot on paper or the blackboard, or by using the intersection of two lines to portray it. None of these are adequate ways to describe the concept of the point. An honest mathematician might do better. He would be likely to ask the student to apply the method of reduction. In this method he can mentally take away, one by one, the dimensions of objects visible to the eye. This will lead to the concept of a pure location, which can be referred to by the mathematical symbol "p."

This point is very well brought out by Lewis Carroll in *Alice in Wonderland*,[10] when he gives the example of the grin of the Cheshire cat, which remains even after the vanishing of the cat. When a geometry student considers the theory of the mathematical point, he is expected to pinpoint the "grin" and forget the "cat." Dimensions vanish, but the point remains. Humorous though the analogy may be, the problem remains a severe one.

While the point is considered merely as location there is little difficulty. But if the point moves, it makes a line; and the line can be straight or curved. In either case it has only two dimensions: those of location and length. Since the point in its essential nature is location only, it follows that it has no breadth. Therefore the line that is formed by its displacement has no breadth either. It is a one-dimensional construct. But now we can postulate that the point, having reached the end of the line so to speak, moves at a right angle to the original line. This gives us the second dimension of breadth or width. When the point again moves at a right angle we have the third dimension of height. By moving from a point to a three-dimensional figure we accomplish either a pyramid or a cone. We can reverse the order by going from the apex to the base, imagining an inverted cone or pyramid.

Two obvious ideas which are recognizable even prior to geometric studies are space and time. The location of a point is a location in space, and the movement of the point to form a line marks a duration from point "A" to point "B." Thus, placing the three-dimensional world in the time-space continuum is most reasonable, even though this recognition came only recently.

The third possible approach to this problem is shared in common by physicists and Indian philosophers such as Kapila of the Sānkhyan school and Kaṇāda of the Nyāya. Even after the discovery of the mysterious abdomen of the atom, the atom continues to have the symbolic status of being the furthest terminus where matter slips into mind, or where mind assumes its physical dimension. The *aṇu* of Kaṇāda needs no revision today even after taking into account all the findings of modern physics. It satisfies the requirements of a physically conceivable atom and a spiritually discernible monad. In the ultimate analysis, modern science cannot lead us into any more firm ground than that established by Kaṇāda or Kapila.

The stumbling block of every serious thinker has been the convertibility and complementarity of spirit and matter. In clarifying this enigmatic principle here, it is considered to be the most brilliant and dynamic aspect of *māyā*. Hence it is called *pradhānam* — the principle of irrefutable dynamism to both make and unmake. The *pradhāna* of the Sānkhyans is equated with the supreme principle, *mahāttattva*. The parallel concept in Vedānta is *mahas*, which is the glorious principle in which the beginning is complementary with the end. The same is also glorified as the supreme aspect of the Divine to which one should ultimately turn, as his final destination, to experience his inherent and adorable intimacy with the Absolute.

VERSE 10

karotīti prakarṣeṇa
prakṛtyaiva guṇān pṛthak
nigadyate'sau prakṛti-
ritīha triguṇātmikā

As by its very nature, it diversifies
the modalities marvelously; this,
which is of three-fold modality,
is well known here as *prakṛti.*

prakṛtya eva — as by its very nature
pṛthak karotīti — it diversifies
guṇān — the modalities
prakarṣeṇa — marvelously
asau — this which is
triguṇātmikā — of three-fold modality
nigadyate iha — is well known here
prakṛtiḥ iti — as *prakṛti*

Darśanamālā is a textbook of the Science of the Absolute. The intention of the author, and what should be that of the student, is not the gathering of information for the sake of scholarship. The prime motives are to attain a lasting happiness and to free the mind from the dual conditionings of pain and pleasure. The overall idea of *māyā* is here presented as an epistemological theme of intimate human experience to be critically scrutinized. For this purpose the Guru kept in mind a structurally conceived scheme of correlation.

The opening definition of *māyā* was given in the first verse of this *darśana* as "what is not known, that is *māyā*." *Māyā* literally means, "what is not, that is (*māyā*)." This *darśana* ends with reference made to the proliferation of the several items which constitute the world of empirical validity commonly recognized as "nature." The structural development of the scheme reminds us of the opening statement of the Holy Quran. It is an affirmation of absolute faith, not only in the supremacy of Allah, but also in the belief that Allah will lead the worshiper safely through the tortuous paths of *māyā*. It is written thus:

In the name of Allah, the Beneficent, the Merciful.
Praise be to Allah, Lord of the Worlds,
The Beneficent, the Merciful,

Owner of the Day of Judgement,
Thee (alone) we worship; Thee (alone) we ask for help.
Show us the straight path,
The path of those whom Thou hast favored;
Not (the path) of those who earn Thine anger nor of those
who go astray. (Ch.1)[11]

As we go from verse to verse we are asked to take full cognizance of every detail of the transactions of life. Between the concepts of *māyā* and *prakṛti* we are given every opportunity to trace the development of manifestation from what "is not" to what is irrefutably "out there."

In his search for happiness man is confronted by many objects which exist at the physical level externally to himself. But what exists as an external factor does nothing for him until he relates to it his subjective awareness of its meaning or significance. We are concerned with neither the phenomenality of inner awareness, nor the content of that awareness which is hypothesized as something belonging to the external world. The main concern of man is the potency of affectivity implied in the gestalt formation of each experience.

Mind makes, as it were, alternate movements between the constant "I" and that pair of variables — subjective consciousness and objective perception — which occur in a one-to-one correspondence with things. The figure of eight movement of consciousness operates in both a centrifugal and a centripetal way. On the physical side, comprehension comes as the awareness of "dis-ease." In the awareness of the subjective world, connation is complementary with cognition "my friend" or "my foe." Thus, the limits of cognition and connation mark the centrifugal periphery of the figure of eight movement of consciousness. On the other hand, the significance of a given situation centripetally affects the agent of awareness, and is experienced as "I am pleased" or "I am threatened." This figure of eight movement of consciousness should not be seen as being a construct of parts. It is a free-flowing unit in its own right, so to speak, and, as a unit, has a totality of its own.

Thus, our awareness fluctuates from one experience to another: between joy and sorrow, hope and despair, threat and security, fulfillment and frustration, excitement and boredom. The whole area of this fluctuation is the arena in which we have to live and work out our development, so as to have a precise knowledge of what is happening. But most people go by their conditioning, and so suffer the natural consequences of the significance of each gestalt.

Unfortunately for us, such a response pattern is considered to be normal and natural. A critical enquiry into our human state will quickly make it clear that a great chunk of our life experience is carved out of the store of prejudice — partly those prejudices handed down in the course of history as racial, national, or tribal conditionings, and partly the prejudice arising from the innate tendencies or *vāsana*-s of the individuated self. Truly it is the radiant Self which becomes individuated as man, though few of us experience this. Individual selves each have a uniqueness which comes as a result of the structuring of three modalities. In Vedānta, these modalities are considered to be the constituents of that aspect of phenomenality called *prakṛti*, or nature.

These three modalities are called *satva*, *rajas*, and *tamas*. *Satva* is the state of all-purity, which has a transparency capable of giving to consciousness a great clarity and a power to mirror all aspects of truth with exactitude. *Rajas* operates as a kinetic principle. It is the cause of the diversification of unified states. In the process of diversification it brings various colorations of the mind which can falsify perception of, and conceptualization relating to, the thing-in-itself. It also engenders a state of excitation in which the view of truth-as-itself is obscured. The example of a beam of sunlight passing through a prism, the consequence of which is the effect of a spectrum of colors, is suggestive of the falsifying aspect of *rajas*. A further example is that of a piece of pure crystal which, when placed on a red carpet, itself appears to be red in color. *Tamas* is essentially the state of inertia. Its nature is exactly opposite to that of *satva*. Where *satva* is transparent, *tamas* is opaque. One who is the embodiment of *satva* cannot be imprisoned in any particular state, but *tamas* inhibits the development or cessation of an existential experience, thus producing a noncreative steadystate. If we examine ourselves closely, we shall see that our state of being arises from one or another or a combination of these modalities. All men, at whatever level of development, are subjected to the play of the modalities. A man can be judged by which modality consistently affects his being, and by the extent to which he can inhibit *tamas* when it arises, and can avoid the desires and excitations of *rajas*, thereby changing to a state of *satva*. The higher the development of a person, the more consistently is his state of being *satvic*.

Although these triple modalities are obvious in their effects, what eludes our comprehension is the mechanics by which each one is given priority with an apparent randomness. They come and they go — often, it seems, without reason. This is what makes it so difficult for us to maintain a consistent lifestyle and have consistently appropriate responses to situations. For those who wish to make a deeper study of the modalities, it is suggested that the Bhagavad Gita be consulted. It is somewhat frustrating that even after a critical examination of *māyā*, we are not fully enlightened about this negative factor which is responsible for all the enigmatic riddles of life. Entering the world of *māyā* is like being caught between the Oracle giving mystical *pitia*, and the cunning Sphinx who rejoices in causing misery.

Through his presentation of the two fields between and in which consciousness alternates, the Guru has prepared our minds for a more penetrating study of consciousness in the next *darśana*, called ***Bhāna Darśana***, "A vision of Awareness."

IV. MĀYĀ DARŚANAM

1 Robert Ernest Hume, *The Thirteen Principal Upanishads*, Oxford University Press, p. 363 - 364
2 William H. Marshall, (Editor), *The Major English Romantic Poets*, Washington Square Press, New York, p. 203
3 Nataraja Guru, *The Bhagavad Gita*, R & K Publishing House, Delhi, Ch. III v. 5, p. 180
4 ibid, Ch. XII v. 15, p. 525
5 ibid, Ch. II v. 14, p. 123
6 The Bible, *The Gospel According to St. John*, I. 1-5
7 ibid, *Genesis*, I. 1-2
8 ibid, *Genesis*, I. 3-4
9 Plato, *Collected Dialogues*, Bollingen Series, Princeton, Theaetetus, 201. d, p. 908
10 The Penguin Complete Lewis Carroll, Penguin Books, p. 66-67
11 A. Yusuf Ali (Trans.), *The Holy Qur'an*, American Trust Publications, p. 14

V. BHĀNA DARŚANAM

A Vision of Awareness

Man seeks happiness. In the here and now he is either happy, unhappy, or in a neutral state. Both happiness and sorrow can vary considerably in degree. In the English language there are three degrees of adjectives: the normative, the comparative, and the superlative. Examples of these are 'good, better, best' or 'bad, worse, worst'. This shows that we have in our minds a scale with which we can gauge the hierarchy of values.

Mostly we live our lives between two extremes. Either our hearts feel heavy and tears trickle down our cheeks, or we are overcome with hilarious laughter that shakes our bodies and brings on uncontrollable convulsions. Yet we know there is another kind of happiness. This is the constant state of beatitude which is totally free of any agitation of the nervous system. Beatitude transcends comparison with other states of awareness.

In the mind of a wisdom seeker a distinction is made between 'what is' and 'what ought to be'. 'What is' belongs to the ontology of existential factors, whereas 'what ought to be' has a teleological reference to a goal, which the seeker tries to approximate in the present with the hope of someday achieving it in reality. The understanding we seek is mainly to help us to know where we stand at present, and in which direction we should move to further our future aims.

In the previous *darśana* we discussed 'what is' without relating that state to the one of 'what ought to be'. Now we are confronted with the need to search for the meaning of the second state. The search can become fruitful only if we know both the structure and function of the totality of human experience. Within this totality individuals are like the pawns on a chessboard. Yet there is a difference: there is no player who moves us about. The choice and responsibility of movement is on every occasion assigned to the pawn itself.

Before we go into what may be the nature of the end we seek, let us make a cursory review of our immediate stand. The person called 'I' is not very much like a guard in a watchtower. For short periods we may be very wakeful, observing with full vigilance what is going on. But if our activity is monotonous, this wakeful state can pass quickly into one which is a form of reverie. A motorist driving on a fast and straight freeway sometimes finds it difficult to keep himself from slipping into a momentary slumber, coming back to himself only when some new thing attracts his attention — a turn-off sign perhaps, or a stop signal.

In our daily life we are kept awake, or nearly so, by a constant barrage of new stimuli. If we do not have a continuous series of confrontations demanding our full awareness to deal with them, then consciousness slips into a second- or third-rate condition of clarity. It is, for example, not uncommon in a parliament or senate chamber, or even the General Council of the United Nations, to observe members with drooping heads, partially asleep or even snoring, to the amusement of their less sleepy colleagues.

Where do we go when we begin to snore? Are we then still engaged in the program of our search for truth? We cannot escape these occasional bouts of physical and mental lassitude. Fortunately, such states prevail only for short periods. Then the glow of life again resumes its brightness, and we can feel in our navel the urgency to prepare for a fresh venture. Again and again we become dissatisfied with what we have already achieved. We look around for a symbol of inspiration to arise, giving us fresh energy and impetus. Such inspiring examples can be thought of only in the superlative.

In this description of our present stand we have touched on four aspects of awareness. The first is the state of clear discernment wherein we can easily initiate and sustain transactions with other people. In this state we have all the shrewdness and cunning that is needed for success in the workaday world of constant competition. The counterpart of this is the world of the dream. Here the operational efficiency of the maneuvering consciousness is reduced to its minimum, and awareness is very much of the nature of a passive witness to the phantasms of imagination. The man who escapes the boredom of a parliamentary session by handing over the responsibility of his metabolic maintenance to his respiratory system exemplifies the third level of awareness. In this state he transcends, without knowing it, the uncouth details of the wakeful and dream experiences. The fourth level is one many of us eagerly wait to experience. The possibility of this is seen by us in the examples of those living, gifted luminaries who guide the destiny of the world, and who can show man how to attain peace on Earth and happiness in the Inexpressible.

Narayana Guru invites us in the first verse to enter a field of absorbing interest. In this *darśana* he will make us familiar with the sixteen aspects of the altering states of awareness.

VERSE 1

antar bahirvadāsīnam
sadā bhramaracañcalam
bhānam dvidhaiva sāmānyam
viśeṣa iti bhidyate

Present within as without,
constantly fluttering like a bee,
awareness is divided into just two kinds:
generic and specific.

āsīnam — present
antaḥ — within
bahirvat — as without
sadā — constantly
bhramara cañcalam — fluttering like a bee
bhānam — awareness
bhidyate — is divided
dvidhā eva iti — into just two kinds
sāmānyam — generic
viśeṣaḥ — specific

After wading through some of the intricacies of the diverse aspects of *māyā*, we closed the previous chapter on the happy note that the key to the enigma of *māyā* could be found in the *Bhāna Darśana*. In the general introduction to this *darśana* we located the four limits of human experience, which are interpreted basically in terms of varying states of awareness. The best German Idealist, who categorically declares that the world is an idea, and the Vedāntin, who agrees with him that everything is created by the mind, will both give up their reasoning, fantasizing, and philosophizing when the German is interred in his graveyard and the Vedāntin is cremated or immersed in the holy River Ganges with a big stone tied around his waist. The grey matter of the brain conceals in it many secrets which neither the biochemist nor the psychologist know anything about. One thing is certain: that a well organized physiochemical system should be there to produce psychophysical and psychobiochemical phenomena.

We do not at this stage wish to raise argumentation to support either of the following propositions: 1) that consciousness is an epiphenomenon produced by the molecular functioning of organized matter; or 2) that the molecular organization is itself the result of a program created by the primary intelligence of the ever-individuating consciousness to produce the kind of awareness it desires to achieve its end. What we can say is that we have made our own body a holistic system, thereby enabling us to think, move, feel, judge and evaluate. And in doing so we have drawn a line of demarcation between the 'outer' and the 'inner'. The most easily perceptible aspect of this line is our own body outline. It may sound very simple to say that awareness is within the body and the objects of perception are outside it. But this is not true in fact. The boundary of the 'outer' and 'inner' aspects of consciousness is as unstable and hard to define as many politically oriented geographical boundaries. On many occasions even the best minds cannot distinguish between what is seen as outer and inner.

If a certain man is told that by the will of a deceased person he has inherited properties in another country, or some place that he has never seen, and if he is also told that a person totally unknown to him is going to snatch away his rightful inheritance, he may become quiet upset and even go to the extent of signing a power of attorney in favor of a solicitor in that unknown country. In such a situation, the man looks at the place and people involved as factual units existing in his external world. It is not difficult to see that all these are fabrications created by the power of composition of his own mind and then projected onto an externality which is as mythical as the place and persons he created.

In the same manner, an actual person who is perceived, listened to, and directly transacted with, can become part of one's own psyche. Thus, a number of experiences connected with an external person are experienced as alchemic changes happening within one's self. At the very outset, the Guru wants to caution us about this difficulty in discerning the placement of awareness as either internal or external, because of a dynamic movement which marks the main characteristic of consciousness. This is the pulsation of awareness as it alternates between the subject and the object in a centripetal and centrifugal movement.

This pulsation of consciousness is so rapid that the Guru uses the analogy of the fluttering of the wings of a bee. The analogy is very apt: as a bee moves from flower to flower, so does awareness move from one interest to another. Even when the bee settles on one flower to extract the pollen, its wings continue to move with the utmost rapidity — so fast that we cannot fix the location of the wings at any given point. The oscillation of awareness between subject and object, and between all things within the sphere of consciousness (hypothetically considered to be placed 'within' and 'without') is also very rapid. If we take a coin between finger and thumb and spin it so that it rotates at great speed on its edge, we see the head and the tail at the same time. Our conscious experience is somewhat like the vision we have of the coin.

In this study we should always bear in mind that the purpose of this book is to show us the path to the attainment of a constant state of happiness, and how to ward off what is inimical to such a state. The duality of happiness and unhappiness is to be thought of as arising from a more basic duality which causes the bifurcation of consciousness into the inner and the outer. So far as what we experience as the 'inner' is concerned, we tend to close it off as much as possible and to see it as a kind of a secure haven. When things go badly for us in the world, this inner haven is like a shell into which we can crawl to reassure ourselves and recuperate. As Freud puts it, it is the womb of the mother into which we can withdraw.

The notion of the external is oversimplified either as what is experienced as being external to the physical body, or as what is outside the personal interest, termed by existential psychologists as the 'ego-boundary'. Problems creep into our daily life when what is termed external is both seen and confronted as being alien to us, bringing us to our wit's end. From there, either the door of the internal can be hospitably opened to the alien to make him a friend, or a passage can be found into the alien so that he or it will cease to be an external factor. If we look at the data presented from this angle, we understand the relevancy of knowing the inner and outer worlds. The effacement of the duality cannot be effected until one discovers the false criterion adopted to make this dichotomy.

Narayana Guru also turns our attention towards two other factors, both of which can cause a qualitative difference in our reactions to all the eventualities of life to which we are exposed: the general nature of consciousness, and its specific modulations. What is specific cannot find its place without sharing the quality of the generic. The generic may be understood as an inductive process of grouping the qualitative sameness of many specific modulations of consciousness, all of which are held together by an inherent homogeneity.

A newspaper report of the sudden death of a million people as the result of an unexpected earthquake has not the dynamism to knock us off balance. For many it may be no more than an interesting conversation piece at the breakfast table, though some might feel vaguely sad or sympathetic. A death in one's family is an altogether different matter. It is indeed specific, and not at all something about which we can generalize. The death of a beloved person may break our heart and cause our soul to bleed for many days. So we can easily see the two pairs of counterparts operating in consciousness — inner and outer, generic and specific — which interpret every experience to us and determine its very meaning and significance.

The first verse of the *Bhāna Darśana* is given in the original text as a somewhat causal cataloguing of the classifications of the modulations of awareness. But an earnest student wishing to use this wisdom text for his immediate guidance should ask himself why the Guru spoke of the external and internal, and the generic and specific, even before going into an examination of the material of consciousness. Such a critical approach will naturally turn the student to the need to look for the axiological importance of the present study.

VERSE 2

sthūlam sūkṣmam kāraṇam ca
turīyam ceti caturvidham
bhānāśrayam hi tannāma
bhānasyāpyupacaryate

Gross, subtle, causal, and the fourth —
thus, the bases of awareness are of four kinds;
the same names
apply to awareness also.

sthūlam — gross
sūkṣmam — subtle
kāraṇam — causal
ca turīyam — and the fourth
iti — thus
bhānāśrayam — the bases of awareness
caturvidham — are of four kinds
tat nāma hi — the same names
upacaryate — apply to
bhānasya api — awareness also

The good earth under our feet is stable. That which is stable and irrefutably concrete is called *sthāṇu*. When a thing is hard and cannot easily be done away with, such as a massive block of stone, it is called *kūṭastha*. In these terms we can notice an interesting etimological relationship between the sounds 'st' in stable, '*sth*' in *sthūlam*, and '*sth*' in *kūṭastha*. Again the same sound occurs in the word *sthiti*, meaning the state of existence, as well as in the word 'state' itself. The common notion that pertains to all these terms is the idea of the concrete. Day after day we wake up to the world of concrete facts and transactionally relate ourselves with people, things, and events. It is in this world of so-called external transactions that we experience misery and happiness.

Although pains and pleasures and the experiences of elation and misery are subjective states, we very often link them with what appear to us as concrete facts belonging to an external, physical world. The one unitive value that all beings seek is happiness. If that has any direct or indirect bearing on external entities, often called the "harsh facts of life," we should look into the nature of the concrete world called *sthūlam*.

The term 'concrete' may have different meanings to different people. The motivation to know the physical world can also vary. The physicist is concerned with whatever quality of concreteness is inherent in all our experiences of the physical world. His concern is with the measurable items, such as light, heat, hydraulics, magnetism, and so on. In the physicist's search for truth he watches the position and velocity of the movements of planets, and busies himself with the equations of motion derived from the values of the coordinates. Or he watches the motion of an electron through a cloud chamber and writes and rewrites theories, only to be contradicted and reversed again and again, and ultimately coming back to "the idea of an objective real world whose smallest parts exist objectively in the same sense as stones or trees exist, independently of whether or not we observe them."[1] This is not our interest. We are students of *brahmavidya*, the wisdom of the Absolute, and so are concerned not with the concreteness of the various modulations and projections of consciousness, but with the consciousness of concreteness. What we want to understand is how consciousness can assume a certain quality when it interprets a modification as something to be loved or discarded, adored or abhorred. What decides our happiness is not the coordination of different sets of molecules in the brain cells, but a more basic causal factor that decides which molecules are to be moved and in what manner. Let the physicist examine the effect; we want to know the cause.

The ground of the manifestation of the quality of concreteness stands in contradistinction to the modification undergone. This is the first aspect studied in *Bhāna Darśana*. Awareness of the concrete is called *bhāna*, and the ground of the modification of consciousness into a concrete mold is called *bhānāśraya*. The modification as such is called *vṛtti*. Thus, *bhāna* and *bhānāśraya* come as counterparts of *bhānavṛtti*. In other words, the modulation of consciousness consists of the original unmodulated consciousness and the causal factor that transforms the basic consciousness into the awareness of a concrete experience.

We now speak of the world of harsh facts. Jesus said:

> If a son shall ask bread of any of you that
> is a father, will he give him a stone?
> Or if he ask a fish, will he for a fish give
> him a serpent?

> Or if he shall ask an egg, will he offer
> him a scorpion?[2]

The first quarter of our study belongs to this world of necessities. Karl Marx, among other economists, thought that man's most vital problems belong in this sector. He begins his book *Das Kapital* (a critique of political economy) with the following definition of a commodity.

> A commodity is, in the first place, an object outside us, a thing that by its properties satisfies human wants of some sort or another. The nature of such wants, whether, for instance, they spring from the stomach or from fancy, makes no difference.[3]

The urgent and pressing desire to satisfy economic want is not the only one confronting and motivating man. According to Freud, sex is the hub on which the wheel of man's activities turn. C. G. Jung asserts that the spiritual need of man is stronger and more profound than any other.

We do not wish to join in the controversy of these intellectual giants. Our intention here is only to make note of the part played by that sector of the world lying outside the confines of our individuality or self. It is this sector which caters to the fulfillment of our many wants and needs — for example, those of nourishment, love and companionship, moral and physical security, and spiritual fulfillment.

The concrete facts of life involved in all these spheres have two aspects. One is that aspect of consciousness which goes into the mold of a specific perception, and the other is that mysterious element which is being interpreted by the basic consciousness as being of a particular value or significance. We will have the occasion to examine the psychological process of experiencing concrete facts later on.

Although Marx is a confirmed materialist, in the above definition of commodity he could not leave out the place of imagination as part of human wants. Nicholas Barbon comments on this in "A Discourse on Coining the New Money Lighter" in answer to Mr. Locke's "Considerations":

> Desire implies want; it is the appetite of the mind and is as natural as hunger to the body. . .the greatest number of things have their value from supplying the wants of the mind.[4]

This criticism of Marx brings us to the counterpart of the factual world of objective phenomena. In this world we hear Jesus giving another maxim. He says that "Man does not live by bread alone."[5]

What is the world that lies beyond transactional actualities? To have an idea of this we should go back to our earlier analogy of the point and the circle, which mark the two extreme limits of a cone: the point, the apex; and the circle, the base. The pulsation of the mind that we spoke of earlier has to touch these two limits. It touches the gross when it expands centrifugally, and loses itself in the subtle when it returns centripetally to the core. Although the subtle does not look as impressive as a hot loaf of bread just taken from the oven, the bread would not have been brought into existence without the intention and skill of the baker. This is a case where one turns away from the facts of life in order to understand the very feasibility of facts. This aspect is called in Sanskrit *sūkṣmam.*

There is a proverb which says that a wound caused by a sword can be healed, but not an injury caused by a word. Some of the greatest tragedies written in the time of the ancient Greeks, such as those of Sophocles, deal mainly with this second quarter of our interest, where the mind is exposed to subtle factors such as love and jealousy, and compassion and revenge. The mechanism of consciousness undergoing modulations which make the individual either happy or miserable is not very different from the mechanism involved in consciousness assuming qualities of what is considered to be objectively factual. As our search is for happiness, the quarter of consciousness dealing with subtle elements cannot be treated as secondary to the objective factors of life.

The greatest miracle in the sphere of consciousness is the recognition of people's names, ideas and meaningful compositions. The word 're-cognition' implies in it a prior knowledge. If we have prior knowledge of everything, then there is nothing to learn. In an actual experience, however, we are ignorant of many things until we learn them from some person or some other source.

This brings us to the problem of knowing initimately the whole process of basic awareness interacting with a ground to assume the special quality that belongs to each item of manifested consciousness. A probe into this is recognized in the West as the study of depth-psychology. In each act of cognition two other factors have to arise from a depth in order to recognize the meaning of what is cognized. The cognition brings only the awareness of a presentation, which can be qualified as *idanta*, the 'thisness' of every experience. As each presentation is first apprehended only as a presentation of a new theme of awareness, it is also indicative of the homogenous factor of the Self that is entering into every experience as a subject to be predicated.

For this reason, 'thisness' belongs to the world of generality. This 'this' is different from that 'this' because of the what of this 'this' and the what of that 'this'. The 'what' is the qualifying element. If 'this' is the subject, 'what' reveals the predicate. Assigning the predicate to the subject, as we have already said, is an act of judgement. This judgement is made feasible by bringing from the depth of one's own psyche a concept or a number of associated concepts with which a newly presented entity can be re-cognized.

A concept does not arise leaving behind all the shades of meaning and emotional content which have gone into every such formulated concept. The newly presented data becomes meaningfully effective only when the central core of consciousness is affected by the recognized presentation. Although the central focus of awareness is operating at the periphery, its counterpart is a consistent, built-in I-consciousness that has on it the fingerprint of every experience that has been and is being shared between the basic consciousness and the modulated consciousness of the individuated self. This value-bearing and value-interpreting ground of I-consciousness, which is always hiding beneath the threshold of consciousness, reveals its recognition, registers its protest, offers its recommendation, and releases its feelings of pleasure or excitement. It keeps its identity concealed when it promotes an incipient memory. It also advocates the cause of social mores. It is a real mystery how the substantial essence of social tradition can be part of the subjective operation of the individuated self. This subtle operation that is going on as the root cause of individuation is called the causal consciousness, or *kāraṇacaitanya*.

After drawing a thick line between the conscious and the unconscious, Jung undergoes a great struggle to spotlight whatever is going on in the unconscious and the items that are lurking there, such as the archetypes or, say, the malignant seeds that can sometimes erupt as a pathological catastrophe. In the psychology of Narayana Guru, as in other writings of Vedānta, the depth is the domain where *tamas* can envelop the individuated consciousness in such a way that *satva* is cut off from opportunities to come in contact with external things, so it turns to the fundamental nature of the Self, i. e. to *cit*, and remains passive. We can describe such a state as *suṣupti*. It is as if the personal self is in a deep sleep. This is similar to a sperm imprisoned in a seed waiting for an opportunity to come up. Thus, in every act of recognition, a seed which is confined in the depth of consciousness brings both meaning and affectivity to the person concerned. This is the third state, which the Guru describes here as *kāraṇa*.

The factual world of empirical experience allots each entity its own exclusive placement, and in that realm one thing is not in another. The space occupied by a physical chair cannot be occupied at the same time and in the same physical sense by any other physical body. In the factual world of transactions it is not possible to pass off a piece of charcoal for a diamond or a lump of sugar, although in principle they are all constituted of carbon atoms. Exclusiveness is the hallmark of empirical actuality. For twenty people to sit and study, a classroom should be at least ten feet by eight feet by seven feet, but for a person to see the whole class he can just use his eyes, which can cover the whole span due to the peculiar shape of the lens. In order to visualize, the brain does not have to provide for a large space within the skull; the entire image is perhaps worked out within the physical space of a certain nerve center in the brain. Thus, even the biochemical basis of perception can undergo fast and efficient transformation to regard and interpret the empirical world without losing much of its psychobiochemical qualities, and can yet leave behind an epitomized replica of each neuropsychic operation for future reference as a memory. Here we have a play between heterogeneity and homogeneity, conducted with great skill, to provide for the subject corresponding to all objective experiences. The shifting of the cortical function to the subcortical and back again to the cortical is the physiological explanation to piece together the objective data and the subjective interpretation of the data.

Scientists who are not satisfied with the mere labeling of functions with Latin, Greek, or German names want to know the real villian behind the scene. This is why Dr. John C. Lilly, in his book *Programming and Meta-Programming in the Human Bio-Computer*, put a most pertinent question: "Who is the programmer?" As early as the second verse of his *Atmōpadēśa Śatakam*, Narayana Guru reverses the arrow of stimulus-response so that we begin with the programmer rather than the program. The programmer is what we have already spoken of as causal consciousness.

It is hard to say what comes first, individuation of a self or the emergence of causal consciousness. Śankara brings in his theory of the indescribability of *māyā*, which casts the shadow of ignorance as a counterpart of *cit* in the Absolute. This very postulation brings to our mind a sense of duality. Śankara had only one alternative, and that was to treat the manifested world as unreal. Rāmānuja, on the other hand, never thought it necessary to postulate the superimposition of ignorance on the Absolute.

According to the Upanishads, existence as such, knowledge as such, and happiness as such are neither good nor bad. Viewing all this through the colored glass of morality is only a preoccupation of the human mind. What is filth to man is delicious food for worms and, in a country like India, even to dogs and crows. Marriage between the children of brothers is highly appreciated among the Arabs, while it is considered sinful in India. Even within India, marrying a niece is sacrilege in Kerala, while it is the best sort of alliance in the neighboring state of Tamilnadu. The sacred cows of Tamilnadu are all marched into Kerala to be served at the lunch table.

These socializing aspects are not at the level of the Absolute. They come only at the level of transactions. Great credit should be given to Freud for postulating the superego, which operates simultaneously at the ego-level and also at the unconscious level of the libido. Although most conditionings occur at the transactional level, they percolate through the ego and become the accumulated sediments of built-in social norms that can have full control over manipulating what we have called the causal consciousness. Narayana Guru gives a very good illustration of this in the *Ātmōpadēśa Śatakam*:

> As countless grains of sand ceaselessly blown onto
> the surface of a pond generate ripple after ripple,
> by untruths successively blown,
> the inner self is transformed from within into various forms.[6]

Each time sands fall onto the surface of the water the surface becomes turbulent, and it causes patterns which are not natural to still water. Apart from the surface disturbance, the formation of the bottom of the pond is also altered by this phenomenon. But there is one thing that participates in all these transformations and yet is not affected by either the changing bottom or the surface disturbance. This unchanging reality is H_20, the essential nature of the water itself. In the same manner the Absolute is unaffected by the three levels of modulations: the causal, the subjective, and the transactional. It always remains the same. Hence, in the present scheme Narayana Guru calls it *turīyam*, the fourth.

VERSE 3

dṛśyatāmiha kāyo'ham
ghaṭo'yam iti dṛśyate
sthūlamāśritya yadbhānam
sthūlam taditi manyate

See here: "I am the body;
this is a pot." Thus, based on the gross,
the awareness which is experienced,
that is considered to be the gross.

dṛśyatām — see
iha — here
aham — I am
kāyaḥ — the body
ayam — this is
ghaṭaḥ — a pot
iti — thus
sthūlam āśritya — based on the gross
yat bhānam — the awareness
dṛśyate — which is experienced
manyate — is considered
tat sthūlam iti — to be the gross

In our daily experience we approach life cosmologically, psychologically, and theologically. Those who do not believe in God or the Absolute substitute for the theological a universal normative notion of values in general. As far as cosmogony is concerned, the belief of materialists, like the previously mentioned Cārvākas, is different from that held by Vedāntins. To both the materialist and the Vedāntin a star is a star, the sun is the sun, and a physical body is a physical body. Both recognize objectively perceivable entities as being the outcome of the action of consciousness. But there the similarity of belief ceases.

When a materialist speaks of a thing as an experience of his consciousness, he means that he sees it as an independent entity separated from the mind which perceives it. He thinks of nature as being a fabulous system of inertial matter operated upon and modified by innate physical and chemical laws. He does not know where these laws come from or why they are so meticulously constituted as the ground plan of the universe. To him they are mysteriously initiated. He understands the consistency in the apparent coherence, coordination and correlation of the physical and chemical operations. But what is the purpose? The materialist does not leave that question alone. He snatches away from God his purposiveness and makes a gift of it to nature. In his eyes it is imperative for nature to evolve. He knows that nature's compulsion to evolve presents itself as a well regulated physiochemical, biochemical and psycho-biological system. But the materialist does not know why this should be so. He also looks upon his own body as one of the entities belonging to the general system, and his consciousness as an incidental by-product that evolved as part of the general evolution of things. The greatest paradox in physical science is that the scientist questions every little detail of the obvious, and takes for granted what is absolutely mysterious and much more than a miracle.

The Vedāntin thinks differently. For him the cosmos of each person is an extensive expansion of his own consciousness. Nature, as he understands it, is a product of the objectivization of the conceptual configuration of what he thinks he perceives and reacts to. This does not mean that there is no objectivity in experience. Every phase of awareness, such as the apprehension of weight, light, heat, joy, infatuation, and so on, can have its precise experiential qualities. Bertrand Russell refers in a humorous way to the awareness of physical qualities: "Atoms are waves of probability, and the physicist says the waves are in his formulae, and his formulae are in his head, from which, however, you must not infer that the waves are in his head."[7]

It is true that we can use our physical senses to touch, to weigh, and to see in order to ascertain qualities of an objective or tangible order. But on further scrutiny it will become evident that we do not know what we touch, we only know that we experience touching. We do not know what causes the sensation of weight, except perhaps the postulated idea of gravity of which we have a conceptual idea. We do not know what we see, other than the sight of form, size, and colors experienced by the mind and projected in a space that is also generated by the same consciousness. However, our mind is so structured that we can assure ourselves of the concreteness of objects. For most people this is not an easily reconcilable position.

At the close of every invocation, the enlightened seers of India repeat the words *śāntiḥ*, *śāntiḥ*, *śāntiḥ*. This means "peace, peace, peace." It is the affirmation of a universal hope among men that one day, in some mysterious way, a grace will come upon them and they will know the peace that is a relief from the burdens of everyday life. We seek peace at all the three levels mentioned at the beginning of the commentary on this verse: the cosmological, psychological, and theological (or the Unknown). Peace at the cosmological level can never be secured if the awareness of it is thought to lie outside our own consciousness.

Both Patañjali in his *Yoga Sūtra*-s and Vyāsa in the Bhagavad Gita insist on a sameness of attitude toward heat and cold. These are used as examples of the concrete. In the empirical world heat and cold are indeed concrete factors. But if these factors are seen as being entirely external to ourselves we cannot mitigate the effects of their action, and thus fashion, change, adapt to, and ultimately transcend their impact. For all this to happen we must accept them as being part of our consciousness.

What we should remember again and again is the purpose of this study. The Guru has specially given the *Bhāna Darśana* so that we may arrive at that state of certitude that alone is valid. Instead of taking this verse as mere theorization about the brute forces of actuality, it should be used as a *mantra* for meditation. Then the annoying externality of consciousness can be truthfully incorporated into one's all-embracing awareness, and the separation of individual and cosmic consciousness can be finally erased.

VERSE 4

atra kāyo ghaṭa iti
bhānam yattad viśiṣyate
tathā'hamayamiti yat
sāmānyamiti ca smṛtam

Here, such awareness as "body" and "pot,"
that is the specific;
similarly, "I," "this," and such
are to be remembered as the generic.

atra — here
iti — such
bhānam — awareness
kāyaḥ — body
ghaṭaḥ — pot
yat tat — that is
viśiṣyate — the specific
tathā — similarly
aham — I
ayam — this
iti yat ca — and such
smṛtam — are to be remembered
sāmānyam iti — as the generic

The two examples given in the previous verse, "this is a pot" and "I am the body," are not examples chosen at random. Each has been selected to represent a sphere of concreteness. To recognize a pot as a concrete reality is a different matter from recognizing one's own body as a concrete fact. When someone says "I am the body," the conceptualized body content is construed out of a partial perception of the external form. This arises from their awareness of the response of the external boundary of the body to sensation. Wherever the surface of the skin is in contact with anything which can exert pressure on it, there awareness flows in the 'I am' context. Very seldom do we experience the totality of our body boundary.

So far as subjectivity is concerned, man experiences difficulty in limiting this field to within the physical form. Despite his awareness of various sensory impressions, moods, thoughts, feelings, and so on, it is difficult for him to draw a line where he can say, "My body is this, but not that." He cannot say, "The field of my subjective being finishes here, and beyond that is the body." It is evident from the example given that such a dichotomy is not considered necessary. A person merely identifies the subject 'I' with its predicate 'body'. Just as in one example 'pot' is the predicate of 'this', so in the other 'body' is the predicate of the 'I' factor.

At the very outset of the Guru's teaching we were shown how man erroneously and habitually engages in the superimposition of the quality of one thing onto another. The most fundamental quality that makes a thing what it is, that is to say, makes it unique among all other classes of things, has been previously noted as its differentia. The 'clayness' of clay can never be taken away from it, even when the clay is fashioned into a pot or some other artifact. As far as the clay is concerned, being fashioned into a pot is incidental — it could just as easily have been a jug, a vase, or a plate. Of course, when clay is fashioned into a pot the incidence of the pot is promoted into a class of differentia to identify it in relation to jugs or jars. At the same time it becomes classified with all other pots.

This turning of clay into a pot has only a transactional acceptance. The fundamental truth of a pot is the clay, or, rather, the 'clayness'. This truth is veiled from the observer by the transactional emphasis on the artifact, on the 'potness', so to speak, of the transformed clay. This happens to us in every field of experience. It occurs in the apprehension of external entities indicated by the subject 'this', and also in the more intimate aggregate of psychophysical constituents which come under the type of experience indicated by the phrase "I am this body." It is true to say that body is a collective impression, the central locus of which is that focus of awareness called 'I'. But the converse of these statements is not true. It is as wrong as the fallacy in the syllogism: "All animals are sentient beings; men are sentient beings; therefore all animals are men."

To speak from a spiritual viewpoint, it is very advisable that a man should see his own self as being everything. It is obvious that this is not usually the case. Such a perception comes only when the fundamental differentia of the one universal Self is positively apprehended throughout the entire field of manifestation, and when specifically modulated incidents are not taken in confusion for the true nature of the Self.

In one regard the spiritual is like any other aspect of life: it can be imitated. Many people do enact a passable imitation of spirituality — passable, that is, to others as deluded as themselves. It is even possible to imitate the aspect of universalized sameness which can be seen in its true expression in a Self-realized man. We can fool ourselves for awhile, and fool others, but very soon we shall discover that we can go all the way only with the realized man. What he is on the surface he is all the way through. To claim realization is one thing; to be realized is very much another.

Let us take the example of *The Imitation of Christ* by Thomas à Kempis. Very many aspirants must have read this book and felt a warm glow of devotion, together with a determination to be worthy disciples of the master Jesus. All professed Christians glorify the sufferings of Jesus the Christ. The crucifixion, with all its terrible agony, has become the central focus of the Christian religion. Yet when it comes right down to what Jesus expected of his followers, how many come anywhere near to it? We may glorify the crucifixion and the part Jesus played, but how many of us, in full consciousness, deliberately, and with a loving, spontaneous acceptance, would, for the love of God or man, accept even a pinprick?

It is very clear from what Jesus said that the path to God is hard and is "all or nothing." Many of us claim to be followers of the Christ, but how many are prepared to pay the price of "all or nothing?" The "all" is the entire life of the would-be devotee. Doubtless we would willingly allow a beautiful harlot to wash our feet with perfume and kiss them. In this we could imitate Jesus. Many no doubt would go even further than he, and reward the woman with a hug and a kiss. But how many of us would deliberately go into the desert alone to contest the personification of all the evil in the universe? Imitation and protestation are not nearly enough — how far can we actually walk with him?

Using the statement "this is a pot," a true contemplative can extend the undiscerned 'thisness' to obviate all its 'potness'. In the same manner, when we say "I am the body," all the variegated moods, tendencies, sensations, and impressions can be sublimated by a contemplative if he turns himself into a blazing fire of pure I-consciousness. However, most of us are not contemplative at all, and we pay only lip service to the hope of Self-realization. We limit ourselves, in both the above cases, to the accidental and partial knowledge of what seems to be concretely manifested, or to the conception of the limits of our own bodies.

In this verse the Guru shows how what is presented to our awareness fluctuates between the generic and the specific. But mere cognition without substantiation of the experience with a meaningful awareness is no experience at all. In a dream one may be weeping inside himself because he is separated from his beloved. Deeply asleep, he may be quite unaware of external events. At the same moment he weeps for his loss in the dream his beloved may be with him in bed, fondling and kissing him, but she is awake in the external world and he is asleep in the internal. No matter what her actions, if he is not aware of them it is for him as though nothing has happened. Awareness draws a line around a relevant meaning, significance, or value associated with what is chosen by the percipient to be promoted as a perceptual entity. In the present case it is a pot: "this is a pot."

In the *Yoga Sūtra*-s of Patañjali, commented on by Vyāsa and further annotated by Vācaspati Miśra (known as Vicārādi), the psychology of perception is throughly examined. In this work every conscious recognition of a particular awareness is called *prakhya*, "knowing in a special way." This knowledge is accompanied by its recognition as an existential verity called *sthiti*. When an awareness comes to stay as a meaningful entity, the whole person becomes affected and the affectivity is expressed as a reaction to that unit of consciousness. It is called *pravṛtti*. For one conscious factor to sustain its interest, it should be highlighted by the concealing of all other irrelevant stimuli. In *Vyāsa bhāṣya* it is called *nirodha*. Further accentuation of the interest may come to such a pitch of infatuation that the percipient will become blind to all other factors. This state of infatuation is called *mūḍha*. The net result can be a concentration of interest in one item at a time, and it is called *ekāgrata*.

The quality of the interest lies dormant in an incipient memory (*vāsana*) that is seeking fulfillment. The quality of interest arises out of the depths of the causal consciousness and activates the memory. This in turn brings a conceptual mold into which the object of interest can be fitted. If the object of perception does not exactly fit into the conceptual mold, then the concept is readjusted and modified to accomodate what is new and peculiar in the presented object of interest. If there is a strong reciprocity from both sides, that is, between the object of interest and the incipient memory, then the experience gains the quality of interest. In between there is a kind of blackout when consciousness flows from one item of interest to another.

The second example given — "I am the body" — is suggestive of a greater dynamism that exists in the aggregate of the body. This dynamism can permeate the I-consciousness with the painful and pleasurable experiences of the body. In either case there is movement from the general, unmodified aspect of consciousness toward a highly specific modality. The Guru clearly says here that both the 'this' and the 'I' factors are indicative of the general aspect of basic consciousness, *bhāna*. The 'pot' and the 'body' are specific modulations of that consciousness, wherein there is a coming together of the item of interest and of the occasional presentation of what we infer to be the object of our interest.

In the *Ātmōpadēśa Śatakam*, Narayana Guru explicitly instructs his votaries to meditate on the full implications of 'thisness' in order to be freed from the easy slide of consciousness into the pitfalls of relativity.

VERSE 5

indriyāṇi manobuddhī-
viṣayāḥ pañca vāyavaḥ
bhāsyante yena tat sūkṣma-
masya sūkṣmāśrayatvataḥ

The senses, mind, intellect,
items of interest, and the five vital breaths —
the awareness which constitutes
the subtle nature of its basis is the subtle.

indriyāṇi — the senses
manaḥ — mind
buddhi — intellect
viṣayāḥ — items of interest
pañca — five
vāyavaḥ — vital breaths
yena bhāsyante — the awareness which constitutes
asya sūkṣmāśrayatvataḥ — the subtle nature of its basis is
tat sūkṣmam — the subtle

In this verse the Guru calls our attention to the senses, mind, intellect, the objects of interest, and the five vital principles (breaths). He asks us to find out for ourselves what it is that makes these factors known to us. What is important is not what we know, but the exact nature of the ground of that knowledge. The items enumerated above cover all that occurs in the two hemispheres (psychological and somatic) of our total beingness. The first group we should examine contains the five organs of perception. Of these, the two major organs of perception are those of the auditory and visual systems.

In Western psychology the experience of hearing is studied from the side of the concrete. The anatomy and physiology of the faculties involved in hearing, which occur in the central nervous system, are the main focus of Western interest. The Indian approach is totally different. In it the organs of action are named after their primary functions, such as the ear being related to the recognition of a simple and harmonious pitch constituted from sound waves, called *śruti*. In Sanskrit the organ of hearing is called *śrotram*. Sound waves may be pitched in the ranges of high or low frequencies. In addition, there can be distinctive patterns formed by the action of microtones. Indian psychologists do not concern themselves with the general study of such patterns; they pay attention only to those able to produce a resonance within the totality of consciousness of the person experiencing sound. Resonating pitches are the most fundamental sound units. It is from the action of these units that the meaningful world of hearing is created for all of us.

Unlike Western psychology, wherein attention is given only to agitations taking place in the neurons, the Indian psychologist calls our attention to a selective structuring of pitches. The structuring of pitches is shown to be relevant in terms of meanings that can be visualized in a holistic manner by the psyche of a person. It is through the action of such selection that an incipient memory can find an occasion to actualize its potentials.

Western psychology speaks of the 'apperceptive mass', and Gestalt psychologists are aware of the miraculous and mysterious composition of sounds and forms. But little is done in the West to discover the true nature of the bilateral relationship between psychological and somatic functions, even in such a simple instance as that of one pattern of waves making a resonant tone while another pattern produces a note of dissonance. The patterns as such have neither the quality of resonance nor dissonance. It is we who give to these patterns the aspects of positivity or negativity. The human auditory system may be likened to a radio receiver. Input in the form of wave patterns is received and transformed into various sounds which are pleasant or otherwise to the self. What is a pleasing transformation to one may be an almost unendurable cacaphony to another. It all depends, as does every experience, on the nature and conditioning of the percipient psyche.

Depending on social and geographical boundaries, a given people may never properly articulate some sounds, or they may not structure some sound patterns semantically; this is especially noticable in music or poetry. The same sounds may be structured and highly appreciated by another people in another geographical area who use a different language grouping. It is evident that the musical harmony with which we are familiar is conditioned at the personal reflex level, and also at a deeper racial level where the easy mutations of such a conditioning are carried by the genes. The faculty of hearing should be studied and understood at a much deeper level than the one which psychologists and neurologists are presently aware of.

The complexity of the hearing process can better be understood when hearing is contrasted with listening, and listening is understood in terms of both comprehension and recall. The whole process enters a more complicated field when a person is multilingual. Then what is thought of using the semantics of one language must be mentally translated into another before it is articulated. At this level of complexity the neurophysiologist tends to assign superhuman or supernatural powers to every neuron. Although in our daily experience the meaningful compositions of nerve energy, which facilitate the requirements of pragmatics, logistics, and syntactics during the process of semiosis, pass unnoticed, neither the neurophysiologist nor the psychologist have succeeded in getting a vivid picture of this complex phenomenon.

Truth, it is said, is stranger than fiction — and it may well be so. But we are not dealing with truth when we consider the explanations of auditory experience given by neurophysiologists, even though they certainly do sound strange. The relative ease with which a child learns its mother tongue cannot be altogether attributed to the child's racial conditioning. Should an infant be taken from its birthplace to a country in which a different language is spoken, it will learn that language with the same ease. For this reason, Indian psychologists begin their studies with the absolute ground of semiosis, and identify it as the unmanifested aspect of sound. This ground is named *para*, after the Absolute itself.

The first stirring of manifestation in the world of sound should not be assigned to the activity of electromagnetic waves. The faculty of hearing is actually born of a particular kind of seeing. Extraordinary though this statement may sound to most of us, it is by no means just a pet idea of Indian philosophers. Scientists of the caliber of Whitehead and Bertrand Russell acknowledge this fact. However, the kind of seeing meant here should not be confused with normal external sight, nor even with the visualizations of the dream world. It does not fall within the field of what is usually considered to be the subjective. The most primary transformation of what is formless into the realm of form, which takes place in the causal consciousness, is here referred to as the primary act of seeing. In Sanskrit this is termed *paśyanti*.

Psychologists of the school represented by Jung want us to accept the inference of the possible inherence of archetypes in the collective unconscious. This is an idea not so very different from the concept of the primeval transformation of a formless incipient memory into something that can initiate a meaningful formation, which can in turn be presented to and accepted by the conscious mind. Modern semanticists have referred to this unconscious process as the 'idea evolving' area of pragmatics. The word 'pragmatics' is related to an ontologic motivating urge, and to a teleologic expectation of the result produced. In this case the expectation is of a result which is advantageous to the person concerned. Between the ontologic urge and the teleologic goal of actualization, a flow of psychic energy is directed by the holistic purpose of the total person. In this holistic aspect the person is termed *jīva*. This process has not yet entered the world of logical structuring. Nor is there yet a specific arrangement of words able to present it in an acceptable form of language. It cannot yet be introduced in a simple way into our effortless and spontaneous articulation. If it could, it would easily reveal to us the fact of an intermediary process occurring. The process happens with such secrecy that even as we speak we do not know how the ideas we put forward enter consciousness. They arrive fully formed and clothed in a logically coherent language. How often have we been slightly astonished to hear what we are saying? If a man is "thinking aloud," he knows his own thoughts only by the words that articulate them in such quick succession. The process is one of such natural ease that one could almost say it was shy about being detected. This intermediary function is called *madhyama*.

A more refined aspect of articulation is given priority in the present study. This is the articulation of sounds in terms of the pictorial images seen in dreams. There is a difference between the visual imagery of the dream and the articulated sound. This is to be explained by one more item in the process of transformation: that by which mental images are converted into sound symbols. The place of sound symbols can be taken by language signs, such as written words, or meaningful characters like those used in the Chinese language. This is called *vaikhari*.

If the reader reviews what we have said on the subject so far, he will have an approximate idea of the primary and subtle ground that is responsible for producing the consciousness of hearing. The only valid method to arrive at the highest truth that man seeks comes from the testimony of the Word. The word of God, or the Word of the Guru or scripture, is the Word that is revealed both to see and to hear simultaneously. This may sound like dogmatic fiction. We will come to know the importance of the Word that guides and transports us to the higher realm of realization as we proceed further.

In the Indian concept of perception there are three factors: the organ of perception, the object of perception, and the interest of perception. The object of perception is a mysterious factor. It has an existential status. However, this is fully established only when it induces the percipient, through the organ of perception, to visualize it in a picture which is in agreement with his basic interest. The liaison which is established between the interest, the organ of perception, and the object need not necessarily always cater to a favorable interest. The thwarting of an interest has as much importance as its fullfillment.

Each sense organ is bombarded with countless millions of stimuli. No ordinary human organism could avoid distintegration if all the stimuli entering the field of awareness were to be registered and recognized simultaneously. An automatic screening process takes place, and only those stimuli relevant to the structuring of a meaningful picture are consciously recognized. These stimuli are accepted as the obvious hall-marks of a re-cognized perception. Out of the remainder of the stimuli, whatever is relevant to a specific perception is incorporated into the picture as secondary phenomena, while most remains as passive background and much is shielded away by the negative principle already alluded to as *nirodha*.

The two major patterns of perception which become integrated are the visual and the auditory. The most significant aspect of visual perception is form, and of auditory perception, name. On the whole we can say that the immediate world is an aggregate of forms and names. Forms are important because they have the capacity to present a subject in its most vivid, tangible, and objectively existential status. The disadvantage of form is its being fixed in a special location. A form cannot persists in a person's experience except when it is in his immediate presence. However, it can cast a lasting impression which the percipient retains as a mental image.

The continuity of an experience, and the sharing of it, are very much dependent on the nominal factor. Names are not only semantic signs, they are also the memory tags of our information system. Mentioning a name can trigger recall, information, conceptualization, and incipient memories, to list only a few items. The mention of a name is as efficient as, or more efficient than, pressing the printout button of a computer to obtain the data of previous programming. Hence the auditory fields, especially that of language, have a more enduring and dynamic place than any other factor in the social fabrication of our transactional world.

The world of the senses is intrinsically related with memory. Consequently, the learning process consists of endless and variegated chains of established coordinations between patterns. These patterns are formed by the action of two or more of our sensory systems, and also by the establishment of links with corresponding motor systems. This structuring ensures that a volition initiated by an individual or given to him in the form of a request or command can be immediately and efficiently carried out at the level of action.

This takes us from our study of the senses to the consideration of the coordinating agents: the mind and the intellect. The observing faculty of awareness can be turned to the movements of thoughts and feelings, just as it can be a witness of perception when the senses are engaged in the act of perception. It is not difficult for one to stand apart from the mainstream of mental events and act as a witness, listening to the arguments and counter-arguments going on in our intellectual sphere, until the volitionally bent intellect passes a resolution to be ratified by the I-consciousness, which either promotes the incipient memory or suppresses it as a matter of expediency or prudence.

What is important in our study is not the mere recognition of the *modus operandi* of the functioning of the intellect, mind, and senses, it is how the individual expresses himself in and through all these formations. We do not refer here to overt expressions which are exposed to the public gaze. Our reference is to the unfoldment of the hidden potentials which are tied up with the personal drives, urges, and concealed desires of the individual. In the present case we are not dealing with the concrete factors of what is seen or heard. Our interest is with the inner development in awareness which facilitates sense perceptions and motor responses to the best advantage of the value visions of the individual. This development is of a subtle nature, and so awareness of this kind is called *sūkṣmabhāna*. In this verse our own inner faculties are recognized as the subtle ground of awareness, *sūkṣmabhānāśrayam*.

Apart from the senses and mind, the five vital principles called *prāṇa* are also included in this verse. The most obvious aspect of *prāṇa* is respiration. Although there is never a moment when we are not respiring, we seldom consciously think of this action. It comes forceably to our attention only if a head-cold or a chest infection makes breathing difficult. Sometimes we may think about it if we come across a book about yoga or decide to watch the workings of our own organism. This gross aspect of breathing is only one of the many functions of *prāṇa*, relating to only two of the five *prāṇa*-s that are always functioning in us.

Like the Yogis, Vedāntins also recognize five *prāṇa*-s (*pañca vāyavaḥ*). Of these, *prāṇa* and *apāna* are conceived of as a polarized parameter to explain the ascending and descending breath. Western psychologists see this action as a physical one: the inhaling of oxygen and the exhaling of carbon dioxide. Both Yogis and Vedāntins consider *prāṇa* and *apāna* to be of a more vital significance than merely physical. The physical organism is a part of nature and, as such, is also subject to the eternal flux of becoming. We usually think of birth and death as being events which happen only once in a lifetime, but this is far from being the case. The physical organism is in a constant state of birth and death as cells die and are replaced. The metabolic function of the body includes several binary functions which all depend on the alternating phases of incoming and outgoing breaths. These two major principles which vitalize the organism are supported by two other forms of *prāṇa*.

Our body and our mind are both exposed to contrasts, such as heat and cold, pleasure and pain, depression and elation, and so on. If we did not have an equalizing principle, our metabolic balance would be adversely affected and the mind thrown into a quandary. This function of balancing and equalizing, which continues without cessation, is assigned to the action of a *prāṇa* called *samāna*.

The gross aspect of *prāṇa* is the respiration of air. Its most subtle function affects the psychological and physiological systems of the organism. *Prāṇa* makes those systems express themselves in the total functioning of the organism, as in the activity of reasoning and in various emotional states. These states include the appreciation of higher values as efficient tools of the individual to tap many latent psychic energies and cognize and discern the qualities and significance of sounds and colors, ranging from the most sublime to the most unpleasant.

Another aspect of the *prāṇa* is to burn the fuel that is ingested in the form of nourishment: turning food into energy. The entire process of digestion occurs under the direct supervision of *prāṇa* and through the action of its biochemical engineering. The resultant energy and the body-building materials are taken to the appropriate parts of the body by that aspect of *prāṇa* called *vyāna*, which plays the role of the grand distributor. The final aspect of *prāṇa* is that which unifies the others and holds them within the physical body. It acts not unlike the nucleus of a magnetic field. When it dissipates or unwinds, the other *prāṇa*-s become inefficient. This is called the *mukhya prāṇa* or *udāna*. When this last *prāṇa* leaves the body, its animation ceases and the physical organism disintegrates.

We have some sort of access to *prāṇa* and *apāna* from within ourselves. The other three can be inferred from the general effect of the organism in its totality of activity. Therefore these three also come in the category of *sūkṣmabhāna* — the subtle operation of consciousness. The will to live is the ground of the operational efficiency of *prāṇa*. That ground can be considered as *sūkṣma-bhānāśraya* — the ground of subtle consciousness — when we come to discern the modulations of awareness in the operational field of *prāṇa*.

The *Bhāna Darśana* is conceived in accordance with the frame of reference of the *Māṇḍūkya Upaniṣad*. Of all the Upanishads, the *Māṇḍūkya* is favored by the non-dualistic school of Vedānta. It is considered to be an ideal book to present the case of monistic or non-dual philosophy. This Upanishad has had many commentaries written on its teachings, but the two most formidable were produced by the master-mind Gauḍapāda and his great-disciple Śankara. The master Gauḍapāda originally was of Buddhist affiliation, and he made use of the *Māṇḍūkya* text to revalue and restate the nihilist doctrines of the school of Nāgārjuna. When the teaching of Nāgārjuna is taken to its logical end, the final conclusion is nothingness. Gauḍapāda critically examines that position and refutes it. He establishes beingness as the final truth.

The polarization in Gauḍapāda's mind was between nothingness and beingness. The historical circumstances of that time added a new stress to the theme of revaluation, especially when it came to the time of Śankara. The nihilists were the anterior skeptics who had to be conclusively dealt with by Gauḍapāda. After the work of his master, and in the representation of it, Śankara found himself beset by a number of adversaries. These included the four schools of Buddhism, the school of Jainism, the Indian schools of materialism and realism, Sānkhyan dualism, and the orthodox school of Vedic ritualism. Śankara had to meet and deal with objections from every quarter, offering a counter-argument to establish the non-dual reality of the Absolute. Because of this, he could not treat the transactional world of wakefulness and the subjective world of dream in a summary fashion as Gauḍapāda did, so he took special care to differentiate dream from wakefulness.

Narayana Guru, who was established in the same spiritual lineage of non-dual philosophy, was fully aware of all the developments that had occurred and were occurring on the Indian subcontinent. Formal schools of Vedānta became well established in the post-Śankara period. Apart from that, the growth of Śaivite philosophy in South India was historically as important as the growth of Vedānta philosophy. Thus the Guru was in a position where in himself he could integrate and assimilate the awesome and penetrating vision of all those previous masters. The Light of the Absolute was again embodied as man in the contemporary vision of the Guru, and the ancient teachings were given their right and honored status.

The result of Narayana Guru's integrated vision of the Absolute is the composition, among other works, of the *Darśanamālā*. Gauḍapāda and Śankara relied on the scheme of correlation given in the *Māṇḍūkya Upaniṣad.* The Guru has also adhered to the same scheme.

When we pass on from the *sthūlabhāna* (concrete basic consciousness) to *sūkṣmabhāna* (subtle basic consciousness), we move from the positive aspect of transactions to the negative aspect of subjective responses. The positive aspect may be called the 'horizontal-plus' and the negative aspect the 'horizontal-minus'. Subjective response is a two-pronged reaction. The first reaction has to meet the demands made by the horizontal-plus side of transactions. This is the field of the actualization of interests, and also of active defense against possible, probable, and actual threats. In the second reaction, the horizontal-minus is polarized with the vertical-minus as urges, drives, irrational phobias, and manias, which are all presented directly to the subjective consciousness in the form of desires of acquisition or rejection. Such attraction-repulsion dynamics gain priority when the sense data arising from environmental factors bring with them indications of the presence of wish fulfilling possibilities.

Strictly speaking, this aspect does not come within the dream experience, even though it falls within the ambit of subjectivity. But a number of subliminal impressions and unconscious urges are presented to awareness through the activation of symbols of myth in the dream. There is a no-man's-land between perfect dreams and subjective wishful thinking or phobias. Here, actual images of pleasure or threat are made use of instead of the dream symbols of archetypal variables. These finer shades of the dream experience should be kept in mind for one to understand the exact nature of the ground of subtle consciousness and to be able to dismiss the entire field of horizontal phenomenality as unreal. And though the field of phenomenality be dismissed as unreal, this cannot be of real help in emancipating the Self, that is to say, in freeing the Self from the clutches and hooks of the transactional world and the subjective world of dreams, including a wide spectrum of pathological deviations that can manifest both in the transactional world and the world of subjective fantasy. This aspect of the teachings of the *Bhāna Darśana* should be treated with the utmost care, although the Guru gives us only a simple hint. Students of psychology can take this aspect as a challenge and, using it as a springboard, dive deep into the mystery of dream experiences.

Compared to the unconscious, the *kāraṇa caitanya* (causal consciousness) covers only a small area. Even within the conscious world of experience, the truly wakeful and transactional items occur only as small islands in the vast and deep ocean of our subjectivity and dreams. After presenting the mystery of the dream here, the Guru takes us into the depth of causal consciousness in the next verse.

VERSE 6

ajño'hamiti yad bhānam
tat kāraṇam udāhṛtam
atrāham iti sāmānyam
viśeṣo'jña iti sphurat

"I am ignorant" — such awareness
exemplifies the causal;
here, what is revealed as "I am" is the generic,
"ignorant" is the specific.

aham — I am
ajñaḥ — ignorant
iti yat bhānam — such awareness
udāhṛtam — exemplifies
tat kāraṇam — the causal
atra — here
iti sphurat — what is revealed
iti aham — as "I am"
sāmānyam — is the generic
ajñaḥ — "ignorant"
viśeṣa — is the specific

When a man says "I am ignorant," is he admitting knowledge or non-knowledge? If he is in a total state of ignorance, then how does he relate that ignorance to himself? If ignorance is total, the awareness of the I-consciousness cannot be present. If nothing is known, then nothing is known. However, if a person has no knowledge of anything, yet knows that he exists, and is also aware that his mind is neither perceiving nor conceiving anything, then he has knowledge of the state of his mind. In that case he is not and can not be ignorant. If we ask a man, "Do you know Einstein's special theory of relativity?" and if his answer is "I am ignorant of that," can we say he is not telling the truth? In this case, what is the status of ignorance?

The person who denies knowledge of the theory of relativity arrives at that denial after a quick mental review of what he does know. The conclusion he draws is that the special item mentioned to him is not within the range of his knowledge. Though he may know nothing about relativity, he does know that relativity is not something as yet known to him.

In the same way, when someone says "I do not know God," or "I do not know the Self," he is categorically denying that whatever it is that he has so far known could be God or the Self. Such a statement includes a paradox: to make it he must have a weak, but still formulated, knowledge of God or the Self. In other words, before knowledge of a thing can be denied there must be an *a priori* knowledge of that thing. We cannot affirm or deny knowledge of something we know nothing about.

In this verse we are discussing the third aspect of the altering states of awareness. This aspect is identified with the state of deep sleep. If we think of deep sleep as having neither the wakeful awareness of the world of objects, nor the mental images that are presented in dreams, then we might think of it as being a void. Indian psychologists do not hold that opinion. Far from thinking of it as a void, they treat it as being a mass of consciousness. This is why it is called *prajñāna-ghana*, the state of being 'totally permeated by consciousness'. Paradoxically, the deep sleep is considered to be a mass of consciousness and at the same time to be devoid of consciousness. This mass of consciousness is also identified with 'causal consciousness'. All images appearing in dreams and the emotional content of every such perception, together with the recognition of external aspects and a right adherence to their names and forms, can be traced to the causal consciousness.

If all the knowledge in dreams, as well as the power of discerning with apodictic certitude things in the objective world of wakefulness, both come from what is known as deep sleep — or a total state of ignorance — how can that state be described as one of 'non-knowledge'? Resolving this paradox is a vital necessity, and crucial to an understanding of Vedānta. Both Gauḍapāda and Śankara praise this state as being identical with that of the Lord who creates everything.

The states of consciousness, moving from wakeful perception to subjective awareness and from there to deep sleep, are conceived in the order of a regressive hierarchy. Wakeful perception is symbolized by the right eye; subjective awareness is attributed to the eye of the mind; the state of the non-operation of consciousness is located in the non-physical space in the heart metaphorically referred to as the 'cave of the heart'.

In Indian mythology and iconographic symbolism, the right side of the body represents the spirit and the left side the creative dynamics of nature. Seeing or perceiving is conceived of as being like the action of a fire in its consumption of fuel: it is a process of alchemy. In other words, the spirit is entering into the tri-basic matrix of modality, into the ever-changing flux of the interactions between *satva*, *rajas*, and *tamas*, and, at the individual level, the knower, the known, and knowledge.

The entry of the spirit causes variations in the patterns, and the kaleidoscopic changes produced by the spirit acting as a catalyst are visualized by the 'eye of the mind'. This visualization includes the subjective replica of what is interpreted to be the picture of objective presentation. The action of the spirit is also experienced as the self-luminous and self-projected mental imagery of the dream experience.

Neither the fire in the right eye nor the power of perception inherent in the mind are independent of their common causal source, here called the space or cave in the heart. Heart in this sense is not to be understood as the physical organ which circulates blood through the body. It should be recognized as the central nucleus of the psyche. An analogue of this can be seen in the mystical Heart of Jesus worshiped by many Catholics. In the Bible, God is seen as "knowing the secret of the heart,"[8] and it is also said that "as a man thinks in his heart, so is he."[9] Jesus himself said, "Blessed are the pure in heart for they shall see God,"[10] and "Why reason these things in your hearts?"[11]

It may be difficult to understand how the indiscernible mass of consciousness in the 'space of the heart' can bring about such a wide variety of experiences divided between the dream and wakeful states. When a man and a woman come together, see each other, talk to each other, and touch each other, they are operating in the realm of concrete facts. Their experiences are understood in terms of the concrete. But when their hearts melt in love and they enter into an orgasmic state of consummation, their concrete duality vanishes. What remains is a subjective recognition of a blissful state of ecstasy. During that moment of ecstasy it may be that the essence of the man and the essence of the woman become unified in the fertilization of the ovum by the sperm. In that fertilized ovum we cannot discern what belongs to the shapes of either the male or female bodies, nor can we say what traits of each parent have entered into it. However, if the ovum is given sufficient time to develop the indiscernible will become discernible. In its maturity it will display the concrete physical aspects of the bodies from which it took the blueprint for its shape. In addition, it will give evidence of the vital functioning and animation we have referred to under the term *prāṇa*. The subjective traits will also be displayed, some of which may have lain dormant not only in the parents but in the genetic inheritance of several family generations. All this and more occurs in the wonderful mystery that is human birth. The mass of consciousness depicted as being located in the deep sleep state is to be equated with the rich potentialities of the fertilized ovum.

In order to present to his readers his own ideas concerning the nature and operations of the collective unconscious, C. G. Jung quotes three poems by Holderlin in his book *Symbols of Transformation.* In the works of this poet Jung traces the path one takes as he enters willingly or is drawn into the unconscious. The first is a poem to Achilles:

> Lordly son of the Gods! Because you had lost your beloved,
> You went to the rocky coast and cried aloud to the flood,
> Till the depths of the holy abyss heard you and echoed your grief
> In the stillness, where far from the clamour of ships,
> Deep under the waves, in a peaceful cave, the beautiful
> Thetis dwells, your protectress, goddess and nymph of the sea.
> Mother she was to the youth, for the powerful goddess
> Had once, on the rocky shore of his island, lovingly
> Nursed the boy at her breast, had made him a hero
> With the might of her strengthening bath and the powerful song of the waves.
> And the mother, lamenting, heard the cry of her child,
> And rose like a cloud from the gloomy bed of the sea,
> Quieted with tender embraces the pains of her darling.
> And he listened while she, caressing him, promised to help him.
> Son of the gods! O, were I like you, I could trustingly
> Pour out my secret grief to one of the Heavenly Ones.
> This I shall never see, but must bear the disgrace, as though I
> No more belonged to her who still thinks of me, even with tears.
> Beneficent gods, who disdain not men's prayers, then hear me!
> How raptly and fervently have I not loved you, holy light,
> Since I have lived, the earth and your fountains and woodlands,

Father Aether – this heart has felt you about me too
  ardent and pure.
O soften, ye kind ones, my sorrows, that my soul be not
  silenced too early,
That I may live and thank you, heavenly powers in the
  highest,
With joyful song till the last, hurrying day,
Thank you for gifts gone by, for the joys of lost youth,
Then take me out of my loneliness up to yourselves.[12]

Next Jung quotes fragments from the poem "Patmos":

Near is God
And hard to apprehend.
But where danger is, there
Arises salvation also.

In darkness dwell
The eagles, and fearless across the abyss
Go the sons of the Alps
On lightly built bridges.[13]

In the chapter giving these quotations Jung also gives us his theory of the collective unconscious:

> The parable of Jonah who was swallowed by the whale reproduces the situation exactly. A person sinks into his childhood memories and vanishes from the existing world. He finds himself apparently in deepest darkness, but then has unexpected visions of a world beyond. The "mystery" he beholds represents the stock of primordial images which everybody brings with him as his human birthright, the sum total of inborn forms peculiar to the instincts. I have called this "potential" psyche the collective unconscious. If this layer is activated by the regressive libido, there is a possibility of life being renewed, and also of its being destroyed. Regression carried to its logical conclusion means a linking back with the world of natural instincts, which in its formal or ideal aspect is a kind of *prima materia*. If this *prima materia* can be assimilated by the conscious mind it will bring about a reactivation and reorganization of its contents. But if the conscious mind proves incapable of assimilating the new contents pouring in from the un-

> conscious, then a dangerous situation arises in which they keep their original, chaotic, and archaic form and consequently disrupt the unity of consciousness. The resultant mental disturbance is therefore advisedly called schizophrenia, since it is a madness due to the splitting of the mind.[14]

Although we shall not quote here from Sigmund Freud's contribution to the theories of the unconscious, we make passing reference to it. In his study of the unconscious he was too preoccupied with the pathological aspects of cathexis and countercathexis. If we consider the vast and orderly creative function of the causal consciousness, both as an experience of the individual and as part of the collective universal experience in which the individual participates as an integral factor, we shall see the pathological aspect as being a mere trifle, something like a freak of nature. In Western psychology the freakish aspect is highlighted. Volumes are written about it with only scant attention being given to the wonder of wonders which lies hidden within ourselves. This is beautifully stated in the "Patmos" verse already quoted: "But where danger is, there arises salvation also."

It is no wonder the Upanishads describe the mass of consciousness, operating as causal consciousness, as the Lord of all creation. Again, what was quoted in "Patmos" is very relevant: "Near is God, and hard to apprehend."

The state of deep sleep is described in the Upanishads as blissful. When encountering such an assertion, it is likely that we would take it to mean a state wherein our feeling of pleasure is at its maximum. Nothing could be further from the truth. In fact, it cannot be true. To experience pleasure, there must first exist an I-consciousness capable of doing so. In the state of deep sleep there is no I-consciousness to know what is happening. Moreover, nothing is happening.

A happening or event exists within a time span; it is accompanied by a sequential consciousness that is aware of the beginning of the happening, its development, and its final cessation. In the state of deep sleep, no one is aware exactly when he enters it, nor is there awareness of its termination. Our "awareness" of the non-happening is nothing more than a presumption we make upon waking. Because there is no memory of the deep sleep state (how could there be?) it is called a happy state in comparison with the dream state and wakefulness.

If this be the case we have to admit a break in the contiguity of one's personal identity. Do we exist or do we not exist in the state of deep sleep? If we exist, what assurance is there to prove it? How can we prove this mass of consciousness did exist, even though there was no personal awareness of it? This question can be answered, but only by penetrating into a much deeper and more profound aspect of the self expressed in the state of deep sleep itself.

In order to understand this phenomenon we should begin again from the wakeful consciousness. We have already said that the wakeful consciousness is constituted by our impressions of concrete facts. The world of concrete facts, to a very large extent, imposes universally binding laws on physical nature. Even if there were one hundred percent collective popular consent to do so, these laws could not be altered. The laws of thermodynamics, electromagnetism and many others in the physical, chemical, and biological world are precise and categorical. It was from such a world that Lewis Carroll dropped Alice into the bottomless pit where she found the bottle of magic liquid which asked her to drink it. What happened to her is exactly what happens to us when we close our eyes and roll into the mysterious world called sleep. Like Alice, we find ourselves in a new world of freedom. And like her also, we have to surrender a major part of our mind in this state; we are not allowed to make any conscious choices.

Elsewhere we have shown the selective structuralism implied in our conscious perception. In the world of dreams there is also a selective structuralism, but with a difference. There, we ourselves cannot consciously select the themes or factors which are structured into the composition of our dreams. Anything can and does happen, and the logic of the objective world goes by the board. An elephant may walk on its hind legs, shake hands with us, give a lecture on metaphysics, or offer us a cigarette. It would not seem strange or impossible in the dream that all the laws of nature may be set aside.

Dreams liberate us from rigid codes of ethics. All the repressions of apparently moral men are let loose, and everyone enjoys the freedom of being amoral. Strange, hideous, obscene, and excessively cruel aspects of our characters are objectified in dreams. Many saints have lamented this very fact when they view the less pleasant aspects of their dreams from the purity of their waking states.

How can it be possible for a well tutored and disciplined mind to accomodate within itself another sphere with which it is incompatible? Such paradoxes are relevant only when the non-transactional sphere of the mind is dragged into the transactional and judged with the exclusive norms of that region of the mind. There is an epistemological violation involved in such examinations.

Now we have to add the third dimension of mind, which can transcend even the need to have a center of awareness. Nor does it need any orientations of ideas which could be termed units of consciousness.

So far, we have gone from the most horizontal aspect of personal consciousness to its vertical depth. This is not in fact the correct method of Indian psychology. We should begin with the most universal, and we should understand the particular as an integral part of the universal whole. The unconsciousness of deep sleep is not to be taken as one of the three altering states of consciousness. What is present in that particular state called deep sleep is present also when we dream and when we make deliberate transactions in the wakeful state. It is also to be understood as having a peripheral formation which is individualistic, as well as a depth wherein it belongs to the universal mass of consciousness. For these reasons it is called *cetomukha*, "that which has its consciousness everywhere."

When we began the study of the first *darśana* of this series, we attributed the appearance of the world to the universal volition of *parameśvara*. This still holds true. At the universal level of consciousness there is uniformity in its projection. Hence all men are, for example, likely to shout aloud and become bathed in the perspiration of fear if they experience a nightmare. All men recognize the sun to be the sun, a tree to be a tree, and water to be water. No one recognizes the moon to be an orange. There is a huge area of recognition common to all in the collective society. Side by side with our common recognitions we experience our own personal certitude and convictions, together with our individual phobias and manias. Thus, in all states of consciousness, the universal aspect of the mass of consciousness and its individuated aspects exist as a composite whole. Such is our state that we can agree and differ at the same time. Our agreements rest on the projection of the universal that is experienced in and through us; our differences arise when we have individual angles to emphasize. Total agreement is possible when the individual can release himself from the fixations of his locus of awareness. A Guru is sometimes described as *sarvaloka anurūpāya* — one who can enter into complete empathy with all states of everyone, transcending all barriers of convention, tradition, and structural norms.

This is what happens to us each time we go into deep sleep. In that state we have no name or form, neither morality nor immorality, nor are we ignorant or learned. The entire matrix of values and relationships is obliviated, and it is this freedom that is glorified as true bliss. Such a state remains for only a short time. A sleeping pill can help a person transcend the pressures of wakeful life and the ghastly nightmares of the dream, but it cannot change the wakeful and dream worlds one bit. However, there is an all-consuming fire of wisdom that can burn away the seeming transparency of wakefulness, the translucency of the dream, and the opacity of deep sleep. This power of the highest form of wisdom is poetically personified as *tripurāntaka*, "the burner of the three cities." The counterpart of its action is that having once burned away the apparent meaning of these three states, all states are seen as being equally beautiful. It is as if we are witnessing in all states the phenomenal drama of *māyā*. Then we see why *tripurāntaka* is allegorically counterbalanced with *tripurasundari*, "the beautiful one of the three cities."

This fourth state will be described in the next verse. Before going into that, we should understand the person who says "I am ignorant" as having the basic consciousness "I" as the generic experience in the totality of all experiences. The predicate "am ignorant" can mean any one of, or a number of, specific states of ignorance, ranging from the idiotic ignorance of one's inability to understand even simple things to the grand philosophical ignorance which opens the gateway to the floodlight of wisdom. The first card in the greater Arcana of the Tarot is the Fool — the personification of ignorance, one might think. But that Fool is the one who points his finger to indicate the way to his big brother and methodological counterpart, the Magician, who is a wonder unto himself and also to the whole world. This aspect of causal consciousness should be construed as being the specific ground of *kāraṇa bhāna*, the third state of the altering states of consciousness.

VERSE 7

aham brahmeti yadbhānam
tatturīyamiti śamsyate
sāmānyamahamityamśo
brahmetyatra viśiṣyate

"I am the Absolute" — such awareness
is praised as the fourth;
here, the element "I am" is the generic,
and "the Absolute" is the specific.

aham — I am
brahma — the Absolute
yat bhānam — such awareness
śamsyate — is praised
tat turīyam iti — as the fourth
atra — here
amśaḥ — the element
aham — I am
sāmānyam — is the generic
brahma iti — the Absolute is
viśiṣyate — the specific

To say that two plus two equals four could be as incorrect as saying that two plus two equals three; yet it could be correct to say that the sum can be seven, or fifteen, or any other number. Arithmetical integers are only artificially created semantic symbols to be applied in the transactional world for the purpose of categorization and classification. A thing-in-itself is what it is; it is not a mathematical entity. Either there is only a nondifferentiated reality, or every unit is unique — so unique that it cannot be treated as a substitute if all the aspects of its uniqueness are compared and contrasted with those of another. Therefore there are not two and two anywhere, to equal four. Such a statement may seem absurd to those who are familiar with mathematical tools — a familiarity, by the way, which helps to make our everyday life coherent. Without the means to translate the visibles into terms of the calculables, we cannot communicate to another even the simplest of the things and events which enter our lives.

In the present verse we are asked to leave the familiar ground of all cognizable and recognizable forms, names, and ideas. A Guru once asked his disciple to meditate on the world without seeing himself in it. Another Guru advised his disciple to meditate without seeing the world as existing around him. If it were possible to juxtapose both of these meditations simultaneously, what would result is the theme we are discussing here. In the first case the subject is excluded from the context of the meditation. In the second case the object is excluded from the meditation. This is a technique very efficiently used by Zen masters. However, what we are discussing here is not what people arrive at with the aid of techniques. The prop in the previous verse was described as shouting to the unknown for a response, and the response coming from the mysterious depths of the unknown. In the present verse any such kind of bipolarity is given up.

The all-illuminating light emanating from the sun is asked here to recoil upon itself and know that it is light. Rivers flowing into the ocean are directed to return to their sources; the beginning and the end are canceled out. Philosophers attempt to establish the verity of this elusive truth by piling hypothesis upon hypothesis. Yet the experience given to us here is not amenable to the conclusiveness of logic. Here we have to shift our camp from the well-systematized and neatly structured world of the logician to the awesome, silent, and mysterious world of the mystic. And we must do this without losing touch with the plain world of natural common sense.

The fourth state is called the 'witness' of the other three states. If a state is to be witnessed, then the witnessing consciousness should also be present in that state. The consciousness that is present in the wakeful, dream, and deep sleep states cannot be treated as a consciousness separate from those states. It cannot be classified as the fourth in the sense in which the wakeful can be differentiated from the dream state. Even so, the nature of what is termed in this verse as the fourth is at variance with the functional qualities of the other three states. The fourth state is treated therefore as a part and as the whole. It is the whole because it is present in all experiences. It can be termed as a part only for the methodological purpose of contrasting its positive, vertical character with the negativity of deep sleep, and with the horizontality of the dream and wakeful experiences.

In the Bhagavad Gita there are a number of models given of contemplatives of the highest order who are fully established in the Self.[15] The qualities of one who is well-established in the Self are: (1) he is established in the awareness that the world of subjective and objective transactions is formulated by the projection of incipient memories; (2) that these are only negative factors lying buried in the mass of consciousness; and (3) that one returns again and again to that mass of consciousness in deep sleep. Such are the qualities of one who is a *sthitaprajña*, well-established in the Self.

Another model is that of one whose actions are not motivated by any personal gain whatsoever. The good of all beings is recognized as the collective goal of all sentient beings. When all one's thoughts and activities are directed to the actualization of the general good, such a person is freed from the dictates of the social ego. In such a case he attains the status of a man of unitive action, which makes him a *karmayogi*.

There is also the model of one who is overawed by the beauty of this wonderful universe, and overawed, too, by the cosmic phenomena of systems complementing systems and laws regulating laws. In every atom of the universe and in all the coordination of the world order, such a person sees the one supreme God and is overjoyed that he is also a part of that creation. Such a notion restores him to his divine heritage. The result is that he feels in his very being the magnanimous benevolence of his Lord. In every impulse he experiences a divine passion to glorify his Lord through the offering of his personal contribution, however small it might be, in the form of sharing his love with and caring for everyone, and in making himself a divine tool. This makes him a true devotee, or *bhakta*.

In all these models the supreme consciousness is certainly present. As a result, the transactions of the wakeful life and the visions of the dream life become permeated with the beauty, sweetness, fragrance, and inexpressible bliss that truly belong to the Absolute.

In these models the ego center is not surrounded by any thick cloud of socially colored relativistic attachment or hatred. The ego of such people is like a roasted seed which no longer has the potency to germinate. No ego boundary exists to separate the 'I' or 'me' from the 'other'. For such men there is no other; the spirit center is functioning as the ego center. There is, however, the retention of memory for the purpose of orientation. The great love of the Self for itself, or to be more precise, the natural abundance of bliss generated by the union of the existentiality of the persona with the all-pervading awareness of bliss, finds the spirit center to be like a floodgate through which the unlimited joy of the Self can be channeled towards all sentient beings. This naturally assigns to such blessed souls the role of guiding, spiritually nourishing, and ultimately saving whomsoever comes under the influence of their attention.

In Chapter XIII of the Bhagavad Gita, entitled "Unitive Understanding of the Distinction Between the Actual and Perceptual" (*kṣetra kṣetrajña vibhāga yoga*), the following verses are given to describe the state of one who is fully established in the Absolute, *brāhmīsthiti*:

> He who sees the Supreme Lord abiding in (a state of) equality in all beings, within the perishing as the non-perishing, he sees.
>
> For he who sees the Lord seated equally everywhere, destroys not the Self by the Self; and so he attains the Supreme goal.
>
> He who sees that all actions are done by nature alone, and likewise that the Self is actionless, he (truly) sees. (v. 27-29) [16]

In these verses the relative pronoun 'he' is used only for the purpose of communicating the sense of an indescribable experience. In the first verse quoted above the word *parameśvara* is used. We have discussed and amply explained *parameśvara* in the first *darśana* as the ground of the phenomenal world, as well as the manifested elaboration which we empirically experience. The visions of this Absolute as filling the perishable and the imperishable alike are treated here as counterparts to be canceled out in the light of the equality of the projected, the projection, and the projector. When such an impression permeates consciousness, the individual factor has little or no operational significance. Thus, it is not the experience of a person seeing equality, it is a recognition by the author of the equality of beingness. This equality of beingness is present in the immanent world which is of a perishable nature, and in the transcendent which is imperishable. Thus, in *brāhmīsthiti*, the state of being absorbed in the Absolute, there is no *bhāna* or *bhānāśraya*.

The basic consciousness and the ground of basic consciousness are indivisible. Therefore we cannot speak of anything as being general or specific in the state of *brāhmīsthiti*. The word *samam* used in verse 27 above, is of great significance here. In Nataraja Guru's commentary he says:

> The word *samam* (equal), as used here, does not merely imply a horizontal distributive equality of the high principle of the

> Supreme in all entities, which includes animate and inanimate according to the previous verse. According to what was suggested in respect of the two opposing factors, the field and the knower of the field, the word *samam* (equal) indicates an equilibrium between two opposing forces, one tending towards spirit, the other towards nature. [17]

In verse 29 above it is explicitly stated that one who truly sees, sees the Self as actionless. To the view of such a person, all actions are performed by nature alone. From this it is evident that one who has entered into this high state of spiritual absorption does not retain an ego center. He neither acts nor does he react.

In Chapter XIV of the Bhagavad Gita, Arjuna asks Kṛṣṇa, his Lord and Guru, by what signs such a man might be recognized:

> Arjuna said:
> By what marks, O Master, does he who has transcended those three modalities of nature become recognized? What is his conduct and how does he transcend those three modalities of nature?

In answer to this question Kṛṣṇa gives the model of one who has transcended:

> Kṛṣṇa said:
> Light and activity and delusion when present, O Pāṇḍava (Arjuna), he is not dissatisfied, nor hankers for them when absent.
>
> He who, seated as a neutral, is not moved by the modalities of nature; who, thinking that the modalities of nature operate in rotation, who, standing apart, is unmoved;
>
> the same in pain and pleasure, at rest in himself, to whom a clod of earth and a stone and gold are alike; firm in attitude (alike) to loved and unloved; who regards his being blamed or praised equally;
>
> the same in honour and disgrace; taking no sides as between friends or foes, abandoning all initiation of works — he is said to have transcended the modalities of nature (*guṇa*-s).[18]

These verses are self-explanatory. The model described here is of one called a *guṇātīta*. A similar description is given in Chapter XVIII of a sañyasi *par excellence*:

> Becoming the Absolute, blissfully serene in the Self, he neither despairs nor hankers; equal minded towards all beings, he attains a devotion to Me supreme (in character).[19]

The first three models given (XIII, 27-29) describe a knower of the Absolute; the second group (XIV, 21-25) describes a total merging in the beingness of the Absolute. The fourth state of the *bhāna* described in the present chapter has reference to only the first group of models. This is because there is a retention of the center of individuation, at least in principle. This is not present in the second group. Therefore, the fourfold division of basic consciousness, the ground of basic consciousness, the universal references, and the specific references are admissible in the case of the first group.

VERSE 8

yatra bhānam tatra bhāsyam
bhānam yatra na tatra na
bhāsyamityanvayenāpi
vyatirekeṇa bodhyate

Where there is awareness there is an object of awareness;
where there is no awareness there is no object of awareness;
thus, by agreement,
and also by difference, certitude comes.

yatra — where
bhānam — there is awareness
tatra — there
bhāsyam — is an object of awareness
yatra — where
na bhānam — there is no awareness
tatra na bhāsyam — there is no object of awareness
iti — thus
anvayena — by agreement
vyatirekeṇa api — and also by difference
bodhyate — certitude comes

Patañjali speaks of the state of aloneness. Plotinus speaks of the "flight of the alone to the Alone." Gautama Buddha speaks of the dewdrop falling into the lake and losing its identity. Jesus the Christ continually affirms "I am That I am" The Sufi Al Husayn ibn Mansur Hallaj said "Anal Haq" (I am the Absolute Truth). Wherever he looked, St. Francis could see none but Jesus. St. Teresa speaks of consummation with the Divine Spouse in the central chamber of the Interior Castle. Arjuna had a vision of the Absolute as the cosmic Person. St. John of the Cross speaks of the highest state of being at the summit of Mt. Carmel. Of all the great mystics, it was St. John of the cross alone who described that state as "nothing, nothing, nothing — on the Mount also, nothing." Here it is neither the basic consciousness of the subject nor the ground of consciousness that is being illuminated. How many know this is the peak they are looking for?

Even such a great soul as Sri Ramakrishna shuddered at the thought of it. He preferred to live as though a bee sipping at the honey in preference to being drowned in honey. It was not that he did not know the highest state. He knew it indeed, and described it as a doll made of salt diving into the ocean to measure its depth. The hesitation of God-lovers to move into this white heat of realization is humorously described in *The Conference of the Birds* of Attar.

Although this is the highest spiritual truth, all around we see the marketing of aids and techniques which claim to produce it within us. Across the world the whole field of spiritual endeavor is being degraded by the so-called Mahatmas and Yogis. Doubtless we shall soon even have "Mr. Yogi of the Universe" contests, or perhaps a contest to discover the Mahatma with the longest beard. In the U.S., "Wah Guru Chew" is a favorite candy. The truth is not to be found in slick marketing techniques, nor in the fervor of countless devotees seeking to find an antidote to meaningless and mediocre lives. All that these show is our utter ignorance of the spiritual worth of the "nothing, nothing, nothing" that the Masters have been glorifying.

In the *Kaṭha Upaniṣad*, the claim "I have experienced" is said to be merely the prattling of an ignoramus. This is because where there is *bhāna* (basic consciousness) operating as a personal awareness, it is of necessity circumlimited by an object or subject of interest. To that extent it still belongs to the individuated consciousness, which is held together by the mutual coherence of incipient memories. When this last vestige is gone, the individual awareness is gone also.

For methodological purposes the principle of agreement and difference has been elucidated in this verse.

VERSE 9

yathā dṛg dṛśamātmānam
svayamātmā na paśyati
ato na bhāsyate hyātmā
yam paśyati sa bhāsyate

As the eye does not see itself, even so
the Self by the Self; because the Self is not
an object of awareness, what the Self sees —
that indeed is the object of awareness.

yathā — as, even so
dṛg dṛśaṃ svayam na paśyati — the eye does not see itself
ātmānam ātmā — the Self by the Self
ataḥ — because
ātmā — the Self
na bhāsyate — is not an object of awareness
ātmā yam paśyati — what the Self sees
hi — that indeed
sa bhāsyate — is the object of awareness

From the day of our birth our senses are constantly turned towards objects of perception. Most perceptions make a demand on us for an immediate reaction. The mind of a new-born baby is not conceptually equipped to understand the significance of every stimulus. Its actions, therefore, are more or less regulated by the basic instinct of seeking pleasurable stimuli while avoiding painful ones. The actions of a baby may look very simple to us. Opening and closing the mouth, sucking or dribbling, turning the head, reaching with its hands, and kicking or wriggling may all seem simple actions, but they play a vital role in the formulation of concepts. The formulation and structuring of concepts, the perception of values, and the correlation of them with signs and symbols are the activities which keep the child busy until it comes to possess a satisfactory working vision of mind.

Just as the lower animals take the air they breathe for granted, so do we take consciousness for granted. We feel no pressing need to know from where consciousness comes. As we grow older and encounter situations where it is necessary to make precise observations free of any natural fallacies and erroneous vision due to personal defects, we begin to pay some attention to the structure and function of consciousness at the transactional level. This need has created a sound and systematic methodology of science. When mature minds entered this field, it became imperative to withdraw the mind from immediate impressions so that things of like nature could be abstracted and generalized for classification under one head. In this connection, the mind has developed the power of analysis and synthesis to a very high degree. Even so, the mind-stuff that has become expert in what may be called the application of the subjective technology of consciousness has not bothered to find out the nature of itself. Only after big cracks have appeared in the foundations and edifice of the general network based on the concepts of the functional mind in its individual and social aspects, have some adventurous people begun to look into the depths of the mind itself. They have been awed and thrilled to discover that mind has a profound depth, and that behind and beneath it is an unconscious mass. No one has dared to jump into it, but they have stood precariously on the edge and speculated about its nature. The work of such men has given a new dimension to the meaning and significance of dreams. And the majestic edifices of the transactional world have begun to seem unimportant in comparison to the buried cities of man's inner reality. Beyond this point, Western psychologists have not yet dared to go.

After the recent confluence of the minds of East and West, ushered in by the advent of psychedelic drugs and the study of parapsychology, along with a social catharsis in the field of personal freedom and the revaluation of the existential meaning of sex, a new field of psychology has been created in the West. This new school could easily, and to some extent has, introduced into itself the traditional psychology of oriental mysticism. A very great contribution to the understanding of man and his place in the universe is to be found in such places as India, Africa, the Middle East, Persia, China, Japan, and in the lore of the native Americans. Although at present this field is a conglomeration of the promiscuous mixing of many disciplines, the muddy waters will soon settle into a clear fountain. This will be to the advantage of the whole world.

Like the discovery of the awesome truths which only a study of dreams can bring to man, the discovery of the Self will turn our understanding of the world one hundred and eighty degrees from where it stands now. The world of positive transactional significance will be revalued. It will be seen to be a negative shadow. All that has been accumulated for centuries as knowledge will turn out to be mere phantom details of information. What is now thought to be important will be seen as trivial in comparison to the one truth that governs all life.

When this revolution of understanding occurs, we shall find our way into the secret chamber of the programmer of the universe. This reality now hidden behind the passing shadows of the phantom transactional world is called in this verse the Self. The Self is the one seer behind all that is seen, though it sees not itself; the one listener behind all hearing, though it hears not itself; the one knower behind all knowing, though it knows not itself; and the one enjoyer behind all enjoyment, though it enjoys not itself. When the tri-basic error is corrected, the knower and the act of knowing disappear in knowledge, and the enjoyer and enjoyment disappear in a nondifferentiated joy. With this verse the Guru has prepared our minds to go beyond the last frontier in the world of personal awareness.

VERSE 10

yad bhāsyate tad adhyastaṃ-
anadhyastam na bhāsyate
yadadhyastam tadasada-
pyanadhyastam sadeva tat

What is the object of awareness, that is superimposed;
the non-superimposed is not an object of awareness;
what is superimposed, that is unreal;
what is not superimposed — That alone is real.

yat bhāsyate — what is the object of awareness
tat adhyastam — that is superimposed
(*yat*) *anadhyastam* — the non-superimposed
(*tat*) *na bhāsyate* — is not an object of awareness
yat adhyastam — what is superimposed
tat asat — that is unreal
api (*yat*) *anadhyastam* — what is not superimposed
tat eva sat — That alone is real

One man says, "I believe in God because I can conceive the attributes of God given in the scriptures. When I meditate upon and pray to God I have a clear idea of his existence and my relationship with him." Another man says, "I do not believe in God because he is not tangible as is the world of objects. I believe what I can see. I can perceive the world through my senses and understand the qualities of matter with my mind. So I believe only in the material."

From a cursory examination of these two statements it may seem that we are listening to two people in total contradiction to each other. On closer examination we shall find that both are speaking of the validity of impressions. Neither yet knows God; both are enchanted by their own ideas. One is very much impressed by what his mind can conceive in itself, the other by what the mind can perceive through the functions of the senses. The apparent difference between them is really no difference. For each it is only a preference for one experience of mind over another.

The God conceived by the individual mind is a fabricated idea only. It is as much a fabrication of values and their interactions as is a gestalt of mental images deliberately constructed from perceptual data and correlated in terms of associative ideas or objects of interest. In either case there is a subjective factor which separates itself from the 'other', and so giving rise to ignorance and falsehood. We mostly do not believe what is true, but rather what gives us the most satisfaction or comfort. It is always the manufacture of the 'other' which deludes us.

In the above examples, the first case illustrates the 'other' as God; the second replaces God with matter, but the 'other' remains. Whatever is conceived of as 'other' is only a superimposition of a mental image on what is discernible. That is to say, subjective and objective notions are only modifications in consciousness; they have in themselves no validity in an absolute sense. What is thought of as 'God' or as 'not God' is an invention of mankind. And like all inventions, it has a psychological existence; we shall undoubtedly be confronted by the products of our own hypothesizing. But they will turn out to be as ephemeral as our own I-consciousness which created them.

In the two cases given, each person emphasizes what he has perceived or conceived. The references are only to personal ideas concerning the nature of existence, not to Existence as such. Existence does exist as the ground for the projection of all ideas of existence. What is experienced as existence is its many conceptual modifications. Sheer existence is to be known as the Self or Absolute. Hence the Guru says *tadeva sat*, "That alone exists."

From a reading of the previous verse, one might have formed the idea that the Guru was dismissing the existential reality of the Absolute by transcending the ontology of the wakeful, the dream, and deep sleep. Contrary to what might be our expectation, the Guru takes us into the heart of ontology in the next *darśana*. The cryptic formula "That alone exists" is both the precious pendant and the secret key of the entire "Garland of Visions." With this we close this first part of our commentary of Narayana Guru's *Darśanamālā*.

AUM TAT SAT

V. BHĀNA DARŚANAM

[1] Werner Heisenberg, *Physics and Philosophy*, Harper, New York 1962, page 129.
[2] *The Bible*, St. Luke, 11: 11, 12.
[3] Karl Marx, *Kapital*, Charles H. Kerr & Co., Chicago 1906, Pages 41-42.
[4] *Barbon*, 1696
[5] *The Bible*, Deuteronomy 8: 3
[6] Nitya Chaitanya Yati, *Neither This Nor That But Aum*, Vikas, Delhi, page. 160
[7] As quoted by Donald Hatch Andrews in *The Symphony of Life*, Unity Books 1966.
[8] *The Bible*, Psalm 44: 21
[9] ibid. Proverbs 23: 7
[10] ibid. St. Matthew 5: 8
[11] ibid. St. Mark 2: 8
[12] C. G. Jung, *Symbols of Transformation*, Bollingen Series XX, Princeton University Press, 1956, page. 406
[13] ibid. page 407
[14] ibid page. 408
[15] Nataraja Guru, *The Bhagavad Gita*, R & K Publishing House, Delhi, see, Ch.II, 55–72; Ch. IV, 18–24; Ch. V, 23–28; Ch. VI, 27–32; Ch. XII, 12–20; Ch. XIII, 27–32; Ch. XIV, 22–26; and Ch. XVIII, 50–57.
[16] ibid. pages. 566-568
[17] ibid. page 566
[18] ibid. page 590-591

PART TWO

INTRODUCTION TO PART TWO

Science is described as the search for truth. Although the term 'science' nowadays covers a very wide field and an increasing number of specialized disciplines, it can surely be maintained that while some of the activities of science contribute little or nothing directly to the improvement of the quality of life, the best of scientific effort adds much to the general good.

Philosophy is the love or pursuit of wisdom. To love wisdom can be said to be the highest possible ideal. Why should man want to be wise? Of what use is the truth that he seeks? Man searches for happiness — not the transient happiness which is all that most of us ever know, but an abiding, constant, unshakeable state of joy and delight in life which our inner certitude tells us is possible. In this context, of what use is truth if it does not bring us happiness? Why should wisdom be loved and pursued if the effect of its attainment is not happiness?

Truth is not pursued for the sake of truth, nor wisdom for the sake of wisdom. The acquisition of either or both should make our life on earth a better one. The old proverb says, "Necessity is the mother of invention." Necessity is a more direct term than either 'truth' or 'wisdom'. It represents the impelling force welling up from unconscious levels of the psyche that gives man no rest. It is that in man that seeks to be happy, and that which makes him relate himself and his efforts to the pursuit of happiness.

The scientist may be willing to use his knowledge in the forging of tools to minimize the labor of man and to increase his productive capacity. However, as a general rule sentiment is not seen to be a motivating force in science. Sentiment and the search for truth do not usually go hand-in-hand in the scientific field. We can say that science is mindful of the general good and the upliftment of mankind to the extent that it aids man with the applied science of technology. When the scientist disregards the hunger of the human soul for sublime values, he very much limits himself and the scope of his science.

Philosophy also is not without its negative aspects. Sometimes locked securely away in ivory towers, philosophers too become out of touch with the human needs of mankind. The exercise of intellect for its own sake can be a self-satisfying activity: there is a beautiful elegance to a well ordered mind. No one can doubt the powers of high intelligence, nor escape seeing the elite class into which it puts a man.

What we seek should have relevancy to the here-and-now of our immediate life situation. In the experience of our present enjoyment and the vision of a prospective enjoyment, we visualize the state of the good. In other words, we have a comprehension of truth as the good in such experiences. That state which the common man envisions as being good may, in the long run, turn out to be not so. What men usually consider to be good is based on the expedient needs of the individual, not on what is best for the collective society. Thus the necessity arises for a normative notion of what is truly good; that is to say, the good that can ensure its value as the good for all. The good for all and the good which is so at all times is identical with truth. It is in the expression of a general good that truth gains its operational connotation. Truth then ceases to be merely an abstraction or a speculative edifice and becomes a way of life.

Sometimes we are fortunate, and what is presented to our senses and mind enables us to forget the woes of life — at least for a little while. For a time we can stand observing life from a state of wonder and joy. It is then we enjoy the delight and freedom which result from the release of our consciousness from the shackles of the annoying and pestering sense of our ego awareness. At such a time we begin to experience life as beauty; beauty gives another dimension to truth.

The science of philosophy — or the philosophy of science — can become complete in itself only when it can interpret to us that which is truly good, and do this without freezing or mummifying the functional unfoldment of what is experienced as the good when that good enhances the ability of the mind to admire and appreciate beauty in all its richness. So often our scientific masters are happy to condition us to prefer the shadow to the substance. For example, we can now obtain plastic flowers which at first sight exactly mimic those which a garden will give us. It is not that plastic flowers are in themselves evil — nothing is intrinsically so — but they act as one of the innumerable ways in which modern economic structuring separates us from that Nature which is our own nature. Increasingly man is conditioned and manipulated for the sake of business profits to accept the spurious in preference to the real.

In this second part of *Darśanamālā*, Narayana Guru wants to bring us closer than we have ever been to the very source of what is good and beautiful in ourselves. For this purpose he reverses the usual methodology of the search for truth by exhorting us to grapple directly with the original cause. In doing so (and if we can follow him far enough) we shall find that the original cause will ultimately prove to be the final cause also.

We can see a similar exhortation in the teachings of Jesus. Christianity is the plant which has sprouted from the good seed of the benevolent life of Jesus. He exhorted all men of his day to be good and to do good. We note particularly that "he taught them as one having authority." (Matthew, 7:29).[1] Jesus lived his own life as a divine flower of eternal beauty. After the Church which bears his name became institutionalized, it lost much of this aspect of the Master's teaching — the emphasis he laid on a life of the good and the beautiful.

Despite the cruel bigotry of the Christian Church and its lapse into the mundane, by no means do all the best members of it fully subscribe to its mediocrity. Some Schoolmen and several mystics turned to the ideas of the good and the beautiful found in the writings of Plato, Julian the Apostate, and Plotinus. Some of the later mystics such as St. Theresa of Avila, St. John of the Cross, St. Francis of Assisi, and Meister Eckhart were to suffer severe persecution from the very Church of which they were the most glorious flowers. They brought to the Christian life a fresh legacy of how to live the good in the most beautiful manner. What is true in any religion is true in all. The Christian mystical notion of life, light and love is identical in meaning with the Vedāntic notion of *sat-cit-ānanda*.

The first *darśana* to come in this second part of the *Darśanamālā* is called the "Unitive Vision of Action." In Sanskrit, action is called *karma*. Action has a gross aspect, and gross action is considered to be an evil. There are obvious and practical reasons for this viewpoint. Gross action takes place in the objective world of cause and effect. It initiates a chain of reaction which may reach far into the future, and which may indeed ensure a "future" at the objective level of pain and misery which might not otherwise have eventuated. Thus the agent of gross action finds himself caught in a structure of obligations and forced to respond to the inevitable consequences of his actions. In short, the performance of gross action guarantees the continuing lack of freedom for man.

Unlike theoretical knowledge of some prospective state (such as the promise of a future kingdom of God) action belongs to the immediate present. Every form of transaction in our transactional world has within it the dynamics of action. The existential verity of such action is irrefutable. Action is not something that happens in the fanciful world of a dreamer's imagination. It has an immediate impact on the present. And it has the power to transmute the potentials of the future so that these become experiential facts of the present. Thus action has a solid basis in the ontological world of existence. This we have already termed as *sat*.

The Vedāntic concept of the Absolute is contained in the phrase *sat-cit-ānanda*. The most primary fact in this is *sat*. In the vision of action which follows as the sixth in the series of the *Darśanamālā*, Narayana Guru is going to relate *karma* directly to the primordial existential aspect of the Absolute.

INTRODUCTION TO PART TWO

1 *The Bible*, St Mattews 7: 29

VI. KARMA DARŚANAM

Cosmo-Psychological Functionalism

Human experience is representative of what is presented to the person as a whole. The cognitive, conative, and affective consciousness functions like a unique mirror with a mysterious and inestimable power to interpret all cognizable items of experience in terms of an intelligible predication of each and every subject presented to it. What is presented is the cosmological phenomena, and the same is mirrored or reflected in the psyche of every individual who is organically related to the same cosmologic matrix. Whatever is the actual state of the presented object, and however independent it is in its substance, the only way it can be mirrored is as an image of consciousness.

This can be illustrated with a crude example. If a mirror is held up to an object there will be a corresponding reflection of the object in the mirror. If the mirror is colored, the reflection will also be colored. If the mirror has a concave surface, the image looks enlarged; and if it is convex, the image looks shrunken. However, there will be a general similarity between the various images. In spite of the differences, there is a unanimity in all the items of correspondence. If we have several mirrors, mirroring the universe from all possible angles, we cannot say which reflection gives the most perfect image. However distorted each item looks in individual mirrors, on the whole there exists a collective image of the cosmic phenomena psychically reflected.

These reflections are not of 'stills' or static bodies, but of an unceasing process of flux. Therefore every represented image is to be interpreted in a manner and language with which the individuated mind is most familiar. Man acts and reacts, or so he universally thinks, and therefore it is only natural that man understands all perceived changes in terms of action and reaction, cause and consequences. When the presented phenomenon is commented upon, two major errors are unconsciously committed. The commentator forgets that he or she is only describing the representative image and has no access to the original. Further, the verbalism involved in cogitation restricts the expression to a conceptual level which is entirely the product of the culture of human intelligence. In other words, every experience is a confection of the observer and the observed. Summing it all up, the world of phenomenal becoming consciously perceived and appreciated is a cosmo-psychological function.

VERSE 1

ātmaiva māyayā karma-
karoti bahurūpadhṛk
asaṅgaḥ svaprakāśo'pi
nidrāyāmiva taijasaḥ

The Self alone, through *māyā*, does
action by assuming many forms,
though detached and self-luminous,
like the *taijasa* in sleep.

ātma eva — the Self alone
māyayā — through *māyā*
karma karoti — does action
bahurupadhṛk — by assuming many forms
api asaṅgaḥ — though detached
svaprakāśaḥ — and self-luminuous
nidrāyāmiva taijasaḥ — like the *taijasa* in sleep

In the four altering states of consciousness, the fourth, which is called *turīya*, has no limitations of time and space. Truly and substantially there is no difference between the fourth state of one individual and the fourth state of another. In other words, it is the exact opposite and perfect counterpart of our unified conceptual notion of matter. We can qualify it as the pure spirit or pure consciousness or the undifferentiated substance of pure awareness. It can remain at the level of the unconscious, and can become manifested at different levels, such as the repository of all dormant memories, or at the level of lending its awareness to incipient memories to formulate the several imageries that constitute the world of dreams, or at the level of the clearly demarcated I-consciousness with the coloration of a social ego and the awareness of a self identity with which it can get into various kinds of polarization with whatever is postulated as the other or the non-self. Thus, the concept of altering states of consciousness, when viewed from the fourth to the first, will structurally resemble a broad-based cone, tapering to and culminating in the pinpoint of an I-consciousness of the wakeful world of individual transaction. We have to interlace this structural image of consciousness with another broad cone which has for its base the awareness of the physical universe of the wakeful state, tapering into the depth of pure consciousness where the apex of the cone vanishes into the infinitude of pure consciousness.

In the present *darśana* we are dealing with the notion of action as it manifests in a cosmic manner as well as that action deliberated by an individual. We have already said in our introduction that from here on we have a reversal in the methodology of our presentation. The action-reaction theme is studied by philosophers and scientists at the surface level where one can observe forms of activity such as attraction and repulsion. Both physicists and philosophers have tried various explanations to account for the world of flux, which bristles with all kinds of conjunctions and disjunctions, integrations and disintegrations, and formations of compounds of all sorts. But here Guru is asking us to look at the entire field of action from the side of what is termed as the fourth, instead of looking at it from what is described as the wakeful consciousness of the individual who is confronted with the otherness of a vision of the universe which stands in contrast to the subjective consciousness of the "I" as its irrefutable, objective world.

Here we are facing a paradox of the worst sort. From the description of the fourth which is given in the *Bhāna Darśana*, there is no likelihood of it ever becoming interested in causing anything which has the quality of the other or the non-Self. It is free of the duality of the world of cause and effect. We have also made a summary dismissal of the wakeful world of phenomenal forms and names as the potential causal factor, because they are only the consequential resultant of some other causal factor. Thus spirit as the basis and matter as the basis are both discredited from being instrumental in making action of any sort. Here we naturally are led into an area where the two above mentioned structural cones of consciousness interlace or interlock. We have diagramed this idea on the next page.

The figure shown has one disadvantage: an ever-moving scheme cannot be represented by a static figure. The pure consciousness given as the fourth itself is to be alternated in our mind as playing the roles of both alpha and omega. This we cannot illustrate with a figure. Neither is it possible to show how a vertical principle manifests itself infinitely and incessantly into the horizontal dimensions of subjective mental images and objective concrete factors. This seemingly contradictory happening within the range of our total consciousness cannot be adequately described by any term other than *māyā*. In the present context, *māyā* stands for the mystery

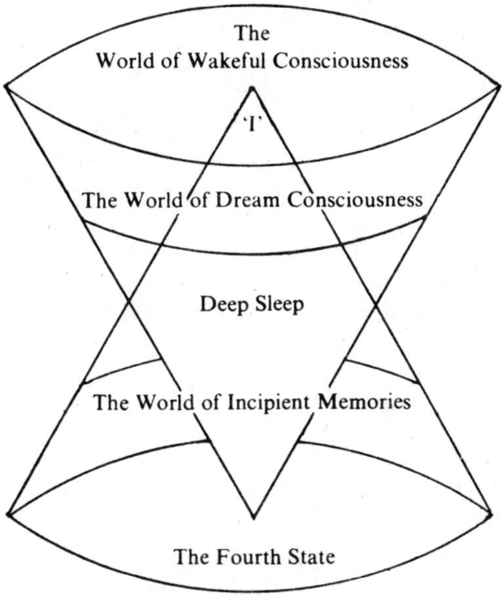

of both being existent and nonexistent at the same time, giving possibilities of being viewed diversely. The area where we locate *māyā* is in what is shown in the above figure as incipient memories. The world of incipient memories has in it the admixture of the personal incipient memories of the individuated consciousness and the universal potentialities which we have dealt with in the earlier chapters of the book. This is somewhat akin to the confluence of the two worlds of the archetypes of the personal unconscious and of the collective unconscious of which Jung speaks.

The pure Self in the present verse is compared to the sky and the sun. The sky is the universal concept of the void. When the Buddhist school of Nihilism compares nirvana to the great void, *śūnyata*, it agrees with the Vedāntin's concept of the nonqualitative Absolute, the *nirguṇa*. It has no function. The second analogy given is of the sun. The sun has no motivation. It simply radiates its effulgence. Yet as far as we are concerned so many things are caused by the sheer presence of the sun, such as the formation of the planets, their motions, the earth becoming habitable, and the solar energy and moisture getting into various kinds of alchemy to produce life of all sorts on this planet. In the same way, the mere presence of the Self initiates many actions without taking upon itself the agency of action. This will be further elucidated in the next verse.

VERSE 2

manye, vadāmi, gṛhṇāmi,
śruṇomītyādi rūpataḥ
kriyate karma paramā-
tmanā cittendriyātmanā

I think, I speak, I grasp, I hear —
all such forms of action are done
by the Supreme Self
through the agency of consciousness and the *indriya*-s.

manye — I think
vadāmi — I speak
gṛhṇāmi — I grasp
śruṇomi — I hear
ityādi rūpataḥ — all such forms
kriyate karma — of action are done
paramātmanā — by the Supreme Self
cittendriyātmanā — through the agency of consciousness and the *indriya*-s

We are not tired of calling the attention of the reader to the fact that this is not a book to discuss hydraulics, thermodynamics, or electromagnetism. We have to keep before our mind the purpose of our pursuit: discovering our lost treasure of happiness. From the study of earlier chapters we now know at least vaguely that returning to the Self in its purest form is the sure path of regaining our happiness. What seems to obstruct our path is the continuous hindrance caused by unavoidable propensities that make us act or react. The point where action ceases altogether is described by the Buddha as nirvana, *nibbāna*. Some of his disciples have even gone to the extent of describing nirvana as nothingness or the pure void. According to the riṣis of the Upanishads, the transcendence of all action as well as the causal urges to act is *mokṣa*. *Mokṣa* is not equated with nothingness or the void. It is the rediscovery of beingness. In this context beingness is equated with the Absolute. Three ways of understanding the Absolute are: the recognition of the irrefutability of the existence of beingness; the appreciation of the intensive and the extensive possibilities in terms of awareness; and the meaning of appreciation centering around a value stemming from an unalloyed state.

In the present verse Narayana Guru carefully uses the term *cittendriyātmanā*, which we have translated as 'the agency of consciousness and the *indriya*-s (senses)', as an instrument of the Supreme Self, or *paramātma*. It is only after bracketing these two terms that he attributes action to the Self. Nataraja Guru, in his exhaustive commentary on *Darśanamālā*, reminds us that in this chapter we are relating the Self to the non-Self, rather than the non-Self to the Self.

To have a correct perspective of our immediate problem, we call the reader's attention to the figure of two interlocking cones given in the previous verse commentary. In the cone which has the base below and the apex above we have already pointed out that there is no action happening at the base. It is only at the apex, where the I-consciousness is functioning at its gross physical level, fully aided by the senses and the mind, that we act and react. For the sake of clarity let us repeat our problem in more specific terms. How can the base, devoid of any urge, prompting, desire, or latent possibility of action, remain ever unrelated to the perceiving mind and the organs of action when they are dependent factors on this one basis, without which nothing can exist? To get a complete picture of the situation, let us draw our attention to the cone in the figure which is drawn with its base at the top and its apex resting on the base of the other cone. In this particular cone the base represents the cosmic phenomena of change and becoming. Here each individual has a separate existential status. This is the world of transaction. It is here we see people roaring with laughter and weeping with bitter tears. All the snares and treacheries of life are experienced here. Action looms large in this sphere. That is why it has become imperative on our path to question the origin, nature, consequences, and meaning of action.

If we take separate individuals only as bodies, we are confronted with a problem which Dewey rightly put when he asked, "How does a body understand another body and make itself understood to the other?" This riddle can be solved only by tracing the common source of all bodies to one unified or unitive reality or beingness. This explains the interlacing of the two representative cones in our figure. The mind that reasons, the senses that perceive, and the organs that act are all to be animated by consciousness. Pure consciousness in Sanskrit is called *cit*. However pure it is when it lends itself as the only existential reality that can give meaning to mental or sensual operations, it is bound to be delimited and stained with the triple modalities of nature: transparency, translucency, and opacity. As a result, the awareness becomes either a positive recognition of a partial manifestation of happiness, or the denial of this positive value in a given context in which an individuated organism is coming into relation or encounter with other forms of specific manifestations of like or unlike species or order.

Now it is clear to us that the dependent factors cannot be treated separately, nor can we look for a cause of action as originating from that sphere alone. Such being the case, the Absolute Self should be looked upon as the sole ground of action, at least in principle. Yet we know that this pure ground is devoid of any sense of agency. Still, individuation arises from it; and the reasoning self cannot function without deriving its reality from it. All actions of the individual are interactions between the modes that arise in the process of manifestation. As the Absolute Self is not directly known to the self as an item of awareness, the reasoning self goes on taking upon itself all agency of action until the psychophysical embodiment of the individual falls apart as a demolished instrument.

The relation between the pure Self and the self that animates the individual is further examined in the next verse.

VERSE 3

ātmaiva karmaṇaḥ pūrva-
manyat kiñcinna vidyate
tataḥ svenaiva karmāṇi
kriyante nija māyayā

Prior to action the Self alone is;
nothing else is known;
therefore, actions are done
by itself with its own *māyā*.

karmaṇaḥ pūrvam — prior to action
ātmaiva — the Self alone is
anyat kiñcit na vidyate — nothing else is known
tataḥ — therefore
karmāṇi kriyante — actions are done
svena eva nija māyayā — by itself with its own *māyā*

There is an interesting symbolic account in the *Aitareya Upaniṣad* which describes how the primeval Self created the four worlds, the cosmic person, and cosmic powers:

1. In the beginning, Ātma, verily, one only, was here — no other winking thing whatever. He bethought himself: "Let me now create worlds."
2. He created these worlds: water (*ambhas*), light-rays (*marīci*), death (*mara*), the waters (*ap*). Yon is the water, above the heaven; the heaven is its support. The light-rays are the atmosphere; death, the earth; what is underneath, the waters.
3. He bethought himself: "Here now are worlds. Let me now create world-guardians." Right (*eva*) from the waters he drew forth and shaped (*mūrch*) a person.
4. Upon him he brooded (*abhi* + *tap*).
   When he had been brooded upon, his mouth was separated out,
   egg-like; from the mouth, speech (*vāc*); from speech, Agni (Fire).
   Nostrils were separated out; from the nostrils, breath (*prāṇa*); from breath, Vāyu (Wind).
   Eyes were separated out; from the eyes, sight (*cakśus*); from sight, Āditya (the Sun).

Ears were separated out; from the ears, hearing (*śrotra*); from hearing, the quarters of heaven.
Skin was separated out; from the skin, hairs; from the hairs, plants and trees.
A heart was separated out; from the heart, mind (*manas*); from mind the moon.
A navel was separated out; from the navel, the out-breath (*apāna*); from the out-breath, death (*mṛtyu*).
A virile member was separated out; from the virile member, semen; from the semen, water (*ap*).[1]

We get a similar version of the creation of the manifold world from the Unitary Soul in the *Bṛhadāraṇyaka Upaniṣad*:

1. In the beginning this world was Soul (*ātma*) alone in the form of a Person. Looking around, he saw nothing else than himself. He said first: "I am." Thence arose the name "I". Therefore even today, when one is addressed, he says first just "It is I" and then speaks whatever name he has. Since before (*pūrva*) all this world he burned up (*uṣ*) all evils, therefore he is a person (*pur-uṣ-a*). He who knows this, verily, burns up him who desires to be ahead of him.
2. He was afraid. Therefore one who is alone is afraid. This one then thought to himself: "Since there is nothing else than myself, of what am I afraid?" Thereupon, verily, his fear departed, for of what should he have been afraid? Assuredly it is from a second that fear arises.
3. Verily, he had no delight. Therefore one alone has no delight. He desired a second. He was, indeed, as large as a woman and a man closely embraced. He caused that self to fall (*pat*) into two pieces. Therefrom arose a husband (*pati*) and a wife (*patni*). Therefore this (is true): "Oneself (*sva*) is like a half-fragment," as Yajñavalkya used to say. Therefore this space is filled by a wife. He copulated with her. Therefrom human beings were produced. . . . . .
7. Verily, at that time the world was undifferentiated. It became differentiated just by name and form, as the saying is: "He has such a name, such a form." Even today this world is differentiated just by name and form as the saying is: 'He has such a name, such a form.' He entered in here, even to the fingernail-tips, as a razor would be hidden in a razor-case, or a fire in a fire-holder. Him they see not, for (as seen) he is incomplete. When breathing, he becomes breath (*prāṇa*)

> by name; when speaking, voice; when seeing, the eye; when hearing, the ear; when thinking, the mind; these are merely the names of his acts. Whoever worships one or another of these — he knows not; for he is incomplete with one or another of these. One should worship with the thought that he is just one's self (*ātma*), for therein all these become one. That same thing, namely, this self, is the trace (*padanīya*) of this All, for by it one knows this All. Just as, verily, one might find by a footprint (*pada*), thus — He finds fame and praise who knows this.[2]

From these two accounts of creation it is not difficult to see that the unmanifested primeval Self itself is the manifested world. The idea of a Supreme Person creating the cosmos from out of Himself is not confined to the Upanishads. (Genesis from the Bible is another example). The cosmic world that is spoken of here should be understood in terms of the self-created worlds of our own interests, which primarily arise from the I-consciousness. The I-consciousness we speak of here is not to be taken as the personal, individuated 'I'. The reader should refer again to the figure in verse one. There the I-consciousness meant here is indicated by the apex of the inverted cone where it penetrates the base of the upright cone. This 'I' may be understood as that which impels the non-differentiated Absolute to manifest itself as the multitudinous universes. It can be equated with the 'will' of God in Christian terminology, though we should remember that any term of division is purely a semantic convenience. The truth is that the consciousness which creates universes from out of itself is whole and complete. What is created is a projection of its own self. The apparent 'otherness' of the creator arises from ignorance and fear. The 'creator' and the 'created' are one and the same thing. This is described with great clarity in verse seven of the *Bṛhadāraṇyaka Upaniṣad* previously quoted. It is we who are the Divine, expressed as both created form and ongoing creative activity. The Self is our own Self.

The seers of the Upanishads have a down-to-earth and matter of-fact attitude when they consider the basic interests, moods, and urges which impel a person to action. The fear of loneliness, the need for delight, the search for companionship, and the emotional and physical intercourse between husband and wife — all these factors and more are not ignored as being outside the scope of spiritual wisdom. The wisdom of the Upanishads firmly rests on the existential factors in daily life, but at the same time the ultimate goal of human life is not forgotton. That goal is the discovery of the Paramount Person (*puruṣottama*), hiding in all and behind everything as the totality of experience.

There is a magical quality in life. We can see it in the mysterious changes of moods, in the sudden birth of new interests and in their often equally sudden vanishing, and in the surging up of unexpected situations. All these can fill us with a sense of wonder, or one of tragic and disastrous catastrophe. This evasive, magical element that enters into consciousness, and which assigns name and form to everything, accounts for the experiencing of our world of varying interests. It is not we who experience anything — all is the experience of the Paramount Person, including its experience of itself as the individuated beings we call 'ourselves'. The magical element is an intrinsic feature of the action-reaction complex in which the individual self becomes almost inextricably tangled. Under the heading "The miserable condition of the individual soul," the *Maitri Upaniṣad* puts it this way:

> 2. Now, it has elsewhere been said: "Like the waves in great rivers, there is no turning back of that which has previously been done. Like the ocean tide, hard to keep back is the approach of one's death. Like a lame man — bound with the fetters made of the fruit of good and evil (*sad-asad*); like the condition of one in prison — lacking independence; like the condition of one in the realm of death — in a condition of great fear; like one intoxicated with liquor — intoxicated with delusion (*moha*); like one bitten by a great snake — bitten by objects of sense; like gross darkness — the darkness of passion; like jugglery (*indrajāla*) — consisting of illusion (*māyā-māyā*); like a dream — falsely apparent; like the pith of a banana tree — unsubstantial; like an actor — in temporary dress; like a painted scene — falsely delighting the mind."
>
> Moreover it has been said:
>
> Objects of sound and touch and sense
> Are worthless objects in a man.
> Yet the elemental soul through attachment to them
> Remembers not the highest place.[3]

In the *Bṛhadāraṇyaka Upaniṣad* (fourth Brāhmaṇa: 4) all

actions are traced to the Supreme Self. This body, these senses, and this mind serve only as an instrument belonging to the Self. In the quotation above, death is mentioned only as a gathering together of all the manifested faculties for a final abstraction of them, so that again as an integrated unit they can be reincarnated in another physical form. The Upanishad says:

3. Now as a caterpillar, when it has come to the end of a blade of grass, in taking the next step draws itself together towards it, just so this soul in taking the next step strikes down this body, dispels its ignorance, and draws itself together (for making the transition).
5. Verily, this soul is Brahma, made of knowledge, of mind, of breath, of seeing, of hearing, of earth, of water, of wind, of space, of energy and of non-energy, of desire and non-desire, of anger and non-anger, of virtuousness and of non-virtuousness. It is made of everything. This is what is meant by the saying "made of this, made of that."

The cycle of action is described as follows:

6. On this point there is this verse: —

> Where one's mind is attached — the inner self
> goes thereto with action, being attached to it alone.
> Obtaining the end of his action
> Whatever he does in this world,
> He comes again from that world
> To this world of action.
> — So the man who desires.[4]

From all the above teachings of the relation between action, the individuated self, and the Supreme Self we get a clear picture of the meaning of the verse now under discussion. It should be clear now what we meant when we said that man is not what he thinks he is. And clear also on what man should do to find the lasting happiness he seeks. Nothing stands between man and the truth that is bliss — except his wrong notions concerning his own nature and an incorrect polarization of interest.

In the next verse Narayana Guru describes the link between the individuated self and the universal Self.

VERSE 4

śaktirastyātmanaḥ kāci-
ddurghaṭā na pṛthak svataḥ
tayaivāropyate karma
nikhilam niṣkriyātmani

The Self has some kind of power,
inseparable from it, difficult to define;
by that alone all actions are
projected in the actionless Self.

ātmanaḥ — the Self
śaktirasti — has some kind of power
na pṛthak svataḥ — inseparable from it
kācid durghaṭā — difficult to define
tayā eva — by that alone
nikhilam karma — all actions
āropyate — are projected
niṣkriyātmani — in the actionless Self

In the context of Vedānta, the worst paradox to which a person is exposed is when he is asked to postulate realities, the nature of which are opposed to his daily experience, and when he is asked to consider what is already known to him — and held by him to be self-evident truth — as ignorance. Moreover, he is asked to seek after and experience as the only true knowledge that which now eludes his knowledge or experience. Man has a physical body equipped with sensory organs and a mind. Each of these faculties has its own field of experience.

The mind is capable of feeling, reasoning, and willing. If feeling is taken as our example, we know it to be a response to a given experience, itself experienced as pleasure or pain. For the most part we seek what gives pleasure and try to avoid what gives pain. Thus we are motivated in an attempt to construct situations giving rise to a pleasurable feeling and to avoid occasions which may bring painful or threatening experiences. All our behavioral patterns are centered around one motivation or another, and the nucleus of every motivation is formed in the depths of our feelings. In most cases such motivation (sponsored by feeling) has little or no relation to the rational faculty of the mind. Usually experiences are self-related. We say, "I am happy," "I am unhappy," "I am angry," "I am elated," and so on. In every instance there is an unmistakeable identity of the quality which is the I-consciousness with that quality of the particular feeling that is predicated on a given experience. In other words, experience is not thought of as belonging to the non-self. Whatever may be the experience, it is always considered to be an intimate event, happening within the self.

The faculty of reason is used by most of us in the formulation or the attempted formulation of precise judgements. This faculty relies greatly on its capacity to detach itself from the irrationality of emotional urges, and to make itself follow as closely as possible the laws of logically structured argumentation. Logic and mathematics are considered by most to be natural forms of the finest expression of the reasoning faculty. What is called 'science' today is very much a product of logical and mathematical reasoning. Science seeks certitude, and bases that certitude on evidence. But the highest form of evidence is always that which is self-evident. In the case of science, self-evidence is not confined to the logical sufficiency that may be experienced by one person; it is taken to be that seen as self-evident by all whose minds are logically disciplined.

The third faculty of mind is that of willing. The evocation of every feeling and the rational conclusion reached in every instance of judgement affects the whole person. Decision follows the arousal of each feeling and the structuring of every judgement arrived at by the process of reasoning. The outcome of decision is resolution — the making of a resolution to act or not to act. Between the choices of action or nonaction lie a wide range of possibilities available to help in the decision as to what the mode of action shall be. Both feeling and reasoning enter into the decision-making situation by altering the proportions of their confluence. Either feeling or reason may choose to remain in abeyance in a given situation, while action of any kind may be postponed if feeling and reason are at loggerheads.

Almost all the transactions of our lives are structured and modified by the three aspects of mind: feeling, reasoning, and willing. In the expression of all or any aspect, the I-consciousness assumes the roles of agency — such as those of the enjoyer, the knower, and the actor. It becomes a case of "I am the enjoyer," I am the knower," and "I am the actor." For most of us these are perfectly valid assumptions, but in Vedānta any such identifications are looked upon as mistaken identities of the self. Such a view is likely to confuse the reader.

It is said that the true Self has an existence that does not undergo change. Such a view does not tally with the experience of beingness of a person suffering the vicissitudes of birth, growth, change, decay and death. What is considered by most to be existential is treated by the Vedāntin as an illusory experience of existence — as being not real existence. So it is that Vedānta asks us to turn away from nonexistence to existence. The true Self is defined as pure consciousness. When consciousness is mentioned, what usually comes to mind is the awareness of knowing things, people, events or ideas. Knowledge is not normally available to us without the dichotomy of the knower and the known, or so we believe. The Vedāntin rejects such a view as nonsense. To him all are the effects of the modulations of consciousness, and as such are only appearances. At this point one may feel a sense of despair because the majority do not understand "what is pure knowledge" without dividing the conscious experience into the knower, knowledge, and the known. Thus we can see that our commonly held notions concerning existence and knowledge are not only challenged but are rejected by the Vedāntin as being of little consequence when it comes to being truthful or knowing truth.

When we come to that experience which is recognized as happiness, we see it as being in opposition to what is experienced as pain. In the *Kauṣitaki Upaniṣad* both pain and pleasure are considered to belong to the body. In that Upanishad even the experiences of bliss, of delight, and of procreation are considered to be generated by the organ of procreation. Such experiences are not the *ānanda* that the Vedāntin speaks of. Thus, in Vedānta the whole concept of self is questioned and contradicted at one and the same time. The Vedāntin emphatically upholds the reality of the Self as one without a second. If there be nothing other than the Self, then all that we experience should belong to that Self. If that is so, there cannot be any power existing outside of the Self which can generate feeling, reasoning, or willing.

If we take the two sides of this question together we are confronted by a paradox which is inherent within the nature of the Self. That is, the Self is capable of producing a state of duality: that of the Self and the non-Self. Moreover, it can within itself cause the illusion of mistaking the attributes of the non-Self for those of the Self. At the empirical level this is an insurmountable paradox. The Guru calls it *durghaṭā*. The literal meaning of this term is 'something of incomprehensible structure'. If the structure of a thing is not known, we are at a loss to understand the exact nature of its function. Be this as it may, we need to free ourselves from the enigma if we are finally to achieve emancipation from the riddles of life. In the next verse the Guru discusses the possibility of doing this.

VERSE 5

sarvadā'saṅga evātmā-
jñatayā karma saṅgivat
karoti na karomīti
na jñaḥ karmasu sajjate

The Self is always detached alone;
by ignorance action is done as if attached;
"I am not acting" — thus,
the seer remains detached in action,

ātma — the Self
sarvadā'saṅga — is always detached
eva — alone
ajñatayā — by ignorance
karma karoti — action is done
saṅgivat — as if attached
na karomi — I am not acting
iti — thus
jñaḥ — the seer
na sajjate — remains detached
karmasu — in action

Mankind is composed of individuals. The problems of a man are the problems of an individual who has to relate himself with other individuals within the framework of a structured society. He also has to cope with the rigors of nature when it is malevolent, and channel to his advantage the resources of nature to maintain his life on earth. Obviously, great demands are made on man by these circumstantial factors. The further demands made by his own personal urges and needs are no less powerful as they impel him to action. It is a matter of daily experience that the action-reaction situations in which he finds himself bring him to various states and shadings of emotion. Some of these emotional impacts on the organism tend toward being pathologically compulsive and inhibitory. How can we deny these as being of no consequence or suggest that they do not affect the personal awareness of an individual? It cannot be denied that they do indeed have an effect. In this verse the seeming affectivity of the individual self is attributed to ignorance.

When we generalize the term 'ignorance', it may seem as though it is an entity standing apart on its own. Is there anything existing anywhere to which we can give the name 'ignorance', except the malfunctioning of our reason, the instability of our emotional states, or the making of wrong decisions which are not fully supported by logical and ethical data? The answer is an emphatic no. If it is true that ignorance is a malfunction within an individual's range of consciousness, how can we say that it does not affect the individuated self?

Let us take an example in which some individual feels the pinch of emotional affliction or irrational addiction. Let us suppose that 'x' falls in love with 'y'. In this state 'x' will see many virtues in 'y' which will stimulate him to take the initiative to do many things to please 'y'. The days and nights of 'x' will be filled with emotional excitement and anticipation. His mind will be in a condition of fantasizing, which will seem to him to be sound reasoning and planning. Despite his condition, 'x' knows the value of consistency and will resolve to act with a calm firmness, even in regard to circumstances beyond his capacity to control. Everything about 'y' will be full of meaning for 'x'. His chief feelings will be of care, sympathy, and love. No matter what the situation is, he will believe his feelings to be reciprocated by 'y'. In short, 'x' is in a state of infatuation with 'y'.

Then, for some reason unknown to him, 'x' begins to experience a cooling attitude emanating from 'y'. Fear sets in. He becomes increasingly apprehensive, lonely, estranged, deceived, unwanted, and finally discarded. All through the affair the emotions of 'x' were aroused. In effect he was saying, "I am excited, I'm inspired, I'm floating on air. Now things are changing. I don't understand; I'm hurt, I've been betrayed." So it often goes. Despite the ferment of arousal that once enveloped 'x', after some time 'y' will become just a memory, a thing of the past, a nobody. Then what happens in the life of 'y' is of no concern to 'x'.

If the earlier experiences had truly belonged to the 'I' self, they, or at least the feelings connected with them, should have persisted. But the 'I' that is the man 'x' continues just as it was prior to knowing 'y'. After regaining the neutrality of the self, 'x' may dismiss the whole episode from his mind as being one of the hangups of immaturity. When Narayana Guru says it is through ignorance one thinks the self to be afflicted, we should understand it in this sense.

As a further example let us take a man who very much relishes a certain kind of food. The food may be spicy, rich, flavorsome, and so on. For some time the gourmet is able to continue to make and enjoy his favorite dishes. Then his physical system becomes damaged in some way and he is forced to consult a physician. Dispassionately the physician advises him to change his diet, and forbids him to eat his favorite foods. This is a hard blow for one who enjoys food, and at first he may revile his doctor as a sadist who enjoys denying him the joy of his life. The patient may vehemently defend his eating habits, findings many arguments he thinks will prove the doctor to be unimaginative and wrong in treatment and prognosis. Finally he succumbs to the pressure and changes his diet. His health greatly improves, and, now convinced of the value of his new diet, he becomes a fervent protagonist of it. Now he looks upon those who revel in the enjoyment of rich and spicy foods as being ignorant and intractible. In this case also we see that the self has no continuing preferences. In an earlier verse the Guru spoke of a blind spot in the self — the structure of which is not known to us. The individual mind is very much influenced and overshadowed by this blind spot.

In psychoanalysis the analyst attempts to show his patient that a mistaken notion has germinated in the patient's psyche, a notion capable of generating a neurotic or psychotic syndrome, a foreign element that has found a place for itself in the psyche. The recognition of this alien factor that previously lay hidden from conscious awareness in the patient's mind often brings a full recovery from his illness. In the same manner, an ignorant person can recognize the possibility that the erring mind can lead the I-consciousness far from its own natural neutrality. Then automatically comes the realization of the oneness of the individual self with the universal Self.

We have still not accounted for action yet. The Guru wants to show us that individual action is part and parcel of cosmic action. In the next verse he will tell us how cosmic action is actionless action, having no actor behind it.

VERSE 6

jvalati jvalano vāyur-
vāti varṣati vāridaḥ
dharātmā san dharati kha-
lveko vahati vāhinī

The one Self alone
burns as fire, blows as wind,
showers as rain, supports
as earth, and flows as river.

ekaḥ khalu — the one Self alone
jvalanaḥ (*san*) *jvalati* — burns as fire
vāyuḥ (*san*) *vāti* — blows as wind
vāridaḥ (*san*) *varṣati* — showers as rain
dharātmā san dharati — supports as earth
vāhini (*san*) *vahati* — flows as river

The Self is equated with the meaning or value (*ānanda*) of existence (*sat*) that operates within the wide field of consciousness (*cit*). What we term here as 'consciousness' ranges from the infinitude of the unconscious to the finitude of conscious awareness. In the field of awareness there is an area, or the possibility of a quality of awareness, that can be called pure (*turīya*). In this quality of awareness no duality or possibility of duality exists; the dichotomy of subject and object is not present. In addition there is a vast area of subjective awareness which includes within its field the dream state. Finally there is that kind of awareness which draws a sharp division between the 'knower' and 'knowledge'. In the context of this last case, knowledge can be of that which is subtle or that which is concrete. The concrete aspect refers to our empirical experiences of the physical world. Only when we include all of the above aspects of consciousness in a unified notion of the self do we get some idea of what is meant by 'Self' in this verse.

When we experience a concrete entity such as a mountain or a river, the experience is the result of an ingrained tendency to abstract the concrete as a factor outside of the self. In this way many things which arise within our consciousness are treated as non-self. One who recognizes the self as being comprised of the concrete, the subjective, the unconscious, and the transcendental has no difficulty in seeing his own concreteness as being part of the concreteness of the physical universe. In the same way he can see that the consciousness pertaining to all the details of the nature and meaning of the cosmos is not in any way different from the consciousness experienced within as his own personal self. A statement such as this may make this kind of looking at oneself and the world seem easy. It is not so. This kind of awareness requires continuous meditation on the nondifferentiation of the homogeneity of that one reality which constitutes both the personal and the universal Self. When a person endowed with such a realization critically examines the course and validity of action, he will see action as part of the flux of becoming which is natural to the phenomenal aspect of the universal Self.

In the process of becoming can be seen various movements which include contraction to a point, expansion into wide dimensions, and motion upward, downward, and horizontally. In all these natural functions, as well as their outcome, there is no agency who wills the varieties of movement. The physical universe is so constituted that physical and chemical properties are produced without the intervention of any personal will which could be said to operate it. This is also true of the biologic factor. For example, it is the nature of the sun to shine. When we form sentences relating to natural functions we say, "*the* sun shines," or "*the* wind blows," or "*the* cloud rains." Thus we unconsciously attribute personification to natural events. Such a habit is a semantic defect in the description of facts. The radiation emitted by the sun and the nerve impulses which disturb the tranquility of the brain belong to the same order of physical events. Man is not a stranger in or a visitor to the universe; he is an integral part of it.

If we do not project our individual notions or prejudices onto natural functions, then we see only occurances. In the present verse the Guru gives the action of fire, of wind, of clouds, of rivers, and of the concrete inner cohesion of the earth as examples of occurances in the cosmic Self. These and many others are all natural events, and they are governed by the precise laws of nature. As integral parts of the cosmic nature, we are also governed by the same laws. In the next verse the Guru equates our bodily functions with the same functioning nature.

VERSE 7

ūrdhvam prāṇohyadho'pānaḥ
khalveko yāti niṣkriyaḥ
nāḍyantarāḷe dhamati
krandati spandati sṭhitaḥ

Going upward as *prāṇa*,
downward as *apāna*,
remaining actionless, the one alone
beats, murmurs, and pulsates in the nerves.

yāti prāṇaḥ (*san*) *ūrdhvam* — going upward as *prāṇa*
apānaḥ (*san*) *athaḥ* — downward as *apāna*
niṣkriyaḥ sṭhitaḥ — remaining actionless
ekaḥ khalu — the one alone
dhamati — beats
krandati — murmurs
spandati — pulsates
nāḍyantarāḷe — in the nerves

In the previous verse we have seen all the actions of the cosmos as being activities which do not proceed from the conscious will of an agent. However, the cosmic forces do work in an orderly way. This inspires us to compare these workings with performances which are preprogrammed. We see them as though initiated by an intelligent mind able to look far into the future, and with the ability to shape the present as a consistent continuation of the past. The sun rises in the east, becomes warm and bright in the midday, then sets again in the west. Night follows with its gentle moonshine and starlight. These movements seem like alternations of the cosmic consciousness to our view. Clouds which rise from the bosom of the ocean to float in the sky and to discharge rain on the farmers' crops have been taken for granted for thousands of years as a kind of gesture of the elements. Our conscious mind is so entwined with the physical events of the universe that we are unable to tell which event should be treated as belonging to the cosmos and which as belonging to our own psyche.

The same apparently purposeful principle of the Absolute operates in our own psychophysical organism. However much we try to unravel their mysteries, there are things we shall never know. We shall not discover the secret force which makes a heart rhythmically pulsate to circulate blood, nor why lungs expand and contract for the intake of life-giving breath and the purging of our inner pollution. The fine network of the nervous system, the conveyance of nerve impulses, the secretions from our glands, and the metabolic changes in the body all operate with perfect inner coordination. What is happening in our bodies is a secret so far as we are concerned. For the most part what happens is autonomous. The conscious mind has very little access to the correction and restructuring of these mysterious and complex faculties that mainly function as instruments of nature and as an integral part of nature's program for life on earth. Even the functions of the mind originate from a depth concealed from an individual's conscious awareness.

When one attempts to relate the individual self with the universal Self, one turns inward and tries to pacify the stream of consciousness. The attempt is to still the mind and to look for the desired union in a passive consciousness. Narayana Guru here suggests that we should look to an entirely different field of operation to experience union of the individual and the cosmic. He first makes us look at cosmic function, then invites us to look for the continuation of the same function in the individual organism. In this way we keep our eyes open to everything and try to follow and understand the multitudinous courses of action engaged in by the supreme nature. The same nature makes no distinction between life when manifested as a tree, a fish or a philosopher. No line is drawn between what science calls organic and inorganic matter. The pigeonholing of data seen in scientific understanding is an artificial creation of the mind made for the purpose of examining things piecemeal. Nature exists and functions as a whole. In it is no categorization, classification, or labeling of its items.

Once again we ask the student of Self-realization to read this as a textbook of the science of realization, not as a book of cosmogony or natural science. The world we see around us is part and parcel of our consciousness. This consciousness is focused with the awareness of an I-consciousness, which is itself stained with the social coloration of an ego, and this is only a very small part of the greater consciousness in which all sentient beings participate and in which they share the unfathomable depth of cosmic consciousness.

When we understand all events — from the wink of an eyelid to the birth and death of stars — they will all be seen as happenings within the realm of awareness of our self, that is, so far as the individual experience of self and the world is concerned. Thus, from the cosmic side we trace the continuation of nature into individual nature. We make that understanding of the origin of events complementary to extending the individual's consciousness beyond the frontiers of his awareness. Then his consciousness becomes one with the universal or collective unconscious, of which the individual is an integral part.

In the next verse the Guru will enumerate the six phases in the process of becoming which are common to all living beings and to all manifestations in the physical universe.

VERSE 8

asti janmardhi pariṇa-
tyapakṣaya vināśanam
ṣadbhāvamiha yo yāti
sa nānyo'vikriyātmanaḥ

From the unmodulating Self,
and not another, the six aspects —
existence, birth, growth, change,
deterioration, and extinction — happen here.

saḥ avikriyātmanaḥ — from the unmodulating Self
na anyaḥ — and not another
ṣad bhāvam — the six aspects
asti — existence
janma — birth
vṛddhi — growth
pariṇāma — change
apakṣaya — deterioration
vināśanam — and extinction
iha yaḥ yāti — happen here

Everything in the universe, from mighty stars in the galaxy to tiny atoms, is subject to change, decay, and diffusion. For a long time scientists held the view that atoms are indestructible. In 1913, Niels Bohr presented to the world a model of atomic structure that many thought to be the final picture of the atom. Bohr's model explained not only the fundamental chemical properties of each element, but also such physical properties as spectrum (characteristic of an element when it is emitting or absorbing light). However, there are serious difficulties with this model. According to electrodynamics, the moving electrons would ceaselessly emit electromagnetic waves. Thus the atomic structure would not exist in a stable state but would always be losing energy. The motions of the electrons would gradually decrease and finally cease entirely.

When we look at our own life on earth we can easily recognize the six phases mentioned by the Guru: existence, birth, growth, change, decay, and extinction. These phases are true of consciousness as well as the physical organism. Thus the worlds of the macrocosm, the microcosm, and of subjective phenomena all belong to the same order of change and transformation. However, these changes are of a relativistic order. All changes occur within the changeless substratum. When we examine the changes experienced within the range of consciousness, we find them all to be modulations of the same consciousness.

Earlier we explained how a minute scrutiny of the material world leads us from the concrete to the subtle and from the subtle to the pure subjective notion that can vanish in the transcendental. In the present verse the Guru is preparing our minds to enter the pure realms of wisdom, doing so without ignoring the possibilities of action being experienced both within our minds and outside our bodies — in the mind as the clash and conflict of interests, outside the body as the movements of harmonious and discordant combinations resulting in union, congregation, or catastrophe.

The *darśana* immediately following this one is of knowledge (*jñāna*). The vision of knowledge will lead us on to that of devotion. For those who seek the liberation of Self-realization, the verticalizing of their tendencies is an inevitable discipline they must undergo. Unlike the method of repression found in *haṭha yoga*. Narayana Guru adopts here a method which is in agreement with the teachings of the Bhagavad Gita (Chapter 2, verses 49-52). Here Kṛṣṇa teaches Arjuna how to transcend action through the cultivation of the unitive way of reasoning. Mere repression of action will produce only inner conflict, and as a consequence more action of the worst kind. In the next verse Guru describes the Self as the basis of all apparent action. Knowledge or wisdom lies in knowing the secret of the impetus of action and the phantom-like manifestations of the phenomenal world.

VERSE 9

svayam kriyante karmāṇi
karaṇair indriyairapi
aham tvasaṅgaḥ kūṭastha
iti jānāti kovidaḥ

In spite of action becoming self-accomplished
by the psychic dynamism and the senses,
the wise one thus knows — "I am the
unattached *kūṭastha*."

tu karmāṇi — in spite of action
svayam kriyante — becoming self-accomplished
karaṇair — by the psychic dynamism (inner organs)
indriyairapi — and the senses
kovidaḥ — the wise one
iti jānāti — thus knows
aham asaṅgaḥ — I am the unattached
kūṭastha — *kūṭastha* (literally, firmly established as a rock)

In theistic religions we often hear people speak of carrying out or conforming to the 'will of God'. Non-dualistic Vedānta is opposed to such a view. Vedāntins do not philosophize in terms of a personalized God using people as instruments to carry out his will. The highest reality to a Vedāntin of the monistic school is Brahma or the Absolute. The Absolute is not to be seen as a Being having desires, nor is it an agent who initiates action. Consequently, it cannot be said that the Absolute 'wills' any thing.

In the previous verse we have seen how everything in this world is subjected to the six kinds of change (existence, birth, growth, change, decay and extinction). We also discussed the five kinds of motion seen in bodies (contraction, expansion, and movement upward, downward, and sideways). With the constant interaction of all these variables it is clear that a great number of activities are ensconced in a totality of marvelous complexity. How does all this arise? If Brahma or the Absolute is the only reality, then the existence of the world should be understood as a dependent factor of that Absolute. If the world has no independent reality of its own, then clearly its actions also should originate from a source other than itself. This reasoning brings us at once to a paradox. The world does not arise as an independent structure. The Absolute, by definition, must be the ground of all existence, but it does not engage in any action. The world cannot act — the Absolute does not act. From where then does action arise?

This paradox is recognized in the Bhagavad Gita. There a correct elucidation of its meaning is given by Vyasa:

> On what is action and what is inaction
> even intelligent men here are confused.
> I shall indicate to you that action on knowing which
> you will be emancipated from evil.
>
> One has to understand about action
> and understand also what is wrong action;
> again one has to have a proper notion of non-action;
> the way of action is elusively subtle (indeed).

After describing the difficulty in understanding *karma*, the Gita suggests the proper attitude one should adopt for such an understanding:

> One who is able to see action in inaction
> and inaction in action, he among men is intelligent;
> he is one of unitive attitude (*yogi*)
> while still engaged in every (possible) kind of work.
>
> (IV: 16, 17, 18)[5]

The usual recourse to solve this riddle is to accept the Absolute as an anthropomorphic Being. In such belief systems this Being has personal wishes and a planned program of action. In the execution of this program He is said to exercise His will through the medium of the lives and actions of all creatures. He displays the attributes of omnipotence, omnipresence, and omniscience. Those who subscribe to such a belief speak of the 'will of God' and tell us what that is. But often we can see that human action runs counter to the professed belief. So if this position is accepted, the problem arises of finding a separate footing for the freely-willed actions of individual human beings who often are tempted to act in a manner which can only be described as 'vicious' or 'immoral'.

It will be difficult for God-fearing people to attribute the source of immoral action to God. If, apart from the will of God, man can have his own power to will and act by free choice, the omnipotency of God is certainly curtailed. It becomes unnecessary to introduce a God at all to account for the very many virtuous and benevolent actions of man. If the actions of an individual can be explained on the basis of his own free will to choose and to act, then God becomes superfluous.

The theistic posture, with all its strains and tensions of argumentation, is not acceptable to Vedāntins. So they give up the dichotomy of an omnipotent God, and man, His creature, and adopt in its place the concept of the 'Self'. The ramifications of the Self extend throughout the whole range of consciousness — from what is experienced when a person says 'I' to what he can ultimately realize as the Absolute. Thus duality is reduced to a way of looking at the real from absolutist and relativistic viewpoints. To account for these fluctuating angles of vision the principle of *māyā* is introduced. *Māyā* implies an alternation in comprehending the real and the unreal, just as we experience, for example, Edgar Rubin's illustration of the gestalt of a white figure on a black ground. When we concentrate on the black ground we see two faces looking at each other. If we concentrate on the white figure, it becomes a vase. When one alternative is real, the other becomes unreal.

Even those of us who never engage in any serious contemplation occasionally experience the world as unreal and our personal self as signifying nothing. After a couple of minutes we again become active and reestablish the importance of our role. The Vedāntin does not place action as arising either in the Self or in the non-Self. Instead, he places it in the magical alternation that takes place in consciousness and calls it *māyā*.

Māyā is described as beginningless, but it is not endless. Although the mystery of *māyā* is fantastic, each item of its composition is by itself short lived. To illustrate the transient nature of *māyā* let us take a man's loving acts of self sacrifice. When he is in a state of passionate infatuation such action is very meaningful to him. He thinks he is doing something of tremendous import which is sure to please his beloved, and enthusiastically devotes himself to that end. Or we can take the action involved in a well planned act of revenge. Such an act may be carried out with the utmost foresight and meticulous attention to detail. Both love and hatred are powerful motivating forces. In each of these examples the time will very likely come when cool reason supervenes and passion diminishes. Then both agents will begin to question the validity of the attitude previously held to justify their actions. What previously was a consuming interest may well begin to seem mere stupidity.

They will be ready to admit that they acted as though possessed by some irrational spirit. It is the alternation of moods that makes an action at first seem to be worthy but afterwards seem to be worthless.

In the individuated self are two aspects. One is pure consciousness which is identical with the Self as existence, knowledge, and value sense. The other is a negative factor which remains crystalized (*kūṭastha*) as an embedded source of incipient memories or potentials. From this source various colorations and conditioned reflexes can arise to saturate and modify any item of awareness experienced in the dream or wakeful states. Just as the concept of the Self ranges from the individual 'I' to blissful identity with the Absolute, so too the Self should be seen in another dimension. This ranges from the individual field of value-vision and interest to include the whole collective consciousness of all sentient beings.

The field for action is not limited within the private fancies of an individual; it happens within the extensive range of collective interaction. The psychophysical tool that becomes involved in the mystery of alternating its emphasis between passive witnessing and the actualization of incipient memories, of both the individual and collective groups of the biologic order, finds its instrumentality in the senses of perception, organs of action, and the monitoring mind. Taking this into account Narayana Guru says, "By means of the inner organ and the senses, action becomes self-accomplished." However, our consciousness basically belongs to pure consciousness, which has within it no desires to fulfill and no volition towards action. A wise man therefore can always look upon himself as having no program of action. This the Guru illustrates when he says, "However, the wise man knows 'I am the unattached, inner well-founded one'."

In the next verse the Guru calls our attention to the operation of *bhāna*, as described in the previous *darśana*. Once again he assures us that what seems to be ontologically true of the empirical world is only a superimposition, and that the ground of its reality rests with the Absolute.

VERSE 10

dṛśyatvāt bhāsyamahama-
pyato'ham śuktiraṅgavat
adhyastameka evādya
śvo'pi sarvopariṣthitaḥ

Because "I" is seen as an object of
awareness, I-consciousness is also a superimposition,
like the silver in the mother of pearl;
above everything else, today and tomorrow,
the one alone exists.

ataḥ dṛśyatvāt — because "I" is seen
bhāsyam (bhavati) — as an object of awareness
aham api — I-consciousness is also
adhyastam — a superimposition
śuktiraṅgavat — like the silver in the mother of pearl
sarvopariṣthitaḥ — above everything else
adya śvo'pi — today and tomorrow
ekaḥ evaḥ — the one alone exists

In the preceding verse specific mention is made of the nature of a wise person. He is described as one who is not affected by what is happening around him, nor is he affected by what he himself seems to be doing. In any action the sense of agency can arise only when one experiences consciousness of oneself as a person. It is as individuals that we seem to ourselves and others to initiate action. Narayana Guru calls our attention to this central core of any experience, which itself determines the meaning of all experience.

As we have already seen, the inner organs operate continually in the areas of enquiry, memory and recall, judgement, decision-making, and affectivity. The organ of affectivity and its operation is attributed to the ego consciousness. The *kovida* (wise man) described in the previous verse is one who has realized that the Self is not his personal ego. He does not act, therefore, from an egocentric base. The deliberation of any action or the manner of any reaction to a situation is very much based on a person's identification with his own self image, as well as how, through that self image, he relates himself to various value-factors.

As an example we can cite a man who looks upon himself merely as a physical body animated with vital forces arising from the input of nourishment. His main interest will be in his body and in finding nourishment to assure its continuance. From his point of view it will not be seen as wrong to kill an animal for food. The consideration of sentience in beings other than himself will not arise, and if it should he would most likely dismiss it as irrelevant to the main issue of sustenence. Such a man may come to realize that the intrinsic nature of all beings, including those he has been used to eating, is the very same nature as his own: that his own Self is the Self of all beings. Such a realization will very much change his attitude toward other living beings. Indeed, his attitude may be so revolutionized that he is likely to adopt a different behavioral pattern altogether, and this not only in the matter of sustenence.

The most gross level at which we are exposed to the pains and pleasures of life is that of action. To decide whether it is worthwhile to engage in any action one should know who he really is and, moreover, why he is doing what is being done or what he is proposing to do. The main purpose of this *darśana* is not to confirm that there is action, nor to deny it. It is to help us in the realization of the Self, to help us to achieve a state of continual serene happiness — even when the senses and organs of action are all geared up for the performance of action.

In this verse the Guru refers to the final verse of the previous *darśana*. That verse says:

> What is the object of awareness, that is superimposed;
> the non-superimposed is not an object of awareness;
> what is superimposed, that is unreal;
> what is not superimposed — That alone is real.

When a person says "I," that is what he experiences — the individuated 'I-ness' of egocentricity. Such a state is a conditioned one, and all conditioned states are nonexistent. Therefore such an ego has no real existence, and it and the experience of it are founded on ignorance. As a consequence, the attempt to please by pampering a nonexistent ego must lead to futility in action. Be that as it may, most of us are all the time engaged in actions designed to lead to self-gratification. A wise man realizes the worthlessness of such pursuits. He knows that "his" senses, physical organism, and mind are all integral parts of the phenomenal universe.

Change and becoming are part and parcel of the universal system, so a wise man will also manifest these factors. He will appear to act in any given situation as any other person would act. One who is wise performs action as it needfully arises as part of the physical necessities of life, but in so doing no unnecessary disturbance will arise in his mind. Though engaged in the most complex of actions his inner serenity will not be disturbed. No matter what the action or what demands are made on him, he will maintain the sameness of vision which is characteristic of a yogi. He will keep himself always in a state of 'neutral zero'.

This is not all. Every action of a wise man will arise from and contain within itself an altruistic or mystical quality of love, kindness, compassion, or beauty. Such a man is in harmony with the universal Self, so he sees everywhere nothing but truth. This truth is the light which illuminates the oneness of all things. As a result of this his understanding will be unitive in its nature. What he continually sees and understands as truth are the unalloyed expressions of goodness and beauty which are the most adorable qualities of the Self. When in a state of appreciation of goodness and beauty, one experiences nothing but happiness. One who is wise does not limit such happiness to the egoistic appreciation of an object of pleasure or pain. He transcends the limitations of all individualistic circumscriptions likely to coerce a person or make him obligated in a relativistic fashion. The actions of one who is wise are unitive and resonate with wisdom.

Consciousness ranges from relativistic sensations such as heat and cold to the highest appreciation of supreme truth. In the next *darśana* Narayana Guru will elaborate on the nature of knowledge.

VI. KARMA DARŚANAM

1 R. E. Hume, *Thirteen Principal Upanishads*, Oxford University Press, (Aitareya Upanishad, First Adhyaya, First Khanda: 1, 2, 3, 4). pages. 294-295.

2 ibid. (Brihad-Aranyaka Upanishad, First Adhyaya, Fourth Brāhmaṇa: 1, 2, 3, 7). pages 81-83.

3 ibid. (Maitri Upanishad, Fourth Prapathaka -2). pages 420-421.

4 ibid. (Brihad-Aranyaka Upanishad, Fourth Adhyaya, Fourth Brāhmaṇa: 3, 5, 6). pages 140-141.

5 Nataraja Guru, *The Bhagavad Gita*, R & K Publishing House, Delhi, Ch IV, 16 , 17, 18. pages 234-236.

VII. JÑĀNA DARŚANAM

Consciousness and its Modifications

There are two prominent views held by rival groups to estimate the significance of consciousness. The traditional view sanctified by religious people and idealists of all sorts stems from the categorical acceptance of a primordial spirit which is identical with the *logos* or Word of God. The theistic coloration of it can be very pronounced as in the writings of theologians, or quite subdued and philosophically subtle as in the philosophy of Hegel. The other view upholds the theory of a self-created matter which is omnipotent by itself, and has within its continuous program of structuring the proliferation of systems governed by an implied mechanical intelligence which can ultimately project and synthesize the generality of all principles in the form of an evolving consciousness, and having for its basis the physiochemical matter imbued with life. In the views of the former, matter is an evolute of spirit. According to the latter, spirit is an evolute of matter. This riddle is overcome by the Sānkhyan philosopher Kapila with the postulation of mind and matter as a reciprocally functioning binary principle.

Narayana Guru, who identifies himself as a monist philosopher favoring integral philosophy, treats both matter and spirit as semantic variations of two modes of philosophical visions, characterized by the immediate requirement of the physio-spiritual enigma in which a discerning mind is caught from time to time. When consciousness is bereft of modification stimulated by any particularized or personalized interest it is treated as free and universal, as if it is pure consciousness by itself and for itself. In such a case it is called *parajñāna*, transcendental knowledge. What is diametrically opposed to it is the specific focusing made to this or that particular object of sense interest, called *indriyajñāna*, sensory knowledge. All other modifications come between these two extremes like a spectrum interwoven with intelligence and sensations.

As the behaviorist would easily refer to the responding consciousness as the natural psychophysical counterpart of the sensibles, Narayana Guru also recognizes the responding consciousness, which makes itself felt as 'I' and 'mine', to be *jivajñāna*, individuating consciousness. In such specific instances knowledge is inferred from the instance of the object illuminated or the sensuousness recognized as one's operational self. Such conditioned forms of consciousness are called *sopādhikajñāna*, relativistic knowledge. If one can intuitively estimate the unmodified state as a prior existence of conditioned knowledge, it is called *nirupādhikajñāna*, unconditional consciousness.

The common experience is to make a dichotomy of the subject and the object. Objective knowledge is empirically supported as originating from a factual thing 'out there', existing independently. The fact that it can be directly perceived gives it the designation of *pratyakṣajñāna*, direct perception. Direct perception can be factual or erroneous. When it is factual it is called *yathārthajñāna*, valid knowledge, and when it is erroneous it is naturally *ayathārthajñāna*, invalid knowledge.

Certitude can come through inner perception also; for example, "I am happy." Such cases are recognized as inwardly perceived knowledge, *aparokṣajñāna*. This literally means 'not perceived by another'. A large percentage of cursory information received for storage comes from indirect perception, such as verbal testimony or inference from partial data, giving us *parokṣajñāna*, literally 'perceived by another'. Inferential knowledge comes from the partial presentation of a cause and effect duality, of which either of the two are available for perception. This is *anumitijñāna*, inferential knowledge. When a case is illustrated, the inference following from it is *upamitijñāna*, comparative knowledge.

Either a person is caught within a plethora of changing and proliferating things, events, and ideas, or they get into a contemplative absorption. In a state of absorption, when the witnessing consciousness has nothing to witness except itself, it is called *ātmajñāna*, knowledge of Self-realization. This is a rare occurrence. On all other occasions there is only the consciousness of the non-Self, which is *anātmajñāna*, knowledge of the non-Self.

Such is the wide variety of modifications that are taken in the present *darśana* of our study.

VERSE 1

jñānamekam hi nirupā-
dhikam sopādhikam ca tat
ahamkārādihīnam yaj
jñānam tannirupādhikam

Knowledge is one indeed — unconditioned
and conditioned; that, devoid of
I-consciousness and so on,
is the knowledge which is unconditioned.

jñānamekam hi — knowledge is one indeed
nirupādhikam — unconditioned
sopādhikam (ca) — and conditioned
yat ahamkārādi hīnam — that devoid of I-consciousness
ca tat — and so on
jñānam — (is) the knowledge
tan nirupādhikam — which is unconditioned

In the *Karma Darśana* we saw how Narayana Guru traced all the activities of our body to the Self. In this he included autonomous as well as voluntary activities. In the same way he showed that all kinds of motions and phenomenal happenings — clouds giving rain, rivers flowing, fire burning, and so on — are also to be traced to the expression of a universal will. In earlier chapters the identification of the individual self with the universal Self was also established. In the cases of both individual self and universal Self, the term 'Self' has only one connotation: *sat-cit-ānanda*, existence-knowledge-bliss. The pure existence of the Self is seen manifested in and as the existence of individual entities. Such entities come and go, differentiations of the Undifferentiated; they occur in time and space, then pass away again into that unknown or nothingness from which they originated.

In terms of pure duration, the existence of things is to be treated as a relativistic factor. Only the Self has absolute existence. In other words, the Self is to be seen as none other than Absolute Existence. The Self is the source of all awareness, and nothing can illuminate the Self that is not its own pure awareness.

All items of awareness at the individual level originate at a certain point in time within our consciousness. After existing for some time they disappear in the same consciousness. That short span of recognition is the individualized conscious awareness. Such an awareness must be described as relativistic. And though the form of awareness may seem to us to be our own, in fact all individual items of awareness are illuminated by the absolute awareness of the Self.

In our daily life we continually experience items of affectivity which very much influence our response and outlook. We are affected by pain and pleasure and many other shades of value. Although we may not be aware of doing so, we measure the affective quality of every experience against that absolute norm of happiness which is the very nature of the Self. Except in the case of Self-realization, this value of sublime happiness is experienced only as a momentary flash. Our ordinary value-sense remains on an individual, relativistic level.

Now we have come to the *darśana* on "vision by knowledge." This introduces us to the holistic vision of the total awareness of the Self. A clear understanding of this teaching will enable us to discover the relevancy of all individualized forms of existence. These forms come to us as the result of individual notions which imply a number of specific values. Such values range from the highest possible joy, satisfaction, sense of fullfillment, or peace to the most disturbing, agonizing, and painful misery.

In the present verse the Guru makes a broad division of the awareness of the Self into the unconditioned and the conditioned. In Sanskrit these are known as *nirupādhikam* and *sopādhikam* respectively. When a man observes a pot and comments "this is a pot," then the pot becomes a condition (*upādhi*) which modulates his awareness into the specific features of it. The literal meaning of *upādhi* is 'intelligence that has undergone conditioning'. *Upā* means 'with' or 'together with', and *dhi* means 'intelligence'.

The question may now arise: how can pure awareness, which is none other than the Self, be related to anything when nothing other than the Self exists? Such a question has already been answered in the first three *darśana*-s — *Adhyāropa*, *Apavāda*, and *Asatya*. The negative aspects of the Self are equated with darkness, which stands in contrast to light.

We have gone deep into a scrutiny of awareness of the external world and come to the conclusion that the world is being and non-being together. Its beingness belongs to pure knowledge and its non-beingness to nescience. This again brings forward a broad division, such as for example the Self and the non-Self. Non-Self is a factor which can condition Self. At this stage we should recall to mind the commentary on verse four in the first *darśana.* There the Guru attributes the manifestation of everything to the interaction between cosmic light and darkness. The cosmic light of pure awareness can be likened to water without ripples or any motion on its surface. Even though the water remains substantially the same, a motion on its surface may be seen as many things, such as ripples, waves, or a high tide. Thus the light of pure awareness is obscured by the darkness of differentiation but the water remains water, just as the Self remains pure.

Using water as an analogy brings to mind many different notions about the varying conditions of it. These are all examples of *upādhi.* When there is no conditioning, the Self remains as pure awareness or nonmodulated intelligence. In that case it is called *nirupādhikam* — the unconditioned state.

Pure awareness animates all individuated beings as well as animating the cosmos. This is true of all sentient beings. There are those among us who believe that only humans can be said to have a soul or an indwelling divinity. Certain sections of the Christian community attempt to justify the killing of animals and birds for food on the ground that these "have no souls." Many scientists believe that only man has intelligence, that the so-called lower forms of life are motivated by instinct only. Such outmoded beliefs are seen today to be untenable not only so far as animals are concerned but also in regard to the vegetable kingdom.

Many years ago such beliefs were proved to be without foundation by Sir Jagadis Chandra Bose, an Indian physicist, plant physiologist, and psychologist. In his book *The Secret Life of Plants*, he proved to the world that plants have an emotional response just as do human beings. In more recent years scientists like John Lilly have shown that dolphins and whales have intelligence. Such intelligence is shown in the ability to plan a collective society and to articulate ideas and feelings even at an interspecies level.

The ṛṣis of India see universal consciousness as the warp and woof of the cosmos. Sir Arthur Eddington came close to this idea when he described the universe as "fringes and folds in the space-time continuum." Sir James Jeans said, "the universe begins to look more like a great thought than a great machine." The ṛṣis place time and space as modalities of mind.

In order to arrive at the notion of unconditioned consciousness we should think of the immanence of a consciousness that has the quality also of transcendence. When that pure consciousness becomes circumlimited, it produces a central locus and a boundary. The central locus produces the notion of individuation, and that notion is recognized as 'I' in the case of human beings. Repeated recourse to circumlimitation and the recurrence of the idea of 'I' makes one egotistically oriented. Thereafter the ego alone becomes real and experience is considered valid only when it is an affectation and expression of the ego. In short, one becomes a person of conditioned consciousness and a stranger to the unconditioned consciousness from which his individuation is derived. In fact the unconditioned state of awareness is our reality and it is always present.

VERSE 2

ahantayā'ntar bahira-
stiyadevam idantayā
bhānavṛttyā'nvitam yattu
jñānam sopādhikam matam

That knowledge modulated as I-consciousness inside,
likewise that which is modulated
as knowledge of thisness outside,
such knowledge is known as the conditioned.

yat — that
bhāna — knowledge
vṛttyānvitam — modulated
ahantayā — as I-consciousness
antaḥ — inside
evam — likewise
yat tu asti — that which is (modulated as knowledge)
idantayā — of thisness
bahir — outside
jñānam — (such) knowledge
matam — is known
sopādhikam iti — as the conditioned

This verse gives a definition of conditioned consciousness. As a matter of fact, all our subjective and objective experiences are conditioned. In the world of Western psychology, the term psychology itself is very much associated with the Pavlovian theory of conditioned reflex. Narayana Guru is not using the term *sopādhikam* in that sense here. Every explicit statement that is made by man in the form of a judgement refers either to his own personal identity and its relation with other things or to the objects of his own experience. The personal reference is to 'I' and the objective reference is to 'this' or 'that'. To illustrate this general division the Guru gives us the terms *idanta*, which means 'pertaining to thisness', and *ahanta*, meaning 'pertaining to the self or I-consciousness'.

Earlier, when we were discussing the Vedāntic concept of perception, we explained how pure consciousness becomes circumlimited and modified to assume definite forms of awareness. Such modification of consciousness is called *vṛtti*. According to Narayana Guru, *vṛtti* is the *upādhi* or condition we are discussing in this *darśana*. It is very important for us to know what these conditions are, how they arise, and how they constitute experiences of pain, pleasure, and indifference. The sole purpose of our present study is to release the mind from all painful conditioning and to lead it to its original state of pure unconditioned consciousness.

Any person one encounters is an object of experience. We cannot ignore the presence of an external object when our sensory system is stimulated by it because then the idea of 'this' arises. When the presence of 'this' is registered, questions arise in the mind: "What is this? Where does it come from? How am I related to it? Is it acceptable, or should I avoid it?" And so on.

To answer such questions, mind operates in the function of the recall of associated memories. In this way one modification of consciousness begets another. Even though the object in question is experienced as a factor external to self, the joy or aversion generated by it is experienced internally. When we experience an external object, a number of subjective questions arise to keep the mind busy with modifications of consciousness, mainly of a conceptual nature. It is in this way that concepts and percepts become conditions (*upādhi*) capable of creating states of consciousness.

In addition to concepts and percepts there arise in the mind factors of affectivity or value. Some of these value factors are conceptual qualities; others come in the form of relationships.

It should not be thought that the whole of consciousness is involved in this subjective activity. Only a minute fraction of our unconditioned pure consciousness undergoes modification. Yet even from this fraction arises the infinitely large world of the time-space continuum. Such a world is constituted of millions of names and forms, together with a sequential train of emotionally charged thoughts and willfully deliberated actions.

The most brutishly ignorant man who, in addition to ignorance, suffers from the excruciating physical pain of some dreadful disease, and the philosopher-seer of the most sublime vision, meditating on the Absolute, are equally subject to the conditioning of consciousness. Whether a person is saying "this is a pot," or "I am the Absolute," there is no substantial difference in the conditional aspect of consciousness.

In the next verse Narayana Guru will define for us the unconditioned state of consciousness.

VERSE 3

anātmanāmahamkārā
dīnām yenānubhūyate
sākṣī tadātmajñānam syā-
dyenaivāmṛtamaśyate

That by which one experiences the witnessing of the non-Self,
such as I-consciousness and so on,
is Self-knowledge, by which alone
immortality is enjoyed.

yenānubhūyate — that by which one experiences
sākṣī anātmanām — the witnessing of the non-Self
ahamkārādīnām — such as I-consciousness and so on
tat ātmajñānam — is Self-knowledge
ena eva syāt — by which alone
amṛtam aśyate — immortality is enjoyed

The Self can be compared to a light that can see and is always witnessing whatever it illuminates. Its experience of such illumination ranges from the witnessing of deep sleep to the witnessing of empirical transactions with gross objects in the wakeful state. In and through all experiences runs a golden thread of pure consciousness. This is not affected by the changing modes of consciousness which occur in the shifting of interest from one item of experience to another. Comprehension of this pure consciousness is obliterated in the minds of most people because they become so intrigued by the values in each item illuminated by the Self.

Among the items that are Self-illuminated are subjective notions such as "I am," "I am happy," "I am unhappy," "I am ignorant," "I am enlightened," and so on. In all such cases the term 'I' stands for the ego. Although its epistemological status is that of non-Self, properly speaking the ego is neither the non-Self nor the Self. It is, so to speak, a negative shadow of the Self. Even in the case of unenlightened people there are moments when the limitation of normal consciousness is transcended. Then consciousness refers neither to the cognizing agency of the ego nor to any factor of the non-Self made specifically interesting by any particular value. Such a state may perhaps best be described as the awareness of an awareness which does not necessitate the dichotomy of the seer and the seen.

The nondifferentiated consciousness of the Self prevails at all times. It is like the ocean which, though seeming to take on the forms of waves, never in fact changes its fundamental nature as water. Recapturing the original nondifferentiated state of consciousness can be identified as realization — that is, Self-realization. What is real in that state is the Self. The non-Self, together with the shadowy ego, are found to be unreal.

In our everyday lives we proliferate experiences of the unreal by our endless search for novelty and variegation. It is the perpetuation of differences that makes knowledge conditional. The awareness of any conditional state implies also the experiencing of existential factors as conditional states of experience. The value derived from such knowledge automatically becomes a relative value only, colored by prevailing conditions. Realization means to discover one's total identity with absolute existence, with nonmodulated consciousness, and with the unbroken blissful state of the Self (*ānanda*).

In the English language the term 'bliss' is associated with intense feelings of pleasure or enjoyable emotional states. This is not the meaning of *ānanda* as the term is used in Vedāntic philosophy. Two important characteristics of *ānanda* are the total abolition of duality and the attainment of the state of immortality. Immortality here is to be understood in a special sense. It does not refer to the perpetuation of a certain substance or substantiality in time and space. Indeed, it refers to a total transcendence of the relevance of the time factor which is the main medium of the state of becoming.

A special word employed by the Guru in this verse to ensure the certitude of pure consciousness is *sākṣī*, meaning 'the witness'. The act of witnessing can also be considered as a modification of consciousness. Previously we mentioned that the term 'modification' carries the same meaning as the Sanskrit word *vṛtti*. The meanings in these two terms, *sākṣī* and *vṛtti*, should be carefully examined.

An eyewitness to a motor accident or a crime may be called upon to give evidence in court. There his witnessing is meaningful only if he can give exact descriptions of objective factors which he perceived through his own senses. Such descriptions, recalled to his conscious mind, are descriptions of the modifications of consciousness which took place in him while he was perceiving the incident. In this example the non-Self has so prevailed upon the light of the Self that the Self can be said to have undergone a total transformation and lost all its transparency. Also in this example the act of witnessing is seen not only at the egoistic level but also at the level of the Self. The first aspect is not an impartial witnessing. The witnessing agency is totally colored and transformed, and has become identical with all the characteristics of the non-Self that is witnessed.

When we speak of the Self as the eternal Witness, it should be understood that we refer to its neutrality. Pure consciousness, without becoming a participant in the 'I' and 'mine' roles of the ego and without identifying itself with the objectivity of the non-Self, always retains its pure state. At the same time it is aware of the game of life projected as though a shadow play.

A playwright who sits in the theater to witness the staging of his own play has a transparency of vision towards the play different from that of the rest of the audience. He, too, may feel to some extent the same empathetic identification towards the characters in the sequential development of the play as the rest of the audience does, but he has an additional awareness also. What is seen on the stage is a projection of fantasy arising in his own mind. He can at any time withdraw himself from the projection of his own fantasy. This means that a playwright has two witnessing roles. One is to witness the projected fantasy; the other is to witness the action of his creative mind which is prone to make such a fantasy.

Now we should take the possibility of witnessing to another more subtle level. There what is to be witnessed is not the non-Self but the Self itself. The most subtle form of witnessing the Self comes in the state of deep sleep. In this state consciousness prevails without having anything in particular of which to be conscious. Deep sleep is an occasion in which consciousness is subjected to a dense form of inertia. It is therefore not an ideal state in which to realize the Self.

The three constituents of nature, *satva*, *rajas*, and *tamas*, are the prime factors present in the structuring of all the items in experiences of the non-Self. *Satva* is the pure-clear aspect of nature that can reflect a thing-in-itself as it is. *Rajas* brings exaggerations and deformities in affective perceptions and conceptions. *Tamas* is opaque. It causes a blackout of both the objectivity and subjectivity of consciousness. Realization comes only when all three of these modalities of nature are transcended. The transcendent state then obtained is called *samādhi*, and it occurs when the Self witnesses the Self. So we can see that to understand all the implications in the present verse, the word 'witnessing' must be appreciated in its correct sense.

From what has been said it should be evident that the Self, when in the state of knowing itself, does not accomplish that experience through the modulation of consciousness in any manner whatsoever. Nor does it engage itself in any exertion in an effort to perceive something, as in the case of the perception of the objects of the non-Self. When such a high state of unconditional, nonmodulated consciousness prevails without its transparency or sameness disturbed by the awareness of 'I' or 'this', it is called Self-knowledge or *ātmajñāna*.

In the next verse Narayana Guru will tell us what is the conditioned state of the knowledge of the non-Self.

VERSE 4

ahamkārādi kāryam ya-
danātmakam asaṅkhyakam
yenāvagamyate'nātma-
jñānam tadavadhāryate

That by which I-consciousness and innumerable
such effects, which belong to the non-Self,
are known, is said to be
knowledge of the non-Self.

yat yena — that by which
ahamkārādi — I-consciousness
asaṅkhyakam kāryam — and innumerable such effects
anātmakam — which belong to the non-Self
avagamyate — are known
tat eva dhāryate — is said to be
anātmajñānam — knowledge of the non-Self

That which cannot be described as the Self is called the non-Self. We have already defined the nature of the Self as being pure existence (*sat*), pure awareness (*cit*), and the supreme value (*ānanda*). In our wakeful life and in our dream life we experience many things having specific names and forms. All of these have some significance for us.

In trying to grasp intellectually the nature of the Self we can say the meaning of pure existence is that which neither originates nor becomes extinct in time. What we perceive through the action of our senses and conceive by the action of mentation comes into existence at a certain point in time, furthering the flow of our awareness as far as we are concerned. It follows that the existence of such perceptions and conceptions, when seen against the meaning of pure existence, must be of a relative and not an absolute validity. Knowledge of the existence of such entities also originates in the stream of consciousness, and vanishes after presenting the idea of the object. From the above it is evident that most items of our consciousness are only relative notions, not an ever-abiding awareness.

The meaning-value or significance of things which we experience may appear to us to be of great importance or of none. This means that within ourselves we have a normative notion of value. We automatically make use of this notion as a measuring rod to evaluate the significance of each item of experience that crosses the field of our mind. In that field items are not referred to an ever-abiding value. In short, the objects of experience are only relatively existential, relatively subsistential, and of relative value significance. Therefore they all come into the category of the non-Self.

Let us take an example from the transactional world of everyday experience. A man staying in a hotel is called to his dining table for a meal. On arrival he looks at the table and finds the tablecloth to be of a design not agreeable to his taste. This immediately arouses some irritation in him. He looks closer as he seats himself and discovers the various items of cutlery to be wrongly placed according to his own ideas of genteel custom. Moreover, the butter smells stale and the bread looks moldy. This further annoys him, and his irritation rises again when an unhandy waiter spills a few drops of soup on the tablecloth. The soup is too salty for the diner's taste but he is very hungry and eats the meal, distasteful though it is to him. Of course his digestion suffers since he eats in a state of irritation and resentment.

After the meal our unhappy diner returns to his room in a state of disgust. He flops down in a chair and moodily switches on the television set. Onto the screen comes a picture of a glamorous and famous artist, who sings a beautiful lyric which is very evocative for the watcher. At once his irritability and disgust and his memory of the unsavory dinner vanishes. Now in a mood of elation, he switches off the television and picks up a writing pad to set down a poetic couplet that flashes into his mind. Effortlessly the mental image is transposed onto the paper, and the delighted writer sees it to be beautiful. In a state of euphoria he sits for a moment enchanted by his creation, his mind empty of thoughts.

In this example we have mentioned a number of individual items. Each item has a definite place as an object of experience. The value of the stale butter is different from the necessary bread that has appeased his hunger. The soup drunk from the bowl has a value different from that of the soup spilled on the table. The song of the television performer, much as the listener enjoyed it, did not have a value as immediate or satisfying as did his own poetry. Despite all the pluralities and variegations in the objects of experience, there is one central factor which again and again becomes involved in the experiences. This is the subjective I-consciousness of the man in our example. Two men placed in identical circumstances may have quite different reactions to them. The one who is not aware that he is dealing with non-Self entities, with which he is interacting from his ego center, will be tempted to treat all facets of the experiences as truly existential factors. He may argue with the waiter, and even throw the cutlery at him instead of quietly reordering its position on the table. Every item in our life can pull us off on a tangent, and may take us far away from our center. This accounts for the eccentricity displayed by most people.

One who has a clear understanding of the Self and the non-Self knows his ego to be only a tool for him to witness the manifestations of the transactional world. To him all factors which are of social importance to others, and which are projected by them onto his ego, are easily seen to be only parts of the transactional game. He may agree to play a conventional role, as an older man might agree to pretend to be an elephant for his grandson to ride. The man will not lose his own sense of identity when he plays games with a child. In the same way, one who is fully aware of the Self is inwardly amused by the game in progress between the individuated ego and its several objects of experience.

One who is Self-realized has an understanding of the transactions in the world of objectivity no less sharp than that of one who thinks the external world to be the only reality. Indeed, he probably has a better sensibility to appreciate, for example, a well arranged and savory meal. However, he remains cognizant of the fact that it is only an ego dealing with non-Self entities. When a person does not have such an awareness, his knowledge is called *anātmajñānam* — that is, knowledge of the non-Self.

Empirical science, developed mostly by Western thinkers, considers external factors as causal entities that produce the effects of sensations on our senses and mind. According to such thinkers, a stimulus is the cause and a response to it the effect; the stimulus comes from outside and the effect is experienced in the self. Vedāntins look upon this theory as putting the cart before the horse. To return to our example of the unhappy diner, the tablecloth which appears to be ugly or beautiful has something to do with the preconditioned aesthetic taste of the man who found it disturbing. We have already mentioned the selective structuring that is implicit in the perception of objects. On account of this, Vedāntins look upon external objects as *kāryam*, that is, effects. The causal factor is seen to be in the preconditioned ego. Thus both the cause and effect are conditioned. This is why Narayana Guru calls knowledge of the non-Self *sopādhikam*, knowledge that is conditional.

Even in the case of knowledge of the non-Self there can be right knowledge and erroneous knowledge. Both are conditional. The Guru will describe these in the next verse.

VERSE 5

yathāvad vastu vijñānam
rajjutattvāvabodhavat
yattad yathārtha vijñāna-
mayathārthamato'nyathā

When things are known as they are,
as in the knowledge of the truth of rope,
that is factual knowledge,
and fictitious when it is otherwise.

yathāvad vastu vijñānam — when things are known as they are
rajjutattvāvabodhavat — as in the knowledge of the truth of rope
yathārtha vijñānam — that is factual knowledge
yattad ayathārtham ato'nyathā — and fictitious when it is otherwise

In their search for truth, the tyranny of the meanings of words can be a major hurdle for most people. For most, mentation is verbalized — a kind of inner dialogue — and we think in the language which is most familiar to us. For some this will be their mother tongue; for others it might be a foreign language which they are obliged constantly to use because of their placement in life. The basis of language is words, but in themselves words express no truths. A word is, so to speak, a frame which encloses a meaning which stems from collective agreement. A word therefore may express a scientific or symbolic meaning, for example. The relation between language and truth may be compared to that existing between a road map and actual places: "the map is not the territory."

In common usage we find terms such as 'armchair philosophy' and 'theoretical physics'. In these kinds of speculative studies the material people work with is concepts. The relevancy or validity of a concept is judged according to the rules of semantics, logic, or mathematical feasibility. We have to differentiate the conceptual from the actual in everyday practice. For example, the proverb "the proof of the pudding is in the eating," does not relate to any actual pudding. It is purely conceptual and means, of course, that the value of a thing can only be determined by test or experience.

But "two and two make four" is both conceptual — when used as an affirmation of a known constant in any field — and practical in reference to daily objective life. One who receives two dollars from each of two friends can in actual fact pocket four dollars. In our search for truth we very often find ourselves in a semantic jungle wherein words are considered as objects of interest in their own right. Some people spend professional lifetimes lost in that jungle, devoting endless energy to the roots of language, or what conjugates should be used, or which inflection is the more correct one. They perfectly illustrate another popular adage: they cannot see the forest for the trees.

Unfortunately we do not minimize the problem when we draw a line between a concept and an actual entity. Instead, we find ourselves in a strange kind of confrontation with the actualities of life. The main and pressing question before us we find to be whether the actual is also the real. Usually we consider the word 'real' as being synonymous with the word 'actual'. In the present *darśana* Narayana Guru makes a distinction between *ātmajñānam*, knowledge of the Self, and *vastu vijñānam*, knowledge of things.

In the Random House Dictionary the word 'actual' is given these meanings:

1) existing in act or fact;
2) existing at present; current; real as of now;
3) pertaining to or involving acts or action.[1]

The corresponding Sanskrit term is *yathārtha*, which means 'conforming to the true meaning of the word'. The truth that is referred to here is of an empirical order. Such truth as this is to be contrasted with absolute truth. Absolute truth in Sanskrit is called *paramārtha*. We would very much like to use the English word 'real' to mean absolute truth, in contradistinction to the word 'actual'. Such a concept is not attached to the word 'real' by lexicologists. However, in the present study we intend to attach that concept to the word so that the reader will always distinguish the real from the actual.

The scientific discipline given to us in schools is to observe, to weigh and measure, and to judge with precision the properties of things perceived. This is done so that our understanding of the transactional world can be as accurate as possible. When a person turns his mind to seek the truth of the Self, he enters a field where there is nothing to observe objectively and nothing which can be measured with any device whatsoever. The truth he is seeking is the truth of all things. The scientist has a method he can use to arrive at the truth he seeks, but the seeker of higher truth has to know what gives validity to any method, and why truth is truth. The latter's questions are much more basic and fundamental.

In the present verse Narayana Guru calls our attention to a traditional example, that of the correct perception of rope as rope and the erroneous perception of rope as snake. He says that to perceive rope as rope is actual knowledge, *yathārthajñāna*, but to see the rope as a snake is illusory knowledge. After making these distinctions he categorizes both these kinds of knowledge as conditional (*sopādhika*). At the commencement of the *darśana* he spoke of real knowledge of the Self as unconditional. From this it is clear that the certitude we arrive at in the world of transactions has reality only within the frame of reference of an actual transaction. The real or absolute knowledge is the *beingness* of knowledge. It is not the knowledge of any thing.

It is not necessary for a great Guru to come and tell us that to see rope as rope is right knowledge and that to see rope as snake is wrong knowledge. Even a child knows this. The reference to certitude and actuality is to call our attention to what we miss in our endless pursuit of details and precision in the empirical world of our search. We seldom, if ever, notice the unbroken existence of pure knowledge, which is none other than the Self. This pure knowledge, when experienced, enables the individuated consciousness to transcend the fixations in which it is riveted, that is, to transcend the empirical and the transactional.

If we walk into any library we shall see large stocks of impressive-looking books, the authors of which lay claim to the revelation of truth. How many billions of trees have been reduced to pulp to provide the paper for this endless output of books and how many man-hours have gone into their production is unknown, but it can be called a labor in vain. Even the best of those books contain only information, bits of conditional perceptions or conceptual ideas. They cannot of themselves give us or engender in us that which he who seeks the Self is looking for. It is likely that one who does seek the Self will eventually turn away from such treasuries of recorded wisdom to the unrecorded truth of his own beingness. There he will be obliged to leave behind the cumbersome burden of memory. We do not have to seek externally; we carry around within ourselves a very great treasure. To know this treasure it is perhaps necessary to compare it with relativistic or conditional knowledge, the discovery and propagation of which takes up a sizeable amount of all national incomes.

Before examining the basic methodology applied by all seekers of truth, whether of the relativistic or absolutist orders, the Guru calls our attention to the basis of certitude which he describes in the next verse. As a prelude to verse six it will be necessary to discuss the psychology of perception as understood by the Vedāntin — which is different from that popularly held in Western countries.

In the West perception is considered to be the sensory response to stimuli caused by the flow of a physical energy such as light or heat. Thus a stimulus comes from an object and is received by the appropriate sense organ such as the eye, the skin, or the ear. So now we have that which is perceived — the object — and he who perceives it — the subject. The externality of the object is taken for granted. The source of perception is always taken to be in the energy that stimulates the organ of perception; for instance, light waves excite the optic nerve to produce the perception of sight. Here light is an external agent which illuminates the object of perception, and it travels from the object to the sense organ in which it causes stimulation. The causal factor of vision in this viewpoint is naturally the illuminating light which is external to the subject.

When he examines the perceptual experience, the Vedāntin introduces the theory of certitude as a prerequisite to the understanding of perception. In Sanskrit certitude is called *pramā*. This corresponds to the term 'self-evident' used by mathematicians and logicians. True certitude comes only when the self of the person concerned is fully convinced of that truth which the person knows or understands. One who is in a state of certitude is called *pramāta*.

After pointing out the need for 'self-evidence', and fixing the knower as the central person involved in the context of knowing a perception, the Vedāntin raises the question of the testimony of certitude. How does a person determine that his testimony is valid? The testimony by which knowledge is validated is called *pramāṇa*. In the complete testimony that is *pramāṇa*, the act of perception is only one of the parts; the other parts are inference, analogy, and word-wisdom. Vedāntins consider the immediate perception and the personal awareness arising during the perceptual experiences as both being aspects of the total perceptive action. Immediate perception is called *pratyakṣa*. *Akṣa* means 'eye', and *prati* means 'corresponding to'.

In the case of sight, the knowledge which corresponds to what is experienced by the eye is called *pratyakṣa.* An object held in one's hand, such as an apple, needs no further proof of its actual existence. When we say "I exist," the evidence of our existence is equally certain. In this case we arrive at this knowledge not by looking at our physical body. The evidence for self-existence comes from within the person. This kind of inner perception in which the sensory organs play no part is called *aparokṣa. Para* means 'another', and so *apara* means 'not another'. Thus the word means 'a perception which does not come from another'. In other words it is a self-evident perception.

After bracketing sensory perception and intuitive perception together and calling them by the general term 'perception', the Vedāntin looks for a causal factor. For the sake of unitive understanding the whole experience is treated as the inseparable concomitance of one unit of modulated consciousness. To understand this let us take the example of a man saying, "I perceive this apple by seeing it, touching it, smelling it and tasting it." Let us suppose also that he says, "I know that I exist." Both these experiences — of the apple and the self — are experiences of certitude. In the statement "I perceive this apple," the subject is 'I' and the object of perception is 'this apple'. In the statement "I know that I exist," the subject is 'I' again and the object is the existence of the subject.

What is the basis for the awareness of the subject? In other words, who is this 'I'? In answer we may say that in this case the 'I' is an entity of consciousness, aware of its own centrally focused consciousness. That is to say it is an aspect of consciousness modulated as a percipient and also as a knower. There is no difference between he who perceives and he who knows. That which perceives the apple and that which perceives the self are both modulated forms of consciousness. The entity is described by the Sanskrit word *pramātṛcaitanya,* meaning the consciousness that recognizes itself as the knower of a certain knowledge or an evident instance of perception. In both the above examples the subject asserts the experience of knowledge or perception. What is that knowledge or perception? It is consciousness recognizing a special modulation of itself. This is called *pramāṇacaitanya,* which means 'a modulated consciousness of evidence'. The consciousness modulated with the identical properties of the object is called *prameyacaitanya.*

Now, finally, let us look at an object of perception such as an apple and an object of knowledge such as the self. What are these items of experience again? These are also modulations of consciousness — two kinds of impressions or ideations. They are both merely modulations of consciousness, different only in the quality of the properties that constitute the experiences.

After thus presenting his case, the Vedāntin introduces the principle of homogeneity. The subject 'I', and the evidence, knowledge, or perception of it; the apple as an object and the perception of it; and the evident knowledge of the self, all have one common factor. They are all aspects of consciousness. What is this one consciousness that permeates the subject, the experience, and the object of experience? It is this the Vedāntin calls the Self. Without the presence of this Self neither the mind nor the senses can produce any effective modulation of consciousness. The Vedāntin now draws the conclusion that the primary cause of knowledge, whether of immediate perception or of intuitive perception, is the self-luminous consciousness which is none other than the Self.

All experiences are a confection of *pramātṛcaitanya* (the knowing consciousness), *pramāṇacaitanya* (the validating consciousness), and *prameyacaitanya* (the objectivized consciousness). When the Self is equated with consciousness it is to be understood as indivisible consciousness. In Sanskrit this is called *akhandacaitanya.*

We can have either a holistic view of perception or a circumlimited and relativistic consideration of a particular aspect of knowledge or perception. The behavioristic school of Western psychology treats only the relativistic aspect as an act of perception. With the above distinctions between the Western view of perception and the Vedāntin's view clearly held in mind, let us now try to understand the Guru's presentation of the following verse.

VERSE 6

yatsānnidhyādeva sarvam
bhāsate svayameva tat
pratyakṣajñānamiti cā-
parokṣamiti lakṣyate

By the mere presence of which alone
everything is illuminated —
that is characterized as knowledge of
immediate perception, and also as inner perception.

yatsānnidhyāt eva — by the mere presence of which
svayam eva — alone
sarvam — everything
bhāsate — is illuminated
tat lakṣyate — that is characterized as
pratyakṣajñānam iti — knowledge of immediate perception
ca aparokṣam iti — and also as inner perception

From our introduction to this verse it should be clear to the reader that the one indivisible Self, which we described as *akhanda-caitanya*, is the sole illuminator of everything that is consciously experienced. It is consciousness that illuminates everything — even the light which falls on and illuminates an external object so we may see it is itself an object of perception. Unconsciousness perceives nothing. The brightest sun will make no impression on an unconscious person, even if its light falls directly into his eyes. This Self is the same consciousness that is described in the *Kena Upaniṣad*:

> That which is the hearing of the ear, the thought of the mind,
> The voice of speech, as also the breathing of the breath,
> And the sight of the eye. Past these escaping, the wise
> On departing from this world, become immortal.
> (section 1; v.2)[2]

The same absolute Self is also referred to as the primeval cause of all the experiences of sentient beings in the Bhagavad Gita:

> Presiding over the ear, the eye and touch,
> taste and smell, and also the mind,

this one avails himself of the values
relating to the senses.
(XV:9)[3]

The present section deals only with the transactional aspect of knowledge. When the Eye behind the eye knows itself to be the indivisible Self, that is pure knowledge. We have already seen this mentioned in verse three of this *darśana*, where the Self is shown to be the all-witnessing consciousness (*sākṣi*).

The individuated consciousness suffers an enigmatic severance from the indivisible Self through wrong identification of itself as a separate person. This presumed severance of consciousness from its original state of indivisibility causes a further dichotomy of the same consciousness into subject and object. Although both subject and object are experienced as separate entities, neither one in reality can be separated from the one consciousness. When this dichotomy is established, the whole cyclic movement of becoming begins to operate. This in turn generates endless bifurcations of consciousness into names and forms, ideas of cause and effect, notions of time and space, and identifications with actors and actions. In this ontologic world of empirical substantiality we find categorizations such as substance, quality, generality, specificity, time, space, action, relationship, inherence, and nonexistence. When placed in this situation an individual should have definite and precise knowledge of all the above categories to be able effectively to transact the business of everyday life.

The demand for apodictic certitude automatically raises the question of standardizing the norms of accuracy. In consequence of this, valid thinking is based on the application of logical methods. These methods are well known as perception, inference, analogy, and word-testimony. Inductive methods such as those of agreement and difference, noncontradiction, and arriving at the residual factor by a process of consistent elimination, are also relevant. So far as an individual is concerned, direct experience comes only from perception or self-evident intuitive cognition. The Vedāntin treats both perception and intuition as two aspects of illumination which can be traced to the Self. The process of the same luminous consciousness producing out of itself both the subject and the object has already been described in verse seven of the second *darśana*. There we presented the theory of perception as elucidated by Dharmarāja Adhvarindra in his *Vedānta Paribhāṣa*.

The main point to be understood here is the manifestation of perception as part of the self-luminous function of the *ātman*. When the Vedāntic concept of perception is properly understood, it will come as no surprise to find intuitive cognition also classed as perception. For the Vedāntin, existentiality is substantiated by awareness. The context of awareness is permeated with its affective value or meaning which alone decides the difference of one perception from another. In spite of the directness of this experience, the spiritual value of it is negative.

The apodictic certitude of the details of external objects stabilizes the conviction of the reality of a concrete world as a self-founded entity; such knowledge comes as the greatest stumbling-block in the attempt to transcend the duality of subject and object. It is in recognition of this fact that Nataraja Guru translates *aparokṣajñāna* as 'nontranscendental awareness'. However valid such experiences are within the transactional frame of reference, they are only relativistic and conditional.

In the next verse the Guru describes that kind of knowledge which is derived from the inferential method.

VERSE 7

yayā'nusādhakam sādhyam
mīyate jñāna rūpayā
vṛttyā sā'numitiḥ sāha-
carya saṃskārajanyayā

That form of the modulation
of knowledge, by which the appraisal of
the possibility produced by concomitant inherence
is deduced, is inference.

jñāna rūpayā vṛttyā — that form of the modulation of knowledge
yayā anusādhakam — by which the appraisal of the possibility produced
sāhacarya saṃskāra janyayā — by concomitant inherence
sādhyam mīyate — is deduced
sā anumiti — is inference

In the first verse of the opening *darśana* of the *Darśanamālā*, the primeval world-cause is presented as a dreamlike volition (*svapnavat saṅkalpa*) of the Supreme Lord. In the next verse the concept of dream is supplemented by that of incipient memories (*vāsana*-s) which are shown as being in the universal mind. The relationship between dreams and incipient memories is one of intimate functional dynamism. Just as the synonyms and antonyms of words are classified and grouped together in a thesaurus, so, in somewhat the same manner, associated ideas are grouped together in our mind. There are some who may not agree with this proposition. William James, for instance, would have us believe that it is not ideas but things which form associations in the mind. In his *The Principles of Psychology*, he says:

> *Association*, so far as the word stands for an *effect*, is *between* THINGS THOUGHT OF — *it is* THINGS, *not ideas, which are associated in the mind.* We ought to talk of the association of *objects*, not of the association of *ideas*.[4] (Author's emphasis)

It seems that William James forgets that we cannot carry things (objects) in our mind, only the ideas associated with things. He admits this fact more clearly:

> Association occurs as amply between impressions of different senses as between homogenous sensations. Seen things and heard things cohere with each other, and with odors and tastes, in representation, in the same order in which they cohered as impressions of the outer world. Feelings of contact reproduce similarly the sights, sounds and tastes with which experience has associated them. In fact, the 'objects' of our perception, as trees, men, houses, microscopes, of which the real world seems composed, are nothing but clusters of qualities which through simultaneous stimulation have so coalesced that the moment one is excited actually it serves as a sign or cue for the idea of the others to arise.[5]

The idea of association leads us naturally to the fact of contiguity that occurs in the stream of consciousness. James defines his law of contiguity as follows:

> Time-determinations apart, the facts we have run over can all be summed up in the simple statement that *objects once experienced together tend to become associated in the imagination, so that when any one of them is thought of, the others are likely to be thought of also, in the same order of sequence or coexistence as before*. This statement we may name the law of mental *association by contiguity*.[6] (Author's emphasis)

Bain, in his *The Senses and the Intellect*, says:

> Action, Sensations, and States of Feeling, occurring together or in close succession, tend to grow together, or cohere, in such a way that, when any one of them is afterwards presented to the mind, the others are apt to be brought up in idea.[7]

It is not hard to see that ideas of things become interrelated, and how such interrelation produces matrices. How does the mind store and build into stacks such an immense quantity of information, and retrieve it almost instantaneously when it is needed? What our mind does can be compared to the activity which gives rise to "paperless books," described here by Earl C. Joseph:

> What is meant by "paperless books" is the total production, dissemination, and display of magazines, journals and books by electronic methods. The process starts with the initial draft of the manuscript by the author either dictating, writing or typing his/her thoughts directly into a type of remotely located

> TV-like computer terminal. The computer then edits the material, acting like a combined secretary and technical editor. It corrects spellings, suggests better sentence structuring, culls out repetitious material, suggests reorganization of thoughts, abstracts, collects key words, compiles citations and builds descriptors. The system plays it back to the author in real time and together they produce further tapes. The resulting tapes, (manuscripts, cataloging information, bibliographical information and abstract) are sent directly to the publisher when the author is satisfied he has a final draft.[8]

What is described here as the function of the "paperless book" is analogous to the process occurring in our mind each time the mind moves from problem detection to decision making.

In the present verse Narayana Guru speaks of inference drawn from the consolidated memory of things associated in the mind, in terms of generalities that govern the relationship between causes and effects. According to Richard Semon, "Memory is a physical residue in the nervous system formed as a result of neural activity during learning. Once formed, the residue remains in a static, dormant state, ready to be recalled."[9]

The following questions arise. Is the sum total of our dormant memories consolidated during the present life only? Where do they all remain stored? According to geneticists, the storage of memory has a history of billions of years. In fact, our complexity is to be judged by the minimum information content in the organism's genetic material. In *The Dragons of Eden*, Carl Sagan says:

> A typical human chromosome has one very long DNA molecule . . . . This DNA molecule is composed of smaller building blocks, a little like the rungs and the sides of a rope ladder. These blocks are called nucleotides and come in four varieties . . . . A typical chromosome DNA molecule in a human being is composed of about five billion pairs of nucleotides. The genetic instructions of all the other taxa on Earth are written in the same language, with the same code book. Indeed, this shared genetic language is one line of evidence that all the organisms on Earth are descended from a single ancestor, a single instance of the origin of life some four billion years ago . . . . Since there are four different kinds of nucleotides, the number of bits of information in DNA is four times the

> number of nucleotide pairs. Thus if a single chromosome has five billion nucleotides, it contains twenty billion bits of information.[10]

If this account is true, our memory is not limited to the physical residue in the nervous system formed as a result of neural activity during the learning process in this life only. Sagan traces the historical origin of memory to four billion years!

Carl Sagan arrives at a limit of four billion years in consideration of where on the time scale he fixes the origin of bacteria in his "cosmic calendar." In *The Dragons of Eden*, the references to both time and space are equivalent to myths. An animal cell is itself a small body, and its nucleus occupies very little physical space. Within the nucleus are the chromosomes. Within each chromosome is the DNA, made up of nucleotide bases of guanine, cytosine, adenine and thymine twisted together in the form of a helix. This is the farthest we can go in the search for the memory deposit at the physical level where objectivity and tangibility can still hold good in the most minimal sense. Beyond this, speculation is based on imaginary mathematical data.

One major argument between the vision of the mystic and the speculation of the scientist is the nature of the common origin of all individuated beings. The scientist traces the history of the latent potentials in a living organism to a genetic history of billions of years, while the mystic traces it to the timeless primeval cause — the incipient will of the Supreme Lord, *parameśvara.* We are not unaware of the fact that this conclusion is repugnant to empiricists like Warren S. McCulloch. He makes this clear when he says:

> The reasons for excluding them (ideas) from physics is that they must not be supposed to be either stuff or process in the causal sequences of any part of the world. They are neither material nor efficient. So, to my mind, Newton, Planck and Jeans sin by introducing God as a sort of mind at large in the world to account for the physical effects, like the action of gravity at a distance.[11]

He is entitled to his opinion, but we would value the honorable company of Newton, Planck and Jeans over and above the postulations of McCulloch.

Let us now consider the model of the physiological psychologists, and compare it to that of Narayana Guru. Hebb's model of memory consolidation is as follows:

learning —	short-term memory (electrical) —	consolidation process —	long-term memory (chemical)

According to Hebb, short-term memory exists in an electrical form that reverberates and eventually results in long-term memory.[12] But Edmund Husserl does not think the process is as simple as that, saying:

> Every actual now of consciousness, however, is subject to the law of modification. The now changes continuously from retention to retention. There results, therefore, a stable continuum which is such that every subsequent point is a retention for every earlier one. And every retention is already a continuum.[13]

The modification and the continuum of retention of which Husserl speaks cannot be limited to that phase of the evolution of consciousness within the lifespan of any one organism. Primary impressions are lying scattered in several previous genetic serializations of prior manifestations. We can therefore change Hebb's model of consolidated memory to the following:

presentation in awareness —	retention continuum —	modified recall —	reconsolidated memory
pratyakṣam	*sāhacaryavṛtti*	*anumānam*	*saṃskāra smṛti*

There is no agreement among neurophysiologists about the actual storage of memory. McCulloch describes memory as a reverberating dynamic which is erasable. Dr. Von Neumann thinks memory is static, unerasable, and the result of an irreversible change.[14] Carl Sagan suggests:

> Short-term and long-term memory reside mostly in different parts of the brain. Classical conditioning — the ability of Pavlov's dogs to salivate when the bells rang — seems to be located in the limbic system.[15]

Schneider and Tarshis hold the following view:

> Long-term memory is chemical in form *but it is not clear what chemical is involved.* If long-term memory calls for an enduring

> chemical change in the nervous system, the obvious place to look for the change is in the synapses. But the chemistry of the synapse is complex. Production of neuro-transmitters is the final step in a chain of events that begins with DNA directing the action of RNA and ends with RNA determining the production of protein. Therefore, if, indeed, the chemical counterpart of long-term storage lies in the synapse, it may involve any one of, or a combination of three factors: DNA, RNA, and protein.[16] (Our italics)

The search for a chemical basis of memory is a wild goose chase. Firstly, the physiologists have no idea what chemical might be involved. Secondly, the RNA in a synapse seems an easy concept when we consider RNA only as a physiological term. The bewildering world of RNA is well described by Carl Sagan in his typical language which actualizes mythical fantasy. He says:

> If each human brain had only one synapse — corresponding to a monumental stupidity — we would be capable of only two mental states. If we had two synapses, then $2^2 = 4$ states; three synapses, then $2^3 = 8$ states, and, in general, for N synapses, 2^N states. But the human brain is characterized by some 10^{13} synapses. Thus the number of different states of a human brain is 2 raised to this power — i.e., multiplied by itself ten trillion times. This is an unimaginably large number, far greater, for example, than the total number of elementary particles (electrons and protons) in the entire universe. . . . These enormous numbers may also explain something of the unpredictability of human behavior and those moments when we surprise even ourselves by what we do. Indeed, in the face of these numbers, the wonder is that there are any regularities at all in human behavior.[17]

The real difference between the approach of Narayana Guru and that of the above-mentioned scientists is in deciding the nature of the cause and effect complex. Halgen Hyden, a pioneer in the study of the relationship of RNA and memory, has theorized that although sensory and motor processes may elevate absolute levels of RNA, only learning can produce *new* RNA. The whole crux of the problem lies in deciding what produces what. It is the motivational dynamic of the whole being that produces not only new RNA but also enzymes and hormones.

The Guru envisions the cosmic volition of *parameśvara* as the primeval cause of the phenomenal world. According to him, the creative and motivational imagination (*saṅkalpa*) triggered by the incipient memories (*vāsana*) of the individual (*jīva*) is the causal factor of the making and undoing of the personality structure. The Guru relates our inferential awareness to our associative inner disposition. This inner disposition is to be understood in depth. Narayana Guru's definition of inference is:

> That retention continuum generated by associative value integration in the form of consolidated memory which can be recalled on the presentation of a work that is partially related to the associated value integration is inference. *Yayā sāhacarya samskāra janyāyā jñānarūpayā vṛttyā anusādhakam sādhyam mīyate sā anumitiḥ.*

This may be compared to Dignāga's definition: "Inference is made on the testimony of characteristic similarity in form." *Sārūpya lakṣaṇam pramāṇam anumānam.*

Dignāga refers only to the formal similarity of the inferent to the inferred. The Guru touches the fundamentals of memory consolidation, and the consequent awareness of modified consciousness, as the causal factor that decides the appropriateness of the inference that is being drawn. There is, however, a significant similarity between Narayana Guru's views on methodology and those of Dharmakīrti.

Among Western logicians, Bradley and Bosanquet also came close to Narayana Guru in giving a separate status to 'this' as the universal subject of all perception and judgement. However, the majority of European logicians think judgement is a "predicative connexion between two concepts."[18] Kant, of course, is an exception to this general view. In his opinion judgement is nothing more than the mode of bringing given cognitions into the objective unity of apperception.

Narayana Guru's special emphasis on 'thisness' corresponds to Aristotle's *Prima Essentia*, the first substance; this can be illustrated by the 'this' in the phrase 'this is a pot'. In the *Ātmopadeśa Śatakam*, Narayana Guru points out the importance of the first substance 'this', which he categorizes as the *viṣama*, that which is difficult to discern. It is interesting to note that Hegel also refers to 'thisness' (*das Diese*) as unutterable, going on to say that modern philosophy has not yet progressed to an understanding of this concept.

A further illustration of Narayana Guru's teaching on this subject may be found in the *Ātmopadeśa Śatakam*:

> In sameness and in the other each one's
> qualifying force always comes and becomes established;
> by the fluctuating function of these two,
> which comprise all, everything becomes the object of awareness.
>
> "This is a pot"; in that, what comes first, "this,"
> is the difficult to discern; "pot" is its qualifying predicate;
> for intellect and such *mahendra* magic to manifest,
> "this" itself becomes the *karu*; thus one should see
>
> "This is knowledge"; in that, what comes first, "this,"
> is sameness; its qualifying predicate is awareness;
> for intellect and all such to vanish, and for the true path to come,
> this should be meditated on. (v. 40-42)[19]

According to Dignāga and Dharmakīrti, judgements are of two kinds, direct and indirect. Indirect judgement is called *anumāna*. *Pratyakṣa*, or immediate perception, according to these teachers, is a synthesis between a sensation and a conception, and inference is a synthesis between a sensation and two concepts. In other words, inference is a cognition of an object through its mark (*lakṣana*) by another mark in which it has its conceptual inference or logical extension called *vyāpti*.

In his book *Buddhist Logic*, Th. Stcherbatsky puts it this way:

> In a perceptual judgement we cognise the object "X" through its symbol which is the conception "A". In an inferential judgement we cognise the object "X" through its symbols "A" and "B". The symbols A and B are related as reason and consequence. When one of them, the element A, is cognised, the cognition of the other, of the element B, necessarily follows. Since the element X, the substratum of the qualities A and B, or the subject of both these predicates, is indefinite, always the same, its expression can be dropped; its presence will be necessarily understood without any formal expression. In that case the two interrelated elements or qualities A and B will represent the whole inference or the whole inferential judgement. This judgement will then apparently consist of two

conceptions only, but related as reason and consequence, the one being necessary ground for predicating the other. The inferential judgement will then become a judgement of concommittance, *vyāpti*.[20]

Vyāpti is the same as *sāhacarya sambandha*, concomitant inherence, as Narayana Guru puts it. Vasubandhu's definition of inference, given in his *Vāda-vidhi*, is *anantaraīyaka artha darśanam tadvido anumānam*.[21] This means "a consequential vision of an implied significance is inferential judgement." This is not as explicit as Narayana Guru's definition.

As universals are bound to be too wide, including concomitant marks, loosely structured language can mislead and cause faulty inferential judgements. To guard against this, modern logicians such as Bertrand Russell and Ludwig Wittgenstein prefer to use symbols which stand for *and*, *or*, *not*, *if . . . then*, such as are used in propositional calculus. Examples of such symbols are as follows:

	$p\,q$	means	p and q
v	$p \vee q$	means	p or q or both
$+$	$p + q$	means	p or q but not both
$\sim$	$\sim p$	means	not p
$\supset$	$p \supset q$	means	if p then q, or not both p and not q
$\equiv$	$p \equiv q$	means	p if and only q, or either p or q or not p and not q

When this is applied in categorical syllogisms using S, M, P, as minor term, middle term, and major term respectively, the first figure, *barbara*, will come as:

$$M(x) \supset = P(x),\ S(x^{\supset} = M(x))$$
$$S(x) \supset = P(x)$$

and *celarent* will be:

$$M(x) \supset = \sim P\ (x),\ S(x) \supset = M(x)$$
$$S(x) \supset = \sim P(x)$$

The trouble with this kind of abstraction is that it takes us away from the whole meaning of our pursuit. Life is not lived in terms of mathematically reduced atomic propositions. Our interest in the mark (*lakṣana*) and concomitance (*vyāpti*) is that we are on the lookout to see how our life in the transactional world, where we have to be concerned with specific characteristics, catches hold of us and makes us identify with particular individuals, things, and events, and also how our consciousness is vivified into multitudinous, morbid formations. This makes our return to universal concomitance of the one existence which is the ground of all existence, to the one knowledge that makes all awareness an illumination of the Self, and to the one norm or criterion which makes all individual cases instances of the endearment (*priyam*) of the Self, difficult if not impossible.

Even in experimental science we do not begin with proof. A general law is postulated as a working hypothesis and is given as an *a priori* ground to work with. After enumerating the hypothesis, we adopt a methodology to see if that hypothesis yields a result. If so, the result is seen as proof. The proof in a single case is one of simple enumeration. Even if the experiment is repeated a thousand times, all that the scientist presents to us is an analogy — an analogy based on the conviction of his testimony. In 99% of cases we believe the word of the scientist, until another scientist contradicts the finding and makes known to the world what was wrong with the analogy of his predecessor. So Narayana Guru in the next verse calls our attention to the testimony of analogy. This leads naturally to the emphasis on the *a priori* acceptance of Word-wisdom.

VERSE 8

gatvā samīpam meyasya
mīyate śrutalakṣaṇaḥ
yayā samvitsopamitir
mṛgo'yamiti rūpayā

On going near the object to be ascertained
and recognizing, "this is the form of the animal
whose marks have been heard of" — that by which
such knowledge comes is analogy.

gatvā — on going
samīpam — near
meyasya — the object to be ascertained
mīyate — and recognizing
iti rūpayā — this is the form
ayam mṛgaḥ — of the animal whose
śruta lakṣaṇaḥ — marks have been heard of
yaya — that by which
sa samvit — such knowledge (comes)
upamitiḥ — is analogy

The example given in this verse to illustrate comparison is similar to the story of the man who is going to the forest in search of the wild bull. He has heard from an informant by what marks the wild bull can be recognized. It has the same marks as a domesticated bull. In the Zen story, the seeker first recognizes the footprints of the bull, following which he finally comes to the bull itself. Then comparing the domestic bull with the wild one he concludes: "This is the form of the animal whose marks have been heard of." Such knowledge is called analogical inference or comparison.

Comparison is the most familiar form of logic which we consciously or unconsciously adopt, as much in science as in poetry. As a matter of fact, the entire theme of our conscious life is a continuous deciphering of the immediate present with the aid of antecedent marks of an analogous previous experience. In other words one's whole life is a continuing series of metaphors and similes. To make a point clear even common folk give examples. All the elaborate performances of experiments in the scientists' laboratories are nothing but the proof of a postulated hypothesis through the arrangement of an analogous experiment with which the hypothesis can be compared. The poet makes full use of the technique of comparison by devising many metaphors which are simple or intriguing, direct or suggested.

Inference by analogy or comparison is of extreme importance to a seeker of Self-knowledge. In the second chapter of the Bhagavad Gita, Arjuna asks for the marks of a wise person who is established in the firm foundation of his intelligence. He specifically asks how such a person sits, speaks, and conducts himself. Sri Kṛṣṇa obliges Arjuna by giving a full description of such a knower. Again in the Gita, Arjuna asks Kṛṣṇa for the marks of a yogi who has transcended the triple modalities of nature. In the Bible, Jesus gives many examples to illustrate the Kingdom of God. Even the phrase "Kingdom of God" has in it a suggested comparison. The marks to be ascertained, whether for recognizing the wild bull or one's true Self, are held before one's discerning eye and take the form of an *a priori* notion. An experiment conducted by a scientist is to experience the proof of the assumed hypothesis. In spiritual life also the proof stands squarely on experiement. Then alone does *a priori* knowledge become ascertained with *a posteriori* conviction.

VERSE 9

aham mameti jñānam ya-
didam taditi yacca tat
jīvajñānam tadapara-
mindriyajñānam iṣyate

The knowledge of "I am," "mine," and so on,
is individual knowledge;
the other, such as "that," "this," and so on,
is spoken of as sensory knowledge.

yat jñānam — the knowledge of
aham — I am
mama iti — mine and so on
tat jīva jñānam — is individual knowledge
tat aparam — the other
idam tat iti yat ca — such as that, this, and so on
iṣyate — is spoken of
indriyajñānam — as sensory knowledge

In expressions like "I am," "I think," "my feeling," "my head," "my wife," "my hat," "this house," and "that star," how the subject relates himself or herself with the object of knowledge with several forms of subtlety is worth examining. In the expression "I am," the subject introspectively gathers all the awareness which the individual can wield at one time and designates it as 'I'. After doing so, that 'I' is made the object of the same awareness and its existential verity is emphasized with the assertion 'am'. Although it sounds like a subjective statement, the person who is saying 'am' is the subject and the 'I' is an alienated object. This implies an ignorance which lurks at the very bottom of the individuation of personal awareness. In the expression "I think," the process by which individuation is effected is similarly alienated as a witnessable process that is going on as "other than I," and it is objectivized. This kind of scrutiny lays bare the anatomy of individuation.

When one says "my feeling," a part of consciousness that lies entrenched in sensitivity is highlighted, and thus, for the purpose of discussion, it is separated from the entirety of the organism and abstracted as a separate entity. This is a classic example of a general notion or total awareness which is often vivified, with separate significance given to fragmentary knowledge.

In expressions like "my head," there is a sort of symmetrical balancing between the subjective and the objective, because the term 'my' refers to an invisible agency of cognition and 'head' refers to an object that can be objectively observed by another person. What is more surprising and yet taken for granted is the ease with which a subjective notion and an objective notion are fused into an organic whole.

In an expression like "my wife," the agent 'my' and the object 'wife' are both subtle abstractions residing in two entirely different persons. The objective tangibility of both the individuals is pushed aside as a matter of no consequence, and emphasis is laid on two private notions of the subject. No one can for sure comprehend the exact awareness that is present in a person when he says "my" and "my wife." The objective, observable woman to whom the reference of wife is made has nothing biologically or physiologically present which gives the distinguishing marks of a wife. Although the mind creates several such confections of knowledge spontaneously, we hardly notice how facts belonging to a heterogeneous order are treated as if they all belong to a homogeneous system.

In expressions like "my hat," and "this house," the objectivity of 'hat' and 'house' are both of the same order, with the exception that there is an introjected subjective notion of an attitude of possessiveness in "my hat," whereas "this house" stands alone as a pure object. Even when the house is presented as an altogether independent entity, it has behind its presentation a fully concealed subject. This becomes evident when we contrast the spatial relationship which the subject has with 'this' house and 'that' star. Rarely do we come across in psychology such a thorough-going analysis of individuation as the Guru has presented here in such simple words.

VERSE 10

aum tat saditi nirddiṣṭam
brahmātmaikyamupāgatam
kalpanādivihīnam yat
tat parajñānamīryate

Aum tat sat — what is thus instructed,
arrived at as the union of the Absolute and the Self,
devoid of functions like willing —
that is said to be absolute knowledge.

aum tat sat — *aum tat sat*
iti nirddiṣṭam — what is thus instructed
upāgatam — arrived at
brahmātmaikyam — as the union of the Absolute and the Self
vihīnam — devoid of
kalpanādi — functions like willing
yat tat īryate — that is said to be
parajñānam — absolute knowledge

Aum tat sat is one of the great dictums which seers arrive at. *Tat sat* literally means 'that is', and in this special context 'that alone is'. In the *mahāvākya*, or great dictum, *tat tvam asi*, meaning 'That thou art', 'That' stands unqualified. However, in this present case 'that' is indicative of *aum*, hence this dictum can be translated as 'that *aum* alone is', or, more precisely, '*aum* alone is'. In the opening verse of the *Jñāna Darśana* knowledge was said to be two kinds, conditioned and unconditioned. In the present verse we have come back to discuss that unconditioned knowledge. Unconditioned knowledge is indescribable, so riṣis use the sound *aum* to indicate it. In the Upanishads we come across expressions like: *aum itiyetat*, 'this is *aum'; aum ityekākṣaram brahma*, 'the monosyllable *aum* is the Absolute'; *aum iti brahma*, '*aum* is the Absolute'.

Indivisible and all-embracing knowledge is *aum*, and that is indicated here as the Absolute. The cosmological aspect of the Absolute and the psychological aspect of the Absolute are indivisibly united. In Patañjali's *Yoga Sūtra*, the same *aum* is mentioned as the indicative symbol of God, *tasya vacakaḥ pranavaḥ*. In the *Chāndogya Upaniṣad*, *aum* is mentioned as the word of consent. As the Absolute is everything, it can be indicated by any nomenclature.

To make it explicit that no name can fully describe the Absolute, it is merely mentioned as 'That'. According to the seers, words and mind recoil upon themselves on making an attempt to describe the Absolute. As *aum*, *tat*, and *sat* are employed differently to describe the indescribable, all three terms have become so semantically rich as to each stand singularly for the Absolute.

When consciousness of the subject stands circumlimited as the subject, and the object is both seen and described as the immeasurable infinitude which lies spread out in time and space as having no bound and yet having for its central locus the perceiving and conceiving subject's I-consciousness, a twofold conditioning is implied: the psychologically conceived 'I' and the cosmologically conceived 'that'. One can experience the cosmological conditioning of 'that' only as units of relatively delimited particulars. which at the most can be classified under generic heads which are also of finite nature. The various forms of conditionings to which the subject and object are exposed have already been dealt with in the previous verses. As *Darśanamālā* is intended to aid the student to realize the union of the Self and the Absolute, the present verse is given as a conclusive teaching that the nondifferentiated knowledge of the Absolute and the Self can come only when all vestiges of conditionings, both psychologic and cosmologic, have fully disappeared. *Jñāna Darśana* is placed between *Karma Darśana* and *Bhakti Darśana* in the present composition. In *karma* the duality of the actor and action is inevitable. Such a duality is admissible in the field of conditioned knowledge. *Bhakti*, on the other hand, is going to be defined in the next *darśana* as a continuous process of knowledge being weaned away from the conditioned to become undifferentiated from the unconditioned. So it is only appropriate that the present *darśana* discusses both the conditioned and unconditioned kinds of knowledge.

The imperiential union of the psychologic and the cosmologic indicated in the present verse is not a knowledge that is one among many items of information that one gains through an act of ratiocination or by dualistic cognition. It is a tremendously sweeping and overwhelming denial of all the limiting adjuncts of an individuated self. After one has embraced this indescribable union, even when the previous individuation returns it does not gain the dynamic status of an ego-centred individual again. Both the psychologic 'I' and the cosmologic 'other' are reduced to mere appearances, and a strong bond of union prevails as a substratum for the superimposition of both 'I' and the 'other'. This knowledge has the existential verity of irrefutability and the subsistential transparency of a boundless Self-knowledge that is not alienated anywhere as a part torn off, or even modulated as an objectivization of any kind. In its absolute value-content it is intensely ecstatic, which can be poorly illustrated by such examples as the total union which is experienced in love. Finite experiencing of love between two people is prized above everything because that is the nearest individuals can arrive at with their conditioned knowledge to the appreciation of the blissful nature of the Self nondifferentiated from the Absolute. It is this blessed state that is going to be dealt with progressively in the next three *darśana*-s

VII. JÑĀNA DARŚANAM

1 Laurence Urdang, ed. in chief, *The Random House Dictionary of the English language, College Edition*, Random House, New York, 1968

2 R.E. Hume, *Thirteen Principal Upanishads* Kena Upanishad, First Khanda, verse -2, Oxford University Press, New York, 1975, page. 335

3 Nataraja Guru, *The Bhagavad Gita*, R & K Publishing House, New Delhi, Ch. XV, v.9, page. 605.

4 William James, *The Principles of Psychology*, Dover Publications, New York, 1950, p. 554.

5 ibid. p. 555

6 ibid. p. 561

7 Alexander Bain, *The Senses and the Intellect*, Appleton and Co., New York, 1974, p. 327.

8 Earl C. Joseph, "Cybernetics and the Management of Large Computer Systems," in *Cybernetics and the Management of Large Systems*, ed. by Edmond M. Dewan, Spartan Books, New York, 1969, pages 82, 83.

9 Allen M. Schneider and Barry Tarshis, *An Introduction to Physiological Psychology*, Random House, New York, 1975, page. 431.

10 Carl Sagan, *The Dragons of Eden*, Random House, New York, 1977, pages 22–24

11 Warren S. McCulloch, *Embodiments of Mind*, MIT Press, Cambridge 1965, pages. 72–73

12 Schneider and Tarshis, op. cit., page. 433

13 Edmund Husserl, *The Phenomenology of Internal Time-Consciousness*, Indiana University Press, Bloomington, 1973, pages. 50, 51

14 See dialogue McCulloch / Neumann, *Embodiments of Mind*, page. 92

15 Carl Sagan, op. cit., pages, 74, 75

16 Schneider and Tarshis, op. cit., page. 439

17 Carl Sagan, op. cit., 42

18 Th. Stcherbatsky, *Buddhist Logic*, Dover Publications Vol. 1, New York, York, 1962, page. 227

19 Nitya Chaitanya Yati, *Neither This Nor That But Aum*, Vikas, New Delhi, 1982, pages. 82–87

20 Th. Stcherbatsky, op. cit., Vol 1, page. 231, 232

21 ibid. Vol 1, page. 236

VIII. BHAKTI DARSANAM

Contemplative Devotion

Love, devotion, compassion, empathy, and consequent rapture of mind come spontaneously rather than as a result of mechanically practiced discipline. Although concentration is prized as a high value both in public life and spiritual pursuit, people quite often forget that it comes as a result of the evoking of a deep interest which is centered around a value that is most dear to one's mind.

Our entire life can be described as an aggregate of values and a network of relationships connecting or coordinating one item of value to another. Every value has a self-luminous nucleus which characteristically triggers a sense of joy ranging from an intense experience of bliss to a moderate sense of satisfaction or well-being. Individual items of sensuous experience are part of the passing parade of phenomenal flux, and hence cannot hold the mind in rapture for more than a given time, which is likely to be short if not momentary.

When such an exteriorized apprehension of physical joy is object-oriented, mind has a tendency to seek a neutral midway point between the subject and the object. Such a joyous state obliterates the duality of the subject and the object, and the mind refuses to be descriptive in the cognizance of such an experience. It is as if the state of awareness becomes identical with a self-induced hypnosis. Afterwards the quality of its affectivity recurs many times, and the joy roused by previous sensuousness becomes more and more abstracted and generalized. Such recurring experience of abstraction becomes aligned with several other closely related experiences, and thus becomes capable of remaining at sublime levels of an abstract sense of the lovable, the beautiful, the adorable, the wonderful, etc. . In such a state there is little or no identification either with the individuated subject or the object ground on which the joyous experience is projected. For this reason it is normal for a person to remain at home in his or her personal center. The Guru describes such a spontaneous involvement with oneself as a joyous and effortless beatitude, and act of contemplative devotion.

In fact it is not an act unless one understands it as *actus purus*, pure action.

It is in this pure joy that one experiences one's natural alignment with the Absolute. In the present case the Absolute should not be confused with anything astounding, voluminous, or infinite. It is absolute in the sense in which the roseness of a rose is absolute, the cheerfulness of a smile is absolute, or the quality of a teardrop is absolute. The glow of a value in itself and the awareness of the Self are not two separate experiences. For this reason one's identification with the total apprehension of one's imperiential selfsameness with a value automatically generates the contemplation of the Self and an affinity with the Absolute.

The most popular experience in which people can easily transcend the sense of duality is when loving mates are overwhelmed with the thrill of each other's inseparable presence as the pearl of one's heart's sweetness. Holding this sense of rapturous fulfillment as the model to measure love and one's consequent devotion to it, Narayana Guru presents in this chapter a scheme which can serve us as an intelligent key to unravel the science of values and their interrelationships. As the entire process is woven around one's awareness of the ever-attracting and resplendent Self within, *bhakti* is defined as the continuous contemplation of one's Self.

VERSE 1

bhaktirātmānusandhāna-
mātmā'nandaghanoyataḥ
ātmānam anusandhatte
sadaivātmavidātmanā

Meditation on the Self is *bhakti*.
That by which the Self is blissful, with that,
the knower of the Self always meditates
upon the Self by the Self.

anusandhānam — meditation on
ātma — the Self
bhaktiḥ — is *bhakti*
yataḥ — that by which
ātma — the Self
ānandaghana — is blissful
tataḥ — with that
ātmavit — the knower of the Self
sada eva — always
anusandhatte — meditates upon
ātmānam — the Self
ātmana — by the Self

Nataraja Guru, in his translation and commentary on the *Darśanamālā*, calls *Bhakti Darśana* the vision by contemplation. Treating *bhakti* as contemplation is in conformity with the traditionally recognized scholastic use of the word as it applies to Christian mystics. In our own times, meditation and contemplation are used as synonyms: both the terms have lost their precise connotation and have become vague in meaning. So it has become necessary to revaluate and restate the terms 'meditation' and 'contemplation'. Sequentially, meditation comes as a prelude to con- contemplation. The way to know something, as Henri Bergson puts it, is not by going around it, but by first entering into it and then being it. Meditation is an active process of applying one's mind to make a total 'imploration' of the depth of whatever is to be known. The state of actually being it is what is achieved by contemplation. It is a passive but steady state. In modern days this distinction is seldom thought of, and *dhyāna* is often translated as meditation. For the purpose of the present study, we translate *anusandhānam* as meditation and *bhakti* as contemplation.

The present verse is closely related to a verse from the Bhagavad Gita. It says:

> But for him who happens to be attached to the Self alone,
> who finds full satisfaction in the Self —
> for such a man who is happy in the Self as such, too,
> there is nothing that he should do. (III: 17)[1]

An individuated mind finds rest only when it returns to its original state. It is conjunction with the non-Self that creates restlessness or disturbance in the self. In individual cases of suffering one can always notice an incidence of the self identifying itself with what it is not, such as when one says, "I am sick." This is a clear case of mistaking the miserable condition of the body for the nature of the Self. One knows the Self only when the 'be-ness'* of the Self (*sat*) is identical with happiness through and through, and there prevails the knowledge of that happiness with nothing else to limit or shade it to any degree. It is for this reason that the Guru says the knower of the Self is always in a state of meditating on the Self by the Self. Because of the ever-prevailing happiness, the mind is fully absorbed in that nature of the Self.

Śankara defines *bhakti* in the *Vivekacūdāmaṇi* (*The Crest Jewel of Wisdom Discrimination*) as *sva svarūpa anusandhānam bhaktiḥ*, which means 'contemplation is the continuous meditation on one's own true nature'. The word *anusandhānam* holds in it the entire key to *Bhakti Darśana*.

This chapter could easily have been called the 'Vision by love'. In Narada's *Bhakti Sūtra*, *bhakti* is even defined as absolute love, which can also mean love for the Absolute. Love is a much used and abused term that should be examined carefully in the present context in order to know how and in what sense *bhakti* is love.

In the context of love it is only normal to think of the reciprocation of giving and receiving love between the lover and the beloved. The terms lover and beloved are also mutually exchangeable. What characterizes a loving couple is their ever-abiding need for togetherness and the undiminishing appreciation of each other as the most lovable and truly loved reality of their beingness of a here and be

* 'Be-ness' is used here in the sense of at-one-ment with the Absolute.

state. This overwhelming recognition of 'be-ness' transcends the fragmentation of time, and thus the experience is so total and realistic that it does not allow the intrusion of any desire for anything else. As a result of such a spiritual compulsion to be ever persisting in the union of what is most adored, the absorption of consciousness implied in that state requires no deliberation to maintain the union. Only where there is such an irrevokable persistence of absorbing interest does the word *anusandhānam* become meaningful.

All beings are always, by their own nature, driven to seek such union that can give at-one-ment with supreme happiness. Unfortunately, on the periphery of life the unreal is very often mistaken for the real; hence every identification with an imaginary source of bliss is automatically repulsed by the inevitable disillusionment that follows on the heels of identification. The fact that the search for happiness is never given up even for a split second shows how dear the value of happiness is. Such being the universal urge to be happy, it is not surprising that a seer of the Self sees the Self as bliss through and through (*ānandaghanam*), and that such a knower is held in total union with what he has envisioned by his magnificent obsession for the hidden splendor of his own blissful beingness.

VERSE 2

anusandhīyate brahma
brahmānandaghnam yataḥ
sada brahmānusandhānam
bhaktirityavagamyate

Brahma is meditated upon
because *Brahma* is blissful.
Constant meditation on *Brahma*
Thus is known as *bhakti*.

brahma — *Brahma*
anusandhīyate — is meditated upon
yataḥ — because
brahma — *Brahma*
ānandaghanam — is blissful
sada — constant
brahma anusandhānam — meditation on *Brahma*
iti avagamyate — is thus known as
bhaktiḥ — *bhakti*

Brahma is the Absolute. Knowledge of the Absolute is an inevitable corollary of the knowledge of the Self. In this context the Absolute is to be understood not as a noun but as a continuous absolution of everything that comes under the purview of consciousness. When consciousness becomes individuated, it seems to assume several modes such as a sequential motion from the prior to the antecedent, extension in all directions, an objectivization of bodily form, and images of gestaltations. When these and the several other such modes stand one apart from the other to suit the finitude of mind's logistics, individuation becomes fully cramped so as to be confined within the narrow frame of an embodied being. Self-knowledge is a re-cognition of the singular homogeneity that pervades all modes, and the spontaneous reclaiming of all alienated modes into an evenly sustaining existentiality which fills as well as transcends all conceivable limits of space and time, mass and motion, and pairs of opposites such as subject and object, knower and known, actor and action, and the enjoyer and the enjoyed. This sudden and total reconversion of the modulated into its true and original nonduality is the absolution that figures in this verse as an act of meditation on *Brahma*.

In the commentary on the previous verse, love was shown as a unifying dynamic. The same love, in its perfection of actualization, is seen here as an ever-abiding rejoicing in the highest sense of mystical union with all. When such a union is realized, the knower of the Self is absolved of all taints of prejudicial judgements that forbid the natural flow of love in all directions and the embracing of all as aspects of one and the same universal Self. This constant meditation on the all-embracing Absolute is exemplified in the lives of the Buddha, Lao-tzu, Jesus Christ, and other perfected beings who are well known for their compassion and their voluntary admission of unlimited liability to the entire world, for the fulfillment of which they lived every moment of their lives. The constant meditation on the Absolute is not to be understood as a sheer withdrawal and absorption into a faceless and characterless emptiness, but as a positive acceptance of one's cosmic dimension and a universal recognition of the one Self that prevails in all and everywhere as the only joy and meaning of this world.

VERSE 3

ānandameva dhyāyanti
sarve duḥkham na kaścana
yadānandaparam dhyānam
bhaktirityupadiśyate

Āṇanda alone is meditated,
not misery by anyone any time.
That meditation which is blissful
is *bhakti*, it is instructed.

ānandam eva — *ānanda* alone
dhyāyanti — is meditated
na duḥkham — not misery
sarve — by anyone
kaścana — any time
yat — that
dhyānam — meditation
ānanda param — which is blissful
bhaktiḥ iti — is *bhakti*
upadiśyate — it is instructed

Both pain and pleasure are forms of misery. If pleasure is a positive agitation of the sensory system, pain is a negative agitation. Both amount to throwing the equilibrium of the composure of consciousness out of gear. Absolute well-being is perfect 'be-ness', and being devoid of the prospect of becoming. Even the slightest ripple on the surface of water is an indication that its tranquility is disturbed. Consciousness is subjected to disturbance much more easily than the molecular disturbance of air or water. But this does not mean the highest state of harmony has to be inertial. Our own healthy body is a good example of a continuous harmony being sustained as it is engaged in various functions. We are not conscious of our bones, muscles, sinews, skin, circulation of blood, respiratory system, digestive process, or the eliminative functions of the kidney and bladder unless they begin to malfunction. From this it is clearly evident that a perfect state of well-being does not show up in the realm of objectivized consciousness. All objectivizations are the result of a partial modulation of consciousness stimulated by a physical, physiological, or psychological encounter with a force that is alien to the system of harmonious function. Such stimulated modulations become highlighted as affective incidents, and all affective incidents circumscribe consciousness with a nucleic emphasis on an ego identity. The ego can never be aroused without a boundary being provided for it. An ego boundary marks the threshold of confrontation and the line behind which the ego is propelled to stand in abeyance, defending individuation against being absolved of its uniqueness. It is this threat that is experienced at several levels, such as the physical, psychological, and societal, and which perpetuates man's preoccupation with egogenic problems, the main source of human misery.

Dhyāna is defined in the Bhagavad Gita as a state of being devoid of imagination of any kind. The elementary disturbance that crops up in consciousness is in the form of a self-induced interrogation, such as "What is this that I perceive?" or "What is happening to me?" This first ripple in the calm surface of consciousness is the call to make a judgement of a projected situation. An instantaneous phenomenon that arises in such a contingency is the dichotomization of consciousness into the perceiver and the perceived. Now it becomes obligatory for the perceiver to separate the characteristics of the perceived from the generality of its existence as a predictable attribute, and then to formulate the judgement "This is such and such." What is predicated as 'such and such' is the conceptual projection objectivized to satisfy the initial question "What is this?" *Dhyāna*, or the pure state of contemplation, is said to be a state wherein such objectivization, conceptualization, and judgement are not warranted.

The state of meditation ascribed to all in the first line of the verse is to be understood not as a conscious action but as a state of pure 'be-ness', and if it implies any action at all it should be treated as inaction in action. As the individual is inhabiting a hypersensitive organism that can be easily equated with a beehive, with the bustle of several urges and potentialities, he is easily exposed to provocation. Every provocation is an exposure to misery. No being likes to be thus provoked. Even a worm wriggles to get out of a disturbing state to a more comfortable or tranquil one. That is why the second line mentions that no one at any time meditates on misery.

In the two previous verses, *bhakti* was identified with *ātma* and *Brahma* respectively. *Bhakti* can be both *ātma* and *Brahma* only if *Brahma* and *ātma* are the same. In the Vedantic frame of reference there are related terms like *parābrahma* and *aparābrah-*

ma, and *jivātma* and *paramātma*. The *aparā* and *parā* aspects attributed to *Brahma* describe states of the Absolute being understood in terms of the manifested phenomena of nature and the unmanifested or transcendental 'be-ness' of the Absolute. When the physical phenomenality of the cosmos is viewed as an affective manifestation of the Absolute, there emerges before the individual the vast world of unlimited time and space checkered with all kinds of names and forms to contend with. Similarly, when the individuated Self, qualified as *jivātma*, is cut out into a separate entity with specific dimension and unique character, the undisturbed state of consciousness that goes into the making of such an individual becomes substituted for by a series of peripheral mentations intrinsically connected with human physiology and its conditioned reflexes. That being the common lot of people, hardly anyone is in a state of meditation. *Ātma*, *Brahma* and *ānanda* fall into the vertical line of *bhakti* only when the manifested phenomena, conditioned consciousness, and the dual state of pain/pleasure affectivity are all reduced to the nondual reality of 'be-ness'. Such a reduction is not a mere intellectual exercise. In the present case, *bhakti* means embracing the universal; and hence the lover of the Absolute, who is seeking union through a state of nondual bliss, has to enter into a wholesale commitment to effect harmony whereever there is the likelihood of a disturbing element raising its head to tamper with the harmonious functioning of the world order. This is the concept of the merciful Buddha or of the savior that is seen in Jesus Christ.

VERSE 4

ātmaiva brahma, bhajati
nānyamātmānamātmavit
bhajatīti yadātmānam
bhaktirityabhidhīyate

Ātma alone is *Brahma.*
The knower of the Self contemplates the *ātma*, not any other.
This thus meditating the Self
is named as *bhakti.*

ātma eva — *ātma* alone is
brahma — *Brahma*
ātmavit — the knower of the Self
bhajati — contemplates
ātmānam — the *ātma*
na anyam — not any other
iti yat bhajati — this thus meditating
ātmānam — the Self
abhidhīyate — is named
iti bhaktiḥ — as *bhakti*

If ignorance is like an ocean of darkness, knowledge is like an island of light where rises the resplendent sun of pure consciousness. Although darkness is negative, it does have the capacity to conceal truth and obstruct vision. When light comes it does not push away darkness. The very presence of light is the absence of darkness. Light not only causes its own existence but it also automatically reveals its presence. It not only presents itself but also illuminates whatever is within its ambit.

The light that is spoken of here is not physical light but the illuminating and self-revealing qualities of consciousness. The self-revealing consciousness is the *ātma*. The revelation is not to any agent other than the Self because nothing else exists except the negativity of non-knowledge. In the present verse the knower of the Self is said to be ever in contemplation of the Absolute. The word used here is *bhajati* and not *dhyāyati*. To be and to know are here reduced into one and the same nature of the Self. As the Self is boundless and not tainted with any relativistic adjunct, it can as well be recognized as *Brahma*, the Absolute. The ocean can be called water because water is the only content of ocean. *Brahma* and *ātma* are related in the same sense. The term *Brahma* as a self-signifying word is necessitated because the knowledge of the Self can sometimes be circumlimited with ego boundaries, and thus can manifest as conditional states. When a pot or jar is immersed in the ocean, no substantial change takes place either to the ocean or to its content, the water. But if the vessel is lifted out of the ocean full of water, even though nothing has happened to the basic formula of the composition of the water as H_2O, nobody would call it ocean. Now it is only a potful of water. It is this kind of crippling effect that comes to the conditional Self when it is identified as a conscious operation of awareness that is of a sensory, cognitive, or volitional import. This is why, in formal logic, the converse of a universal proposition is said to be not tenable. We can confidently say "All oceans are water," but its converse, "All instances of water are oceans," cannot be accepted. The present verse recognizes knowledge as Self-knowledge only when it is free of any limiting conditioning.

In the previous *darśana*, all forms of conditioned knowledge such as perception, inference, comparison, and sensory- and ego-oriented manifestations were specified. Only *parajñānam*, unconditional knowledge that transcends relativistic notions, can be considered as true Self-knowledge in that respect. It is thoroughly in resonance with the Absolute, and it is that resonance that is described here as *bhajanam*, contemplation. The word *bhajanam* has in it a very subtle suggestion that the state described here is dynamic and not static, open and not closed. Its range is infinite and not finite. No experience of a relativistic order can fully reveal the true purport of *bhajanam* in its immensely rich mystical resplendence. However, we can get a faint idea by comparing it to the striking of a matchstick in an absolutely dark place. Where the flame burns there is no darkness, but as we look farther and farther away from the flame we notice a gradual increase of darkness until it is nothing but intense darkness. Although, logically, light and darkness cannot coexist, physically this paradoxical status exists. Otherwise, an increase in the voltage of light would not alter the intensity of light in an illuminated room. The shimmering self-evidence of a person sitting in the dark and saying "I am" is a case of Self-knowledge, but in a badly limited and grossly conditioned state. The complexity of its relativity only increases when that consciousness is fed with the sense data of perception and the limitless conjectures of a mind that is capable of proliferating compositions of mental images. In this way, a person can have so many informational tags put into his bio-computer as to make him a bursting reservoir of information. This of course is not a case of the knower of the Self, and this knowledge is certainly not Self-knowledge.

Although effort is required for a person to free himself of the ten thousand and one colorations and conditionings that come to his mind, once he is free of the tyranny of inhibitory or obsessive compulsions consciousness effortlessly shines forth without having any need to dismiss the unreal. And although there can be a relativistic increase or decrease in physical light, or in the cognitive clarity of apprehending and discerning objects of perceptual or conceptual import, there exist no such degrees of comparison in consciousness that is pure, simple, and homogeneous. This is not a state that is manifesting, but it is what truly is and what is veiled by the phenomenon of relativism, which is comparable to the kaleidoscopic variegation of patterns and designs in an organically functioning tapestry of mental images. In the conditioned state, innumerable are the objects for the mind to meditate on, but in the unconditioned state the Self alone is, and it has not a second to be with. Hence we can say it has become the all-filling *Brahma* which is never again tampered with by the advent of anything conditional, eventual, or consequential. This pure state is *bhakti*.

VERSE 5

ānanda ātmā brahmeti
nāmaitasyaiva tanyate
iti niscita dhīryasya
sa bhakta iti viśrutaḥ

Ānanda, *ātma* and *Brahma* —
such are the names of this alone, so it is said.
In whom there is such certitude of awareness,
he as a contemplative is well known.

ānanda ātma brahma — *ānanda*, *ātma* and *Brahma*
iti — such
nāma etasya eva — are the names of this alone
tanyate — so it is said
yasya — in whom
niścita dhiḥ — there is such certitude of awareness
sa bhaktaḥ — he as a contemplative
iti viśrutaḥ — is well known

During our wakeful hours every receptor in our nervous system is capable of producing a world of interest widely variant from the one produced a few moments before. Each sense organ is keen to add to the given world of perception its special contribution, such as the formal, tonal, tactual, palatal and olfactory. Every cell in our body can go into panic and raise an S. O. S. alarm. This growing, changing, evolving, decaying, and dying organism of ours is constantly being hit by forces extraneous to our body and mind, just like a billiard ball, because the phenomenal world is a hyperactive cloud chamber in which everything, from the most invisible subatomic particles to the inconceivably large galaxies, is always moving, with each in its own orbit and all with a regulated motion. Clashes, blasts and counterblasts, and alchemic changes both gradual and instant, are continuously taking place at the gross level of solids, liquids and gases, and at the subtle levels of energies and modes of consciousness. Such is the world of a beginningless, chaotic cosmos and an endless cosmic chaos.

The consciousness imprisoned in the psychosomatic matrix of an individual is endlessly drifting, with a nucleus of an I-consciousness which is likely to be infested with the infection of an almost incurable egotism. And yet this ego is commisioned to do the tremendous task of understanding the mini-infrastructure of the individuation given it to monitor as well as the metastructure of the cosmic system of which this psychosomatic sub-system is an organic and integral part. However negligible is the role of an individual in the grand scheme of the known and unknown cosmos, human life is so fated that each individual's universe is physically and conceptually structured around the continuously pulsating notion of 'I' to which every perception, every cognition, every volition, and every aesthetic appreciation, positive or negative, is to be constantly coordinated to preserve the integrity of one's orientation. The I-consciousness in us is expected to act as a baby Hercules or an infant Aṣṭavakra to do the tremendous work of deciphering the hydra-headed myth which is presented to its already contaminated instrument of observation, and each time with a different Gordian Knot. It is no wonder that millions and millions of ego-oriented individuals fail in this task a billion times, to be gobbled by the terrible witch of logical fallacy whom Indians call *māyā*, and others, sin or Satan. However terrible or incomprehensible this myth looks, it is the home, sustenence, and only meaning of our life on Earth and the cosmic whole to which such a life belongs. Deciphering this myth is variously called awakening, liberation, emancipation, knowing the Tao, God-realization, salvation, and Self-realization.

In the fragmentary heap of relativistic notions and impressions that cling onto our sensory or cognitive consciousness with the firmness of a bionic handshake, one is bound to be frustrated about not seeing any trace of the Absolute, *Brahma*, anywhere. Even the idea of a Self is irreparably disfigured because of its substitution with the individual's physical body and the constant shouts and stutterings of the ego. In spite of the ever-raging storm of such adversities there is a ray of hope, because every now and then the senses discover a momentary joy in the objective presentation of a sensation, a cognition, an imagination, or in a constant and contiguous presentation of a certain certitude, which can come and stay as a permanent plank under one's foot. It is by firmly standing on this plank of certitude, the 'be-ness' of life, that one makes a dent in the world of names and forms, causes and effects, and actions and actors, to enter into the ontologic existentiality which sustains every form and name and the causal unity of actions revealed as the governing law of the universe. This law is discovered and appreciated as the constant behind all the variables in the changing worlds of the physical, the chemical, and the biological.

As we become more and more familiar with the inner unity of an otherwise heterogeneous world, we begin to see with more transparency the common anatomy of universal laws in their mathematical logic, and the syntax and inflex of the language of universal myth in the grand drama of life, expressed through the ecstasies of love and the tearful pathos of a wrongly placed love's failure. Then we have already entered the portals of truth and we are no longer outsiders to the secret of creation. We are no longer blindfolded. Individuality does not obstruct us from seeing that the same Self, which one can clearly perceive behind the notion of I-consciousness, continues in its homogeneous and unlimited vastness behind the ever-deceiving symbols of 'you', 'he', 'she', 'it', 'they', 'this' and 'that'. Just as I am dear to myself, the endearment has now magnified a thousandfold and become coextensive and commingled with the Self of all. Fetters of the individual are broken; frontiers of vision are smashed. The perilous separation is averted. Love reigns supreme, and in its clear sky there never comes even once a cloud of suspicion or hatred. Consciousness is freed from the bondages of the past. Time is no longer segmented. Allah alone is. It is as if that 'is' is not an 'is'. It may be called the *sūnyata* of the *nibbāna*, One without a second. Verily, "this Self is the Absolute," *ayam ātma brahma*.

VERSE 6

ānando'hamaham brahmā-
tmā'hamasmīti rūpataḥ
bhāvanā santatam yasya
sa bhakta iti viśrutaḥ

I am *ānanda*, I am *Brahma*, I am *ātma*;
in such forms, for whom
there is always identification,
as a contemplative he is well known.

ānandaḥ aham (*asmi*) — I am *ānanda*
aham brahmaḥ (*asmi*) — I am *Brahma*
aham ātma (*asmi*) — I am *ātma*
iti rūpataḥ — in such forms
yasya — for whom
satatam — there is always
bhāvanā — identification
bhaktaḥ iti — as a contemplative
sa viśrutaḥ — he is well known

The impenetrability of matter and the evanescene of an idea such as "God is Love" are conjectures of mind. How many such conjectures is the mind capable of? No one can say, because mind is replete with millions of such shimmering mentations that glow like fireflies. This is an activity that goes on continuously. In each such glow there looms existence as "this is." Each affirmation of the given existence is immediately predicated as "such and such." Nothing comes so handy as a predicable to be classified. Classification is made on the basis of a mark of distinction. The uniqueness of each mark is based upon its worth or value. Again, this worth is decided upon the predicable's capacity to stimulate the ego to glow with an affective identification.

Any one identification does not preclude the ego from forgetting it in the very next instant, only to assume another identification which is as unique as the previous one. This process of shifting from the 'be-ness' of one identity to another is as compulsive as the flow of time, which no one can inhibit or reverse as in the fictitious case of the commercialized time of modern sophistication. Although a once assumed and experienced identification is cast aside in the next moment like the slough that is molted by a snake, the process by which each identification is arrived at is carefully preserved as a brick in the superstructure of the built-in world of ever-growing dimension in which the ego dwells. When a person dies, he is believed to have come to a total extinction or a transference to some mythical realm of dead souls. But when a memory slips out of consciousness it is only normal to expect the same to reappear with exaggerated or diminished importance on many a subsequent occasion. Thus what is feared as the past that has departed forever goes on coiling around the present, making the present fabulous in its inclusion of the variegation of names and forms and the correlatives of causes and effects. In this great process that is happening in the psychic replica of cosmic evolution, systems are fused into systems.

Although the countless happenings of the cosmos leave almost no room to be observed and studied in isolation, thanks to the scientist's ludicrous way of pretending to see only what he promotes to significance as the observable data for experimentation and verification, one can have a piecemeal approach to this highly intriguing process by which the dimensions of consciousness are altered for fresh emphasis and new evaluation. One such model of change is the continuous transition in form and content of the sprouting and growth of the acorn into a mighty oak. There is nothing flimsy about the existentiality of an oak at any time. All the same, there is a consistent refutation of each antecedent state to nurture and establish the posterior. The capacity of the human mind to leave childhood without remorse, to accept adolescence and pass on gaily into youth, and to be thankful for having matured in old age, conceals in it the aiding and abetting of the invisible hand that is always busy with continuing this passing show of the phenomenal.

Another model of changing the surface designs of consciousness is that of generating convulsions, as in a watery expanse, to push ripples into waves, waves into raging billows, and billows into sweeping tidal currents, thus altering the phases of the ocean between storm and calm. The calm sea which lies at our feet like a tame animal has little comparison with the devastating gale and fury of a cyclone. Still another model is to leave one's body in the comfortable abandon of a siesta and go into the wonderland of fabulous dreams in which imagination promiscuously mates with irrationality and shamelessly generates out of its womb the catharsis of repressed desires or causes the explosion of a ripened neurosis into the most eerie nightmare that can choke the dreamer's soul. Another model is to walk blindfolded into lifelong imprisonment, looking upon every fetter and chain as a duty to be performed in the collectively accepted and believed world of transaction, which houses institutions like home, society, religion, nation, and every form of manmade law. Still another model is of geniuses like Vyasa, Valmiki, Homer, Dante, Shakespeare, Goethe, and others,, who populate the world with countries, people, and all kinds of weird wars and enchanting love affairs with such creative ability that a Ravana, an Arjuṇa, an Agamemnon, an Othello or a Mephistopheles has a more enduring personality grid than anyone who is still in flesh and blood around us.

We cannot exhaust such models. The hand that is busy with the creation of the phenomenal sometimes shares its art with painters, sculptors, architects, musicians, writers, dancers, and even kids in their tender age who gather together to create their enchanting worlds of eidetic creation. In all these inexhaustable formations and elaborations, what is at work is also the One which is always at rest. By remaining One it becomes the many. Even when one is at the height of his hilarity, or pinched in every limb with shooting pain, this One, the purest of all consciousness, sits as gently as a meditating Buddha and witnesses the ongoing drama of pain and pleasure, while the poor ego is tossed on the surface in the tumult of transactional agitations such as of cognition, volition, and feeling. If only it could leave the surface for a split second and dive deep to become enlightened of the 'inside' story, it would become at once free of the multitudinous world and would see in wonder, listen in wonder, and later speak in wonder of the one Absolute all this is. Although such a state of the highest wonder has no need for articulation and has no words for expression, in such a state it is as if one declares one's truth as *aham brahma asmi*, "I am the Absolute."

VERSE 7

bhāryā bhajati bhartāram
bhartā bhāryām na kevalam
svānandameva bhajati
sarvo'pi viṣayasthitam

The wife does not merely worship the husband,
nor the husband, the wife.
By all, their *ānanda* alone is worshiped,
which resides in the sense interests.

bhāryā — the wife
na kevalam — does not merely
bhajati — worship
bhartāram — the husband
bhartā bhāryām — (nor) the husband the wife
sarvaḥ api — by all
svānandam eva — their *ānanda* alone
bhajati — is worshiped
viṣayasthitam — which resides in the sense interests

The Buddhists equate nirvana or Buddha-consciousness to mindlessness, the transcendental counterpart of mindfulness. It is an indescribable state, so it is sometimes referred to as 'that-ness'. It is from the indescribable that the describable arises. The describable is the mind, which is the opposite of mindlessness. Mind manifests in various degrees of awareness. Awareness comes as either a promise or a threat. The promise is the promise of immanent or progesssive union in which awareness can pass through an objectivized euphoria to a passive merger until that aspect of mind is fully absorbed into mindlessness. The threat is the threat of the 'other', which insists on occupying the legitimate territory of the living space of one's persona or even takes the more positive posture of destorying one's existential status. This threat is automatically followed by the conscious recognition of the need to reject the other and erect a wall of defense with one's maximum ability to forestall the danger of any advance the other might make into one's ontologically or teleologically available territory. Mindfulness of defense is hardened by objectivizing one's existential ego and its counterpart, the threat from the other. In either case, there is the expending of one's libidinal energy.

When a person spends his energy in winning bread and consuming it, the energy spent is amply replenished with the breakdown of the food he eats into the required calories and various life-building and life-perserving constituent energies that reside in the food. Therefore, seeking the path of nourishment is a lively activity of a living organism. The need for nourishment described above as experienced on the physical plane is symbolic of the need to be nourished emotionally, morally, psychically, intellectually and spiritually. Life in us is like the *virāt puruṣa*, the universal spirit described in the Vedas and the Upanishads. It has a thousand eyes, a thousand mouths, a thousand hands, and a thousand legs to pursue whatever channel is available, following which one can find one kind of nourishment or another. Going in such paths is a perennial process of spending and replenishing one's libidinal energy. The energy that is required to resist, to reject, to defend, to offend, and to flee is a killer activity. This is the gloomy night of the soul for which everyone seeks redress. Thus, on the whole, life is an interplay between looming destruction and benign sustenence.

Although pain and pleasure are both opposed to mindlessness, pleasure is benignly in agreement with the dissipation of awareness into mindlessness, whereas pain, both physical and mental, has the quality of constricting the frontiers of awareness to the painful actualization of the ontological severity of the here and now of transaction, leading to an acute problem of one's ego being riveted to his physical and social self. As there is no third alternative for an individuated self, almost all the wakeful hours of transaction are diverted to the purpose of relating oneself with as many favorable conditions as possible that can spiritually sustain oneself with the acquisition of opportunities to become mindless, however short such periods may be. Each time awareness dissolves and disappears into mindlessness it is as if one has merged back into the total, and every reemergence into awareness can be like a fresh lease on life. This is the nourishment one seeks in the company of one's spouse, friends, children, pleasures of the senses, delightful entertainments, and positive indulgences in spiritual ecstasies. However varied are the actualizations of finding one's exit into the mindless, all such exits are only differing means to attain the same end. That is why the seer Yājñavalkya tells his wife that it is not for the sake of the husband the husband is loved but it is for the sake of the desire of the Self, and it is not for the sake of the wife that the wife is loved but it is for the sake of the desire of the Self. The seeming motivation of love is only a fictitious label to give the items of love a sophisticated status in the social eye. But in all actuality, one's love is generated by the Self, and its fulfillment is reentering the womb of one's own creativity. For man there is no holiday or escape from his need to be nourished by the love of his own dear Self. All seeming forms of discontentment and rejection are the negative long shadows that are cast by the ever-moving caravan of the unquenchable desires to rediscover and reenter the 'be-ness' of the Self, the mindless beatitude of the final extinction, the *nibbāna*.

VERSE 8

evam paśyati kutrāpi
vidvān ātmasukham vinā
na kiñcidaparam tasya
bhaktireva garīyasī

Thus the wise man sees everywhere
nothing but the joy of the Self —
not even a little of anything else.
His *bhakti* indeed is the highest.

evam — thus
vidvān — the wise man
paśyati — sees
kutrāpi — everywhere
na — nothing
ātmasukham vinā — but the joy of the Self
aparam kiñcit api — not even a little of anything else
tasya bhaktiḥ eva — his *bhakti* indeed
garīyasī — the highest

The given world is a mosaic of sensory impressions perceived as piecemeal pictures further oriented into ensembles of conceptions, the ground of which is intuitively apprehended by a keen intellect. When the alignment between perceived objects and their conceived properties is erroneous, perceptual illusions take the place of objective observation. When the required alignment has a correct one-to-one correspondence, the ensemble reckoned by the mind as the 'other' provides for a valid transactional context for the individuated self to enter into encounters or reactions. In the case of most people, consciousness is more or less filled with the fluctuating details of the illusory and the transactional. The cognitive mind has a tendency to move from multifarious effects to a unitive cause, so that the many can be unified through a process of reduction to arrive at a basic factor in which are seeded all the ramifications of consequential developments. When this tendency is promoted, the philosopher's quest to apprehend the source of everything increases until it culminates in an intuitive vision which becomes more and more organized, holistic, and reliable as a constant ground which has the potential to manifest itself into the variegated world of names and forms.

The orientation of the perceiver changes on shifting the ground of seeing from the perceptual to the conceptual, and from the conceptual to the intuitive. The import or meaning of the subject-object relationship in these three cases varies, although what is presented in all three cases is the phenomenal. In the perceptual appreciation, the operative force that acts as a mechanism of attraction or repulsion is an instinctive conditioning of a vitalistic order which is inherited by all living beings to a certain extent as a device for the organism's self-preservation. This instinct misfires when the previously mentioned alignment between the perception and its corresponding conception is erroneously made. Then it is not very different from the trial and error chance operation one sees in the case of the rat in the maze. The growth from mechanistic gestaltation to a more intelligent appreciation of a consciously apprehended ensemble shows maturity. Yet even this ability brings a person only to a level of the mediocre assessment of subject-object relationships.

Mind is like the confluence of two streams, one bringing in the perceived data of an objective world regulated by physicochemical, biophysical, and biochemical laws, and the other constituted of imaginations, memories, and volitions geared by desires. The confluence of the two streams integrates the contents of both streams into an inseparable whole, and the growing and changing knowledge that accompanies it becomes like its incessant flow. It is in this rapid current of mind that the subtle maneuvering of consciousness enters to give the whole experience a meaning and worthwhileness of a perennial nature.

The three orders of the mosaic that go into the structuring of the world, the two streams that culminate in the confluence of the unified stream, and the three appraisals of the imperiential connotation such as the meaning, the Self, and the Absolute, are all in a muddle until wisdom prevails to sort them out and relate with diligence the triads of the physical, the psychologic, and the cosmologic aspects of the entire situation. All these aspects are replete with enigmas of the worst order. What should be the most tangible, objective, and irrefutably existent can also be the most spurious phantom of an illusion, such as visual fallacies that seem most real until one detects one's mistake. In most cases such defects belong to a generic possibility of error shared by all members of the species and the detection of the error comes to most people only when it is too late to rectify. Pleasure/pain dualities are associated at this level with sense objects which can also be the repositories of sense interests. Thus, what could have been the depth of a thing can also be its most superficial appearance. This is the case of *sat* being rightly sustained by *ānanda* or spuriously substituted for by a fake norm of *ānanda*. Here we are narrating the story of the physico-sensory world.

The second realm which is psychologically at one with the physico-sensory world can be studied as a separate entity only by artificially segregating it with a logical device. Here the central figure that emerges is the *ātma*, in this case the *jīvātma* or the individuated self, which can function merely as the mind propelled by desires and sustained by memories, representing a faulty ego, or it can assume the mighty role of transmuting everything into modes of consciousness as the supreme and primal *cit*. This is the golden link between existence and value, which can rightly be called the subsistent. This dominates the limitless world of consciousness, which includes in it both the conscious and the unconscious, and the known and the unknown. Effecting the most needed purification of this vast realm of consciousness is the mighty challenge which every seeker of the Self has to take upon himself. All the disciplines enjoined in the wisdom texts of religions, all the austerities of mystics, and the self-discipline practiced by yogis are most useful to convert this infinite realm from the ocean of misery to the ocean of knowledge.

We have already noticed a subversion of the order of the trio of *sat*, *cit*, and *ānanda* when we examined the meaning of the visibles in the perceptual world. The converse of the same subversion should be seen in order to understand the mysterious function of the ever-existent *sat*, which is like the imponderable and impenetrable matter which is full of holes and vacant spaces with no part of it stable for even a split second. Here we get the paradox of knowing the existence only by deducing it from the fingerprints or, to be more exact, the mind-prints of the impressions it makes in the realm of awareness of the subjective agent who sits behind the perceptual devices of the sensory system.

Thus, in all three realms of the physical, the psychic, and the cosmic, there is a continuing perpetuation of illusoriness, a continuous validation of transactional integrity, and the irrefutable persistence of the one Reality, which in fact is never fragmented, and its tribasic aspects are only a seeming distinction in one and the same consubstantial reality. The true *bhakta* is one who is established in the consubstantiality of the eternal trios, who is capable of unflinchingly holding on to the one existentiality of the differently perceived, the differently conceived, and the differently evaluated ground of all. In the same way such a contemplative is fully aware of the one Self without whose creative imagination there cannot be names and forms and multifarious appreciations of the ensembles of things and ideas. Only this truest of all contemplatives can lucidly shift his position from one angle of vision to another, so that he can have an unprejudicial appreciation of every individuated being's value-orientation and concealed or expressed motivation. As he sees clearly the triple manifestations of the illusory, the transactional, and the transcendental, he excels in maintaining his position in the neutral zero from where he can easily enter into the transcendent immanence and the immanent transcendence of the most adorable Absolute. It is this efficiency that makes his contemplation the highest of all achievements.

VERSE 9 & 10

lokasya pitari svasya-
gurau pitari mātari
satyasya sthāpitari ca
tat pathenaiva yātari

niyantari niṣiddhasya
sarveṣām hitakartari
yo'nurāgo bhaktiratra
sā parā paramātmani

Towards the Father of the world,
to one's spiritual teacher, father, mother,
towards the founders of truth,
towards those who walk in the same path,
towards those who put down evil,
(and) to those who do good to all,
what sympathy there is, that is *bhakti*,
what here belonging to the supreme Self is the ultimate.

lokasya pitari — towards the Father of the world
svasya gurau — to one's spiritual teacher
pitari — father
mātari — mother
satyasya sthāpitari ca — towards the founders of truth
tat pathena eva yātari — towards those who walk in the same path
niyantari niṣiddhasya — towards those who put down evil
sarveṣām hitakartari — (and) to those who do good to all
yaḥ anurāgaḥ — what sympathy there is
bhaktiḥ — that is *bhakti*
atra — what here belonging to
paramātmani — the supreme Self
sā parā — is the ultimate

Little sparrows, however small in size and meager in strength to defend, will valiantly put up all their might and courage to fight an intruding snake or crow that wants to gobble up their fledgelings. This indeterminable courage which they exercise without the least consideration for their personal safety seems to flow into them from the reservoir of a universal urge to care. What pleases every farmer as he goes around and watches his wheat, rice or cornfield is the delightful sight of a steady stream of vital energy flowing into the seeds that are sown to transform the sprouted plants into a steadily growing crop that culminates in a bumper harvest. Here the farmer is consciously or unconsciously grateful to the amazingly benign hidden hand that promotes his labor and concern at every step to make his farm yield plentifully. The interaction between the sun and the ocean is very much like the shared responsibility of a universal father and mother which replenishes the biosphere of the planet Earth by lifting mammoth clouds out of the sea and distributing them on the surface of the Earth as rain to fill rivers and lakes and to store in subterranean pockets and veins. It is like a free service rendered to all living organisms irrespective of their merits. A thousand and one other instances can be quoted to show that the innate law that holds together every atom of this world has a will to care and a meta-intelligence to design a program with all the caring parents in the world put together.

Although every one of us is a beneficiary and a programmed worker committed to the universal functioning of the world order, most of us are carrying out our roles, even at a high efficiency level, with a compulsive instinct that keeps us blindfolded. We are released from this ignorant plight, which at best is like the obligatory labors performed by a slave, and are changed into the joyful cocreators of this world by teachers of spiritual insight who rouse their fellow men from the stupor of ignorance. Thus God, who hides behind the scene, comes to the forefront wearing the garb of the common man in the street, giving him education and leadership to plan each day and to make this world a veritable workshop of high creative efficiency. It is like a grand sacrifice, beginningless and interminable, which is continuously fed with the oblation of fresh life generated in the assembly lines of physical fathers and mothers. However ignorant they are of the purpose for which they generate and perpetuate the species, they are like the receptors and effectors of the grand body of this world. They receive into them life's retrospective storage of instinct and prospective designs of intelligence only to modify and perfect the worth of these universal gifts and to pass them on to the next in line to continue the divine sport of phenomenality. This highly decentralized and distributed government of countless billions of autonomous units, functioning with crisscrossed alignments and reciprocal empathy, is periodically reexamined, revalued, and restructured by the phenomenal recurrence of law-knowing and law-enforcing super-geniuses that appear among the cream and scum of human society as prophets, poets, and scientists.

This world of ours, which is loosely held together with the matrices of innately inherited and outwardly ordained group discipline, has evolved straitjackets of varying mechanistic determination which are comparable to human devices like dikes, locks, and floodgates so that the system will not be inundated with the wild passions that are periodically released from groups or individuals. Human freedom is actualized and realized by severely curtailing it with the sanctions, blocks, and permits which are nurtured with the consent of those who allow themselves to be ruled. Such is the complex matrix to which every one of us belongs.

In this winding path our safe conduct is vouched for only by a reciprocally generated sympathy that automatically wells up in our heart on meeting another of our kind, both in the public and private cellars of this age-old labyrinth called world. Our habitual choice to walk a path of truth, goodness, and beauty is always a movement or transition from the previously acquired to what is to be passed on in the relay of tradition. This is to be known as a hierarchy of devotion, *paramparā bhakti*. Among those guided by this instinctive devotion there happens now and then the great wonder of one gaining an insight into the entire system of the phenomenal in such an amazing manner as to become convinced of his or her identity with the supremely numinous truth that shines in and through this wonderful world. The devotion of such a contemplative is the ultimate, *parābhakti*.

VIII. BHAKTI DARŚANAM

[1] Nataraja Guru, *The Bhagavad Gita*, R & K Publishing House, Delhi, Ch. III, v. 17, p. 191

IX. YOGA DARŚANAM
Transpersonal Union

Yoga or union suggests the joining of two things. Even though in philosophy the mind/body duality is well known, the schism implied in that situation is appreciated only as a semantic problem and not as one substantially experienced at the levels of feeling and willing (emotion and volition). The real problem stems from the disharmony which arises between two hearts or two minds; and the incompatibility that is grievously felt in the union of two bodies. The answer to such a primary problem comes from the harmony that ensues from the quality of interpersonal union.

The root cause of interpersonal disunity lies in intrapersonal discord. In most people there is a vague understanding of an unchanging ego identity that can take the place of the seer, the knower, the doer, and the enjoyer, but even then the functions of our sense of agency can be widely at variance with each other (e. g. "I hate" and "I love"). The classic discord between these agents has given rise to several speculations, of which a well-known schematic visualization comes from the Freudian School as the id, ego, and superego. In Indian schools the function of the id is assigned to *vāsana*-s, the ego is *ahamkara*, and the place of the superego is assigned to *dharma*. As *dharma* is morally and spiritually identified with righteousness (at least in India) the appetite of the id-like *vāsana*-s is decried as a psychological menace to be effaced. This process is generally recognized as the cultivation of detachment and the repetitive practice of moralizing tendencies so that one's habitual choice will be in agreement with what is rated as one's integrity in *dharma* (righteousness). The sole aim of centering one's I-consciousness around the nucleus of a universal value such as love, compassion, justice or truth is to effect an inner cohesion and unity at the intrapersonal level.

This problem does not end even when a person makes himself or herself whole and psychologically solid to interact with others, because anyone with whom such a person wants to relate cannot be expected to be free from their own intrapersonal heterogeneity.

A great alchemy that can interrelate two persons through a process of fusing their interests in identical values comes from the conflagration of love in which two such individuals are gracefully brought together by the Divine or by Benevolent Chance. Love is universally experienced as a process in which an effort of union is made through conscious aspiration and an effortless union is happening by Providential Grace. In the present chapter *yoga* is said to be such a beautiful incidence, in which the knowledge of togetherness — of being one and identical — is beautifully complemented by the preparedness to live in amity.

When the 'other' is not merely another person but the collective Self to which the individual self also belongs, and one treats the universal Self as the 'other', otherness is not a bar to union because the personal self serves as the nucleus of the universal Self. In this case one may feel like saying "I am the Absolute," or one may feel enveloped by the universal to the extent that one can easily turn to the 'other' and say, "That thou art." When this happens in an enormous and continuous manner, the differentiating quality of the individual becomes more and more flushed with the universality of fundamental existence, subsistence, and value, and then one is no longer tyrannized with the congenital idiosyncracies of the person concerned.

Such an all-out purification, which can ultimately result in the effacing of the 'self' and the 'other', may have to include even physical exercises such as controlling breath and regulating synergic centers. Even in such practices, what matters is not the mechanical adaptability of a certain technique but its worthwhileness in touching at the fountain source of the one bliss to which all forms of happiness belong. In other words, one falls in love with the only love that is, whereby one's existentiality and subsistentiality can both become the structural and functional dynamic of *ānanda*, which is at once the ground of the personal self and the universal Self. The insight of that togetherness is evidenced in *jñāna yoga*, and its functional veracity is vouchsafed by *karma yoga*. In *yoga* there is no duality. The seeming duality of *jñāna* and *karma* is accepted only for the convenience of describing what is otherwise indescribable.

VERSE 1

satatam yojayati yad
yunakti ca cidātmani
manonirodha rūpo'yam
sa yoga iti śamsitaḥ

That which always unites
and also gets united with *cidātma*,
which is in the form of restraining mind,
that is praised as *yoga*.

yad — that which
satatam — always
yojayati — unites
ca — and also
yunakti — gets united with
cidātmani — *cidātma*
ayam — which is
mano nirodham rūpaḥ — in the form of restraining mind
saḥ — that is
śamsitaḥ — praised
iti yogaḥ — as *yoga*

Games are played in freedom. There is no obligation to play. It is in freedom that one resolves to enter into a game of his choice. The choice is so suitable to him that he sees in it a promise of feeding into him and feeding out of him a circulatory happiness. He sets the rules of the game for himself and other willing partners. In all cases the rules are framed by consensus. The rules of a game prescribe how to commence, how to proceed to the goal, what is one's precise role, what are the modes of correct relationship and reaction; and when one errs, how to rectify the error and what penalty is to be imposed for the deception; and, finally, how to bring the game to its graceful close. When it is terminated, it is terminated forever. A game can be played by a big group as in football, on a principle of dichotomy, two teams with one-to-one correspondence, or it can be played alone as a solo performance as in skiing or gymnastics. What is beautiful about a game is that the mind goes into concentration. From the very first moment of the game's commencement to the final second, there is such a union of ends and means that the goal is not to achieve anything other than bringing the game to a close. Success and failure are juxtaposed, and all participants in the game know that these relative possibilities are to be transcended. All parties who come to the field begin the game in loving comradeship and close it with the benign handshake to the victor in congratulation and the victor's embrace of his comrade who lost the game in gratitude for his earnest participation.

Sport is called *līla*. This is the best model of *yoga*. Even when twenty-two people have to deal with only one ball, there is not a flickering second when the entire mind of each player is not brought to full attention on the ball. The concentration of his mind is aided by his keen observation (sensory) and the conduct of his movements which are in full resonance with the changing position of the ball (motor). Concentration, when it is simple, spontaneous, total, and not rebounding in reaction, is called the equipoise of the reasoning self. Pāṇini, the great grammarian of India, calls that union *samādhi* — *yuja samādhau*, which means '*samādhi* is union'. The game spoken of above is an outward performance, a *yoga* or union of the performance of a team. Although this is an excellent diversion to keep both the body and mind well exercised, there is another game which is many times more meaningful and rewarding. The attitude is the same, i. e., of playing games with one's own faculties and the environments of the given world. In this game the field is not spatially delimited like a tennis court or football field. It is rather the field of the knower, the field of the actor, the field of the enjoyer.

A game is a game only when the knower, with full conscience and deliberation, performs his role to promote in full his truest happiness. In such an act, the knower, the performer, and the enjoyer are all fused into the identification of one and the same person. Such a person is fully conversant with the possibilities of his field, its hierarchy or probabilities, and the sequential order in which actualization is to be attempted. Like the rapid, harmonious, and efficient fluttering of the wings of a bee, the consciousness of the performer moves so rapidly from subject to object that one and the same consciousness is facing itself from two poles, which are recognized as the subject and the object. This is similar to the conception of Feynman that there is only one electron which is seemingly countless. This rapid modulation is called *vṛtti*. The intended game of the *yogi* is to effect a total cessation of the consciousness that fluctuates and thereby automatically creates the subject-object duality between a non-temporal, non-spatial, non-physical subject and an object spatially located, temporally contacted or apprehended, and physically assessed. An observation of this phenomenon can never be fully directed to the observed because the source of its illumination is in the observer, and the most active intentionality of perception and conception originates from the self as a vibrant projection of an image which is received back as a vibrant introjection. Thus one unit of modulation is completed. Although this happens as a self-deluding hypnotic function, the *yogi* intensifies the thoroughness of watching the full round of modulation so that he can free that bit of consciousness from being identified as subject or as object, as the accompanying attributes pinned on to the subject as a pain-pleasure complex, or as the attributes of the object such as visual, auditory, or other properties. The result is a total transcendence effected there and then even when the flow of energy does take place. There is no qualitative distinction between the first, second, or third moments of the transcendence of modulation. This is what Patañjali calls *citta vṛtti nirodha.*

The field of the knower consists of the planes of the physical, the vital, the mental, the psychic, and the spiritual. The instruments of the knower to reciprocate with the field are the faculties of contact such as the five senses, and operations like locomotion, manipulation, articulation, procreation and elimination. There is a five-fold performance of five-fold systems: the five elements, five forms of objectified sense contacts, five varieties of interests, five forms of vital energies, and five varieties of motions. This complex is called the quintuplicated world.

Transcending a modulation as described above is a simple act compared to the pacification and transcendence of the quintuplicated activity of the field and the knower of the field dichotomy. In principle, the *yogi*'s successful transcendence of the same is performed through an act of absolute devotion, *śraddha*. This mode of transcendence is what Vālmiki calls *praśamana*, systematic pacification, or *prapañca upaśama*, the pacification of the quintuplicated universe. In Patañjali's and Vālmiki's definitions, the stress is made on the mode of performance. However, Narayana Guru calls our attention to deal with the modulation at the deeper level of removing the incentive from the potential seed of a maturing incipient memory which is about to burst into the actualization of a conscious act. This is like entering the green room of a theater, inviting an actor to free himself of his costume and role, and giving him freedom to sit with the audience. Then, instead of entertaining an assumed false identification, the Self remains established in its truest form because it is freed of its obligation to fullfill the instinctive wish of a *vāsana*, incipient memory. Narayana Guru praises such a reversion of transcendence within immanence itself as *yoga*, and he qualifies it as *vāsanānāśa*, the reduction of the potential into the impotent.

VERSE 2

na draṣṭa, darśanam, dṛśyam
vidyate yatra tatra hṛt
yojayedvāsanā yāvat
yogo 'yamiti yogavit

Where the seer, the sight and the seen
are not known, there the heart
should be joined while *vāsana* is present.
Such is *yoga* — thus the *yoga* knower.

yatra — where
draṣṭa — the seer
darśanam — the sight
dṛśyam — (and) the seen
na vidyate — are not known
tatra — there
hṛt — the heart
yojayed — should be joined
yāva vāsana — while *vāsana* is present
ayam yoga — such is *yoga*
iti yogavit — thus the *yoga* knower

Darśanam is a general term for perception. The organs of perception are the five senses having the faculties of hearing, touching, seeing, tasting and smelling. The Buddhists consider mind as a sixth sense which perceives the orientation of the stimuli fed into the organism by the five senses. In the Bhagavad Gita also mind is referred to as the sixth sense. Perception is plainly the function of the nervous system.

Although not strictly scientific in the empirical sense, people everywhere seem to make reference to their head and heart as if the head is only for cold reasoning and the heart alone can feel the warmth of feelings like love. This being a universal convention, it should not be dismissed as merely a vulgar assessment of the characteristics of consciousness. A more recent theory is the concept of a bi-cameral brain. What is relevant in localizing consciousness in the head and the heart is warranted by two specific features of consciousness. One is the urge to know, the attention that is sustained, the manipulation that one feels somewhat compulsively to make, and relating the goal as the main motivational factor connected with one's primary drive to which every shade of one's behavior is intrinsically related. This is described by Vyāsa, the commentator of Patañjali's *Yoga Aphorisms*, as *pravṛtti. Pravṛtti* literally means strong and spontaneous modulation. 'Strong and spontaneous' is to be taken as having an emotional propensity, and 'propensity', according to William MacDugal, is the dynamic of concentrating an excessive quantity of mental energy to pursue a certain activity. So, on the whole, this aspect of consciousness is responsible for the total involvement of the entire organism to make a performance of action.

When a person has to do some activity, he either does it in the light of the sun or in other artificially produced illumination. This external light that is pressed into service is only to aid the self-luminous light of one's own consciousness, which is roused in the form of an awareness. The act of mentation, which is allegorically said to be of the head and not of the heart, has direct reference to the illumination of a gestalt, a theme, or an ensemble, which is amply made available through perception and the logical orientation of it with one's cognitive ability. This is the second characteristic, although it is the first that comes in the sequential order of cognition, connation, and affection. Vyāsa calls this aspect of cognition *prakhya* or *prakāś. Prakāś* means mere light. *Prakhya* means to grasp clearly with illumination.

In the present verse the Guru speaks of *draṣṭa*, *darśanam*, and *dṛśya. Draṣṭa* is the individuated person who, while cognizing a perceptual entity, also recognizes the illuminating light as belonging to the cognizer. Along with the objectivization which cognizes objects and connotes their import, there is a corresponding act of subjectivization. It is like a thread of two entwining strands: the ego, and the ego's continuous reaction to what is being cognized and connated.

The impact of specified consciousness on the intellect alternates between assessing the theme by making the cognition again and again vivid, and acting upon it in terms of dissonance or resonance with appropriate manipulations of both one's inner attitudes and dispositions as well as the structural composition of the psychophysical matrix with which the interest is tied up for the time being. In other words, illumination and action are simultaneously progressing towards the actualization of a value. The actualization of value belongs to the catering to interests, and that in its turn is determined by the need and capacity of an incipient memory to become expressive at a conscious level. When this process of cognition and action is in progress, there is a retrospective recall of all the associated memories of the incipient memory that is rekindled, and also a prospective registration of fresh interests which has the ability to both mutate and transmute the revived incipient memory. Thus, in this process, which is both consciously and unconsciously monitored by the ego, there is a continuous registration as in the input of a magnetized tape which is the retention for the future. Vyāsa calls this retention *sthiti*, which means 'establishing a status quo'.

Although each unit of the operation of thematic consciousness comes to a close as in a closing gestalt, its operational dynamic is only buried in the unconscious and can reappear as a vivid experience whenever its revival is deemed necessary either through conscious recall or by neurotic or psychotic compulsion. Its reactivating potential is not merely a retentive element. It very much becomes the perennial interest of the ego. That is why Narayana Guru relates it to the heart. If *yoga* is to be understood as *samādhi*, the modulations which spontaneously happen at the cognitive level should be quelled, and they should also be made inoperative at the affective level. This is why the Guru recommends the triple absence of individuation — that is, the perceiver, the perceived, and the act of perception — as an accomplished fact of the pacified heart. All that we have said hitherto is to be visualized entirely to connote the word *hṛt*, heart, used in this verse by the Guru. The affectation of the ego will persist as long as the ego is infatuated with the glamour of the incipient memory.

As both retention and affection are closely linked with the ego, the ego should be further examined. The ego as such has no power to do anything unless it can wield the faculty of illumination and the faculty of discrimination. The Self is the only source of illumination. Self is not the ego. Ego is a projected identity on the subtle aspect of nature which has gone into the procreative matrix of a person. In other words, ego is a shadowy person. It is and it is not. It is this aspect of ego which says "I know" or "I do not know." Its power to discriminate is the more vital and functionally efficient aspect. This, of course, is to be associated with *buddhi*, or intelligence. *Buddhi* is again a link to the Self or the spirit. Its power to perceive and discriminate is the borrowed light of the Self. At the same time, it is loaded with the incipient memories retained by a person. Furthermore, it is subject to the influence of the triple qualities of procreative matter, such as being pure and sublime, being kinetic, and being retentive, inertial, or opaque. Ego vastly depends on the intellect both for discrimination and manipulation. Thus heart, which is said to be the seat of the ego, also becomes the seat of all intrigues continued by the ego and intellect in collusion. An aspirant *yogi* has to become vigilant in stopping this unhealthy alliance between ego and intellect, which are bent on aiding incipient memories. This is achieved by making the light of pure spirit prevail upon heart with a discipline that constantly diffuses the ego's craving for power, glory, and pleasure. Until this is accomplished, *yoga* is not achieved. When the heart has known the undisturbed depth of the silent spirit, *yoga* is achieved.

VERSE 3

nāmarūpamidam sarvam
brahmaiveti vilīyate
yad brahmaṇi mano nityam
sa yoga iti niścitaḥ

All this name and form is
Brahma indeed. Thus, in
the Absolute, mind always merges well.
That is ascertained as *yoga*.

sarvam idam — all this
nāma — name
rūpam — (and) form
brahma eva iti — is Brahma indeed
yad — thus
brahmaṇi — in the Absolute
manaḥ — mind
nityam — always
vilīyate — merges well
saḥ — that is
niścitaḥ — ascertained
yoga iti — as *yoga*

A name is essentially conceptual. At least the first apperception of form comes from perception. Formal appreciation is mainly attributed to visual perception. For fixing in one's mind the appropriate name of a thing or idea either a written word image or a spoken word image is relied upon. Thus conceptualization is generally initiated with a visually or auditorially coined word symbol. By repeated use, names and forms become inseparable in cognitive consciousness and its several forms of transactions. The child's earliest way of getting acquainted with things is more thoroughgoing than the observation of a grown-up. Whatever a child sees it reaches for with its hands. If the thing can be grasped physically, the child will either bring the thing to its mouth or its mouth to the thing. Thus seeing, touching, and tasting go more or less together, and a coordinated experience is unconsciously used as a basis for the child's translucent comprehension and subsequent conceptualization. There are a variety of things which come to the child's attention because of the sound they produce. In the child's interpersonal relationships, along with the association of things, language is evolved as a nominalistic medium to bring the child's mind to meet the adult's mind on the common ground of the perceptibles. Thus, almost from the moment of the child's admission to the empirical world, the great process of the structural composition of the empirico-critical world is commenced, and it snowballs into the 'self and the other' world of the individual. Its growth, concretization, and persistence as the facts and figures of an empirical world continue until one's death.

In this tremendous unconscious creation, names and forms are the two main constituent elements. A form has a unity. It can also have parts, parts that constitute the unity of the whole. Peter can be recognized as different from Paul. The distinguishing marks can be the variation of form in specific parts that make up the whole, such as the shape of the nose or the forehead, the eyes, the lips, the cheekbones, the hair, and so on and so forth. Thus, with a formal system there come many infrastructures of forms. In the same way, each form can belong to the metastructure of a more general classification to which species belong. What is true of form is also true of name, because names also have hierarchies of relationship. Form consists of the visible impression of a color, which is more or less of a superficial order, and a shape, which is unique in the role it plays. However rigid a shape may be, it has the freedom to move within the range of spatial dimension from the most microscopic to the vast macrocosmic exaggeration. A meager pencil sketch can serve the purpose of identification as well as a painting or a three-dimensional model true to the original in size and color.

Thus, when we probe into the mystery of these two simplest of all universals called name and form, we go from one mystery of detail to another; so it is no wonder that the entire world of both the Self and the non-Self is based on these two fundamentals. Nobody can think without using word images in their mind. All word images are concepts. Concepts are processed and recreated memories. The relation between the conceptual memory and the original thing or event is very much like that of a photocopy in black and white or a pencil sketch of the original. Conceptually recalled images are confections of names and forms neatly blended, and each such unit becomes animated with the prevailing mood of the individual whenever it is assigned a place in the range of an experience. Thus all experiences of pain, pleasure, and indifference are stimulated, nurtured, and continued by names and forms.

In the case of a non-contemplative, extroverted person, the proliferation of the images of name and form goes on without the individual giving any special attention to the validity of the impressions created by the name-form complex. Of course, there is not anyone who is totally devoid of contemplation. But in the case of one who is an avowed contemplative, apart from merely experiencing name and form, such a person will also develop a critical faculty to moderate and improve his modes of appreciation so that the presiding consciousness can be in full control of the constant interplay of concepts and percepts. Although at a beginning stage of self-discipline such critical apperceptions of gestalts are far apart and varied, when the discipline increases all the structural details of the presentative consciousness and its representative character are scrutinized for the purpose of integrating all infrastructure and metastructure to become fully harmonized in the idea of the universal.

Narayana Guru calls the specific variance *anya*, and the integrated universal *sama*. Contemplative discipline is to go from the multifarious *anya* to the unitive *sama*. In the present verse the word *brahma*, meaning the Absolute, stands for *sama*. The *anya* or the variant has the ability to color the consciousness that apprehends it with its specific property. To escape from the impact of it at the time of its occurrence is most difficult. Here exactly is the need for disciplining the entire mechanism of mentation, by which one can reverse the power of streaming consciousness from the effect to the cause and from the manifoldness of names and forms to the unitivity and universality of the one Absolute, *brahma*. When this is achieved, one cuts across all forms of phenomenality and gains the transparency of yogic vision. Then he says, "All this is Brahma," *sarvam khalvidam brahma*.

VERSE 4

cittasya tailadhārāvad
vṛttyā'vicchinnayā'tmanı
nirantaram ramyate yat
sa yogo yogibhiḥ smṛtaḥ

By the modulation of consciousness
which is unbroken as in the streak of oil,
what incessant rejoicing is in the Self.
Such is *yoga* — this is the recognition of *yogi*-s.

cittasya vṛttya — by the modulation of consciousness
avicchinnaya — which is unbroken
tailadhārāvat — as in the streak of oil
yat — what
nirantaram — incessant
ramyate — rejoicing
ātmani — (is in) the Self
saḥ — such
yogaḥ — is yoga
smṛtaḥ — (this is) the recognition
yogibhiḥ — of the *yogi*-s

Consciousness is like a stream. It is always flowing. The flow alternates between conscious awareness and unconscious states of non-recognition. The monitoring of the direction of conscious awareness may be voluntary or autonomous. The flow in the unconscious is always autonomous. The mechanism for the incessant flow of consciousness is known as *vṛtti*, modulation. Modulation assumes the specific characteristics of a thing or an idea. This assumption is through an act of cognition accompained by the registration of an interest, which is enhanced with the recall of memory if the interest is suggestive of the promotion of happiness or of endangering threat. Where the potentials of pleasure or pain are meager, both interest and attention are low key.

The yogic discipline is goal oriented. The *yogi* sets *kaivalya*, the primeval, unadulterated state of pure 'be-ness', as his final goal. As every step is to be directed to progress toward the attainment of it, all acts of cognition, volition, and states of affection are to be aligned with this basic goal. Thus the goal has to be both ontologic and teleologic. It is teleologic because it refers to a future possibility, and ontologic because there is an approximation of the goal to a certain degree, however negligibly, in the here and now. Such a discipline enjoins upon the aspirant the conscious monitoring of every modulation in the stream of consciousness. Autonomous modulation takes place as a conditioned reflex. The instinctive behavior of a person has behind it the inbuilt accumulation of the information of his genetic past, and hence the power of the autonomous to produce a modulation is enormous, instantaneous, and mostly of an undetectable nature with regards to the implied unconscious motivation. This is a biologic "black box," zealously guarded by the unconscious, and the challenge it offers to the *yogi* is the transmutation of the autonomous into the voluntary. Our psychosomatic organism is like a mass of psycho-electrical installations kept in complete darkness, with the exception of a little light around the cognizing agent, identified with the ego. This feeble light is experienced by the ego in the form of a desire, a fear, an apprehension, a challenge, a call for reciprocation, the passing parade of impressions, and the vague, broken awareness of incoherent reflexes that fill up the gap between one definitive interest and another. The *yogi*, for the purpose of remaining alert and continuing an attention that is vivid, has to fight with this mechanistic automation generated by his past.

Realizing the enormity of his task, the *yogi* decides to keep his attention as far as possible filled with evenly harmonized modulations consciously monitored, which can become afterwards a sequential movement of consciousness through a series of habitual choices. This is not an easy thing to accomplish, because life is not static and our environments vary continuously with kaleidosopic fickleness. To achieve this, a number of skills are required. The main counterparts involved in the experiencing of consciousness are the Self and the non-Self. The Self, for its alignment with the non-Self, has to do its interlinking through the good office of the ego. The ego is therefore to be equipped with the right orientation to the goal; a favorable mood by which it can amicably exercise its empathy even with the most unforeseen situations; a philosophically enriched disposition of positively wanting to perpetuate love, compassion, fellowship, and cheerfulness; and a vivid comprehension of the total meaning of every passing moment. This comes through an act of *samyama*, which can be somewhat approximated to a creative form of contemplation by which a possibly miserable autonomous presentation of the ever-fleeting phenomena is substituted by a consciously generated theme of a favorable psychodrama, which gives ample opportunities for the ego, in perfect harmony with the Self, to induce a high degree of the numinous in all details of the phenomenal.

The *yogi* continuously promotes his capacity to both reconnoiter the situation and to direct all energies involved to continue the unbroken attention given to a chosen set of values, such as seeing only love where there is a lot of hatred concentrated. This is more easily said than achieved. A unilateral posture of love in a situation of aggression and hatred can turn comical and ridiculous, and can even worsen the situation into an absurdity. So the *yogi*, out of his love for the actualization of a noble ideology, should not lose touch with the facts that are present. In such a complex situation many backward and forward and left and right maneuverings are to be made to arrive at a correct homeostasis of behavior. This explains some of the curt and seemingly drastic measures which a *yogi* adopts when a person of shallow understanding expects him to conform to ritualistic adherence to conventional ideologies. This hard but most fulfilling discipline increases the *yogi's* inner tranquility, and that in turn enables him to have a more clear and correct perspective of all his involvements with persons and events.

The *yogi* also has his assigned niche in a given situation in the phenomenal world. He cannot run away from it. When thus placed for a lifetime, the individual is exposed to both the dark and benign forces of nature. Although it is easy to be in a state of joy when conditions are favorable, the same joy is to be taken across several thorny issues which can be of gruesome pain to the body, the social self, and the moral conscience. To tide over such disasters, the *yogi* has to attune himself with the Self, which is perennially of the nature of existence, subsistence, and bliss. This identification is of course hindered by the ego's longstanding intimate and intrinsic relationship with the body and the mind, which are equipped with a highly sensitive neural system. However hard this game is, it can be achieved. The mark of it is the incessant inward joy reflected in the smile of a meditative Buddha. It is this state of unbroken beatitude that is recognized by the *yogi*-s as *yoga*.

VERSE 5

yatoyato mano yāti
sadā'tmani tatastataḥ
niyamya yojayedeta-
dyogo'yam yujyatāmiha

To whichever mind goes, from all that
this should always be restrained,
and should be united in the Self —
this is *yoga*. In this should remain united.

yataḥ yataḥ — to whichever
manaḥ — mind
yāti — goes
tataḥ tataḥ — from all that
etat — this
sadā niyamya — should always be restrained
yojayet — (and) should be united
ātmani — in the Self
ayam yogaḥ — this is yoga
iha — in this
yujyatām — should remain united

A perennial question that haunts the human mind is, "To be or not to be?" Man is always at a crossroad. He has to choose his next move — in his thought, in his word, and in his action. When he is confronted with such a situation, he needs guidance; the guidance of a norm. Unfortunately, he has two norms before him. Freudian psychologists recognize these dual norms as the norm of the id and the norm of the superego. The *Katha Upaniṣad* speaks of them as the pleasure-giving and the good. Śankara terms the dual values as *anitya*, the fleeting, and *nitya*, the eternal. The Buddhist describes them as the *akuśala*, the evil born of ignorance, and the *kuśala*, the good resulting from wisdom. Knowing this, the *yogi* enjoins upon himself the disciplines of five injunctions and five restraints. The five injunctions are deliberations to exercise. They are: to keep mind, word, actions, body, food, environment, and company clean; to engage in activities that promote serenity and joyfulness; to have programs of self-learning; to carry out the instructions of the preceptor; and to offer service to promote the welfare of the world. The restraints are to refrain: from causing hurt to any sentient being; from the fabrication of lies; from theft; from misappropriation; and from erroneous steps in the path of chastity.

The senses are sometimes compared to cows that go into pastures for grazing, or to brutes of the forest which go hunting for their prey. Mind is always a companion of the senses, both in their commissions and in their omissions. The contact between the senses and an object of perception is like pressing a button in the mind to recall a whole bunch of memories. Once the memories are aroused, the urge to actualize a hidden desire gains momentum and libidinal energy is instantaneously generated for the purpose of actualizing the conscious or unconscious desire. The even flow of consciousness is at once disturbed. A veil of oblivion is immediately cast over all objects other than what is relevant for the mind's immediate pursuit, and also over other latent desires which are lying in wait to be actualized at an opportune moment. This veiling enhances the highlighting of the interest. The sudden release of libidinal energy makes the mind infatuated with the possibility of actualizing the desire. The desire can be meritorious or non-meritorious. It is meritorious when such a pursuit advances one's progress in realization, and non-meritorious when such indulgences cause the intensification of attachment and bondage. Infatuation has a blinding effect on the intellect's normative vision of the Absolute. Only an intensively purposeful conscience of spiritual awakeness can prevail against the moral blindness that afflicts the mind with the irresistable compunction to behave in a certain way.

To mitigate compunction and to promote the morally and spiritually guided behavior of both the senses and mind, the ego in its capacity as the volitional agent should act in accordance with the instructions of a preceptor or the canonical word wisdom made available through the Science of the Absolute. This adherence to the Word of the Guru or of the Supreme Science is known as *śraddha*. *Śraddha*, or devotion to truth, is intensified when a seeker or novice successfully establishes his or her bipolarity with the stable model of an excellent teacher or the ever-inspiring ideal venerated by millions like the Buddha consciousness or Christ consciousness. To graft on to the teaching of world Masters or to one's own preceptor, one has to engage oneself in the purificatory discipline of continuously detaching oneself from all unhealthy distractions and engaging oneself in actions that are wholesome, honest, beautiful, harmonious, and beneficial to the world. It is like rolling a stone uphill. The pressure has to be constant and continuous. The vigil must be round the clock. A moment of lapse is enough to fall or slip. So one has to be extra conscious at all moments of one's life to maintain one's poise.

The usual tendency of the mind is to go out through the windows of the senses. This centrifugal impulse is to be converted into a centripetal interest so that the senses and mind are always turned inward to be united with the ever-resplendent glow of the Self. In the union of the mind with the Self the mind loses its separate identity, and there will not be an agent to claim specific knowledge such as "I am," or "I know." Only where there is an existential confrontation that evokes the idea "I am" or "I will" can the ego have its recognition. To those who are constantly under the spell of their ego-infatuation, forgetting or forgoing the ego is wrought with the fear of being destroyed. Such a prospect always brings to them a plaguing sense of insecurity. So they always prefer to have some sense object to be associated with, or other paranoiac people to make friends with. This emotional dependence and sense indulgence keeps the mind always at the periphery of consciousness, and it becomes incapacitated either to dive deep or to fly high. The Self which transcends time and space is sometimes described as the biggest of the big and the smallest of the small at one and the same time. Such contradictions or opposing characteristics are given to cancel out these pairs of opposites by which alone one can establish oneself in the neutral, indescribable numinosity of the Absolute. The same is also experienced by soaring into the sublime heights, which in effect is like immersing into the deepest depth. The highest and the deepest are the same. This profound experience of seeing the immanent as the transcendental and the transcendental as the immanent is the rare occasion of *yoga*. Gaining that union and not losing it again can be effectively achieved only with the continuous exercise of detachment from the untrue and the unwholesome, and the emphasizing of the mind's union with the Self constantly and forever. Only when such a union is effected is there *yoga*.

VERSES 6 & 7

sarvānartthakaraḥ pumsām
saṅkalpaḥ kalpitaiḥ saha
unmūlya vāsanājālair
yenātmani nirudhyate

dṛśyasya na dṛśo'stitvam
ato dṛśyam dṛgātmakam
iti yuñjīta dṛgrūpe
yaḥ sa yogavidām varaḥ

Saṅkalpa —the cause of all disasters of mankind —
along with projections, should be uprooted
and incipient memories be restrained in the *ātma.*
What is seen has not the perceived
reality, because what is seen
is the seer itself. Who is thus united
in the seer, he is the best among *yoga*-knowers.

saṅkalpaḥ —*saṅkalpa*
sarvān anartthakaraḥ pumsām — the cause of all disasters of mankind
saha kalpitaiḥ — along with projections
unmūlya — should be uprooted
vāsanājālaiḥ (*ca*)—and incipient memories
nirudhyate — be restrained
yena ātmani — in the *ātma*
dṛśyasya — what is seen
na dṛśaḥ astitvam — has not the perceived reality
ataḥ — because
dṛśyam — what is seen
dṛgātmakam — is the seer itself
yaḥ iti yuñjīta — who is thus united
dṛgrūpe — in the seer
saḥ — he
yogavidām varaḥ — is the best among *yoga*-knowers

A kaleidoscopic vision is exciting and entertaining. The kaleidoscope is intended to cause a visual illusion by combining several circularly or polygonically juxtaposed images. In a properly structured kaleidoscope one cannot detect the true nature of the primary form which is magnified into a highly complex form. To produce the effect of optical illusion, properties of light, the logistics of geometry, and laws of reflection are complemented with the encoding of color and form, and their subsequent interpretation is aided by consciousness generated by the molecular patterns of the visual mechanism of the brain. Visual images introjected and reciprocally projected are such a total experience that there is no room left for consciousness to stand outside and have a detached view of the vision so that it can be reduced to the simple form of the primary object out of which the highly magnified elaboration is effected.

Similarly to the optical illusion, illusions of sound, touch, taste, smell, motion, weight or weightlessness, and several such phenomena can be effected by slightly altering the function of the nervous system and the secretion of glands and the various hormones of the body. A living organism is always undergoing psychophysical, psychochemical, and biological changes in accordance with the variation of the physical, social, and psychological environment in which the organism is placed. This is particularly so in the case of human beings. These changes amount to the creation of a series of sensory illusions and hallucinations of all sorts. Although the critical staff of rationality is present to guide the reason of the individual, the amount of hypnotic spell that is exercised on the mind cannot be fully determined.

Thus, the reality of empirical experience is of an absolutely relativistic order. Everything is real and unreal. From deep sleep to absolute wakefulness there is a wide range of consciousness, which has an intensity of darkness at one end and an intensity of light at the other. Between the total darkness of the unconscious and the brilliant light of critical observation lies a diffused area of consciousness which can be identified with the zone of the dream experience. Thus, there are hallucinations relating to the wakeful, the dream, and deep sleep. To put it another way, we can say that the wakeful is composed of perceptual cues molded into empirical facts by the clothing of sensory stimuli with conceptual garments; that in the dream state prior memories are variously fabricated to provide for a psychodrama in which one and the same subject transforms into all and sundry, and becomes every form and meaning of what is experienced as a dream; and that the third aspect of deep sleep is the effacement of all traces of memories. On the whole we can say that consciousness remains uninfluenced by memories for awhile, and then at other times becomes monitored by memory into various elaborations. Yogic insight means to get behind these altering states and to not be deluded by the surface disturbances.

To simplify such a probe and to effect unitive vision, the entire phenomenon is divided into the seer and the seen. These terms in English are a little misleading. First of all, seeing is associated with the eyes and the agency of seeing is attributed to an ego. Therefore, seer can mean a particular person who sees. But this is not the sense in which seer is to be understood. It is a universal operation of consciousness which at the physical level has the adjuncts of psychophysical instruments, such as eyes, ears, etc. as in human beings, or sensitive feelers as in insects. Even the lowest forms of life such as vegetation have this perceiving consciousness to some degree. The seer we speak of is a generic consciousness that is universally functioning, and the seen is a feedback of the same consciousness after it has been modulated with the properties and characteristics of various psychophysical interactions. In understanding the totality of this universal function there is the snag of differentiating the Self and the non-Self. Most people stumble at the threshold of objectivization and will find it almost impossible to fill the chasm between the subject and the object. A number of techniques are adopted by aspiring *yogi*-s such as introjecting more and more consciousness into the muscular and neural activity as one sits in various postures. This of course helps people to get rid of physical rigidities and gives more lucid motion to moribund psychophysical energies. It does not, however, bring the desired union of the individuated self with the universal Self.

At a further level a yogic aspirant may resort to *prāṇayāma* with the intention of uniting the ascending and descending vital energies, which are known as *prāṇa* and *apāna* respectively. In the case of most people, *prāṇāyāma* remains only as a breathing exercise. If it is to mean anything more than torturing the respiratory system, one should go beyond the physical breathing exercise to know who breathes and what is breathed in and breathed out. The smallest unit in the function of breath is pulsation. The entire world of the cosmos is pulsating at different levels. Each pulsation has the complementary functions of a centrifugal expansion and a centripetal contraction. Everything is generated through a spasmodic expulsion and impulsion of energy. The quantas of energy involved in each spasm or pulsation determine the behavior and properties of all the physicochemical constituents of this world. Thus our breathing is a part of the universal pulsation. All living beings are rhythmically pulsating and maintaining their life. Sacrificing one's *prāṇa* into *apāna* and *apāna* into *prāṇa*, or uniting the upgoing breath and the downgoing breath in the heart, is only suggestive of the spirit merging into matter and matter becoming surcharged with spirit or the visible changing into the ideational and ideas transforming into visibles. In the process of *prāṇāyāma* the breathing in or filling in is called *pūraka*. The retention of what is filled in is called *kumbhaka*. The process of exhaustion is called *recaka*. These become spiritually meaningful only when the filling in can be interpreted as knowing everything in the seer that is 'I' — one's own self — to be *ayam ātma brahma*, "This Self is the Absolute"; when *kumbhaka* is interpreted as retaining the consciousness *aham brahma asmi*, "I am the Absolute"; and when *recaka* is the realization of the same Absolute as the manifested world, so that one can confidently say *prajñānam brahma*, "This knowledge is the Absolute." This is the *recaka*, seeing the other as the Absolute.

Even after receiving the secret instruction *tat tvam asi*, "That thou art," from one's teacher, one may not become a *yogi* unless this consciousness of the union of the subject and object is continuously realized by perpetuating the retentive idea "That thou art." This is not possible unless one empties oneself of one's ego. Personal ego is an aggregate of memories called *vāsana*, and it is always active to produce volitional imagery. This is called *saṅkalpa*. *Saṅkalpa* is the root cause of all human miseries. An effective step in withholding from being influenced by the *vāsana* is returning again and again to the true nature of the Self. This withdrawal is called *pratyāhāra*. When once the Self is seen through an act of *samyam*, the Self can be seen in all and as all. When there is nothing extraneous to attract or distract, consciousness becomes steady and *samadhi* is achieved. Thereafter one does not experience the duality of the subject and the object. Such a state is praised as *yoga*.

VERSE 8

yadā piban manobhṛngaḥ
svānanda madhu mādhurīm,
na spandati vaśīkṛtya
yojito yogavāyunā

When mind, the bumble bee, sips
the honey-like sweetness of one's own bliss,
fluttering ceases and is drawn
into union by *yoga vāyu.*

yadā — when
manaḥ — mind
bhṛngaḥ — the bumble bee
piban — sips
madhu mādhurīm — the honey-like sweetness
svānanda — of one's own bliss
na spandati — fluttering ceases
vaśī kṛtya — and is drawn into
yojitaḥ — union
yogavāyunā — by *yoga vāyu*

Various kinds of electrical motors are operated by currents which make a magent resonate and dissonate alternately. Mind also operates with a similar mechanism of being attracted or repulsed. Where one can trust love, mind is easily attracted and it clings on to the object of love such as a beloved. When there is the least suspicion of that trust, mind withdraws and becomes hesitant. And when the distrust becomes serious, mind is repulsed and a context of love no longer exists. The same love manifests in small doses toward any object that has in it a promise of pleasure, however meager, such as a good sound, an affectionate touch, a pleasing form, a good taste, or a fragrant smell. However, an object which is considered to be pleasure-giving cannot keep the mind bound to it for a long time. Even the most pleasing smell can become offensive when its intensity is increased and it fills the entire air one breathes. A taste is enjoyable for a very short period and thereafter can cause nausea. It is monotonous and boring to look at the same form for a long time. One may enjoy an embrace and may become excited, but if it is prolonged for more than one can stand one feels smothered and very badly wants to get rid of it. Even the best of music can become a menace when it is too much. From all this it is evident that mind's attraction to objects of pleasure is caused by short-lived illusions about happiness. When mind is tired of one object of pleasure, it leaves it and goes on to the next.

Just as our hand has five fingers, each with a special kind of structure that enables us to do a number of skillful activities with it, mind has, to aid its perception, five sense faculties, and to aid its execution, five organs of action. Just as there is pleasure in hearing, touching and seeing, there is also pleasure in doing work, moving around, speaking, procreating and excreting. Each one of these has importance over the rest according to the interest it caters to. The eyes are so structured that they can easily be turned from left to right and top to bottom to include in the span of vision a wide variety of objects. If a man goes on drawing all the forms and shapes that please him, there is no end to that. There are several combinations of unified action possible, such as listening and doing, seeing and doing, touching and doing, moving and seeing, moving and touching, and so on. Thus the entire universe offers each person a wide variety of attractions.

Attractions are not all of a uniform type. Whenever a movie comes to town with the most shocking themes and scenes, we see a big rush of people to the theater. A similar attraction can be produced by another picture that has a high aesthetic and moral presentation. The secret of enjoyment is described by two Sanskrit words, *rati* and *rasa*. Allegorically, Rati is conceived as the female spouse of Smara. In the Western world of mythology, Smara is equivalent to Eros and Rati to Psyche. *Smara* literally means 'to remember'. In remembrance there is an implied concept. Each concept is a conditioned state of both the body and the mind. Concepts also act as prejudices. Prejudices can be favorable or unfavorable. The favorably conditioned states of conceptually established prejudices attract the mind. The opposite repulses it. Another name of Smara is Madana. *Madana* is one who maddens. In madness there is a gloating of the ego, and in such a state the ego will be infatuated with a highly emotional need to relate with a certain form or object of love. When the madness is of a negative order, the ego will be under a compulsive spell to destroy the hate-symbol.

The actualization of egotistic pleasures is exploited by the facilitators of all interests in life such as trade, commerce, therapy, religion, etc. In all these spheres a number of devices are used to externalize human interests. The carrot that is held before the ass of the mind is one *rasa* or another. *Rasa* is the essence of a temporary appreciation such as erotics, fear, wonder, or dread. In Bharata's *Natya Śastra* he mentions eight basic moods or *rasa*-s. Bhoja added to these a ninth *rasa* called *śāntiḥ*, the peace that comes when the mind is no longer distracted. This is the enjoyment which a *yogi* seeks. Such a *rasa* can come only when the mind is fully drawn to the most loveable object. Man loves nothing and no one more than his very Self. Even when a man kills himself it is because he pities himself. So the most stable of all *rasa*-s comes when mind is guided to the discovery of the sweetest of all ecstasies that lies buried in the Self. However, the mind is like a brute. It is to be tamed and educated, controlled and disciplined. Any discipline involving threat and suppression will be reacted to by the mind, which in its bitterness and sourness becomes neurotic and psychotic. So it is to be disciplined with great care and with healthy incentives. The flowers that bloom in the forest need the service of bees to pollinate them. However great this need is, no flower leaves its place to go in search of a bee, but the flower can give an incentive to the bee by being fragrant and colorful. The fragrance of a flower can travel to far-off places carried by the breeze. That is enough for bees to set out in search of the flower. Like that, the fragrance of the blissful experiences of *yoga* can be presented to the mind with the winds of *yoga* (*yoga vāyu*) such as *prāṇāyāma*. Attracted by the hidden joys of the Self, once the mind enters the portals of the Self it becomes as excited as a bumble bee caught within the petals of a full-blown lotus flower which is full of honey and pollen dust. When the bee begins to sip honey, it is pacified and does not flutter its wings any more. Similarly, when the *yogi* becomes attuned to his Self, he comes to know that *ānanda* is his very nature and that there is nothing to seek outside. In fact, both the inside and the outside become one universal Self for him.

VERSE 9

dhyānam antar bhruvordṛṣṭir
jihvāgram lambikordhvataḥ
yadā syāt khecarī mudrā
nidrālasyādi nāśinī

When meditation is done with gaze between the eyebrows
and the tip of the tongue fixed above the uvula,
then happens *khecarī mudrā,*
which dispels torpor and fatigue.

yadā — when
dhyānam — meditation (is done)
bhruvaḥ dṛṣṭiḥ antaḥ — with gaze between the eyebrows
jihvāgram — (and) the tip of the tongue
lambikordhvataḥ — fixed above the uvula
syāt (*tada*) — (then) happens
khecarī mudrā — *khecarī mudrā*
nidrālasyādi nāśinī — which dispels torpor and fatigue

There is life in a seed but it sleeps. When it is roused, the sprout comes out like a waking person getting up from his bed and standing erect. A sleeping person cannot stand erect and balance his body on his feet. The head becomes heavy and the neck cannot support it. Even the eyelids become heavy, and it is hard for a sleepy person to keep his eyes open. Even when a person keeps awake, if there is not enough stamina in the body and the system is assailed by lethargy, it is difficult to apply oneself physically to any work or to keep the mind attentive to do any task. The more one becomes attentive, the greater is the clarity of mind and the agility of the body to engage every part to function effortlessly. The polarization between sleep and wakefulness is only an expression of the polarization between *tamas*, inertia, and *satva*, clarity of expression. *Tamas* has the qualities which are usually attributed to inorganic matter. If we arrange in a series inertial matter, biologic function, psychologic activity, cognitive function, intuitive flash, and the highest perception of truth, we get a hierarchy of the gradation that ranges between the morass of the unconscious and the highest sublimity of consciousness. The mounting of consciousness from the inertial to the sublime is like the ascent of a lark from a nest in the valley where it sleeps to a height far above the clouds, from where it pours out its heavenly music. Hence the yogic discipline that arouses consciousness and enables it to soar high is called *khecarī mudrā*, the psychophysical set which is similar to a levitating body.

The jettisoning of a heavy aircraft with several hundred passengers into the thin air of the sky or a spacecraft into outer space needs the propulsion of great energy, exceeding in proportion the gravitational pull of the Earth. We Earthlings do not fall off the crust of the planet because of the gravitational pull which acts on all bodies with a tremendous magnetic force. The same irresistable, blind force keeps our body and mind together by filling our psychophysical organism with inertia at a physical level. *Rajas*, the kinetic energy in us, has the power to shake off inertia, but it has no direction unless *satva*, the clear knowledge of pure wisdom, monitors the psychic energy as it is released from its frigid state.

A model of *khecarī* is described in this verse. As all organs of perception and action are below the eyebrows, the guiding and maneuvering functions of the visual faculty are tied up with the lower parts of the body, such as in directing the feet to walk. It becomes attentive to sexual needs, excretory functions, appeasing of hunger, respiratory needs, manipulation of hands, observation of objects around, localizing and giving orientation to various stimuli received, and even to the introspection that automatically goes on with the silent witnessing of the linear flow of ideas and words when the mind is engaged in active reasoning or passive imagination. Even in a blind person the faculty of vision is extremely active, although such a person is incapable of directing his eyes to the shape and color of objects. This dysfunction is amply compensated for by the person's power to direct his attention to a keen observation of anything in which he is interested. What is eye to the psychological organism is 'I' to consciousness. To get into *khecarī mudrā*, the most essential and dynamic power of the visual faculty is detached from the rest of the organism and is placed in-between the eyebrows. This synergic center is called the *ājña*, the center from which all volitions come in the form of the will to act. Concentration is identical with the con-centering of consciousness in the *ājña*. When this is possible, consciousness has a mastery over all.

The oral and the anal are the two extreme limits of expression. The emission of semen, the excretion of waste, and the mouth are all activated by clusters of nerve endings that are easily tickled. While an adult finds it extremely pleasure-giving to engage in sexual activity, the child enjoys its activity of excretion. The appeasing of two of the major instincts, physical and sexual hunger, is intrinsically connected with the mouth region. From impressing affectionate kisses and mingling of breath to the sweetest whispering of love-promises, the mouth is assigned a great role in love-making. The pleasures of the palate are also not mean. The erection of the sexual organ when it is aroused is suggestive of the organism's preparedness to participate to its full measure. In *khecarī mudrā* there is a wholesale sublimation of the entire libidinal energy by concentrating the arousal in the mouth region. Freud speaks only of the pathological perversion of it in his "Theory of Anal Erotics." Erotic energy is the highest that man can wield. This is concentrated in the mouth, and as a base for sublimation the tongue is erected in a vertical position and inserted through the cavity behind the uvula. Thus the verticalized flow of energy is brought into conjunction with the synergic center of volition, *ājña*, and the aspirant *yogi* roots out all incipient memories that are of an expending nature. Even in an ordinary orgasmic delight one experiences getting high. In the *khecarī mudrā* the elevation that one gives to one's consciousness is a thousand-fold higher than any object-oriented delight, including sexual orgasm. This is a highly cathartic function in which the ego cathexis is transmuted into a spiritual cathexis. In other words, all pent-up libidinal urges to relate the ego to objects are directed to the transcendental. The uplifting effect of this is experienced at all levels, such as the physical, the vital, the moral, the cognitive, and the intuitive.

This is a conscious function, but the consciousness involved is different from the binary function of subject-object oscillation. As both the articulating tongue and the gestalting eye are interlocked to aid meditation, the entire gamut of the semiotic process is put here in the crucible of a psychic alchemy. *Vāsana*-s which are encapsulated in concepts are transmuted into the spiritual awareness of a single unity. The existential verity of the referents of all concepts is reduced to one unifying and unitive existence. As a result of this, differentiating connotations are given up in favor of the one single meaning: awareness without frontiers. This leads to the discovery of the meaning of all meanings, the peak experience of supreme bliss. This is the significance of *khecarī mudrā* in a nutshell.

VERSE 10

jñānam karmeti loke'smin
dvidhā yogaḥ samāsataḥ
anayoryogavistāraḥ
sarvaḥ parisamāpyate

In this world *yoga*, in short, is of
two forms — knowledge and *karma* — thus.
All forms of *yoga* are conclusively comprised
in these two descriptions of *yoga*.

asminloke — in this world
yogaḥ — *yoga*
samāsataḥ — in short
dvidhā — is of two forms
jñānam — knowledge
karmeti — (and) *karma* thus
sarvaḥ — all (forms of *yoga*)
parisamāpyate — are conclusively comprised
anayor yoga vistāraḥ — in these two descriptions of *yoga*

Knowledge comes by listening, listening to the truth that is revealed by one who has met truth by knowing it and being it. Listening is an active process. It becomes fruitful only through meditation on what is heard. Manipulating a rational structure of what is heard is conceptualization or merely improving upon concepts that have been formed earlier. This does not bring wisdom to the listener, it only helps in the acquisition of information. Knowledge, as Socrates says, becomes a virtue only when one fully acquaints himself with the full purport of the secret of a revelation and it is lived in its entirety. Such an act is called *nididhyāsana*. That is why Yājñavalkya instructed his wife and disciple, Maitreyi, to listen , *śravana*, ponder over, *manana*, and actualize the teaching, *nididhyāsana*, when he commenced his teaching of *brahmavidya* to her.

What is spoken about or revealed by the Guru consists of the wisdom of the Self and its relationship with the non-Self. The non-Self is the field of which the Self is the knower, *kṣetrajña*. The field, *kṣetra*, is vast and varied. It consists of the body, its organs of perception and action, and the world, constituted of the three modalities of nature, the five elements, the five basic properties of elements, the five *prāṇa*-s or vital energies, the mind, the intellect, the ego, and the memory. All these categories are always engaged in action. Therefore a *yogi* has to understand clearly the field of action, the purport of action, the instrument of action, the volitional agent of action, and the motivation that decides the character of action.

An individual is part of his society, and interaction between members of one's community is inevitable for anyone. As a result there are many external activities which one is obliged to perform. On the one hand, the individual is thrown off balance by the disequilibrium of his own nature modalities and changing patterns of psychic energy, and this keeps a person busy finding ends and means to gather himself to give him peace. On the other hand, the person is exposed to external challenges, and there also he has to establish his harmonious relationship with everyone in the world around him. The Gita says nobody can remain even for a short while without doing action. For the embodied being action is imperative. If the course of action is left to the push and pull of random chance, it soon becomes so complicated that one loses his ground and will not be able to retract himself from the whirlpools of frightful actions. So it is necessary to know the secret of action and make it unitive with the understanding of the cause and effect involvement of the ego with several programs of action. This problem being very grave, even Lord Kṛṣṇa in the Bhagavad Gita says that the course of action is too difficult to comprehend, even for a wise person.[1]

Action, non-action, perverted action, and unitive action are all to be distinguished very carefully. Unitive action is called *karma yoga*. For achieving *karma yoga* a person has to see that everything pertaining to nature goes through series of changes which are entirely governed by physicochemical and biological laws of nature. These are like the ceaseless formations of waves in the ocean of phenomenality, which an individual can do nothing either to stop or to modify. Whether man wants or not, fire will burn, water will flow, the sun will shine, and the moon will wax and wane. Even his own body will have birth, existence, growth, evolution, and decay. In this vast field of phenomenal changes, action belongs to the 'other' and one need not pin one's responsibility or conscience to it. One has to own actions when they are willed with the motivation of achieving an end. It is here action has to become unitive. When the ego is infatuated with the emotional or value-significance of the end of action, one loses sight of the binding nature of action. So a *karma yogi*, as advocated by the Gita, sees action in inaction and inaction in action.[2] Natural actions, actions to fulfill bodily necessities, and actions to perpetuate the welfare of the world are always relevant. When the relevancy is accepted with full understanding, and actions are performed in accordance with the injunctions of the science of the Absolute, *karma* becomes unitive. Such knowledge of the non-Self distinctly reveals the Self as the Supreme Knower in all sentient beings.

A knowledge of this transcendental aspect of the Self, the *param*, releases the mind from all its cravings. As a result, the lower self comes to know the higher Self in all its glory. This is *jñāna yoga*. *Jñāna yoga* concerns itself with the *tat padārtha*, 'that'-ness of the Absolute; and *karma yoga* enables the individuated consciousness imprisoned in the *tvam padārtha*, 'thou' aspect of all objectivization, to be released. Thus, when the secret of the Self and the non-Self are taken together, it is evident that there is only one *yoga*. It is of both *jñāna* and *karma* and also it is neither *jñāna* alone nor *karma* alone. This is the conclusive teaching the Guru gives on *yoga*.

IX. YOGA DARŚANAM

[1] Nataraja Guru, *The Bhagavad Gita*, R & K Publishing House, Delhi, Ch. IV, v. 16, p. 234

[2] ibid. Ch. IV, v. 18, p. 236

X. NIRVĀṆA DARSANAM

The Finale

Two events which are an absolute certainty in life are birth and death. It is not in the individual's power either to prepare for his birth or to have it gracefully. Likewise, although death is wholly certain, there is an uncertainty as to the time and the mode of its happening. In spite of the unpredictability of death, one can prepare for it so that the journey up to a conscious point of life's final termination can be made abundantly satisfying to oneself and exceedingly beautiful to others.

In one sense the entire life is a preparation for the final departure. What there is after one dies is a big question which can perhaps never be adequately answered. Another pertinent question is to enquire into the state of being as one approaches and enters into death, and the content of the probable continuance of the Being that is punctuated with death on the physical and phenomenal side.

In the two previous chapters the individual psyche is aligned, or rather realigned, with its cosmic counterpart, at first through the establishment of a bipolarity which is rich in its fragrance of love and devotion. That realignment is further homogenized with a process of contemplative absorption of the individualized personal self in the totality of the universal Self. Now there is only one more step to go, the ceasing to be of a name appended to a form marked by a perishable aggregate of an organism.

Death is death. Even then a contented elderly person led into silence with an inwardly growing contentment, finally closing his eyes with a thankful smile after watching with satisfaction his many dear ones standing around him with inexpressible love and veneration, is something remarkably beautiful when contrasted with death caused by a road accident or a suicide committed in desperation. In like manner a well-conceived and personally opted form of merger into one's universal ground is different from dying helplessly, lamenting over the fateful attack of old-age and disease. In the present chapter no mention is made of those who have not made a choice of their final exit.

The burning out of the phenomenal mark of individuation is termed in this chapter as *nirvāṇa*. Three possible groups are presented for evaluation. One group is of such people who have turned to the path of the spirit with the intention of glorifying their power perch in society on the ground of having attained psychic capabilities (*siddhi*). Then there are others who are motivated by the pure intention of releasing themselves from the snares of psycho-physical attractions and who have set emancipation as the only goal of life. The final group is of people who have succeeded in obtaining their liberation with varying grades of success. Among such people again two divisions are made. One refers to people like Buddha who see a meaning to returning to one's folks with the intention of aiding sincere aspirants into the path of liberation. And the other group is shown mainly to demonstrate to what intensity the absolute abandon of liberation can lead, until the physical presence can be totally ignored even though death as such has not yet claimed the most elite among the liberated.

VERSE 1

nirvāṇam dvividhaṁ śuddha-
maśuddham ceti tatra yat
śuddhaṁ nirvāsanam tadva-
daśuddham vāsanānvitam

Nirvāṇa is of two kinds:
the pure and the impure.
That which is the pure is devoid of *vāsana*;
similarly, that is impure which is conjoined with *vāsana.*

nirvāṇam — *nirvāṇa* (emancipation)
dvividham — is of two kinds
iti — (such as)
śuddham — the pure
aśuddham ca — and the impure
tatra yat — that which is
(*tat*) *śuddham* — the pure
nirvāsanam — is devoid of *vāsana* (incipient memories)
tadvat — similarly
(*tat*) *aśuddham* — that is impure
(*yat*) *vāsanānvitam* — which is conjoined with *vāsana*

The body-mind organism of man is only a device. A device is a programmed instrument, and the program is so that a specific end may be achieved. In a complicated organization of an instrument there are many sub-devices and sequential programs. When such is the case, the progressive operation of the plethora of devices results in the continuous actualization of countless motivations. A human organism geared with motivations is not very different from an animated robot that is programed for a specific performance. When the performance is over, the robot comes to rest. In man's case his individuation and programing have their counterparts in a transforming world, which lends itself to be a fertile field to actualize all the specific interests of man. In the case of a robot, its return to rest is the reduction of its activity to nonfunctioning. This is also what happens to man when he goes into an inertial state such as deep sleep.

There is another kind of cessation of his activity: that is, his return to the source. Thereafter he is not a device and he has no program to perform. This is a case of the release of the imprisoned splendor of the Self from the shackles or bondage of a predetermined role-playing. Such a release is called *nirvāṇa*. *Nirvāṇa* literally means 'burning out' or 'extinction'. A candle burns only until there is no more wax left to continue the process of oxidation. From a burned out candle a new candle will not emerge. This is not the case when a plant fruits and its characteristics are posited in a seed. Out of the seed there can again emerge the cyclic life of a plant. Therefore *nirvāṇa* is sometimes compared to a roasted seed which no longer has the potential to sprout.

However, this final cessation does not spell the exit into nothingness. As the glory and grandeur of *nirvāṇa* is inestimable, a number of analogies are given to describe that state. Lord Buddha compares it to the merging of a dewdrop into the infinitude of the ocean. Jesus Christ compares it to the return of a prodigal son to acknowledge the profound love and compassion of an all-knowing father. The source or ground of manifestation is also differently described as truth, knowledge, and the blissful delight of pure love which is the solvent of all dualities. The first and immediate experiential recognition of the release comes from the awareness of a total satisfaction or fulfillment. This ecstatic state of beatitude is called *nirvṛti*, boundlessness. From there on there is no role to play, no program to be fulfilled, no mount to be ascended. The search has culminated in the profound beauty and joy of envisioning. Coming to such a state is called *nirvṛtti*. In such a state only peace prevails. There is no stir in consciousness. This non-modulated aspect is described as *nivṛtti*. The *yoga* spoken of in the previous *darśana* becomes a reality. There is no well-being higher than this to achieve. Therefore it is called *śreyas*. In fact, this final release from all motivations enables one to transcend even the idea of well-being. Hence this state is called *niśreyas*. This is as if the part is reabsorbed into the whole. It is like a piece of iron sucked into a magnetic field where the iron and the magnet become the same. Because of this quality, *nirvāṇa* is called *brahmasamsparśa*. *Brahma* means the Absolute; *samsparśa* means to be actively in contact. Thereafter the status of the individual is only nominal.

In reality the individual does not exist. Only the Absolute is. For this reason, the state of the liberated is indicated as *brahmabhūyam*, identity with the Absolute. In such a state the liberated can be described only as 'is' or 'be'. This aloneness is called *kaivalya*. Only in a state of becoming are there beginnings and ends, births and deaths. Where eternity prevails, death is not relevant. That is why *nirvāṇa* is equated with *amṛta*, immortality. Such a state of perfection is glorified as *pūrṇam*. Even in this final stage there can be traces of previous conditioning. If any such vestige lingers on unresolved, the release should be looked upon as impure. On the other hand, when the attainment is without blemish like pure light and fully harmonized as in a love that transcends duality, it is to be understood as pure. There are grades of purity, and they are going to be elucidated in the following verse.

VERSE 2

atiśuddham śuddhamiti
śuddham ca dvividham tathā
aśuddhaśuddham cāśuddha-
maśuddhāśuddham ucyate

Most pure, pure — thus
the pure is of two kinds, and similarly
the impure also is said to be
impure-pure and impure-impure.

ati śuddham — most pure
śuddham — pure
iti — thus
śuddham — the pure
dvividham — is of two kinds
ca tathā — and similarly
aśuddham — the impure
ucyate — is also said to be
aśuddha śuddham — impure-pure
ca aśuddhāśuddham — and impure-impure

There are seers and seekers. Among the seers there are those who see the psychic potentials within the phenomenality of their being, and there are sages of supreme wisdom who have transcended the phenomenal so as to be in perfect attunement with the numinous. Similarly, among seekers there are passionate ones who are enamored with the magical potentials of psychic attainments, and what they seek is the power of position and the following of multitudes. Occasionally there comes from among the multitude of seekers that rare one who is anguished by his separation from the truthful state of the Self. He seeks only the Self, the truth of his being. Thus there are varieties of experiential and imperiential pursuits in the spiritual path. In the present and succeeding two verses the classification of the emancipated is attempted.

VERSE 3

atiśuddham tridhā paścā-
dvare caikam varīyasi
ekamekam variṣṭhe'tha
śuddham brahmavidi sthitam

The most pure is again of three kinds:
one in the superior, one in the more superior,
one in the most superior; and thus
the pure is established in the *brahma*-knower.

atiśuddham — the most pure
paścāt — is again
tridhā — of three kinds
ekam — one
vare — in the superior
ekam — one
varīyasi — in the more superior
ekam — one
variṣṭhe — in the most superior
ca atha — and thus
śuddham — the pure
sthitam — is established
brahmavidi — in the *brahma*-knower

The ascending and descending dialectics of union with the Absolute is conceived schematically without having any reference to the spatial format of ascension or descension. In this scheme the immanence and transcendence are so poised that the progression from immanence to transcendence can be said to be one of ascension, and progression within transcendence as descending to the inestimable depth of the Absolute. Although all aspects of pure *nirvāṇa* refer to that quarter of the Absolute which is termed in the *Māṇḍūkya Upaniṣad* as *turīya*, the fourth, in the present verse the attainment and perfection of the fourth itself is described as having four quarters. The state of identity with these quarters or absorption in them can be named as *śuddhanirvāṇa*, pure extinction, *atiśuddhanirvāṇa*, more pure extinction, *atiśuddhataranirvāṇa*, even more pure extinction, and *atiśuddhatamanirvāṇa*, the most pure extinction. Those who become established in these four quarters can be respectively named as *brahmavit*, the knower of the Absolute, *brahmavidvara*, superior in the knowledge of the Absolute, *brahmavidvarīya*, the more superior in the knowledge of the Absolute, and *brahmavidvariṣṭha*, the most superior in the knowledge of the Absolute. All these four classes are said to be the liberated even when they are physically alive in their bodies.

In the present verse it is said that the *śuddhanirvāṇa*, perfect extinction, is in the *brahmavit*, the knower of *brahma*. More pure extinction is in the superior knower of *brahma*. The even more pure extinction is in the still more superior knower of the Absolute, and the most pure extinction is in the most superior knower of the Absolute. The characteristics of all these four kinds will be subsequently described. In the next verse we are given a similar categorization of the four kinds of extinctions which are not fully disassociated from the passions and nescience of the phenomenal.

VERSE 4

aśuddhaśuddham viraja-
stamo'nyat sarajastamaḥ
mumukṣau prathamam vidyāt
dvitīyam siddhikāmiṣu

The impure-pure is devoid of *rajas* and *tamas*
and the other is with *rajas* and *tamas*.
The former is known to be in the seeker of liberation,
the latter in those who desire psychic attainment.

aśuddhaśuddham — the impure-pure
virajastamaḥ — is devoid of *rajas* and *tamas*
rajas — passion that leads to action
tamas — inertial state that cause confusion and depression
anyat — and the other
sarajastamaḥ — is with *rajas* and *tamas*
prathamam — the former
vidyāt — is known to be
mumukṣau — in the seeker of liberation
dvitīyam — the latter
siddhikāmiṣu — in those who desire psychic attainment

Man acts by compulsion or impulsion. Compulsion comes from conditioning which is either instinctual or acquired. Instinctive compulsion is a behavioral pattern shared by all members of the species. The dictates of wisdom and the discipline of *yoga* are directed against such compulsive behavior. As a part of the *yogi*'s sublimating discipline, reflexive and autonomous functions are infused with mindfulness and unconscious compulsions are substituted with conscious deliberations. Conscious deliberations, however, can become accentuated and reinforced by obsessive naturalistic passions or depressive inhibitions that come in the form of periodic confusion and clouding of the intellect. In the rare case of those who steer clear of these anomalies, the only passion that survives is the desire to be liberated and the only confusion stems from putting their trust in the envisioning of a state of liberation which they are prone to structure on the basis of their *a priori* knowledge of liberation. In their pursuit there is no stain of evil, and their ardent effort will ultimately bear the fruit of liberation.

Therefore the *nirvāṇa* to which they are drawn is certainly pure. Although their knowledge and volition are free from the modulations of rajasic passions and tamasic confusion, they do not enter the state of pure liberation until their consciousness is freed of their identification with bondage and the notion of liberation as a futuristic possibility. For that reason there is impurity in the conceptual liberation of the seeker. Hence the state is called *aśuddhāśuddha*. *Mumukṣu* is one who has an intense desire to be liberated.

In the path of *yoga* there are many pitfalls and snares that can easily trap the ambitious ego of even an ardent aspirant. In Patañjali's *Yoga Sūtra*, Chapter Three, aphorism thirty-six, it says:

> Thence (from the knowledge of *puruṣa*) arise prescience (*prātibha*), supernormal power of hearing (*śrāvana*), supernormal power of touch (*vedana*), supernormal power of sight (*ādarśa*), supernormal power of taste (*āsvāda*), and supernormal power of smell (*vārtā*).[1]

Vyāsa says that when the knowledge of *puruṣa* is acquired these faculties are developed involuntarily, i. e., without the application of *samyama*.

It is further said in the next aphorism that these powers are impediments to *samādhi* but are acquisitions in a fluctuating state of the mind. In commenting on this Vyāsa says, "In *samādhi* there is only one subject as the probe of a concentrated mind. Hence the attainment of powers mentioned before causes disturbance to such a mind. When aided by the knowledge of the various principles and the practice of renunciation, the mind becomes one-pointed, and is completely closed to permeation of knowledge. Then only can the state of the Self being itself be reached. Attainment of power is inimical to that."

Even in the first chapter of the aphorisms of Patañjali a warning is given, in aphorism thirty.[2] There the impediments which disturb the mind are given as sickness, incompetence, doubt, delusion, sloth, non-abstention, erroneous conception, non-attainment of any yogic stage, and instability to stay in a yogic state. In the *Yoga Vāsiṣṭha*, Vālmiki also laments the fate of the misguided yogic aspirants who are ensnared by psychic attainments. In spite of their discipline, their conceit and ambition to hold positions of power among their deluded fellow humans causes them to perpetuate around themselves a faith in the hallucinative phenomena of the miracle, which drowns both themselves and others in the muddy waters of confusion that are surrogatively looked upon as spiritual. Hence the state of such a yogic aspirant is termed here as doubly impure, *aśuddha-aśuddham*. In the next verse we are given the characteristics of the *brahmavit*, knower of the Absolute, who is a truly liberated person.

VERSE 5

dagdhvā jñānāgninā sarva-
muddiśya jagatām hitam
karoti vidhivat karma
brahmavid brahmani sthitaḥ

Having burned everything with the fire of wisdom,
aiming the good of the world,
doing action according to injunction,
the knower of *brahma* remains firm in *brahma.*

dagdhvā — having burned
sarvam — everything
jñānāgninā — with the fire of wisdom
uddiśya — aiming
hitam — the good
jagatām — of the world
karoti karma — doing action
vidhivat — according to injunction
brahmavit — the knower of *brahma*
sthitaḥ — remains firm
brahmaṇi — in *brahma*

In constant proximity with a magnet, a piece of iron transforms into a magnet. Likewise, in proximity with fire a piece of iron becomes red-hot. In either case the transformation occurs as a result of initimate bipolarity. It is to a similar bipolarity that an aspirant exposes himself through love and devotion when he relates himself to the Absolute. The Absolute is not a thing but an irrefutable certitude that dispels all lurking fear and suspicion which clouds consciousness. Such an intimacy with the Absolute inevitably becomes a purificatory process by which the luminosity of the Self becomes rid of all stains that color individuation. Eradication of the coloration of consciousness is called *vairāgya.* Presence of darkness remains real only until the radiation of light is kept steady and constant. The steadying effect in the form of the clarity and certitude of the Self is realized by living the Word of the Guru and *śāstra*, the science of wisdom.

Even when a fuel is burning with a bright flame, part of it is not fully transformed into light. Similarly, the seer who is in the final stage of his reduction is in a process of diminishing his individuation and maximizing universalization. The whole process is thus one of *vairāgya* and *śraddha*, in other words, of purification and bi-polarity.

The good of the world is turning it continuously from falsehood to truth, ignorance to knowledge, and expenditure to conservation. The Word or *Logos* is identical with the Absolute, and it is this Word that is shining forth as the instruction of the preceptor and the injunction of the scripture. *A posteriori* certitude is preceded by *a priori* revelation. The Absolute transforms the Guru and the scripture into word wisdom. The Guru and the scripture transform a seeker into a seer. By the same token, a seer becomes the refuge and consolation of the world. The energy source of the world is its natural fuel, and the wisdom source of the world is the seer who retains his integrity at the level of interpersonal transaction. The seer described here as *brahmavit* is presented in the fourth chapter of the Bhagavad Gita as the truly wise person:

> One who is able to see action in inaction and inaction in action — he among men is intelligent; he is one of unitive attitude, while still engaged in every (possible) kind of work.
>
> That man whose works are all devoid of desire and wilful motive, whose (impulse of) action has been reduced to nothing in the fire of wisdom — he is recognized as a knowing person by the wise.
>
> Relinquishing attachment for the benefit of works, ever happy and independent, though such a man be engaged in work, he (in principle) does nothing at all.
>
> One free of all expectancy and of subjugated relational self-consciousness, who has given up all possessiveness, and is engaged merely bodily in actions — he does not acquire evil.
>
> Satisfied with chance gains, unaffected by conflicting pairs (of interests), non-competitive, remaining the same in gain or no gain, he remains unbound in spite of having been active.
>
> In the case of one whose attachments are gone, who has gained freedom, whose spiritual being has been founded on wisdom, his works, having a sacrificial character only, become wholly dissolved.
>
> (For him) the Absolute is the act of offering, the Absolute is the substance offered into the Absolute which is the fire, offered by (him), the Absolute, the end to be reached by him

> being even the Absolute, by means of his peace supreme of absolutist action. (IV: 18-24)[3]

Even after the burning of a rope one can see in the ashes the form of the plaited strands. Similarly, there is a semblance of the personal factor of an individual in a person even after his having attained his realization. That is why he is placed one degree below the most pure. At the same time there is not even the slightest stain of the ego which separates his interest from the good of the world. So he is included here among the pure. Such a knower of the Self is again and again alluded to in the Upanishads and the Bhagavad Gita. In the fifth chapter of the Gita we again read of him as follows:

> To those, however, in whom that unwisdom in the Self has been destroyed, wisdom shines sunlike as the Ultimate.
>
> Thus having That for reasoning, That for the Self, That for finalized discipline, That for supreme goal, they go to a state of final non-return, all their (relativistic) dross being cancelled out by wisdom.
>
> In regard to a Brahmin endowed with learning or humility, a cow, an elephant, and even a dog, as also one who cooks the dog (for food), the well-informed ones see the same (differenceless reality).
>
> Even here creative urges are conquered by those whose minds are balanced in sameness; free from blemish and unitively balanced is indeed the Absolute; therefore such persons become grounded in the Absolute.
>
> He should not rejoice on good befalling him nor be disturbed by a mishap; stabilized in reason, delusion-free, as knower of the Absolute, firmly established is he in the Absolute.
>
> (V: 16-20)[4]

In the next verse we are told about the more superior knower of *brahma* who enters into a more pure form of *nirvāṇa*.

VERSE 6

saṃnyasya sarvakarmāṇi
satatam brahma niṣṭhayā
yaścaratyavanau deha-
yātrāyai brahmavidvaraḥ

Having renounced all action,
always established in the Absolute,
who moves about the world merely to conduct bodily life —
he is the superior knower of *brahma.*

saṃnyasya — having renounced
sarva karmāṇi — all action
satatam — always
brahma niṣṭhayā — established in the Absolute
yaḥ — who
avanau carati — moves about the world
dehayātrāyai — merely to conduct bodily life
brahmavidvaraḥ — is the superior knower of *brahma*

A windmill exposed to the wind spontaneously turns according to the course of the wind, and it rotates without any conscious deliberation on the part of the wheel or the mill. The body-mind organism is part of nature's creative device, and it will go on until, by its own wear and tear, the body falls apart. Such automatic functioning is inevitable, and action belonging to this category is known as *prārābdhā*. The psychophysical functioning of a superior knower of the Absolute is similar. Such a person is described in the Karma Yoga chapter of the Bhagavad Gita:

> But for him who happens to be attached to the Self alone, who finds full satisfaction in the Self — for such a man who is happy in the Self as such, too, there is nothing that he should do.
>
> Neither is there anything indeed for him resulting from work done, nor anything from work omitted here, nor is there either for him any dependence in respect of anything derivable from any being whatsoever. (III: 17, 18)[5]

Such a person can be considered as a true *sannyāsi*, as well as one matured in the highest form of devotion. As a man of superior devotion, a *brahmavidvara* is again described in the Gita, in the chapter entitled Bhakti Yoga:

> He who has no hatred toward all creatures, who is also friendly and compassionate, who is free from possessiveness, and egoism, who is equalized in pain and pleasure, and forgiving, such a unitively-disciplined one, who is always contented, self-controlled, firmly resolved, whose mind and reason are dedicated to Me — he, My devotee, is dear to Me.
>
> He who does not disturb (the peace of) the world and (whose peace) is not disturbed by the world, and who is free from exaggerations of joy, hate, and fear — he (too is) dear to Me.
>
> He who expects no favours, who is clean, expert, who sits unconcerned, carefree, who has relinquished all undertakings — he, My devotee, is dear to Me.
>
> He who neither rejoices nor hates, nor grieves nor desires, and who has relinquished both the beneficial and the harmful — such a one, endowed with devotion, is dear to Me.
>
> He who is the same to foe and friend, and also in honour and dishonour, who is the same in cold and heat, in pleasure and pain, and who is free from attachment,
> to whom censure and praise are equal, who is silent (in manner), content with whatever happens to come, having no fixed abode, mentally constant — such a man of devotion is dear to Me.
> (XII : 13-19)[6]

The final absorption that awaits such a superior knower of the Absolute is said to be more pure than that of the *brahmavit*, knower of the Absolute. In the next verse is given the mark of *brahmavid-varīya*, the even more superior knower of the Absolute.

VERSE 7

anyena vedito vetti
na vetti svayameva yaḥ
sa varīyān sadā brahma-
nirvāṇam ayamaśnute

He knows only when informed by another,
does not know by himself —
such a person is the more superior.
He always enjoys absorption in the Absolute.

yaḥ — he
vetti — knows
anyena veditaḥ — only when informed by another
na vetti — does not know
svayam eva — by himself
saḥ — such a person
varīyān — is the more superior
ayam — he
sadā — always
aśnute — enjoys
brahmanirvāṇam — absorption in the Absolute

All psychophysical functions are programmed for only a short display by the individuated self. Within the frame of reference of the time-space continuum, they are controlled by cause and effect dynamics just so long as the individual believes in playing a role-identity. This identity cannot be maintained when the imprisoned consciousness of the individual breaks the ego boundary and expands into a cosmic consciousness. Having once attained that consciousness, individuation is more or less effaced. Senses are withdrawn from the externally illuminated world of name and form and the transactional interrelationships of things. Awareness becomes minimal. All colorations and conditionings of the past begin to fade out. The place of ego-consciousness is substituted by Self-awareness. A short-term revival of the empirico-rational awareness can be effected by an outside agency, though as the suggested meanings of names and forms have become fictitious to such a person, it is unlikely that any real interest can be revived in sense objects or ratiocination of events. Absorption in the universal has now become most natural. This more superior knower of *brahma* is described in *Guṇatraya Vibhāga Yoga,* chapter fourteen of the Bhagavad Gita, as the *yogi* who has transcended the three modalities of nature (*gunātīta*):

> He who, seated as a neutral, is not moved by the modalities of nature, thinking that the modalities of nature operate in rotation, who, standing apart, is unmoved,
> the same in pain and pleasure, at rest in himself, to whom a clod of earth, and a stone, and gold are alike, firm in attitude alike to loved and unloved, who regards his being blamed or praised equally,
> the same in honour and disgrace, taking no sides as between friends or foes, abandoning all initiation of works —
> he is said to have transcended the modalities of nature.
> (XIV : 23-25)[7]

In the next verse the most superior knower of the Absolute is presented.

VERSE 8

svayam na vetti kiñcinna
vedito'pi tathaiva yaḥ
sa variṣṭhaḥ sadāvṛtti —
śūnyo'yam brahma kevalam

Not knowing anything by himself,
even when informed he remains so —
such a person is the most superior.
Always without modulation, he is *brahma* alone.

na vetti — not knowing
kiñcit — anything
svayam — by himself
veditaḥ api — even when informed
tatha iva yaḥ — he remains so
saḥ — such a person
variṣṭhaḥ — is the most superior
sadā — always
vṛtti śūnyaḥ — without modulation
ayam — he is
brahma kevalam — *brahma* alone

The term non-dual implies the transcendence of the dual. The dual alluded to is the dichotomy of the knowing subject and the known object. The arrival at the non-dual holistic appreciation is effected either by reducing the subject into the total immanence of the object, as in the case of monistic materialism, or by reducing the existentiality of the object into the transcendent substantiality of the subject, as monistic idealists do. A third possibility is cancelling out the subject-object duality and placing oneself in the precarious neutral zero where the Word becomes a synonym for both the cause as well as the effect.

In monistic materialism everything is reduced to matter, and the observing mind is treated as an epiphenomenon which has no reality of its own. The non-dual emphasis in such an outlook does not take one beyond a philosophical surmise of the system to which man belongs. This does not alter very much the whimsical characteristic and action-reaction pattern of the percipient's behavior. Of course, it will considerably influence the judgement of such a person in the assessment of values. In the second case, that of the transcendental idealist, the main impact of monism can be seen in his withdrawal from all action fronts. As for the neutral monist, he finds ample excuses to do as well as not to do. Both his restraints and his indulgences are explained away as issues of semantic significance. The *brahmavidvariṣṭha*, the most superior knower of the Absolute, is not a philosopher and he cannot be placed in any of the three above-mentioned categories. In fact, he is a person who defies placement and categorization. He can be likened only to himself. Like an ocean which has come to absolute rest, his passions are appeased and he does not act either with deliberation or with instinct. His sensory faculties are as if they are put out of commission, and his mind does not appreciate either pain or pleasure. Ego, attachment, the lust for life, sleep, and languor have now become irrelevant because the triple modalities of nature — *satva*, *rajas*, and *tamas* — do not any longer monitor his consciousness. Even the oscillation of the ascending and descending vital breaths becomes so pacified that this person seems to have come to a state of suspended animation. Hunger, thirst, and such bodily needs are not known, and all functions, including the excretory, come to a complete stop. The sustenence of the body is not maintained by the intake of nutrients. Except for the continuation of his metabolic balance in some mysterious way, no sign of life is in him. In the Gita it is said:

> But beyond this unmanifested there is yet another unmanifested perennial existence, which among perishables itself does not perish.
>
> That unmanifested is called the imperishable. That they speak of as the highest (spiritual) path, attaining which they return not. Such is My supreme abode.
>
> This is the supreme Spirit, O Pārtha, within whom all existences abide and by whom all this is pervaded, who is attainable, however, by devotion exclusive of all extraneous factors. (VIII : 20-22)[8]

In Patañjali's *Yoga Sūtra* this state is considered as the equalization of the thinking substance and the Self. The aphorism says, "When the purity of the *satva* and of the Self are equal there is aloneness."[9] Here Patañjali equates *kaivalya* with the highest kind of *nirvāṇa*. In the state of aloneness the body-dweller is identical with the eternally pure.

The term *sadāvṛtti śūnyaḥ* can be broken either as *sadā* plus *vṛtti śūnyaḥ* or as *sadā* and *āvṛtti śūnyaḥ*. When taken in the first sense it means the absence of the modulations of consciousness. In the second, it means the absence of any return from transcendence. Both meanings are relevant here. In the next verse final cessation is described.

VERSE 9

heyopādeyatā nahya-
syātmā vā svaprakāśakaḥ
iti matvā nivartteta
vṛttir nāvarttate punaḥ

Of this, there is nothing avoidable and acceptable.
As for the Self, it shines by itself.
Thus having become certain, liberate.
Thereafter modulation does not repeat.

asya — of this
nahi — there is nothing
heyaḥ — avoidable (and)
upādeyatā — acceptable
ātmā vā — as for the Self
prakāśakaḥ svayam — it shines by itself
iti — this
matvā — having become certain
nivartteta — liberate
punaḥ — thereafter
vṛttiḥ — modulation
na āvarttate — does not repeat

Of this universe, what is or is not is not determined by the primary substance which constitutes it. The eidetic configurations conceived as vibrant energy, flying or clustering particles, stabilized atoms, and adhering molecules are not self-contained truths. These are the verdicts of human intelligence in the light of a self-luminous principle which functions through the envisioning of spatio-temporal configurations. By some strange compulsion, human intelligence is never tired of giving a running commentary on the changing patterns which go into the composition of both the presentative and representative awareness. The characteristic of this commentary is its implied logistics, which arranges events or observations in a precedent-antecedent sequence of cause and effect.

Two main concerns of the witnessing intelligence are the discerning of coming into manifestation and dissolving into the mystery of oblivion. Configuring or assuming tangibility is called *upādāna*, and dissolution is called *heya*. A wave emerging into form is an *upādāna*, and merging back into a level of invisibility is *heya*. In such an example water does not become anything other than itself either in the appearance of the wave or in the disappearance of the wave. The rule that governs the generality of the material world is the conservation of energy and the transformation of matter. Only human intelligence creates out of the dual principles of *upādāna* and *heya*, emergence and reemergence, a meaningful story of teleology, evolution, historicity, psychology, existentiality, empiricism, and a thousand and one other exegetic explanations. This truth is pointedly referred to in the opening line of the present verse. If the fascinating or threatening grand dramas of life are only read into the 'folds and fringes' of an apparent flux of phenomenality, the mind which creates the world can also resolve it. When this understanding becomes certain beyond a doubt, one wakes up to the reality of the Self. As a result of such a realization, the phantasmagoria of world-fascination and world wilderness cease. Thereafter there is not a second to be explained or evaluated. No word can explain that boundless radiance of the one light that is without inside or outside. Śankara speaks of that as "the inner light which is also identical with the outer light. It is the first principle of luminosity. It is the twice transcendental. It is the light of lights. It is the self-luminous light of the Self, the light of Śiva, which is the same as I am." In Sanskrit:

> *antar jyotir bahir jyotir*
> *pratyagjyotir pārat paraḥ*
> *jyotir jyotir svayam jyoti*
> *ātma jyoti śivosmyaham*

In the Gita this is spoken of as "establishing the mind reflexively in the Self, without thinking of anything whatever." (VI: 25).[10] In the next verse the non-dual reality of *brahma* is established, and with that both *Nirvāṇa Darśana* and *Darśanamālā* are concluded.

VERSE 10

ekamevādvitīyam bra-
hmāsti nānyanna samśayaḥ
iti vidvān nivartteta
dvaitānnāvarttate punaḥ

The one *brahma* alone is without a second;
nothing else is; there is no doubt.
Thus the knower should liberate from duality.
Thereafter he does not return.

ekam — the one
brahma — *brahma*
eva asti — alone is
advitīyam — without a second
na anyat — nothing else is
na samśayaḥ — there is no doubt
iti — thus
vidvān — the knower
nivartteta — should liberate
dvaitāt — from duality
punaḥ — thereafter
na āvarttate — (he) does not return (does not repeat)

Between the first formation of clay and the final definitive culmination of it into a well-baked, useable pot, there is an untold history which runs into countless billions of years. The evolution of the nebulae, the formation of a galaxy, the manifestation of a solar system, the accidental formation of planets, the cooling of the crust of the Earth, the deterioration of rocks, nature's kneading the rocks into clay with incessant sun and rain, the appearance of life in matter, the amphibian, the organization of matter into biologic and subsequent psychologic evolutes, the Stone Age, the discovery of using implements, the development of the skill of making pottery, the discovery of the use of fire, the baking of the pot, and a million other unobserved details of the flux of the world phenomena have come sequentially as a causal chain to effect even this seemingly least trifle of an event in the universe. When such a causally conceived relationship of things is seen as the inseparable organic continuation of the world system, there emerges from that picture the idea of a purposive evolution and the intelligence of a creative insight which engineers the world phenomenon. This is the *Logos* that is referred to in the very first verse of *Adhyāropa Darśana*, chapter one of the present book, as the incipient will of *parameśvara*, the Supreme Lord. In the tenth verse of the same chapter, the same was compared to the organic expansion and unfoldment of the latent characteristics of a fig tree, which in the course of time becomes manifested as a tree of enormous size, having roots, trunk, branches, leaves, flowers and fruit, each item of which is distinct from the other. In spite of the apparent difference between its microscopic origin and macrocosmic expansion, nowhere in the process of its elaboration is there a severance of the effect from cause; hence the creative principle, *brahma*, the sustaining vitality of the process, *viṣṇu*, and the continuous transmutation that is being effected from stage to stage, *śiva*, is also called *para*, the transcendent Absolute, and *sarva*, the all-embracing single reality.

In the present final verse of the *Darśanamālā*, the same *brahma* combines within its reality the ontologic immanence of the substance of all, the dynamic process of the teleologic evolutionary manifestation, and the all-transcending idea of the Eternal Being. This immanent-transcendent Absolute is alluded to in the *Chāndogya Upaniṣad* as *ekam evādvitīyam*, the one alone without a second. This great dictum also means that the Absolute is one that does not warrant any kind of difference. In Vedāntic terminology the non-differentiated truth of the Absolute is termed as *sajātīya vijātīya svagata bheda śūnyata*. There is only one Absolute and there is not another of the same class. This non-differentiation is *sajātīya bheda śūnyata*. There is nothing other than the Absolute to make a different category of reality. Such a non-differentiation is known as *vijātīya bheda śūnyata*. Within the Absolute there are no parts. This organic non-differentiation is known as *svagata bheda śūnyata*.

The supreme truth that is spoken of here is inexpressible. In the *Taittirīya Upanisad* we read:

> Wherefrom words turn back,
> Together with the mind, not having attained —
> The bliss of Brahma he who knows,
> Fears not at any time at all. (2.4)[11]

In the *Katha Upaniṣad* we read:

> The wise one is not born, nor dies.
> This one has not come from anywhere, has not become anyone.

Unborn, constant, eternal, primeval, this one
Is not slain when the body is slain.

(2. 18)[12]

The knowledge of the Absolute does not come as a cumulative result of any action. We read in the *Muṇḍaka Upaniṣad*:

This Soul (Ātma) is not to be obtained by instruction,
Nor by intellect, nor by much learning.
He is to be obtained only by the one whom He chooses;
To such a one that Soul (Ātma) reveals His own person
(*tanūm svām*).

(3.2.3)[13]

For one who comes to know this there is no return. In the *Chāndogya Upaniṣad* we read:

He leads them on to Brahma. This is the way to the gods, the way to Brahma. They who proceed by it return not to the human condition here—yea, they return not!

(4. 15. 6)[14]

Narayana Guru himself closes another of his books, *Ātmopadeśa Śatakam*, *One Hundred Verses of Self-Instruction*, with a similar verse:

Neither this, nor that nor the content of existence am I
But existence, subsistence, joy-immortal; thus attaining clarity
Emboldened, discarding attachment to being and non-being
One should gently, gently, merge in SAT-AUM.[15]

AUM TAT SAT

X. NIRVĀṆA DARŚANAM

1 James Haughton Woods, *The Yoga System of Patanjali*, Harvard Oriental Series, Motilal Banarasidas, Delhi, 1966, page. 265

2 ibid. page. 63

3 Nataraja Guru, *The Bhagavad Gita*, R & K Publishing House, Delhi, Ch. IV, v. 18–24, pages. 236–240.

4 ibid. Ch. V, v. 16–20, pages. 270–274.

5 ibid. Ch. III, v. 17, 18, page 191.

6 ibid. Ch. XII, v. 13–19, pages 524–528.

7 ibid. Ch. XIV, v. 23–25, page. 591.

8 ibid, Ch. VIII, v. 20–22, pages. 372–374.

9 James Haughton Woods, op. cit., Ch. III, aphorism 55, page. 295.

10 Nataraja Guru, op. cit., Ch. VI, v. 25, page. 300.

11 R. E. Hume, *The Thirteen Principal Upanishads*, Oxford University Press, New York, 1975, Taittiriya Upanishad, second valli, fourth anuvaka, page. 285.

12 ibid. Katha Upanishad, second valli: 18, page. 349.

13 ibid. Mundaka Upanishad, third mundaka, second khanda: 3, page. 376.

14 ibid. Chandogya Upanishad, fourth prapathaka, fifteenth khanda: 6, page. 224.

15 Nitya Chaitanya Yati, *Neither This Nor That But Aum*, Vikas, Delhi, 1982, page. 221.

APPENDIX

दर्शनमाला ॥

॥ ॐ तत् सत् ॥

दर्शनमाला ॥

॥ अध्यारोपदर्शनम् ॥

(प्रथमम्)

आसीदग्रेऽसदेवेदं भुवनं स्वप्नवत् पुनः ।
ससर्ज सर्वं सङ्कल्पमात्रेण परमेश्वरः ॥१॥

वासनामयमेवादावासीदिदमथ प्रभुः ।
असृजन्मायया स्वस्य मायावीवाखिलं जगत् ॥२॥

प्रागुत्पत्तेरिदं स्वस्मिन् विलीनमथ वै स्वतः ।
बीजादङ्कुरवत् स्वस्य शक्तिरेवाऽसृजत्स्वयम् ॥३॥

शक्तिस्तु द्विविधा ज्ञेया तैजसी तामसीति च ।
सहवासोऽनयोर्नास्ति तेजस्तिमिरयोरिव ॥४॥

मनोमात्रमिदं चित्रमिवाग्रे सर्वमीदृशम् ।
प्रापयामास वैचित्र्यं भगवाम् चित्रकारवत् ॥५॥

आसीत् प्रकृतिरेवेदं यथाऽदौ योगवैभवं ।
व्यतनोदथ योगीव सिद्धिजालं जगत्पतिः ॥६॥

यदाऽत्मविद्यासंकोचस्तदाऽविद्या भयङ्करम् ।
नामरूपात्मनाऽत्यर्थं विभातीह पिशाचवत् ॥७॥

भयङ्करमिदं शून्यं वेतालनगरं यथा।
तथैव विश्वमखिलं व्यकरोदद्भुतं विभुः ॥८॥

अर्काद्यथाक्रमं विश्वं तथा नैवेदमात्मनः।
सुप्तेरिव प्रादुरासीद्युगपत्स्वस्य वीक्षया ॥९॥

धानादिव वटो यस्मात् प्रादुरासीदिदं जगत्।
स ब्रह्मा स शिवो विष्णुः स परः सर्व एव सः ॥१०॥

॥ इति अध्यारोपदर्शनम् ॥

अपवाददर्शनम् ।।

(द्वितीयम्)

चैतन्यादागतं स्थूलसूक्ष्मात्मकमिदं जगत् ।
अस्ति चेत्सद्घनं सर्वं नास्ति चेदस्ति चिद्घनम् ।।१।।

अन्यन्न कारणात्कार्यमसदेतदतोऽखिलम् ।
असतः कथमुत्पत्तिरनुत्पन्नस्य को लयः ? ।।२।।

यस्योत्पत्तिलयो नास्ति तत् परं ब्रह्म नेतरत् ।
उत्पत्तिश्च लयोऽस्तीति भ्रमत्यात्मनि मायया ।।३।।

कारणाव्यतिरिक्तत्वात् कार्यस्य कथमस्तिता ? ।
भवत्यतः कारणस्य कथमस्ति च नास्तिता ? ।।४।।

कार्यत्वादसतोऽस्यास्ति कारणं नह्यतो जगत् ।
ब्रह्मैव तर्हि सदसदिति मुह्यति मन्दधीः ।।५।।

एकस्यैवास्ति सत्ता चेदन्यस्याऽसौ क्व विद्यते ? ।
सत्यस्त्यात्माश्रयो यद्यप्यसति स्यादसंभवः ।।६।।

विभज्याऽवयवं सर्वमेकैकं तत्र दृश्यते ।
चिन्मात्रमखिलं नान्यदिति मायाविदूरगम् ।।७।।

चिदेव नान्यदाभाति चितः परमतो नहि ।
यच्च नाभाति तदसद्यदसत्तन्न भाति च ।।८।।

आनन्द एवास्ति भाति नान्यः कश्चिदतोऽखिलम् ।
आनन्दघनमन्यन्न विनाऽनन्देन विद्यते ॥९॥

सर्वं हि सच्चिदानन्दं नेह नानाऽस्ति किञ्चन ।
यः पश्यतीह नानेव मृत्योर्मृत्युं स गच्छति ॥१०॥

॥ इति अपवाददर्शनम् ॥

असत्यदर्शनम्।

(तृतीयम्)

मनोमयमिदं सर्वं न मनः क्वापि विद्यते।
अतो व्योम्नीव नीलादि दृश्यते जगदात्मनि ॥१॥

मनसोऽनन्यया सर्वं कल्प्यतेऽविद्यया जगत्।
विद्ययाऽसौ लयं याति तदालेख्यमिवाऽखिलम् ॥२॥

विजृम्भते यत्तमसो भीरोरिह पिशाचवत्।
तदिदं जाग्रति स्वप्नलोकवद् दृश्यते बुधैः ॥३॥

सङ्कल्पकल्पितं दृश्यं सङ्कल्पो यत्र विद्यते।
दृश्यं तत्र च नान्यत्र कुत्रचिद्रज्जुसर्पवत् ॥४॥

सङ्कल्पमनसोः कश्चिन्नहि भेदोऽस्ति यन्मनः।
तदविद्यातमःप्रख्यमिन्द्रजालमिवाद्भुतम् ॥५॥

मरीचिकावत्प्राज्ञस्य जगदात्मनि भासते।
बालस्य सत्यमिति च प्रतिबिंबमिव भ्रमात् ॥६॥

आत्मा न क्षीरवद्याति रूपान्तरमतोऽखिलम्।
बिवर्त्तमिन्द्रजालेन विद्यते निर्मितं यथा ॥७॥

मायैव जगतामादिकारणं निर्मितं तया।
सर्वं हि मायिनो नान्यदसत्यं सिद्धिजालवत् ॥८॥

विभाति विश्वं वृद्धस्य वियद्वनमिवात्मनि ।
असत्यं पुत्रिकारूपं बालस्येव विपर्ययम् ॥९॥

एकं सत्यं न द्वितीयं ह्यसत्यं भाति सत्यवत् ।
शिलैव शिवलिङ्गं न द्वितीयं शिल्पिना कृतम् ॥१०॥

॥ इति असत्यदर्शनम् ॥

मायादर्शनम् ॥

(चतुर्थम्)

न विद्यते या सा माया विद्याऽविद्या पराऽपरा ।
तमः प्रधानं प्रकृतिर्बहुधा सैव भासते ॥१॥

प्रागुत्पत्तेर्यथाऽभावो मृदेव ब्रह्मणः पृथक् ।
न विद्यते ब्रह्म हि या सा मायाऽमेयवैभवा ॥२॥

अनात्मा न सदात्मा सदिति विद्योतते यया ।
सा विद्येयं यथा रज्जुसर्पतत्वावधारणम् ॥३॥

आत्मा न सदनात्मा सदिति विद्योतते यया ।
सैवाऽविद्या यथा रज्जुसर्पयोरयथार्थदृक् ॥४॥

इन्द्रियाणि मनोबुद्धिपञ्चप्राणादयो यया ।
विसृज्यन्ते सैव परा सूक्ष्माङ्गानि चिदात्मनः ॥५॥

अङ्गान्येतान्यवष्टभ्य सुखी दुःखीव मुह्यति ।
चिदात्मा मायया स्वस्य तत्त्वतोऽस्ति न किञ्चन ॥६॥

इन्द्रियाणां हि विषयः प्रपञ्चोऽयं विसृज्यते ।
यया सैवा पराऽध्यात्मस्थूलसङ्कल्पनामयी ॥७॥

शुक्तिकाया यथाऽज्ञानं रजतस्य यदात्मनि ।
कल्पितस्य निदानं तत्तम इत्यवगम्यते ॥८॥

धीयतेऽस्मिन् प्रकर्षेण बीजे वृक्ष इवाखिलम् ।
अतः प्राधान्यतो वाऽस्य प्रधानमिति कथ्यते ॥९॥

करोतीति प्रकर्षेण प्रकृत्यैव गुणान् पृथक् ।
निगद्यतेऽसौ प्रकृतिरितिह त्रिगुणात्मिका ॥१०॥

॥ इति मायादर्शनम् ॥

भानदर्शनम् ॥

(पञ्चमम्)

अन्तर्बहिर्विदासीनं सदा भ्रमरचञ्चलम् ।
भानं द्विधैव सामान्यं विशेष इति भिद्यते ॥१॥

स्थूलं सूक्ष्मं कारणं च तुर्यं चेति चतुर्विधम् ।
भानाश्रयं हि तन्नाम भानस्याप्युपचर्यते ॥२॥

दृश्यतामिह कायोऽहं घटोऽयमिति दृश्यते ।
स्थूलमाश्रित्य यद्भानं स्थूलं तदिति मन्यते ॥३॥

अत्र कायो घट इति भानं यत्तद्विशिष्यते ।
तथाऽहमयमिति यत् सामान्यमिति च स्मृतम् ॥४॥

इन्द्रियाणि मनोबुद्धिविषयाः पञ्च वायवः ।
भास्यन्ते येन तत्सूक्ष्मं अस्य सूक्ष्माश्रयत्वतः ॥५॥

अज्ञोऽहमिति यद्भानं तत्कारणमुदाहृतम् ।
अत्राऽहमिति सामान्यं विशेषोऽज्ञ इति स्फुरत् ॥६॥

अहं ब्रह्मेति यद्भानं तत्तुर्यमिति शंस्यते ।
सामान्यमहमित्यंशो ब्रह्मेत्यत्र विशिष्यते ॥७॥

यत्र भानं तत्र भास्यं भानं यत्र न तत्र न ।
भास्यमित्यन्वयेनाऽपि व्यतिरेकेण बोध्यते ॥८॥

यथा दृग्दृशमात्मानं स्वयमात्मा न पश्यति।
अतो न भास्यते ह्यात्मा यं पश्यति स भास्यते ॥९॥

यद्भास्यते तदध्यस्तं अनध्यस्तं न भास्यते।
यदध्यस्तं तदसदप्यनध्यस्तं सदेव तत् ॥१०॥

॥ इति भानदर्शनम् ॥

कर्मदर्शनम् ।।

(षष्ठम्)

आत्मैव मायया कर्म करोति बहुरूपधृक् ।
असङ्गः स्वप्रकाशोऽपि निद्रायामिव तैजसः ।।१।।

मन्ये वदामि गृह्णामि शृणोमित्यादि रूपतः ।
क्रियते कर्म परमात्मना चित्तेन्द्रियात्मना ।।२।।

आत्मैव कर्मणः पूर्वमन्यत् किञ्चिन्न विद्यते ।
ततः स्वेनैव कर्माणि क्रियन्ते निजमायया ।।३।।

शक्तिरस्त्यात्मनः काचिद् दुर्घटा न पृथक् स्वतः ।
तयैवारोप्यते कर्म निखिलं निष्क्रियात्मनि ।।४।।

सर्वदाऽसङ्ग एवात्माऽज्ञतया कर्मसङ्गिवत् ।
करोति न करोमीति न ज्ञः कर्मसु सज्जते ।।५।।

ज्वलति ज्वलनो वायुर्वाति वर्षति वारिदः ।
धरात्मा सन् धरति खल्वेको वहति वाहिनी ।।६।।

ऊर्ध्वं प्राणो ह्यधोऽपानः खल्वेको याति निष्क्रियः ।
नाड्यन्तराले धमति क्रन्दति स्पन्दति स्थितः ।।७।।

अस्तिजन्मर्द्धिपरिणत्यपक्षयविनाशनम् ।
षड्भावमिह यो याति स नान्योऽविक्रियात्मनः ।।८।।

स्वयं क्रियन्ते कर्माणि करणैरिन्द्रियैरपि।
अहं त्वसङ्गः कूटस्थ इति जानाति कोविदः ॥९॥

दृश्यत्वाद्ग्राह्यमहमप्यतोऽहं शुक्तिरङ्गवत्।
अध्यस्तमेक एवाद्य श्वोपि सर्वोपरिस्थितः ॥१०॥

॥ इति कर्मदर्शनम् ॥

ज्ञानदर्शनम् ॥

(सप्तमम्)

ज्ञानमेकं हि निरुपाधिकं सोपाधिकं च तत् ।
अहङ्कारादिहीनं यज्ज्ञानं तन्निरुपाधिकम् ॥१॥

अहन्तयाऽन्तर्बहिरस्ति यदेवमिदन्तया ।
भानवृत्त्याऽन्वितं यत्तु ज्ञानं सोपाधिकं मतम् ॥२॥

अनात्मनामहङ्कारादीनां येनानुभूयते ।
साक्षी तदात्मज्ञानं स्याद्येनैवामृतमश्यते ॥३॥

अहङ्कारादि कार्यं यदनात्मकमसङ्कुचकम् ।
येनावगम्यतेऽनात्मज्ञानं तदवधार्यते ॥४॥

यथावद्वस्तुविज्ञानं रज्जुतत्त्वावबोधवत् ।
यत्तद्यथार्थविज्ञानमयथार्थमतोऽन्यथा ॥५॥

यत्सान्निध्यादेव सर्वं भासते स्वयमेव तत् ।
प्रत्यक्षज्ञानमितिचापरोक्षमिति लक्ष्यते ॥६॥

ययाऽनुसाधकं साध्यं मीयते ज्ञानरूपया ।
वृत्त्या साऽनुमितिस्साहचर्यसंस्कारजन्यया ॥७॥

गत्वा समीपं मेयस्य मीयते श्रुतलक्षणः ।
यया संवित्सोपमितिर्मृगोऽयमिति रूपया ॥८॥

अहं ममेति ज्ञानं यदिदं तदिति यच्च तत् ।
जीवज्ञानं तदपरमिन्द्रियज्ञानमिष्यते ॥९॥

ओं तत्सदिति निर्दिष्टं ब्रह्मात्मैक्यमुपागतम् ।
कल्पनादिविहीनं यत्तत्परज्ञानमीर्यते ॥१०॥

॥ इति ज्ञानदर्शनम् ॥

भक्तिदर्शनम् ।

(अष्टमम्)

भक्तिरात्मानुसन्धानमात्माऽनन्दघनो यतः ।
आत्मानमनुसन्धत्ते सदैवात्माविदात्मना ॥१॥

अनुसन्धीयते ब्रह्म ब्रह्मानन्दघनं यतः ।
सदा ब्रह्मानुसन्धानं भक्तिरित्यवगम्यते ॥२॥

आनन्दमेव ध्यायन्ति सर्वे दुःखं न कश्चन ।
यदानन्दपरं ध्यानं भक्तिरित्युपदिश्यते ॥३॥

आत्मैव ब्रह्म भजति नान्यमात्मानमात्मवित् ।
भजतीति यदात्मानं भक्तिरित्यभिधीयते ॥४॥

आनन्द आत्मा ब्रह्मेति नामैतस्यैव तन्यते ।
इति निश्चितधीर्यस्य स भक्त इति विश्रुतः ॥५॥

आनन्दोऽहमहं ब्रह्माऽत्माऽहमस्मीति रूपतः ।
भावना सततं यस्य स भक्त इति विश्रुतः ॥६॥

भार्या भजति भर्तारं भर्त्ता भार्यां न केवलम् ।
स्वानन्दमेव भजति सर्वोपि विषयस्थितम् ॥७॥

एवं पश्यति कुत्रापि विद्वानात्मसुखं विना ।
न किञ्चिदपरं तस्य भक्तिरेव गरीयसी ॥८॥

लोकस्य पितरि स्वस्य गुरौ पितरि मातरि।
सत्यस्य स्थापितरि च तत्पथेनैव यातरि॥९॥

नियन्तरि निषिद्धस्य सर्वेषां हितकर्त्तरि।
योऽनुरागो भक्तिरत्र सा परा परमात्मनि॥१०॥

॥ इति भक्तिदर्शनम् ॥

योगदर्शनम् ॥

(नवमम्)

सततं योजयति यद्युनक्ति च चिदात्मनि ।
मनो निरोधरूपोऽयं स योग इति शंसितः ॥१॥

न द्रष्टा दर्शनं दृश्यं विद्यते यत्र तत्र हृत् ।
योजयेद्वासना यावद्योगोऽयमिति योगवित् ॥२॥

नामरूपमिदं सर्वं ब्रह्मैवेति विलीयते ।
यद्ब्रह्मणि मनो नित्यं स योग इति निश्चितः ॥३॥

चित्तस्य तैलधारावद्वृत्त्याऽविच्छिन्नयाऽत्मनि ।
निरन्तरं रम्यते यत्सयोगो योगिभिः स्मृतः ॥४॥

यतो यतो मनो याति सदाऽत्मनि ततस्ततः ।
नियम्य योजयेदेतद्योगोऽयं युज्यतामिह ॥५॥

सर्वानर्थकरः पुंसां सङ्कल्पः कल्पितैः सह ।
उन्मूल्य वासनाजालैर्येनात्मनि निरुध्यते ॥६॥

दृश्यस्य न दृशोऽस्तित्वं अतो दृश्यं दृगात्मकम् ।
इति युञ्जीत दृग्रूपे यः स योगविदां वरः ॥७॥

यदा पिबन् मनोभृङ्गः स्वानन्दमधुमाधुरीम् ।
न स्पन्दति वशीकृत्य योजितो योगवायुना ॥८॥

ध्यानमन्तर्भ्रुवोर्दृष्टिर्जिह्वाग्रं लम्बिकोर्ध्वतः।
यदा स्यात्खेचरी मुद्रा निद्रालस्यादिनाशिनी ॥९॥

ज्ञानं कर्मेति लोकेऽस्मिन् द्विधा योगः समासतः।
अनयोर्योगविस्तारः सर्वः परिसमाप्यते ॥१०॥

॥ इति योगदर्शनम् ॥

निर्वाणदर्शनम् ।

(दशमम्)

निर्वाणं द्विविधं शुद्धमशुद्धं चेति तत्र यत् ।
शुद्धं निर्वासनं तद्वदशुद्धं वासनान्वितम् ॥१॥

अतिशुद्धं शुद्धमिति शुद्धं च द्विविधं तथा ।
अशुद्धशुद्धश्चाशुद्धमशुद्धाशुद्धमुच्यते ॥२॥

अतिशुद्धं त्रिधा पश्चाद्वरे चैकं वरीयसि ।
एकमेकं वरिष्ठेऽथ शुद्धं ब्रह्मविदिस्थितम् ॥३॥

अशुद्धशुद्धं विरजस्तमोऽन्यत्सरजस्तमः ।
मुमुक्षौ प्रथमं विद्यात् द्वितीयं सिद्धिकामिषु ॥४॥

दग्ध्वा ज्ञानाग्निना सर्वमुद्दिश्य जगतां हितम् ।
करोति विधिवत्कर्म ब्रह्मविद्ब्रह्मणि स्थितः ॥५॥

संन्यस्य सर्वकर्माणि सततं ब्रह्मनिष्ठया ।
यश्चरत्यवनौ देहयात्रायै ब्रह्मविद्वरः ॥६॥

अन्येन वेदितो वेत्ति न वेत्ति स्वयमेव यः ।
स वरीयान् सदा ब्रह्मनिर्वाणमयमश्नुते ॥७॥

स्वयं न वेत्ति किञ्चिन्न वेदितोऽपि तथैव यः ।
स वरिष्ठः सदा वृत्तिशून्योऽयं ब्रह्म केवलम् ॥८॥

हेयोपादेयता नह्यस्याऽत्मा वा स्वप्रकाशकः ।
इति मत्वा निवर्तेत वृत्तिर्नावर्त्तते पुनः ॥९॥

एकमेवाऽद्वितीयं ब्रह्मास्ति नान्यन्न संशयः ।
इति विद्वान्निवर्त्तेत द्वैतान्नावर्तते पुनः ॥१०॥

॥ ॐ तत् सत् ॥

॥ इति निर्वाणदर्शनम् ॥

॥ समाप्तेयं दर्शनमाला ॥

BIBLIOGRAPHY

Reference of Books and Authors

A Discourse on Coining the New Money Lighter
— Nicholas Barbon: 238.

A historical introduction to the postulational foundation of Experimental Epistemology
— Warren S. McCulloch: 100–101.

Advaita Dīpika
— Narayana Guru: 60, 185.

Alice in Wonderland
— Lewis Carroll: 223.

An Anthology of the Poems of Narayana Guru
— Nataraja Guru: vii

An Integrated Science of the Absolute
— Nataraja Guru: vii, xii, 6, 7, 10, 15.

Aparokṣa Anubhūti
— Śankara: 143.

Ātmōpadēśa Śatakam
—Narayana Guru: 6, 148, 172, 181, 183, 241, 242, 250, 355, 356, 452.

Being and Nothingness
— Jean-Paul Sartre: 135.

Bhagavad Gita
— Vyāsa: 3, 4, 18, 82, 84, 99, 102, 120, 120, 150, 158, 169, 171, 172, 175, 183, 206, 207, 213, 228, 245, 271, 273, 274, 317, 319, 346, 360, 369, 374, 401, 425, 439, 440, 441, 444.

Bhakti Sūtra
— Narada: 369.

Bible: 93, 263, 301, 360.
Book of Genesis: 77, 78, 219.
Gospel according to St. John: 170, 220–221, 222.
Psalms: 172.

Brahma Sūtra
— Bādarāyana: 47, 184.

Buddhist Logic
— Th. Stcherbatsky: 356.

Cit Jaḍangal
— Narayana Guru: 133.

Considerations
— Locke: 238.

Strindberg and Van Gogh
— Karl Jaspers: 98.

Subramanya Kīrtanam
— Narayana Guru: 12.

Symbols of Transformation
— C.G. Jung: 264.

The Conference of the Birds
— Attar: 277.

The Imitation of Christ
— Thomas à Kempis: 248.

The Principles of Psychology
— William James: 349.

The Senses and the Intellect
— Alexander Bain: 350.

The Secret Life of Plants
— Sir Jagadis Chandra Bose: 329.

The Tao of Physics
— Fritjof Capra: 102.

The Word of the Guru
— Nataraja Guru: 13.

Tractatus
— Wittgenstein: 221.

Upaniṣads:-
Aitareya 299
Bṛhadāraṇyaka 99, 100, 209, 300, 301, 302.
Chāndogya 99, 363, 451, 452.
Īśāvāsya 205, 207.
Kena 346.
Katha 411, 451.
Kaṭha 277.
Kauṣitaki 306.
Maitri 302.
Māṇḍūkya 59, 258, 259, 433, 452.
Taittirīya 146, 152, 451.

Vāda-Vidhi
— Vasubandhu: 357.

Vedānta Paribhāṣa
— Dharmarāja Adhvarindra: 142, 145, 347.

Vivekacūdāmaṇi
— Sankara: 64, 369.

Yoga Sutra (Aphorisms)
— Patañjali: 178, 245, 249, 363, 402, 436, 446.

Yoga Vāsiṣṭha
Valmīki: 118, 436.

INDEX

Sanskrit

A

B

GENERAL INDEX

A

B

C